JEFFERSON DAVIS

Jefferson Davis:

High Road to Emancipation and Constitutional Government

James Ronald Kennedy

&

Walter Donald Kennedy

Jefferson Davis: High Road to Emancipation and Constitutional Government

Copyright© 2022 by James Ronald & Walter Donald Kennedy

ALL RIGHTS RESERVED. No part of this publication may be reproduced, distributed, or transmitted in any form or by any means, including photocopying, recording, or other electronic or mechanical methods, or by any information storage and retrieval system without the prior written permission of the publisher, except in the case of very brief quotations embodied in critical reviews and certain other noncommercial uses permitted by copyright law.

Produced in the Republic of South Carolina by

SHOTWELL PUBLISHING LLC
Post Office Box 2592
Columbia, So. Carolina 29202
www.ShotwellPublishing.com

Cover Image: Jefferson Davis portrait courtesy of Wikimedia Commons.

ISBN: 978-1-947660-77-9

FIRST EDITION

10 9 8 7 6 5 4 3 2 1

Contents

Preface to 2022 Edition ix

Introduction xi

Chapter 1 1
Defending Our President—Jefferson Davis

Chapter 2 5
The High Road to Emancipation

Chapter 3 15
The Founding Fathers Struggle Against Slavery

Chapter 4 25
Jefferson Davis: The Early Years

Chapter 5 35
Jefferson Davis: The Soldier

Chapter 6 51
Jefferson Davis: The Planter

Chapter 7 63
Jefferson Davis: The Statesman

Chapter 8 129
Jefferson Davis: The Political Prisoner

Chapter 9 147
Jefferson Davis: The Last Years

Chapter 10 165
Conspiracy Allegations

Chapter 11 191
The Federal Government's Teaching of Secession at West Point

Photos 207

Chapter 12 215
The Character of President Davis's Accusers

Chapter 13 267
The Motives of President Davis's Accusers

Chapter 14 293
The Struggle to Prevent a Consolidated Federal Government

Chapter 15 323
A Perpetual or Conditional Union

Chapter 16 341
Secession as an American Political Principle

Chapter 17 357
The Final Argument

Chapter 18 367
Your Verdict - Your Decision - Your Future

ADDENDUM I 371
KENTUCKY AND VIRGINIA RESOLUTIONS OF 1798

ADDENDUM II 377
SOVEREIGN STATES DEFY THE FEDERAL GOVERNMENT'S
UNCONSTITUTIONAL ACTS

ADDENDUM III 383
PRESIDENT FRANKLIN PIERCE DEFENDS STATES' RIGHTS

ADDENDUM IV 389
MARYLAND RESOLUTIONS OF 1861

ADDENDUM V 397
UNITED STATES SUPREME COURT VS. PRESIDENT ABRAHAM LINCOLN

ADDENDUM VI 407
APPEAL FOR JUSTICE FOR MAJOR HENRY WIRZ

ABOUT THE AUTHORS..415

Preface to 2022 Edition

IN AN 1860 SPEECH in the U.S. Senate Senator Jefferson Davis urged Americans to take the high road to emancipation.[1] Jefferson Davis put his words to action by setting up schools at his own expense to educate slaves on his plantations. Yet, Yankee propagandists claim that Jefferson Davis led the South in a war to maintain slavery as a permanent institution in America. In 1860 Senator Jefferson Davis introduced a resolution in the Senate declaring that these United States were a republic of Sovereign States created by the compact of the Constitution. His resolution passed with favorable votes from Senators both North and South.[2] Yet, Yankee propagandists claim that Jefferson Davis led the South in an effort to destroy America's original Constitutional Republic. Who was this man—Jefferson Davis?

This book is a revised, second edition, of a work originally published in 1998 under the title of *Was Jefferson Davis Right?* The revised edition is done to update the original defense of President Davis in light of America's politically correct, wokeness, and cancel culture. The original manuscript was written (1998) at a time in which there was still hope that America would allow the South to continue its tradition of honoring the men who wore the gray in the War for Southern Independence—but unfortunately that day no longer exists! The old North/South Post-War bargain is broken.[3]

---

1 Davis, Jefferson, *Rise and Fall of the Confederate Government*, Vol. 1 (1881, Nashville, TN: William Mayes Coats, circa 1980), 30.

2 The Papers of Jefferson Davis, Rice University, https://bit.ly/3UFrYS8, (Accessed 10/5/2021).

3 See Chapter 18 "The Bargain Is Broken," Kennedy & Kennedy, *The South Was Right,* 3rd edition, (1991, 1994, Columbia, SC: Shotwell Publishing, 2020), 412-20.

In this, the second edition, the authors "take the gloves off" and confront America's neo-Marxist ruling elite with brutal facts, while challenging all Americans who honor traditional, conservative, moral, and political values to take a stand for Constitutional Liberty. After the unfortunate end of the War for Southern Independence Confederate Vice President Alexander Stephens declared, "The Cause of the South is now the Cause of all [Americans]." And so it is that today we see calls for Red State and Red County secession. There are calls to nullify egregious Federal mandates, and an emerging realization that "We the people" are no longer citizens of a Constitutionally limited Republic but are subjects to an all-powerful, supreme Federal Government.

Yes, Jefferson Davis, and all those who wore the gray in the War for Southern Independence, were right! They fought to prevent the dictatorship of an all-powerful, supreme Federal Government; they fought to preserve the principles of the original Constitution; and they fought for our freedom—shall we do less?

James Ronald Kennedy

Walter Donald Kennedy

July 2022

DEO VINDICE

Introduction

ON MAY 10, 1865, the military forces of the United States of America captured Jefferson Davis, president of the Confederate States of America. From the very outset of the war, the authorities in Washington, D.C., had encouraged the idea that they would "hang Jeff Davis from a sour apple tree." After four long and bloody years of aggressive war, the United States—which by then had mutated into the Yankee Empire[1]—at last had the opportunity to bring Jefferson Davis to "American" justice! Within a matter of weeks of his capture, the deposed Confederate president found himself the Yankee Empire's political prisoner, in chains, and charged with treason. From the time of his imprisonment, President Davis demanded a trial on any charges against him, especially on the charge of treason. But, in spite of their former boasting, the Yankee Empire's authorities carefully avoided giving Jefferson Davis his day in court.

Why did the Yankee Empire[2] fail to bring to justice a man whom it had branded a nineteenth-century Benedict Arnold? Why was this American arrested, imprisoned, chained, shackled, and indicted for treason yet never given the constitutional right freely granted the most vulgar of common criminals, the right to a fair and speedy trial? Were the Yankee Empire's authorities afraid of the outcome of such a trial?

---

1   See, Kennedy & Kennedy, *Yankee Empire: Aggressive Abroad and Despotic at Home* (Columbia, SC: Shotwell Publishing, 2018), ix-xii.

2   Throughout this book the post 1861 United States is referred to as the "Yankee Empire." Lincoln and the Republican Party used their political power to unconstitutionally change the original constitutionally limited Republic of Sovereign States into the current supreme Federal Government in which the states are now mere provinces of an all-powerful Federal Government.

Although never convicted of treason in a court of law, Jefferson Davis has been convicted in the court of public opinion. Jefferson Davis and, through him the people of the South, carry the stigma of treason, even to this day. In virtually every schoolbook and official publication of the victor of the War for Southern Independence, Jefferson Davis's motive is questioned and his character slandered as it relates to his actions in 1861-65. Furthermore, his actions and the actions of the South are assaulted by implying that the War for Southern Independence was actually fought to preserve slavery and to destroy the Union. Jefferson Davis's Northern counterpart, Abraham Lincoln, is praised as the great savior of the United States, who not only prevented the destruction of these United States but also destroyed slavery in America. In schoolrooms across the South, one will find photographs of the American icon, Abraham Lincoln. Yet, nowhere in those schools will one find a photograph of the president of the Confederate States of America. So complete has been the South's defeat and pacification that it is no longer capable of appropriately remembering and honoring the sufferings of its ancestors who wore the gray in the struggle for Southern independence. With the publication of this book, Jefferson Davis will now have his day in the court of public opinion. This book will provide a "Southern friendly" view of Davis and the cause for which he fought. This information will be presented to you, the reader, who now represent the "court of public opinion."

This book will serve as the defense for Jefferson Davis against the charge of treason. It is a defense the Yankee Empire, for highly questionable reasons, would not allow—even to this day! The authors will address you, the reader, as Davis's jury, thereby giving you an opportunity, most Americans have been denied—the opportunity to hear President Davis's defense against the charge of treason. This defense is being made after more than a century of the victor's slanderous anti-South, anti-secession, anti-Davis propaganda has been consumed by the American public. After you have had an opportunity to read for yourself the rest of the story about Jefferson Davis and the inalienable right of secession, then you, the jury, will have sufficient facts on which to base your verdict. It has been a long wait but at last, Jefferson Davis will have a fair hearing in the court of public opinion. You, the reader, shall give to the deposed president of the Confederate States of America something the Yankee Empire refused to give him—a fair hearing for the defense, a chance to explain to the world why the people of the South found it necessary, proper, and moral to secede from the United States and establish for themselves a new government ordered upon the American principle of "government by the consent of the governed." Our request is that you, the jury, honor your duty and wait until you have heard all of President Davis's defense before you vote on his guilt or innocence. Your vote will not only reflect how you feel about the charge of treason lodged against Jefferson Davis but it will also reflect upon all Southerners who wore the gray in defense of the South during the War for Southern Independence. The prosecution in this case (i.e., the victors in the war) have had more than 150 years to present and <u>enforce</u> its view of Jefferson Davis and the South's guilt. The prosecution has exercised virtually unchallenged supremacy in presenting its case against the accused. Its well-paid sycophants in postmodern academia, the media, and Hollywood have worked tirelessly to indoctrinate the public with its slanderous, anti-South, views. It is now time for you to hear the plea of the defense.

This court is not composed of those politically correct, woke lackeys who unquestionably endorse the invasion, conquest, occupation, and colonialization of the once sovereign states comprising the Confederate States of America. This court is composed of President Davis's fellow countrymen. After reading this book you will have had an opportunity to acquaint yourself with the principles of our original constitutional Republic of Sovereign States—principles of 1776 that President Jefferson Davis and the South defended in 1861-65. Regardless of your ancestry or where you live, you are President Davis's fellow countryman. You represent an honest and educated jury. You deserve the right to pass Judgment upon the deposed president of a once free and sovereign nation—the Confederate States of America.

Photo part of author's collection. Aubrey Hayden artist.

Chapter 1

DEFENDING OUR PRESIDENT—JEFFERSON DAVIS

ON MAY 10, 1865, the military forces of the United States captured Jefferson Davis. (Hereafter the authors refer to the "United States" as the "Yankee Empire" when the time period in discussion is after 1860.) Jefferson Davis was the democratically elected President of a sovereign nation, the Confederate States of America. From the very outset of the war, the authorities of the Yankee Empire in Washington, DC, had encouraged the idea that they would "hang Jeff Davis from a sour apple tree." After four long years of aggressive and bloody war, the Yankee Empire at last had the opportunity to bring Jefferson Davis to "American" justice! Within a matter of weeks of his capture, the Confederate president found himself a political prisoner of the Yankee Empire, literally bound in chains and shackles, and charged with treason. But, in spite of their former boasting, the Yankee Empire's ruling elite carefully avoided giving President Jefferson Davis his day in court.

Why did the Yankee Empire fail to bring to justice a man whom it had branded a nineteenth-century Benedict Arnold? Why did they avoid bring this Rebel and traitor before the Bar of Justice? Why was this American arrested, imprisoned, chained, shackled, indicted for treason, and yet the Yankee Empire never gave him the constitutional right freely granted to the most vulgar of common criminals—the right to a speedy and fair trial? Were the Yankee Empire's ruling elites afraid of the possible outcome of a fair trial? Were they afraid that the Yankee Empire would lose in court what it had gained in an illegal invasion of a democratically elected, sovereign nation—the Confederate States of America?

Although never convicted of treason in a court of law, President Jefferson Davis (and through him, all traditional Southerners) has been convicted in the Yankee Empire's court of public opinion. Jefferson Davis, and through him the people of the South, have been branded with the stigma of treason to the good ole U.S.A. The slanderous charge of treason is especially evident in the early part of the 2020s. President Jefferson Davis's motive is questioned and his character slandered in every schoolbook and official publication of the victor in the War for Southern Independence. Furthermore, his actions and the actions of the South are viciously slandered by implying that the War for Southern Independence was actually fought to preserve slavery in America forever and to destroy the Union. Jefferson Davis's Northern antagonist, Abraham Lincoln, is praised as the great savior of the United States, who not only prevented the destruction of these United States but also destroyed slavery in America. Today (2022) in American schoolrooms where prayer and Bible reading have been expelled, Lincoln's image looks approvingly down upon the indoctrination of Southern children. Southern taxpayers are financing a federally sponsored, postmodern, left-of-center education system that trains Southern children in the virtues of "one nation indivisible," critical race theory, transgenderism, and radical feminism.

You, the reader, are now empaneled as Jefferson Davis's jury—you will be presented with the defense's evidence that will exonerate President Jefferson Davis from the slanderous charge of treason. You are the jury in the court case against Jefferson Davis—a trial that the Yankee Empire refused to allow the accused. They refused because they knew that the evidence, the facts, would not only exonerate Jefferson Davis but would serve as an indictment of war crimes against their evil Yankee Empire.

This court is composed of open-minded readers of this book. This court is not composed of the politically correct, neo-Marxists who still endorse the invasion, conquest, and occupation of the Confederate States of America. This court is composed of

Americans who are willing to looks at the historical facts and render their judgment based, not upon emotionalism generated by generations of anti-South, pro-Yankee Empire propaganda, but upon a fair analysis of the evidence. This court is made up of Americans, regardless of where the now live, who still honor the heritage of Constitutional liberty as handed down to us from the Founding Fathers. After reading this book you will see that President Jefferson Davis and the Southern people were defending the principles of 1776. If the Colonies had a right to secede from London's oppressive central government in 1776, then the South was right to secede from Washington, DC's oppressive central government in 1861. And as you will see, that right still exist for all American-values voters in Red State, Red County America![1] The War is not over until freedom is won.

---

1 See Kennedy, James Ronald, *Red State Red County Secession: Creating A Nation of Our Own* (Wake Forest, NC: The Scuppernong Press, 2020).

*Isaiah T. Montgomery, Founder of Mound Bayou.
Largest Colored Taxpayer in Mississippi.
Former slave and life-long personal friend of Jefferson Davis.*

Chapter 2

THE HIGH ROAD TO EMANCIPATION

ONE OF THE MOST EVIL and slanderous allegations made by the pre-War North against the South was that Southerners intended to expand and maintain the system of slavery in America forever. Post-War the Yankee Empire's propagandists continue this false and slanderous allegation. They do so to justify the Yankee Empire's illegal invasion and continuing occupation of the South. They arrogantly claim that "The South fought the 'Civil War' to keep their slaves!" Pre-War Northern politicians and other agitators claimed or implied that Southerners were opposed to abolition of slavery and would fight to maintain slavery in America forever. Nothing could be further from the truth. Prior to the capture of the American abolition movement by Northern radicals (around 1830), there were more abolition societies in the South than in the North.[1] The South was motivated to find a way to remove slavery without casting blacks out of their current "homes" and leaving them destitute without any means of support. This is exactly what happened via Yankee

---

1   For a more detailed description of Northern vs Southern motivations for ending slavery see, Kennedy & Kennedy, *Punished With Poverty*, 2nd ed, (Columbia, SC: Shotwell Publishing, 2020), 43-54.

emancipation (Lincoln's low road to emancipation) which resulted in near starvation, disease and impoverishment for 8.5 million black and white sharecroppers in the post-War South.[2]

Although it is difficult for modern-day Americans to understand, for the most part, slaves in the South identified their master's place as their home. There existed a close relation between master and servants that was uniquely different than the image conjured up in Northern minds by radical abolitionist propaganda—*Uncle Tom's Cabin* etc. For example, at the beginning of the War General Forrest took over 43 male slaves with him. These slaves served as soldiers in Forrest's army. During the War Forrest, at his own personal expense, freed these slaves. As free men they could go home or stay with Forrest's army. Most stayed with Forrest until the end of the War. At the end of the War 20 went back "home" with Forrest and worked Forrest's plantation.[3]

Davis, speaking in the U.S. Senate chamber, noted the close relations between white masters and black slaves. Davis saw this close relationship as a direct step on the high road to emancipation:

> There is a relation belonging to this species of property, unlike that of the apprentice or the hired man, which awakens whatever there is of kindness or of nobility of soul in the heart of him who owns it; this can only be alienated, obscured, or destroyed, by collecting this species of property into such masses that the owner is not personally acquainted with the individuals who compose it. In the relation, ... the mere domestic connection of one, two, or at the most half a dozen

---

[2] Chattel slavery morphed into sharecropping slavery after the War. The physical and financial conditions of sharecroppers were far worse for blacks and whites trapped in the system of sharecropping—a system that lasted for over 100 years after the end of the War. In fact, the War did not end slavery, it merely changed its character and swept millions of blacks and whites into the system of tenant farming—a new form of slavery. See, Kennedy & Kennedy, *Punished With Poverty*.

[3] Mitcham, Samuel W., *Bust Hell Wide Open-The Life of Nathan Bedford Forrest*, (New York: Regnery History, 2016), 72-3.

servants in a family, associating with the children as they grow up, attending upon age as it declines, … for this is the high-road and the open gate to the condition in which the masters would, from interest in a few years, desire the emancipation of every one…[4]

Davis expressed this feeling toward slaves in a rebuke of Senator Dix of New York who declared that the black race in America was destined to become extinct. During an 1848 speech in the Senate Senator Dix claimed that "free blacks would continue to be an inferior cast and simply die out." Davis made the following reply to Dix's idea that blacks were destined for extermination:

With surprise and horror, I heard this announcement of a policy which seeks, through poverty and degradation, the extinction of a race of human beings domesticated among us. We, sir, stand in such a relation to that people as creates a feeling of kindness and protection. We have attachments which have grown with us from childhood – to the old servant who nursed us in infancy, to the man who was the companion of our childhood, and the not less tender regard for those who have been reared under our protection. To hear their extinction treated as a matter of public policy or of speculative philosophy arouses our sympathy and our indignation.[5]

Now, contrast Jefferson Davis's attitude toward the black race with those of Northern abolitionists. The Northern idea that black Americans were destined for natural extermination was shared by many officials of the Yankee Empire during the War for Southern Independence. When the Union Army was undergoing a smallpox epidemic it used effective methods to stop the spread of the disease.

---

4   Davis, Jefferson, *Rise and Fall of the Confederate Government*, Vol. 1, (1881, Nashville, TN: William Mayes Coats, circa 1980), 30.

5   Walters, Ryan, "Party Truths," Abbeville Institute Blog, https://bit.ly/3SbXHZN (Accessed 7/10/2021).

When smallpox broke out among blacks in territory occupied by the Northern military, they did little to combat the spread and claimed it was a "natural outcome" of emancipation (Another example of Lincoln's low road to emancipation). It also confirmed their biased opinion that the black race was on the verge of extinction.[6] A correspondent for the *New York Tribune* succinctly summed up the prevailing Northern attitude toward blacks when he advocated a Northern policy toward blacks that would "hem him in and coop him up" leaving the rest of America for "the white man."[7] This was the Northern attitude toward blacks. During the War an Illinois Democrat chastised Republicans and other Northern radicals because of the dire position their war had forced upon "freed" blacks:

> Oh! Ye, honey tongued humanitarians of New England...I would beseech you to go into the camps of the contraband [concentration camps or reservations where free blacks were placed by Northern armies] who are starving and pining for their old homes, and lift them out of the mire into which your improvident and premature schemes have dragged them.[8]

Yet, the Yankee Empire's sycophants in academia and press falsely claim that the North is the center of racial love and respect, while slandering Davis and his Southern countrymen as evil, racist, haters of blacks. The truth is that Davis looked toward the day in which slaves would be free and become a prosperous part of the South. He did more than talk about it, he actively worked for it!

Davis's plantation, Briarfield, was an example of how this would occur. As explained in Chapter 6 Davis set-up a system of judge and jury operated by slaves for judging and punishing breaches in

---

6 Downs, Jim, *Sick From Freedom* (Oxford University Press: 2012), 97, 113.

7 Shepherd Price as cited in, Kennedy & Kennedy, *Punished With Poverty* 2nd edition, 81-2.

8 Cox as cited in, Downs, *Sick From Freedom*, 61.

plantation rules or actual crimes against fellow slaves. Davis saw this as a way to prepare a race that had never formed a democratic society on its own for membership in Southern society:

> ...the preparation of that race for civil liberty and social enjoyment...When the time shall arrive at which emancipation is proper; those most interested will be most anxious to effect it."[9]

From this it is easy to understand why many whites referred to Jefferson Davis as "the friend" of blacks. In this he was only following the example already set by other slave-owning Southerners—many of whom prior to 1830 were active members of abolition societies.

General Robert E. Lee's father-in-law left provisions in his will for the freeing of his slaves. It is said that the only time that General Lee took leave from the Confederate Army was when he went home to execute his father-in-law's last will and testimony. John Randolph of Roanoke, Virginia, left instructions for his slaves to be sent as free men into the open lands of the Northwest Territory but "compassionate" Yankees refused to allow blacks into the Ohio territory.[10] Randolph's words demonstrate the unique and close relation that existed between most Southern slave owners and their slaves.

> With a family of more than two hundred mouths looking up to me for food, I feel an awful charge on my hands. It is easy to rid myself of the burden if I could shut my heart to the cry of humanity and the voice of duty. But in these poor slaves I have found my best and most faithful friends; and I feel that it be more difficult to abandon them...than suffer with them.[11]

---

[9] Davis as cited in, McElroy, Robert, *Jefferson Davis-The Unreal and the Real* (New York: Harper & Brothers Publishers, 1937) Vol. I, 104.

[10] Russell Kirk, *John Randolph of Roanoke: A Study In American Politics* (Indianapolis, IN: Liberty Press, 1978), 186.

[11] John Randolph as cited in *Ibid.*, 159.

John Randolph's words as quoted above are not the words of a cruel, evil, white racist but are the words typical of the vast majority of Southern slave owners.

What impact did Jefferson Davis's attitude toward the black race have on the blacks he owned? Were they filled with hatred toward the man who owned them or were they grateful for the good treatment and opportunities Davis afforded his slaves? The words of three former slaves leave no question about their admiration and love for their former master—all to the astonishment of Yankees then and now.

Below is the text of a letter sent to Jefferson Davis in 1886 from one of Davis's former slaves. Isaiah Montgomery was the President of a large association of "Colored people of Mississippi." The tender and respectable tone of the letter shines through the dark and slanderous propaganda regarding Jefferson Davis and his attitude toward former slaves.

> Vicksburg, Mississippi-Sept. 27th 1886
>
> Hon. Jefferson Davis
>
> Beauvoir, Harrison Co Miss
>
> Dear Sir,
>
> Feeling assured that you would take active interest in any enterprise tending to the welfare and development of the Colored people of Mississippi. We have today mailed you a catalogue of the 1st fair held in /85 and some notices of the second meeting, which takes place at the fair ground near the city from the 10th to 13th Novbr next. If convenient for you to be in this locality about that time, we would be highly pleased to have you visit the Fair. We would also esteem it a special mark of encouragement if yourself and distinguished lady would name a special premium (see pages 12 to

14 in catalogue) (in any line that may suit you) to be put in our catalogue for /86 and completed for at the coming Fair with

Best wishes for your continuous preservation.

I am very respectfully

Your Obt. Servant

Isaiah Montgomery, Prest

In September of 1941 one of Jefferson Davis's former slaves, George Johnson, was interviewed. An audio recording of the interview is held by the Library of Congress. The interviewer was interested in what life was like as a slave on one of Davis's plantations. No doubt the interviewer was surprised when Mr. Johnson detailed the fact that the Davis slaves were all educated!

> Master Jeff sent to Richmond, Virginia an got two teachers. They opened a nice school. Educated all his (Davis's slaves). And made my father a civil engineer. And then made Isaiah Montgomery (another one of Davis's slaves) bookkeeper. And on and on they made different one farmers, carpenters, sawmill (millwright), gin (cotton-gin wright) and all like that... (Davis) had all those (slaves) from different places on those plantations to come to that school. Nice school. He (Davis) give them all a formal education. When they got free, they could take care of they-self... Everyone admired him.

Was slavery, even under a benevolent master, a good, long term, social system? No! Jefferson Davis and the majority of Southerners understood this but the question was not "should slavery be abolished" but how to emancipate slaves without creating a mass of unemployed vagrants roaming across the

South. Jefferson Davis believed it could be done if the North would allow the South to take the slow but steady *high road to emancipation*. But the "high road to emancipation" did not fit into the North's aggressive political ambitions.

William Samford, of Vicksburg, Mississippi, was one of Jefferson Davis's former slaves. He came to New Orleans in 1889 to attend Davis's funeral, to pay his respects to the Davis family, and honor his former master. A Yankee news reporter questioned him, asking why a former slave would shed tears at the death of his former master. This black man's answer shocked the reporter then and, no doubt, it shocks most ill-educated Americans today:

> That I loved him this shows, and I can say that every colored man whom he ever owned loved him. He was a good and kind master.[12]

It was not Northern love of their black brothers and sisters that motivated the Yankee Empire to invade and conquer the South. Just as they do today, the elites of the Yankee Empire use blacks as a tool to advance their own economic and ideological interests. Jefferson Davis called them out in 1848:

> Neither love for the African [recall northern laws against free blacks immigrating into their lily-white states], nor revulsion from property in persons [property transported from Africa by Yankee slave ships] motivated the present-day agitators, ... No sir... the mask is off; the purpose is avowed...It is a struggle for political power.[13]

---

[12] William Samford as cited in, Jones, William J., *A Memorial Volume of Jefferson Davis* (1889, Harrisonburg, VA: Sprinkle Publications, 1993), 500.

[13] Davis as cited in, Allen, Felicity, *Jefferson Davis – Unconquerable Heart*, (University of Missouri Press: 1999) 168.

English journalists who were opposed to slavery could see through the false pretenses put forth by Northern radicals. One English journal ran an editorial that plainly called out Yankee hypocrisy, "They (Northern political radicals primarily of the emerging Republican Party) do not love the Negro as a fellow-man; they pity him as a victim of wrong. They will plead his cause; *they will not tolerate his company.*"[14] [Emphasis added]. Another English journal was even more pointed:

> *Republicans put empire above liberty*, and resorted to political oppression and war rather than suffer any abatement of national power...There was not, in fact, a single argument advanced in defense of the war against the South which might not have been advanced with exactly the same force for the subjugation of Hungary or Poland. Democracy broke down, not when the Union ceased to be agreeable to all its constituent States, but when it was upheld, like any other *Empire*, by force of arms[15] [Emphasis added].

Note this early recognition by foreigners that the once free Republic of the United States had morphed into an aggressive Empire. No, the War was not fought over slavery—although slavery did provide the Yankee Empire with a convenient excuse for its aggressive invasion of a sovereign nation—the War was not fought to preserve the Union because the Constitutional union of free, independent, and sovereign states was destroyed via aggressive war initiated by Lincoln and the Republican Party. The original Constitutionally-limited Republic of Sovereign States was replaced with today's supreme Federal Government. The Yankee Empire went to war for the same reason that King George III went to war in 1776—to preserve an empire. When asked why the North was invading the South an English journalist replied, "For Empire sir, for Empire!"

---

14 As cited in, *The North British Review*, "The American Republic: Resurrection through Dissolution" Edinburgh, British Edition, February 1862, 233-72.

15 *The Times of London*, September 13, 1862, 7-8.

Black lady who cooked for Jefferson Davis while he was in prison

Julia J. Smith was a Woman of Color who cooked for Jefferson Davis while he was in prison. She wrote from Phoebus, VA, November 17, 1903:

> I cooked for the Hon. President Jefferson Davis. Mr. Davis was in prison nine months before I commenced cooking for him; then I was his cook until he went away. The first thing he desired me to cook was to devil some crabs for him, which I did. Dr. Cooper was his physician and Rev. Minnigerode, of Richmond, VA., was his minister. I was very sorry when he left. I never lived with better people in all my life. He and his wife were very grateful for everything that I did for them. Could I see you, I would relate to you many incidents that happened while I was there, which are very interesting. I loved Mr. Davis. May God bless his offspring, and long may they live! [Excerpt from the *Confederate Veteran* Magazine January 1904].

Chapter 3

THE FOUNDING FATHERS STRUGGLE AGAINST SLAVERY

THE MERE MENTION OF SLAVERY in America immediately congers up the image of Simon Legree mercilessly beating Uncle Tom, a poor downtrodden black slave. Unfortunately, Simon Legree is the stereotypical image created and maintained by Yankee propaganda as a description of all Southern slave owners. As we have already seen in Chapter 2, this is far from an accurate description of the relationship between black and white folks in pre-War Dixie. Evidence of the close relation between Southern masters and their slaves is documented by the fact that, "U.S. slaves had much longer life expectations than free urban industrial workers in both the United States and Europe."[1] Free blacks in New Orleans, Louisiana, owned more property and had better living conditions than free blacks in New York, New York.[2] These and unnumbered other facts are carefully censored (hidden) by the Yankee Empire's political, media, entertainment, and postmodern academic propagandists. Maintaining their complete monopoly of facts about the War is a matter of life and death for the Yankee Empire. Without their ability to monopolize the flow of information about the War, they would not be able to maintain the false justification for their criminal invasion,

---

1   Fogel & Engerman, *Time On The Cross-The Economics of American Negro Slavery* (Little, Brown, & Company, New York: 1974), 126.

2   *Ibid.*, 244.

conquest, and occupation of the South. The truth is to the Yankee Empire what kryptonite is to Superman! Even the smallest amount of truth will destroy the Empire's hold on America.

As we have previously noted, the South was at one time the leading section in the American movement to abolish chattel slavery. Even before independence Southerners attempted to halt the nefarious British and New England slave trade. The Founding Fathers were well aware of the need to limit and eventually abolish chattel slavery. *But chattel slavery is not the only form of slavery.* The Founding Fathers understood that the first principle of a free people is to protect their constitutional rights and thereby prevent free people from becoming political slaves.

St. George Tucker

St. George Tucker, (1752-1827) of Virginia was a champion of the original Constitution and an abolitionist. In his treatise against slavery, Tucker described three forms of slavery: (1) *Political slavery*. Political slavery exists when a nation (such as the Confederate States of America) is conquered by another nation (such as the United States of America). Tucker states that the "subjection of one nation or people, to the will of another, constitutes the first species of slavery."[3] In the state of political slavery, the people of the conquered and subjugated nation are denied the right to live under a government based upon the consent of the governed. The day-to-day existence of each member of society may be relatively free, yet it is the ruling government and not the people that has the ultimate authority over the society. (2) *Civil slavery*. Civil slavery exists any time the government encroaches upon the liberties of the citizens more than is absolutely necessary for the maintenance of a peaceful society. According to Tucker, this happens "whenever the laws of a state respect the form, or energy of the government, more that the

---

[3] St George Tucker, *A View of the Constitution of the United States: With Selective Writings*, Clyde N. Wilson, ed. (Indianapolis, IN: Liberty Fund Inc., 1999), 407.

happiness of the citizen."[4] This idea is similar to James Madison's writings in the *Federalist* number 43, "...the safety and happiness of a society are the objects at which all political institutions must be sacrificed." Tucker also notes that civil slavery exists any time laws are unequally enforced or any time there is "inequality of rights or privileges between the subjects or citizens of the same state." (3) *Domestic slavery.* Domestic slavery is a condition in which "one man is subject to be directed by another in all his actions."[5] A little remembered example of Domestic or Chattel slavery is when St. Patrick was held as a slave in Ireland before he escaped and returned as a Christian missionary to the heathen Irish. Chattel slavery is not unique to one race or ethnic group—no race of men has been spared the humiliation of slavery. The very word "slave" derives from the white Slavic people who were captured and sold into slavery by the Muslim Turks.

Statelessness is a prerequisite for political slavery. When viewing the various aspects of slavery as described by Tucker, it becomes evident that modern-day Americans who hold traditional conservative political and moral values are a stateless people. We have no government that protects and (more importantly) promotes our values. The existing government is at war with our values. As such, we are being held in political slavery.

There exists a never-ending struggle between liberty and morality on one side and unbridled power and moral corruption on the other side. That struggle is more pronounced today (2022) in America than it has ever been. Today there exist an *irreconcilable ideological division* between traditional, conservative, Christian values folks (Red State, Red County voters) and postmodern, liberal, neo-Marxist folks (Blue State, Blue County voters). Under the current system of government, one side will dominate and the other side must submit. In contemporary America the neo-Marxist ruling elite in Deep State Washington, DC, use their political control of government, academia, the mainline, and digital media to compel traditional, American-values folks to submit to Deep State

---

[4] *Ibid.,* 408.

[5] *Ibid.,* 409.

(neo-Marxist) legislation, regulations, Supreme Court rulings, and taxation.[6] Meanwhile, "We the people" are derided as "deplorables," "irredeemables," and "bitter clingers." Traditional Americans have no government that will consistently protect and promote our values—we are in fact a stateless people. Historically, stateless people are, at worst, easy targets for genocide or, at best, the ruling elite's political slaves. Political slavery (and therefore statelessness) was of great concern to the Founding Fathers. The following are examples of early Americans pointing out the danger of political slavery:

- Jonathan Mayhew, of Boston Church voiced his understanding that the British people executed King Charles I on January 30, 1649, because "Britons will not be slaves."[7] Note, Mayhew was speaking about political slavery.

- Mayhew delivered a sermon in 1754 in which he declared that "loyalty and slavery are not synonymous."[8] Free people voluntarily give their loyalty to "their" country—a country that protects and promotes their interests. But slaves are *compelled* to swear allegiance to an indivisible empire that holds them captive.

- Samuel Stillman, pastor of the First Baptist Church of Boston preached that Americans had "too great a Sense of the Privileges of Englishmen, too much of the Spirit of Britons, and too great a Conviction of our own Importance, to consent to be Slaves."[9]

- John Adams condemned the British Monarchy as "a race of Kings bigoted to the greatest degree to the doctrines of *slavery*."[10]

---

6 Inflation is an indirect tax. It is caused by government devaluing the purchasing power of its money. Politicians do this by allowing for the issuing of unsound credit and printing of fiat currency that is backed by nothing other than the promises of politicians. Increasing price of goods and services is a symptom of decreased purchasing power of government money. Inflation that average folks see as increasing prices allow politicians to blame greedy businesses for inflation and thereby deflect guilt from themselves.

7 As cited in, Colbourn, Trevor, *The Lamp of Experience* (Indianapolis, Indiana: Liberty Fund, 1965), 74.

8 Ibid., 75.

9 Ibid., 82.

10 Ibid., 92.

- Josiah Quincy noted the courage of the Dutch and Hungarians who were slandered as "Rebels" "they were called so for no other reason than …that they would not be slaves."[11] The English called American Patriots "Rebels" just as Yankees called Southerners Rebels just because they were fighting to defend their country's independence—they would not be slaves.

- John Adams urged the educated classes to dwell upon "the beauty of liberty and virtue, and the deformity, turpitude, and malignity, of slavery and vice." He also warned colonists that "there seems to be a direct and formal design on foot, to enslave all Americans."[12]

- Adams also noted the those who fight for freedom can never lose because "If they die, they cannot be said to lose, since death is preferable to slavery."[13]

- Adams had such a strong faith in annual elections that he declared "where annual elections end, there slavery begins."[14]

- John Dickinson of Pennsylvania was a reluctant Revolutionary but he knew that free people could lose their freedom and become political slaves when "the *mad moment* which slipt [slip] upon them the shackles of slavery."[15] Fabian socialism (creeping or gradual socialism) is an example of how free people can allow their freedom to die of gradualism.

- Dickinson understood that England was no longer America's "friend." He stated "There can be no friendship between freemen and slaves."[16]

---

11 *Ibid.*, 98.
12 *Ibid.*, 108-9.
13 *Ibid.*, 115.
14 *Ibid.*, 120.
15 *Ibid.*, 132.
16 *Ibid.*, 134.

- Dickinson also noted the danger posed to freemen by large standing armies. He described Charles II's use of a large army in 1684 as a way in which a tyrannical King could "make his people *fully sensible of their new slavery...*"[17] The use of military force to pacify a formerly free people is not new in world history.

- He knew that liberty was generally lost by "the decay of *virtue*," that "SLAVERY IS EVER PRECEDED BY SLEEP."[18] Note: "The decay of *virtue*." What would he say about America's current political system of crony capitalism, the unelected Deep State bureaucracy, and the slanderous neo-Marxist propaganda issuing forth from the media and academia?

- James Wilson of Pennsylvania warned that King George III was becoming "a *Tyrant* over *Slaves.*"[19]

- Benjamin Franklin warned Americans that if the King's and Parliament's oppression of rights belonging to all Englishmen continues—rights derived under the ancient English constitution—then the result will be to "enslave us all."[20]

- George Washington argued that the mother country's King and Parliament "are endeavoring by every piece of Art and despotism to fix the Shackles of Slavery upon us."[21]

- Washington warned that if the King and Parliament continue oppressing the Rights of Englishmen "the once happy plains of America are either to be drenched with blood or inhabited by slaves."[22]

---

17 *Ibid.*, 136.
18 *Ibid.*, 138.
19 *Ibid.*, 151.
20 *Ibid.*, 158.
21 *Ibid.*, 189.
22 *Ibid.*, 191.

- Thomas Jefferson noted that it was not just the King who is becoming America's slave master but all 160,000 Englishmen who were allowed to vote in Parliamentary elections. Jefferson declared "we should suddenly be found the slaves, not of one, but of 160,000 tyrants."[23]

- Thomas Jefferson saw the danger of creeping tyranny that slowly, almost without public notice, has its design to reduce a free people to slavery. "History has informed us that bodies of men as well as individuals are susceptible of the spirit of tyranny...Single acts of tyranny may be ascribed to the accidental opinion of a day; but a series of oppressions, begun at a distinguished period, and pursued unalterably though every change of ministers, too plainly prove a deliberate, systematical plan of reducing us to slavery."[24]

- James Cannon declared of Englishmen that they had "lost the distinguishing character between freemen and slaves."[25]

- An American Whig noted "whether you be English, Irish, Germans or Swedes, ...by your residence, and the laws of your country, [we are] freemen and not slaves."[26]

These examples, drawn from America's Colonial past, demonstrate that from the very beginning of our county, our forefathers were greatly concerned about the dangers of political slavery. Neo-Marxists (also known as liberals, progressives, postmodernists, etc.) attempt to detract from America's early fear of slavery by claiming that white Americans expressed no concern about African slavery. The historical fact is that several Southern colonies were the very first to attempt to control or prohibit the African slave trade in America and that prior to the abolition movement being captured by New England extremists, circa 1830,

---

23 *Ibid.*, 200.
24 *Ibid.*, 201.
25 *Ibid.*, 228.
26 *Ibid.*, 232.

there were more abolition societies in the South than in the North.[27] As to the allegation that "white" Americans did not care about African slavery even while white Americans were struggling to gain their independence—it is an illogical but highly emotional charge against our Colonial ancestors. Suppose there are two homes on fire and one of them is yours! Which home do you attend to first? The fact that you do not rush over and help your neighbor fight his fire, while yours burns, does not mean that you are not concerned about his dire situation. Once you save your house, then you are free to go over and help your neighbor. That is the principle that patriotic Americans applied to the issue of African slavery. The fact that some Southern Colonies attempted to pass laws to halt the slave trade prior to the Revolutionary War is proof that they were concerned but gaining their freedom, and thus avoiding political slavery, was utmost in their minds. One of the indictments against King George III listed in the Declaration of Independence was that his government voided (nullified) laws passed by Colonial Legislatures regarding issues such as the slave trade. Once the English Empire's attempt to make political slaves of all Americans was defeated, then a vigorous abolition movement sprang up in America, especially in the South prior to 1830.

The struggle against political slavery requires bold and courageous men and women. The struggle against political slavery requires enlightened folks who can recognize the danger ahead when slavery is slowly creeping upon them. Cowardly, apathetic, timid, and pacified conservatives will cling to their chains in hope of gaining some degree of security but, with the passing of each day, the chains of political slavery become heavier and are fastened tighter. Failure to act when there is a greater possibility that freedom could be won without violence and bloodshed is the greatest sin committed by

---

27 See, Kennedy & Kennedy, *Yankee Empire: Aggressive Abroad and Despotic at Home* (Columbia, SC: Shotwell Publishing, 2018), 179-99; Kennedy & Kennedy, *Punished With Poverty-The suffering South* 2nd edition (Columbia, SC: Shotwell Publishing, 2020), 43-54; Kennedy & Kennedy, *The South Was Right!* 3rd edition (Columbia, SC: Shotwell Publishing, 2020), 79-106.

pacified, cowardly, and timid conservatives. Historically, there are numerous examples of occupied people using non-violent methods to achieve their freedom.[28]

Looking at the generation of 1776 it becomes evident that our forefathers were patriotic heroes because they were NOT prudent men! They could hear the clanking chains of political slavery and boldly risked all for liberty. They were revolutionaries, not like the neo-Marxist mobs in America's streets today, they did not advocate the violent destruction of society. They were seeking to conserve the ancient rights of Englishmen—constitutional rights that were based on the Magna Charter secured by bold Englishmen of prior generations.

Jefferson Davis and his generation of Southerners took a stand in 1861 similar to the stand Colonial Americans took in 1776. The primary points of contention in 1861 were not tariffs or slavery—just as tea taxes and the Stamp Act were not the primary points of contention in 1776. In both cases the primary point of contention was that of protecting constitutional rights belonging to all Americans—rights without which Americans become stateless people and therefore political slaves. Today's generation of Southerners and Americans in general are faced with a similar challenge. Will "we the people" passively accept the neo-Marxist chains of political slavery or will we take the bold action necessary to abolish neo-Marxist political slavery in America? Will we become America's modern-day abolitionists fighting against political slavery?

Some may complain that there is no danger of political slavery in America because they mistakenly believe "we have a constitution that protects our rights." But they seem to be ignorant of the fact that *no word, clause, article or amendment in the Constitution is self-enforcing*! Stateless people have no government to enforce the "protections" inscribed in the Constitution. Stateless people are political slaves. Political slavery is what Jefferson Davis and his fellow Southerners were trying to prevent. The following list will

---

28 See examples of five nations that used non-violence to defend their freedom and culture in, Kennedy, James Ronald, *Dixie Rising-Rules for Rebels* 2nd edition, (Columbia, SC: Shotwell Publishing, 2020), 103-15.

demonstrate how effective the neo-Marxist have been in their effort to destroy constitutional liberty and thereby enslave American-values, conservative, voters to their leftist ideology:

- The right of the people within their state to determine when human life begins no longer exists[29]
- The right of the people within their state to determine if they will allow prayer and Bible reading in their public schools no longer exists
- The right of the people within their state to establish the definition of marriage no longer exists
- The right of the people within their state to define sexual perversion based upon Biblical principles no longer exists
- The right of the people within their state to determine if welfare benefits will be provided to illegal aliens no longer exists[30]

President Jefferson Davis and his fellow Southerners could see the approaching tyranny that would turn Southerners into the Yankee Empire's political slaves. They could see the emerging Yankee Empire that was determine to exploit the South for the benefit of Northern financial, commercial, and political elites. With their victory in the War for Southern Independence, the Yankee Empire has become what General Robert E. Lee, in 1866, predicted it would become, like all other empires, "aggressive abroad and despotic at home."[31]

It takes bold and dedicated men to risk all in the pursuit of liberty. Was Jefferson Davis such a man? Who was this man, Jefferson Davis? Was he the Rebel, the arch traitor the Yankee Empire's propagandists claim or was he an honorable man, willing to risk all for his country, his Southern kith and kin, and for Constitutional government?

---

29 Even if the Supreme Court "allows" states to again exercise these rights, there is no guarantee that said right(s) will be permanent. What master gives; master can take away. Under the current illegitimate Federal system, it is not a "right" but merely a "privilege" graciously allowed by the master, i.e., the supreme Federal Government.

30 Kennedy, James Ronald, *Be Ye Separate-Bible Belt Revival or Marxist Revolution* (Maitland, Fl: Xulon Press, 2021), 99.

31 Kennedy & Kennedy, *Yankee Empire: Aggressive Abroad and Despotic at Home* (Columbia, SC: Shotwell Publishing, 2018), 65.

Chapter 4

Jefferson Davis: The Early Years

JEFFERSON DAVIS, THE YOUNGEST of ten children, five boys and five girls, was born on June 3, 1808, in Christian County, Kentucky. Because of a subsequent subdivision of Christian County, the portion of the county of his nativity is now within the limits of Todd County, Kentucky. The town of Fairview was established in the locale of his birthplace some years after the subdivision of Christian County. The actual site of his birthplace was given to the Baptist church of Fairview by Davis in 1886 for the construction of their church building. The lineage of great men is often the subject of discussion among historians, genealogists, and casual observers. "The brave beget the brave," in its Latin equivalent, are words often used by the United Daughters of the Confederacy when honoring heroic efforts of descendants of Confederate soldiers. Genealogists have a saying that "the apple does not drop far from the tree." Southerners have always held family lineage as an important part of the make-up of an individual. The family of Jefferson Davis exemplifies this tradition.

The origin of Davis's greatness could very well be said to reside in his father, Samuel Davis. Jefferson Davis's father was a native of Georgia and a Revolutionary War veteran. Jefferson Davis stated that his father was "a native of Georgia, and served in the war of the revolution, first in the 'mounted gunmen,' and afterward as

Rosemont, Davis' childhood home, "Where my memories begin."

captain of infantry at the siege of Savannah."[1] Samuel Davis's courage and fortitude in the defense of his home state of Georgia was exhibited when, as a sixteen-year-old boy, he was sent by his mother to assist his half-brothers then serving in the Revolutionary War. He remained in the service and rose to the rank of captain. Samuel Davis's widowed mother died before her children returned from the war. Jefferson Davis's father, Samuel, was wounded during the Revolutionary War battle of Kettle Creek[2] which took place in Wilkes County, Georgia, in 1779. In the battle, four hundred patriots led by Colonels Clark, Dooley, and Pickens routed more than seven hundred British loyalists. This legacy of courage in the defense of liberty undoubtedly was an inspiration to Samuel's children. According to Jefferson Davis, Samuel Davis met Miss Jane Cook of South Carolina while serving in the Georgia militia. Samuel Davis

---

1   Jefferson Davis, as cited in J. William Jones, *A Memorial Volume of Jefferson Davis* (1889, Harrisonburg, VA: Sprinkle Publications, 1993), 27.

2   Janet S. Hermann, *Joseph E. Davis, Pioneer Patriarch* (Jackson, MS: University Press of Mississippi, 1990), 3.

and Jane Cook were married in July 1783. Davis states that his father, Samuel, was Welsh, and his mother, Jane Cook, was Scots-Irish.[3] Of some note is the fact that both of Jefferson Davis's parents were literate, a notable feat for people inhabiting a near-wilderness on the American frontier. The names of Samuel Davis's children are found on the muster sheets of every war that the United States fought from the Revolution until the War for Southern Independence. The patriotic influence of the father was felt by the sons of military age who, during the War of 1812, while Jefferson was a child of three years, joined in the defense of the Mississippi Territory. Of Samuel Davis's five sons, four were of military age at the time of the war. Three of the four served in defense of the United States, two of them winning high praise from Gen. Andrew Jackson for their actions during the Battle of New Orleans.[4] So strong was the patriotic spirit in the Mississippi Territory that the local government had to draft men to stay at home! One of Samuel Davis's sons was prevented from joining the war effort by this draft.[5] Today, when it is so common to hear of draft-dodgers at times of national danger, it is hard to believe that men could be so instilled with love of country that an order had to be issued to keep them at home.

Shortly after the close of the Revolutionary War and before the Davis family left Georgia, their life settled down to a more normal pace. Six months after the birth of their first son, Joseph, Samuel Davis joined with other members of Wilkes County, Georgia, to organize the Phillips Mill Baptist Church. This church was housed in a small log chapel built by the men of the community. About this time, the Davis family acquired their first slave, Winny. Winny and Samuel Davis were both members of Phillips Mill Baptist Church. A curiosity is that, although Winny, a slave, and Samuel Davis, her master, were members of the local Baptist church, Jane Davis was

---

3   Varina Howell Davis, *Jefferson Davis, A Memoir by His Wife* (New York: Belford Company, Publishers, 1890) I, 3, 4.

4   Hermann, 25.

5   Walter L. Fleming, "The Early Life of Jefferson Davis," *University Bulletin*, Louisiana State University, June 1917, Vol. 8, No. 6, 160.

never a member. The membership of a black slave and white master in the same church has often been cited as evidence of the close and cordial relations between the races at this time in Southern history.

> The position of black members in the Phillips Mill Baptist Church reflects the attitude of the eighteenth-century rural society toward the race. Although each new member was listed as "Turner's Sam" or "Chiver's Amy" or "Samuel Davis's Winny," he or she seemed to suffer no restriction in worship.[6]

Although strange to the ears of modern, "politically correct" Americans, this cordial relationship between the races was not unique to Georgia. In Mississippi, and about the same time Phillips Mill Baptist Church in Georgia was being organized, the same friendly relationship has been noted.

> The history of the Palestine Baptist Church, Simpson County, Mississippi, relates such a story. The Palestine Baptist Church was organized in 1786 (one year before the United States Constitution was ratified) by twelve men, eleven white and one black .... The significance of the black members of the church is obvious: the first Baptist church west of the Mississippi River, for example, was established in Louisiana by Joseph Wills, a black preacher.[7]

The close relationship between the races among Baptists in the Old South elicited this response from noted Southern historian Francis B. Simkins: "The Baptists did this less by deliberate missionary efforts than by accepting Negro members on a basis of Christian brotherhood that seems strange in the twentieth-century South."[8] The perception that the evils of slavery could be

---

6   Hermann, 6.

7   *Palestine Baptist Church Pictorial Directory* 1988 Harrisville, Simpson County, MS, 2.

8   Francis B. Simkins, *A History of the South* (New York: Alfred A. Knopf, 1959), 159.

diminished by the civilizing influence of Christianity was to be the hallmark of the South's opinion about the institution of slavery. The Davis family embraced this theory; and the kind and generous spirit demonstrated toward blacks given to their care was typical of the entire Davis family.

By 1793, the Davis family moved to Kentucky where the last child of Samuel and Janet, Jefferson, was born. It was here in Kentucky that Samuel Davis's family was to mature and become a stable, middle-class family. No matter where the family moved after this time, Kentucky had made a permanent influence on the Davis family and would be remembered with fondness. Both farming and mercantile trade kept the family members busy, especially older brother Joseph. Joseph Davis would play the role of a father figure for Jefferson after the death of Samuel Davis. In 1810, Samuel Davis moved his family down the Natchez Trace and into Louisiana to a farm on Bayou Teche. A year in the mosquito-laden low country and swamps was enough to convince Samuel to again move his family. The family abandoned the home in Louisiana after one year and moved one last time to Wilkinson County in Mississippi, where hills and clear-water springs were more to the liking of the former Kentuckian.

Jefferson Davis was four years old when his family settled in Mississippi. Davis's elder brother, Joseph, at that time was twenty-six years old and already a man of means and position in the territory. To understand Jefferson Davis fully, one must understand both Samuel and Joseph Davis. Joseph was not only a planter but also a lawyer and budding politician. As their father grew older and more dependent on his sons for assistance, Joseph slowly began to shoulder the burden of family patriarch. By the year 1816, various elements within the Mississippi Territory (the current states of Mississippi and Alabama) were demanding the admission of Mississippi to the Union. At a convention of delegates of the territory, Joseph Davis was chosen as chairman of the committee to draw up a petition to Congress "praying that the Mississippi Territory might be admitted into the Union as a *free, sovereign, and independent state*" [emphasis added].

In 1817, the western portion of the Mississippi Territory was admitted to the Union as the state of Mississippi. The balance of the territory was organized as the Alabama Territory and awaited its turn for admission into the Union. Joseph Davis was chosen as a delegate from Jefferson County to the Mississippi Constitutional Convention. At the convention, Joseph voted along with other members from his section of the state. Nevertheless, he often broke ranks with many friends in pushing for as conservative a constitution as possible. Joseph demanded and voted for a constitutional amendment that limited the franchise to taxpayers only, opposed outlawing duels, and favored mandatory service in the militia.

The most controversial stand taken by Joseph was in trying to pass a constitutional amendment that would limit the power of masters over slaves. Joseph and other delegates recommended that masters who were cruel to their slaves would have their slaves taken away and sold, with the profits going to the benefit of the poor. The measure did not pass but was an indication of the Davis family's high regard for the care of slaves. It should be noted that Joseph took this position even though it endangered his law practice. To him, it was a matter of principle. The willingness of Joseph Davis to risk the loss of personal gain in the defense of a principle was a characteristic common in the Davis family. One historian notes that this stand by Joseph Davis could be explained because "having grown up with one or two blacks who shared the hardships of frontier life with his family, Davis never lost the ability to see them as humans with the same feelings as whites."[9]

With its work completed, the convention adjourned in August 1817. The constitution drawn up was very similar to and in many ways a copy of the constitutions of Kentucky, Tennessee, and Louisiana.[10] In each of these state constitutions, a clear declaration of state sovereignty is made. The constitutions of both Tennessee and Louisiana declared the intention of their people to form "a free

---

9   Hermann, 31.

10 *Ibid.*

and independent state."[11] In Tennessee's constitution, the people also declared "that government being instituted for the common benefit, the doctrine of non-resistance against arbitrary power and oppression is absurd, slavish, and destructive to the good and happiness of mankind."[12] Earlier the neighboring state of Kentucky had become enraged by the abuse of federal power and requested of Thomas Jefferson that he write a defense of States' Rights. During this crisis the state of Virginia issued a similar request to James Madison. The two resolves became known as the Kentucky and Virginia Resolutions of 1798. These resolutions made the following declaration: "Resolved, that the several States composing the United States of America are not united on the principle of unlimited submission to their general government... each State acceded as a State, and is an integral party [of the compact of union]." The resolutions went on to proclaim that the Federal Government "was not made the exclusive or final judge to the extent of the powers delegated to itself."[13]

When Jefferson Davis was only eight years old, his brother and fellow Mississippians were already waving the flag of States' Rights. Indeed, the people of the South had imbibed the philosophy of States' Rights from the earliest parts of their history.[14] It should come as no surprise that these people, or their descendants, would not surrender their faith in this American principle without a fight. Little did anyone realize at that time that the future commander in chief of that heroic struggle for States' Rights was a mere lad in their community.

---

11   Constitutions of Tennessee and Louisiana, as cited in *The American's Guide to the Constitutions of the United States of America* (Trenton, NJ: Moore and Lake, 1813), 303, 341.

12   Constitution of Tennessee, *Ibid.*, 314.

13   Kentucky and Virginia Resolutions, as cited in Kennedy & Kennedy, *The South Was Right!* 3rd edition, (1991, 1994, Columbia, SC: Shotwell Publishing, 2020), 230-1.

14   Kennedy & Kennedy, *The South Was Right!* 3rd edition, (1991, 1994, Columbia, SC: Shotwell Publishing, 2020), 318-31.

December of 1817, President James Monroe signed the resolution admitting Mississippi into the Union—Joseph Davis was thirty-three years old and Jefferson Davis was nine years old. In the fall of 1819, Joseph was elected to the state legislature where he served on a committee studying the banning of the importation of more slaves into the state. Joseph became known as a man of independent thinking and a man of principle. On July 4, 1824, when Jefferson Davis was only fourteen years old, his father died. From that point until Jefferson's adulthood, Joseph Davis became a father figure to the younger Davis. This view was expressed often by Jefferson Davis in his later years. In September of that year, Joseph, using his political influence, secured an appointment for his younger brother to the United States Military Academy at West Point, New York. The relationship between Joseph and Jefferson Davis was more akin to that of father and son than that of two brothers. Joseph kept a close watch on Jefferson's progress at the academy and even made a trip to visit his younger brother during Jefferson's stay. Yet, the roots of Jefferson Davis's education were far removed from West Point, New York.

As a young man growing up in the frontier environment of Mississippi, Davis was educated by his parents and at a local "academy." At the age of seven, he was sent away to Kentucky for more formal education at St. Thomas Aquinas College, a Roman Catholic school. Young Jefferson made the trip from South Mississippi to Kentucky (a trip of several weeks' duration) on a pony in the company of Maj. Thomas Hinds, former commander of the Mississippi horsemen during the Battle of New Orleans. Near Nashville, Tennessee, the travelers paid a visit to Major Hinds' old commander, Andrew Jackson. At this early age, young Jefferson was to meet a future president of the United States. Davis fondly remembered the kind and courteous treatment extended to him by both Andrew Jackson and Mrs. Jackson. Reflecting on his youthful sojourn with General Jackson, Davis, in later life stated that "in me he inspired reverence and affection that has remained with me through my whole life."[15] Davis and Major Hinds stayed with

---

15 Jefferson Davis, as cited in Fleming, 163.

the Jackson family for several weeks. While there, they noted that General Jackson, a battle-harden soldier, always said grace before eating a meal, a fact that impressed young Davis.

Young Jefferson remained at St. Thomas Aquinas College for two years. Returning to Mississippi at age nine, he continued his education at a nearby academy. At the age of fourteen, in 1821, Jefferson was sent back to Kentucky to Transylvania College in Lexington. At the time, Transylvania College was one of America's premier institutions of higher education. Transylvania offered a regular course of study as well as advanced study in law and medicine. In 1821, Transylvania had an enrollment of 383 students compared to 319 students at Yale and 286 students at Harvard.[16] During the time that Jefferson Davis served in Congress, no fewer than eighteen members of the House and Senate, representing at least nine states, were graduates of Transylvania College.[17] It was at Transylvania that Davis met and became lifelong friends with classmate George W. Jones. Jones, as representative from the Michigan Territory, would one day introduce Davis into Washington, D.C., political society. From Transylvania College, at age sixteen, Davis was admitted to West Point Military Academy. Davis's appointment to the academy was made through the office of Secretary of State John C. Calhoun. How strange is the hand of Providence; one day Senator Davis, whose mother was from South Carolina, would pick up the mantle laid down by Senator John C. Calhoun of South Carolina.

Even at an early stage of his life, Jefferson Davis had already made an impression on those who knew him. Shortly after his departure from Transylvania College for West Point, the following toast was offered by his friends in Lexington, Kentucky, at a Washington birthday celebration: "To the health of Jefferson Davis, late a student of Transylvania, now a cadet at West Point. May he become the pride of our country and the idol of our army."[18]

Summary

---

16 *Ibid.*, 169.

17 *Ibid,*, 170.

18 *Ibid.*, 174.

Jefferson Davis was born and raised during the early days of these United States. Davis's father was a native of Georgia and his mother a native of South Carolina. Davis's family roots ensured that staunch ties of blood to the Deep South would develop. His father was a veteran of the Revolutionary War, receiving wounds during action in some of the most difficult and partisan battles of the near civil war between patriots and Tories in Georgia. When Jefferson Davis was only five years old, three of his older brothers served as members of the Mississippi Territory militia and saw action in defense of their country during the War of 1812. Jefferson Davis grew up in a home that had a deep regard for the Christian religion, his father being a founding member of an early Baptist church in Georgia. He was introduced to the system of slavery at an early age by parents who held to the then prevalent view of biblical slavery, a view that his older brother Joseph would expand upon in an attempt to ameliorate some of the coarser aspects of the institution.

At the death of his father, Jefferson's elder brother Joseph assumed the responsibility of head of the family and became the most influential man in young Jefferson's life. Joseph's standing in the community, both social and political, made it possible for the younger Davis to attend both Transylvania College in Kentucky and the United States Military Academy at West Point, New York. When Jefferson Davis became a cadet at West Point, at age sixteen, that event marked the beginning of the career of an influential American statesman and patriot.

Chapter 5

JEFFERSON DAVIS: THE SOLDIER

JEFFERSON DAVIS was appointed to the United States Military Academy at West Point, New York while he was in his third year at Transylvania College in Lexington, Kentucky. In 1824, at the age of sixteen, young Jefferson moved to New York to begin the life of a cadet. This move would put Davis in contact with some of America's brightest and soon to be most notable personalities. Yet, in the class of which Jefferson Davis was a member, few names appear that would be recognized by modern Americans. A fellow Mississippian, Maj. William T. Walthall, stated, "With the exception, however, of Jefferson Davis himself, but few of his class have attained special eminence—none any brilliant or historic reputation— either in civil or military pursuits."[1]

Although few notable personalities were found within his class, his associates in the classes his junior and senior were to become some of America's best-known leaders of that age. In the graduating class of 1825, one year after Davis was admitted, are found the names of men such as A. H. Brown, an engineer officer who played a leading role in the construction of Fort Sumter; Benjamin Huger, major general of the Confederate Army; and Robert Anderson, Yankee defender of Fort Sumter in April 1861. The class of 1826 graduated such men as Albert Sidney Johnston, the "Stonewall of the West" of

---

[1] William T. Walthall, *The Life of Jefferson Davis* (1908, Biloxi, MS: The Beauvoir Press, 1989), 2.

the Confederate Army and a personal friend of Davis, and Samuel P. Heintzelman, Union general and cadet whose copy of William Rawle's textbook on the United States Constitution would be cited by many Southerners in the defense of the right of secession. The class of 1827 graduated such men as Robert E. Lee, most notable of all American military leaders; Joseph E. Johnston, Confederate general and nemesis of the Confederate president; Leonidas Polk, Episcopal bishop and Confederate general; and Union general Philip St. George Cooke. Of special interest for Davis after the close of the War for Southern Independence was an 1830 graduate, Albert T. Bledsoe. Bledsoe was assistant secretary of war in Davis's administration as well as a noted political scientist and theologian. It was Bledsoe's work *Is Davis a Traitor or Was Secession a Constitutional Right* that would be at the center of Davis's defense against the charge of treason after the Yankee Empire's illegal occupation of the Confederate States of America. Bledsoe's capability as a defender of the Southern cause was noted by none other than Robert E. Lee, who after the war told Dr. Bledsoe, "Take care of yourself, Doctor; you have a great task; we look to you for our vindication."[2]

At West Point, Davis's education centered around the training of a good soldier. Yet, one class that was taught at the academy had implications for all the young men, the class on constitutional law. Two textbooks for this class were noted by Davis as being in use at West Point Military Academy while he was a student there: Rawle's *A View of the Constitution of the United States of America* and James Kent's *Commentaries on American Law*. According to Davis, "Rawle on the Constitution was the textbook at West Point, but when the class of which I was a member entered the graduating year Kent's Commentaries were introduced."[3] The subject of a textbook advocating the right of secession being used at West Point will be discussed in more detail elsewhere in this work. What is to be noted here is that the idea of States' Rights had a strong influence throughout America at that lime, nothing to the contrary having

---

2   Robert E. Lee, as cited in Albert T. Bledsoe, *Is Davis a Traitor?* (1866, North Charleston, SC: Fletcher and Fletcher Publishing, 1995), Introduction.

3   Jefferson Davis, as cited in Edgar S. Dudley, "Was 'Secession' Taught at West Point?" *The Century Magazine* (New York: The Century Co., 1909), LXXVIII, 633.

been taught cadets at West Point. Kent's *Commentaries*, which served as Davis's textbook on the Constitution, makes it clear that the Federal Government could exercise only those powers which were specifically delegated to it, all power not delegated by the states to the Federal Government remained with the states[4] (a concise and fitting definition of States' Rights).

Jefferson Davis graduated from the United States Military Academy at West Point in 1828, at the age of twenty. He graduated twenty-third out of a class of thirty-three. He was appointed a second lieutenant in the Sixth Regiment of Infantry and shortly thereafter was transferred to the First Infantry Regiment. His first assignment was to Fort Crawford in the Northwest Territory in what is now the state of Wisconsin. The territory was sparsely inhabited by white men and under constant threat of Indian and British attack. Davis's chief responsibility was protecting the settlers and strengthening and enlarging the fort. Commanding a detachment of troops cutting trees to strengthen Fort Crawford was one of the more mundane duties performed by Lieutenant Davis at his first post. Mundane as it was, this work was considered hazardous duty because the men assigned to it were in an isolated spot in the wilderness surrounded by Indians, most of whom resented the army's presence. Davis and his command preformed their duty without the loss of a life and in doing so were said to become the first lumbermen in Wisconsin.[5] From Fort Crawford, Lieutenant Davis was ordered to Fort Winnebago, also in the Northwest Territory. The danger inherent in the life and duty of a soldier in such a place can hardly be imagined by men of this age. In later years, Varina, Davis's wife, would write of his frontier experiences:

---

4   James Kent, *Commentaries on American Law* (1826, New York: Da Capo Press, 1971), II, 364.

5   Varina Howell Davis, *Jefferson Davis, A Memoir by His Wife* (New York: Belford Company, Publishers, 1890), I, 61.

> Reconnaissances were made every few days of the most dangerous character. Death rode on the croup with every man who left the fortified posts, so that with the excitement about Indians, the daily round of duties ... Lieutenant Davis passed the time.[6]

On the lonely, snowy frontier of Wisconsin in 1828, Lieutenant Davis was delighted to re-establish his friendship with a former classmate from Transylvania College, George Wallace Jones. Jones' two sons soon became very much attached to the young soldier. According to Jones, "He [Davis] was a great favorite with my boys, whom he used to hold on his knees and fondle as if they had been his own."[7] Jones, an early pioneer and prominent settler of the Northwest Territory, would remain a lifelong friend and supporter of Jefferson Davis. During the War for Southern Independence, Jones was imprisoned by the Lincoln government after returning from Bogota where he was serving as United States Minister. Jones had written Davis requesting a commission for his son in the Confederate Army before his return from Bogota. Relating the events of his arrest, Jones stated:

> I was recalled [from Bogota], and on my arrival was given a diplomatic dinner by Seward. Six days after, I was imprisoned in Fort Lafayette ... on a telegram sent by W. H. Seward.... On February 22, I was released by order of Secretary Stanton, who informed me that he could see no reason why I had been imprisoned."[8]

Jones' two sons, both from Iowa and ever mindful of their friend Jefferson Davis, served in the Confederate Army. After the war, Jones, at the request of Davis, rescued a Davis family photo album that contained photographs of Davis's deceased children and other

---

6   Ibid., 74.

7   George Wallace Jones, as cited in J. William Jones, *A Memorial Volume of Jefferson Davis* (1889, Harrisonburg, VA: Sprinkle Publications, 1993), 49.

8   Jones, 52.

relatives. The album had been stolen from Varina by Northern troops after the capture of the presidential party at the close of the war.[9] The elderly friend of Jefferson Davis, Gen. George Wallace Jones of Iowa, would be numbered among the honorable men of the South and America who served as pallbearers at Jefferson Davis's funeral in 1889. For the reunited friends in the wind-swept Northwest Territory of 1828, all these events were yet to be acted out.

In this wild and frigid country, Lieutenant Davis performed his duty oftentimes wet and profoundly cold. Exposure to the damp, freezing conditions took its toll on Davis's health. He began suffering from pneumonia and was soon losing weight, eventually becoming so weak he had to direct work from his bed. His weaken condition so affected his ability to move that his servant, James Pemberton, had to carry him about like a child "from bed to window." The faithful service of his servant was noted by Davis's wife who stated,

> During this period James carried the arms, the money, and everything of value possessed by his master, knowing that, at any time, he could be free with the simple ceremony of leaving-taking; but he remained throughout the whole period of Mr. Davis's service on the frontier, as tender and faithful as a brother; and he was held as dear as one.[10]

At about this time, a new commander was sent to take command of the First Regiment, Col. Zachary Taylor. Taylor was a man whose fortune would be intertwined with that of Jefferson Davis for many years to come.

Lieutenant Davis received his baptism in battle during the Black Hawk War. Up until this time, Davis had performed many dangerous tasks for the army but had not yet led troops in battle. During his assignment in the Northwest Territory, an uneasy truce existed with several Indian tribes in the area. Most Indians had adjusted to the

---

9 Hudson Strode, *Jefferson Davis, Tragic Hero* (New York: Harcourt, Brace, and World, 1964), 396.

10 Varina Davis, as cited in *Ibid.*, 81.

white settlement of their ancestral lands; however, in 1831 an Indian leader by the name of Black Hawk was threatening the territory of Illinois with war.

A peace conference with the chiefs of the Indian nations allied with Black Hawk was called by General Gaines, ranking United States military officer in the area. Because of the natural distrust of the Indian chiefs for their adversary, the peace conference was held far from the security of the American fort. To display his fearlessness, General Gaines went to the peace conference with only four other men, Lt. Jefferson Davis, an interpreter, and two soldiers. The peace conference was a failure, and Black Hawk, with his confederates, left with every intent to fight for their lands. With the peace conference ending in a failure, General Gaines determined to ask the governor of Illinois to call out the state militia. This being done, General Gaines sent two lieutenants to Fort Dixon, Illinois, to muster in the volunteers.

> On the morning when the muster was to take place, a tall gawky, slab-sided, homely young man, dressed in a shirt of blue jeans, presented himself to the lieutenants as the captain of the recruits, and was duly sworn in. The homely young man was Abraham Lincoln. [One] lieutenant was he who afterward fired the first gun from Fort Sumter, Major Anderson. The other lieutenant, who administered the oath, was, in after years, the President of the Confederate States, Jefferson Davis.[11]

Various accounts of the role played by Davis and Lincoln in the Black Hawk War are cited by different biographers of these men. Many myths have been spawned about these incidents. One myth of some interest is that, years later, Lincoln was overheard stating that the first time he was ever administered the oath of allegiance to

---

11 Reverend Dr. Harsha, as cited in Varina Howell Davis, I, 131. Various accounts surrounding Davis's contribution in the Black Hawk War are reported by different biographers. See J. Williams Jones, Hudson Strode, and Robert McElroy.

the United States it was administered by Jefferson Davis.[12] Jefferson Davis and Abraham Lincoln have attested to the facts as far as the mustering in of the Illinois militia but not to the extent that some have reported.

The Black Hawk War consisted of several raids and engagements starting in 1831 and lasting until late 1832. In an early engagement, at a place known as Stillman's Run, Black Hawk and his warriors won the praise of Davis for their tenacity and valor. Davis told a friend that he had never known anything to compare with the gallantry of the Indians on that occasion. The success of the Indians at Stillman's Run was followed by more savage attacks upon settlers and friendly Indians by Black Hawk. During one of these attacks, a small child was kidnapped by the Indians. Lieutenant Davis was detailed to rescue the child and, to the great relief of the child's parents, accomplished his mission. Lieutenant Davis noted that the child was not harmed by the Indians, and with its suntanned and dirty face the child could have passed for an Indian child.

The final engagement of the Black Hawk War took place at the Battle of Bad Axe. On August 3, 1832, Black Hawk and his warriors were cornered in a marsh near the Mississippi River. Both Jefferson Davis and Abraham Lincoln were reported to be present at this battle, Davis in active service and Lincoln in the reserve force.[13] Black Hawk and his men were forced to surrender, whereupon Lieutenant Davis took charge of Black Hawk and escorted him to Jefferson Barracks. During this time, Davis showed much kindness and respect to his defeated foe, so much so that Black Hawk, in his autobiography, made the following statement about Lieutenant Davis:

> We started to Jefferson Barracks in a steam-boat, under the charge of a young war chief (Lieutenant Davis), who treated us all with much kindness. He is a good and brave young chief, with whose conduct I was much pleased. On our way down we called at Galena,

---

12 Varina Howell Davis, I, 131.

13 Jones, 60.

and remained a short time. The people crowded to the boat to see us, but the war chief, would not permit them to enter the apartment where we were, knowing, from what his own feelings would have been if he had been placed in a similar situation, that we did not wish to have a gaping crowd around us.[14]

At Jefferson Barracks, St. Louis, Missouri, Davis delivered the prisoners to the Federal Government's "tender" mercies. Black Hawk was "confined to the barracks and forced to wear the *ball* and *chain!*"[15] In his autobiography, Black Hawk would note the humiliation inflicted upon him by the Federal Government:

The path of glory is rough, and many gloomy hours obscure it. May the Great Spirit shed light on yours— and that you may never experience the humility the power of the American Government has reduced me to, is the wish of him who, in his native forests, was once as proud and bold as yourself.[16]

Thus closed one of the last "Indian Wars" fought by Americans east of the Mississippi. Both Davis and Albert Sidney Johnston were disillusioned by the way the war had been prosecuted. Johnston noted that the war could have been "averted by foresight and a little timely generosity on the part of the Government."[17]

The unbiased historian will notice that this struggle was made by white men in an effort to secure for themselves rights to Indian lands. In the light of these facts, the vaunted cry by the men of these Northern states, when dealing with the institution of Southern slavery, that they believe in the struggle for the rights and the

---

14   Chief Black Hawk, as cited in Varina Howell Davis, 1, 143. Chief Black Hawk dictated his life story in October 1833, and it was later published.

15   Black Hawk, as cited in Robert McElroy, *Jefferson Davis, The Unreal and the Real* (New York: Harper and Brothers Publishers, 1937), I, 30.

16   *Ibid.*

17   Albert Sidney Johnston, as cited in *Ibid.*

freedom of their fellow man, rings hollow. Indeed, the new states to be formed in the Northwest were "free" states; free from the red and black man. By war and prohibitory legislation, the "rights" of white men were protected, but the same cannot be said for the rights of either the red man or the black man.[18]

One year after the end of the Black Hawk War, an incident occurred that would portend much difficulty for Davis and the nation. In 1832, South Carolina, the home state of Davis's mother, was locked in a struggle with the Federal Government over the state's nullification of the federal tariff. At this time, it appeared that United States troops would be called upon to "enforce" the will of the Federal Government upon South Carolina. This call gave Davis, an adherent to the policy of States' Rights, much concern.

> The nullification by South Carolina in 1832 of certain acts of Congress, the consequent proclamation of President Jackson, and the "Force Bill" soon afterwards enacted, presented the probability that the troops of the United States would be employed to enforce the execution of the laws in that State and it was supposed that the regiment to which I belonged would in that event be ordered to South Carolina. By education, by association, and by preference, I was a soldier, then regarding that profession as my vocation for life. Yet, looking the issue squarely in the face, I chose the alternative of abandoning my profession rather than be employed in the subjugation of, or coercion of, a State of the Union, and had fully determined and was prepared to resign my commission immediately on the occurrence of such a contingency. The compromise of 1833 prevented the threatened calamity, and the sorrowful issue was deferred until a day more drear, which forced

---

18 Kennedy & Kennedy, *The South Was Right!* 3rd ed. (1991, 1994, Columbia, SC: Shotwell Publishing, 2020), 65-70.

upon me the determination of the question of *State sovereignty or federal supremacy—of independence or submission to usurpation.*[19] [Emphasis added]

This was Davis's first time, but not his last, to contemplate how to respond to an unconstitutional act by the Federal Government vis-a-vis a sovereign state. Indeed, Davis's life would center around the very question he first faced as a lieutenant in the United States Army.

With the close of the Black Hawk War, Davis's career as a commissioned officer in the United States Army was coming to an end. After service in Wisconsin, Illinois, Michigan, Arkansas, and Kentucky, 1st Lt. Jefferson Davis resigned his commission from the United States Army on June 30, 1835. With his marriage to General Taylor's daughter, Sarah Knox Taylor, he established himself as a cotton planter in Mississippi. The tragic death of his bride, only six months after their marriage, cast a pall of melancholy upon Davis for several years.

Jefferson Davis continued life as a planter in the Wilkinson County area until elected to the United States House of Representatives from Mississippi. Davis, an advocate for Texas both as a republic and later as a state in the Union, stood in opposition to any demands made by Mexico against Texas. Shortly after Texas was received into the Union as a state, Mexico broke off diplomatic relations with Washington. From that point forward, newspapers in Mexico City acted as if war had already begun. As tensions increased, Washington ordered Gen. Zachary Taylor, Davis' former father-in-law, into disputed areas of Texas. In a last-ditch effort to avert hostilities, President James K. Polk sent an ambassador to Mexico City to negotiate an adjustment of the dispute. The ambassador was John Slidell of Louisiana, the same individual who would later be sent to France on behalf of the Confederacy, on board the British vessel *Trent*, by President Jefferson Davis. On April 24, 1846, the Mexican Army attacked United States troops on the Texas side of the Rio Grande River. As soon as this intelligence reached Washington, the United States declared war on Mexico. Jefferson Davis not only

---

19   Jefferson Davis, as cited in Jones, 61.

voted for all measures to provide troops and supplies to the Texas frontier, but also was willing to cast his lot with those who were called upon to place themselves in harm's way.

While serving in the capacity of a United States representative from Mississippi, Davis received word from Vicksburg, Mississippi, of his election as colonel of the First Mississippi Volunteers. Completing his business in Washington in the summer of 1846, Representative Davis resigned his seat in the House of Representatives. Before leaving Washington, Davis requisitioned one thousand percussion rifles manufactured by a Finn named Whitney of New Haven, Connecticut, for his volunteer battalion. This was a bold and farsighted move on the part of a militia officer. The common weapon of the day was a large-caliber, smooth-bore flintlock musket. General Winfield Scott, Davis's superior, did not like the new weapon and requested that Davis issue the standard weapon to his troops. The old musket was large and slow to load but tried and proven as an infantry weapon. Nevertheless, Davis understood the advantages to a modern military of the new weapon. The percussion firing method had been proven by sportsmen throughout the frontier, and the same men had also shown what a rifle could do against massed troops. Davis would not be swayed from his decision. Therefore, the Whitney rifle of Connecticut, in the hands of Davis's Mississippians, became known as the "Mississippi Rifle."

The first problem faced by Colonel Davis was establishing a system of military tactics for the use of the new weapon. With the efficiency of an officer accustomed to such demands, Davis established the needed system of tactics for his troops. In providing his men with both new weapons and a new organized system of drill for that weapon, Davis was blazing a new trail for America's military. In so doing, Davis was leading the way for others, for within a few years the entire United States Army would adopt Davis's new weapon.

Arriving in Mexico, Davis and his Mississippians encamped at Camorgo and at once began drilling with the new weapon and tactics. Colonel Davis reported to his former father-in-law, the first time the two had seen each other as soldiers since before Davis's marriage to the general's daughter. General Taylor had never fully approved of his daughter's marriage to Davis, and he and Davis had never been on speaking terms since the marriage. Time and the shared grief of the death of Sarah had attenuated any lingering feelings of hostility between the two men. From the day of their meeting in Mexico until the death of Zachary Taylor, even though often political opponents, Davis and Taylor were close friends.

Soon after the arrival of the Mississippians, General Taylor's army was put in motion. The army began its trek into the interior of Mexico with the objective of destroying the Mexican Army under the command of General Ampudia. Ampudia had taken a defensive position in and around the city of Monterey, Mexico. The Mexicans were said to have from 9,000 to 15,000 regulars and volunteers, against which Taylor flung his 6,000 Americans.

Davis and his Mississippians saw their first real action during the Battle of Monterey at a place called La Taneria. Several regiments of regular troops had been unsuccessful in an attack against the position. General John A. Quitman's brigade, consisting of Davis's Mississippians and Colonel Campbell's Tennesseans, was ordered forward. The brigade of volunteers carried the day, with Davis's Mississippians in the fore of the fray. The Mexicans were forced to abandon La Taneria, but, because of orders from General Quitman, the attacking force was unable to complete the victory. The Mexicans retreated to Fort El Diablo, which they abandoned the next day.

The Battle of Monterey lasted three days in which time Colonel Davis displayed much courage and resourcefulness and won the praise of General Taylor and Davis's friend Albert Sidney Johnston, acting inspector-general and a classmate from Transylvania College and West Point. On September 24, Mexican general Ampudia asked for terms of surrender. General Taylor appointed Gen. William Jenkins Worth, Gov. J. Pinckney Henderson, and Colonel Davis as commissioners for the United States Army.[20] Generous terms were offered to and agreed upon by the Mexicans. The last term in the agreement was offered to save Mexican pride, that is, the flag of Mexico would be saluted by the Mexicans' own guns as it was lowered.

---

20 McElroy, I, 86.

Of historical note is the fact that similar conditions of surrender were offered to and agreed upon by Maj. Robert Anderson at Fort Sumter. The only United States fatality during the battle at Fort Sumter happened when a gun exploded while a salute was fired in honor of the United States flag while it was being lowered.

As a result of the American victory at Monterey and the signing of a temporary armistice, relative peace descended upon Northern Mexico. General Taylor concurred with the opinion of his superiors in Washington and consented to the reduction of his army in favor of General Scott in Southern Mexico. Unfortunately for General Taylor's army, the American government in Washington did not approve the terms of the armistice. Thus, hostilities resumed. General Antonio Lopez de Santa Anna, the "Napoleon of the West," seeing the disadvantage of his opponent, moved his army into Northern Mexico in an attempt to reverse the outcome of the late battle. General Taylor's army, having been reduced, had approximately 4,700 troops, the greater number of which were still raw recruits, to contend with Santa Anna's 20,000 Mexican troops.

General Taylor formed his troops close to a narrow pass near a ranch known as Buena Vista. Jefferson Davis's Mississippians were now in the thick of one of the major engagements of the war. General Santa Anna sent General Taylor a curt surrender demand. An enraged Taylor replied, "I beg leave to say that I decline acceding to your request."[21]

---

21 General Zachary Taylor, as cited in Hudson Strode, *Jefferson Davis, American Patriot* (New York: Harcourt, Brace, and Company, 1955), 178.

After some preliminary maneuvering and skirmishing by Santa Anna on the first day, the Mexican Army pressed its advantage of strength on the second day of battle. The left flank of the American line was routed, posing the possibility of a complete flanking of the American line. Such a condition would have spelled sure defeat for Taylor. General Taylor took to the field of battle oblivious to the dangers from shot and shell and ordered Colonel Davis's Mississippians forward against Santa Anna's second in command, General Ampudia. The Mississippians moved forward with the elan of veteran troops. Meeting some fleeing Indiana troops, Davis pleaded with them to join his men in the attack, and several companies heroically responded. Davis's regiment was under a constant barrage of musket and cannon fire during this movement. Receiving a wound that shattered his ankle, Davis, disregarding the pain, led his men forward and threw the enemy into flight. While Davis's Mississippians, supported by a few Indiana companies, were attacking the enemy, a heavy artillery fire was maintained on the Mexican line by Captains Braxton Bragg and Thomas Sherman. As the Mexican infantry retreated, the American artillery withdrew to support another part of the line. While covering the withdrawal of the artillery, Davis noticed a formation of Mexican lancers approaching. To prevent the capture of the artillery and further endangering the American line, Davis formed his regiment on a small ridge. In this position, the flank of the Mississippi regiment was in close proximity to that of the Indiana regiment waiting to receive the attack of the lancers. The angle formed by this deployment of troops formed a shallow "V" that became attached to Davis's legacy at the Battle of Buena Vista. Many historians have cited this formation as the reason for the defeat of the Mexican lancers. In his official report, Davis explained how this event took place:

> The Mississippi regiment was filed to the right, and fronted in line across the plain; the Indiana regiment was formed on the bank of the ravine, in advance of our right flank, by which a re-entering angle was presented to the enemy. ... As the enemy approached, his speed regularly diminished, until when within

eighty or a hundred yards, he had drawn up to a walk and seemed about to halt. A few files fired without orders, and both lines then instantly poured in a volley so destructive that the mass yielded to the blow and the survivors fled.[22]

Bombarded by Captain Sherman's artillery, the enemy was forced to flee the field of battle. Jefferson Davis had remained on the field of battle in total disregard of a painful wound in his right foot. Eight hours after his being wounded, Davis's blood-filled boot was removed. His foot and perhaps his life were saved by the tender care of his friends. In those faithful eight hours, Davis had become the idol of the nation for his valor and martial abilities. After the Battle of Buena Vista, only General Taylor was held in higher esteem than Davis by the nation. Surely, for Davis, the most gratifying response to the events of the day came from his former father-in-law, Gen. Zachary Taylor. According to John Reagan, future postmaster general of the Confederate States of America, General Taylor told Davis, "My daughter was a better judge of men than I."[23]

Jefferson Davis, the wounded hero of the Battle of Buena Vista, returned home amid an outpouring of patriotic zeal from not only his Southern friends but also the entire nation. In reply to the accolades for his service, Davis would reply, "It was our country's necessity, and not our own, which prompted the service there performed."[24] Stepping from a ship in New Orleans on his return from the war, Davis was met by boisterous crowds scattering flowers and laurel wreaths in honor of him and his Mississippians.

Among the letters and messages received by Davis upon his return was one from the president of the United States, James K. Polk. President Polk offered Davis a commission as brigadier general of volunteer troops of the United States Army. In a letter

---

22 Jefferson Davis, as cited in *Ibid.*, 180.

23 General Zachary Taylor, as cited in McElroy, I, 94.

24 Jefferson Davis, as cited in *Ibid.*, 92.

dated May 19, 1847, President Polk stated, "Your distinguished gallantry and military skill while in the battles of Monterey and Buena Vista, eminently entitle you to it."[25]

Summary

Twelve years after Lt. Jefferson Davis had resigned from military service, he was offered a soldier's chance of a lifetime, a commission as a general officer. The temptation must have been great, for Davis considered the offer for several days while consulting with his brother Joseph. But, in the end, it was Davis's adherence to the Constitution, not personal aggrandizement, that won out. Both Jefferson and Joseph Davis held the view that the states had not delegated to the president the right to commission officers of state militia. Clearly, in the minds of the Davis brothers, President Polk was violating the principle of States' Rights. Davis wrote the president and, after acknowledging the honor done him by the offer, Davis stated, "[M]y opinions compel me to decline the proffered honor."[26]

For the second time in his life, but not the final time, Jefferson Davis had his faith in the principle of States' Rights tested. The second time, just as the first, Jefferson Davis disregarded personal interest to uphold the American principle of constitutional government. Thus came a fitting end to the military career of Jefferson Davis. Other than his brief command of the troops of Mississippi, after it seceded from the Union and before his election as president of the Confederacy, Davis's military career as a field officer was over.

---

25 James K. Polk, as cited in Strode, *Jefferson Davis, American Patriot*, 188.

26 Jefferson Davis, as cited in *Ibid.*, 18.

Chapter 6

JEFFERSON DAVIS: THE PLANTER

THE TRANSFORMATION OF DAVIS the soldier to Davis the planter began with his introduction to a charming young lady, Sarah Knox Taylor. Miss Taylor was the daughter of Col. Zachary Taylor, commander of the First Regiment of the United States Infantry in which Davis was a lieutenant. The announcement of the intent of marriage between Sarah and Jefferson was met by scorn from Colonel Taylor. Taylor, having been a professional soldier all his life, did not wish his daughter to suffer as his wife and children had from life on military posts. Also, he felt Davis had not been loyal to him at a court-marshal proceeding several years earlier and had never forgiven Davis for the perceived offense. The "offense" was simple and to most people insignificant. At a court-marshal proceeding in which Colonel Taylor, Maj. Thomas Smith, Lieutenant Davis, and a new lieutenant were sitting as judges, the new lieutenant requested that the court allow him to attend to his duties without wearing his dress uniform. Colonel Taylor voted no; Major Smith, whom Taylor disliked, voted in the affirmative; and Davis voted in the affirmative. From this event, Davis learned that it is not always enough to be right. About this incident he would later state, "I was right as to the principle, but impolitic in the manner of asserting it."[1]

---

1   Jefferson Davis, as cited in Hudson Strode, *Jefferson Davis, American Patriot* (New York: Harcourt, Brace, and World, 1964), 80.

Jefferson Davis Presidential Library, on the grounds of Beauvoir, Jefferson Davis' last home, Biloxi, Mississippi.

Davis and Miss Taylor were engaged for two years while awaiting the blessing of Colonel Taylor. During this time, a certain amount of subterfuge was practiced by the young couple. Often Sarah's young brother would assist in the effort to expedite their rendezvous. The young brother would grow up to be known as the son of President Zachary Taylor and as Gen. Richard Taylor, C.S.A. Even after the defeat of the South and as a paroled Confederate officer, Richard Taylor would use his position as the son of a former United States president to assist his imprisoned friend and brother-in-law, Jefferson Davis. Sarah eventually went to her father and explained that, since he could not offer proof against the character of Jefferson Davis, she would proceed with her marriage. This incident has led many to state that the young couple "eloped" and was married without the approval of their families. Yet, the facts of the matter do not support such an allegation. Taylor begrudgingly relented upon the condition that the marriage take place at the home of Mrs. Gibson Taylor in

Lexington, Kentucky. In a letter to her mother, Sarah thanked her father for money he had sent her for her wedding.[2] Jefferson Davis gave this account of the marriage:

> In 1835 I resigned from the army, and Miss Taylor being then in Kentucky with her aunt—the oldest sister of General Taylor—I went thither and we were married in the house of her aunt, in the presence of General Taylor's two sisters, of his oldest brother, his son-in-law, and many others of the Taylor family.[3]

After the wedding, Mr. and Mrs. Davis proceeded to Hurricane, the home of Jefferson's brother Joseph. Joseph had been successful as a cotton planter and was eager to assist his younger brother and his new bride in establishing a home.

Jefferson and Joseph arranged a settlement of their father's inheritance so as to provide Jefferson Davis with land and slaves near the old Samuel Davis homesite. The land and homesite were in an area appropriately known as Briarfield. With the assistance of his faithful servant and friend, James Pemberton, Jefferson Davis began clearing land for the cultivation of cotton. As the season progressed to what was then known as the "chill-and-fever season," the young couple decided to take a trip to a more congenial climate. Davis made arrangements with his sister, Mrs. Luther Smith, for a visit at her home, Locust Grove, at Bayou Sara, located near the town of St. Francisville, Louisiana. Soon after their arrival at Locust Grove, Jefferson began to show signs of the dreaded malaria fever. Sarah's symptoms followed her husband's by one day as she too fell prey to the fever. The couple were nursed in separate rooms, both suffering from high fever and delirium. It was thought that Jefferson

---

2   Robert McElroy, *Jefferson Davis, The Unreal and the Real* (New York: Harper and Brothers Publishers, 1937), I, 33-34.

3   Jefferson Davis, as cited in Varina Howell Davis, *Jefferson Davis, A Memoir by His Wife* (New York: Belford Company, Publishers, 1890), I, 162.

was in the most danger, yet it was Sarah, who, on September 15, 1835, succumbed to the deadly disease. She was buried in her sister-in-law's family plot in what is now St. Francisville.

Jefferson Davis lingered for weeks; many despaired for his life. With the tender assistance of his friend and servant, James Pemberton, Davis was nursed back to health. Davis was so weak that James virtually carried Davis back to his brother's home in Mississippi. Just as in the Northwest Territory, Jefferson Davis's life was in the hands of his friend and slave. The trust and affection between these two men, slave and master, black and white, would have an influence on Davis years later in the Congress of the United States. Davis could never understand the venomous hate spewed out by notorious Abolitionists against Southern slavery in light of the relationship he had always had with his slaves.

Even though he was slowly regaining his health, it was determined in the fall of 1835 that Davis could not survive a cold, wet Mississippi winter. Therefore, arrangements were made for a winter sojourn in Havana, Cuba. With his health recovering, Davis remained in the warm tropical air of Cuba where it is thought that he spent most of his time in solitude, grieving for his lost love. After a suitable recovery, Davis returned to the United States. His departure from Cuba was marked by the manifestation of a cloak-and-dagger episode. Having been informed that a former United States military officer was in Havana, the Spanish authorities kept a close watch on Davis. When Davis was observed making sketches of military installations, the authorities began to ask questions about the "invalid." On somewhat short notice, Davis took passage for the United States. He landed in New York and proceeded to Washington, D.C., where he met his old friend from the Northwest Territory, Gen. George Wallace Jones. General Jones, at that time, was a delegate to Congress from the Michigan Territory, the last such delegate before the territory was admitted to the Union as a state. Jones introduced Davis to many prominent men in Washington, such as Franklin Pierce of New Hampshire, Thomas H. Benton of Missouri, John J. Crittenden of Kentucky, and many others.

This trip to Washington afforded Jefferson Davis the opportunity to meet an American president for the first time. (Although Davis had met Andrew Jackson at the general's home in Tennessee when Davis was seven years old, that meeting occurred before the general was elected president.) Senator Franklin Pierce introduced Jefferson Davis to President Martin Van Buren while Davis was in Washington for the first time. Taking a liking to Davis, President Van Buren invited him to breakfast at the White House. The meal was highlighted by conversation about military affairs, territorial questions, and other subjects of interest to the president. Van Buren not only was impressed by the manner in which Davis carried himself but also paid him a special compliment on his choice of boots, a point that pleased Davis greatly and was an often-told story by the Davis family. Many historians have wondered if Spanish forts and Cuba were discussed along with Davis's choice of footwear.

With the arrival of spring, Davis began his journey back to his Mississippi plantation of Briarfield. Still depressed from Sarah's death, Davis threw himself into the work of improving the production of his plantation and the condition of his slaves. So engrossing was this effort that Davis had little or no contact with the outside world. Davis's social contact during this time consisted of Joseph Davis, his friend and slave James Pemberton, and the other slaves on his plantation. Davis would remain a semi-recluse not leaving Briarfield for as long as a year at a time during this period. His contact with Joseph consisted of conversations on increasing cotton production, improving the life and condition of their slaves, and, as always, politics. Both brothers were strong Jeffersonian Republicans. In Joseph's library could be found copies of *The Federalist*, the Constitution, *Elliott's Debates*, *Wealth of Nations*, and, of course, copies of the Kentucky-Virginia Resolutions.

> The brothers considered the Constitution a sacred compact, by which a number of sovereigns agreed to hold their possessions in common under strict

limitations; and that, as in any other partnership or business agreement, it was not to be tampered with or evaded without the sacrifice of honor and good faith.[4]

Not only was Joseph instrumental in establishing Jefferson's fundamental political philosophy, but also during Jefferson's absence Joseph "kept an eye" on Mississippi politics.[5]

Throughout his life, Davis was always sensitive to the needs and hurts of other people. As during the transfer of Chief Black Hawk, he never allowed anyone to take unfair advantage of weaker or defenseless people. Seeing one of his employees greatly distressed, Davis inquired as to the problem. The man, a millwright for Davis, told a sad story about his wife's health problems and how she needed care by a physician in Louisiana. The man was distraught because he did not have the money for the physician and trip that were needed. Upon hearing the story, Davis gave the man five hundred dollars and said, "Save your wife, and the knowledge that you have done so will satisfy your debt to me."[6]

Davis's tender regard for people did not stop at the color line. His relationship with people of color was one of love and respect. As with his parents, Davis advocated the biblical view of slavery, a view held by the better elements of Southern slave society. The biblical view of slavery, almost unheard of today, was articulated well by theologians of both Protestant and Catholic churches in the South. Indeed, this very same view was held by New England clerics during the colonial period of American history. Forgotten in the history of American slavery is the fact that the first colony to enact positive laws for the benefit of slavery masters was the colony of Massachusetts in 1641.[7] As long as slavery was necessary for the development of the region, it was maintained. Only after slave labor

---

4   Ibid., I, 172.

5   Janet S. Hermann, *Joseph E. Davis, Pioneer Patriarch* (Jackson, MS: University Press of Mississippi, 1990), 91.

6   Jefferson Davis, Ibid., I, 174.

7   George II. Moore, *Notes on the History of Slavery in Massachusetts* (New York: D. Appleton and Company, 1866), 11.

became a threat to white labor did the people of Massachusetts and, indeed, New England legislate against it. None other than John Adams of Massachusetts testified that the only reason slavery was abolished in the North was because white workers did not wish to have to compete with black workers.[8]

Central to the theme of biblical slavery is the idea that the institution of slavery, just as the institution of government, was made necessary by the sinfulness of man. The institution was not sinful, but it was the product of sinful man. According to this view, God instituted laws to regulate the activity of sinful man; among these were laws that covered the institution of slavery. The recognition that God was central in creation and had title on everything made ownership of a person impossible. With this view in mind, one could only own the *labor* of a person, not the whole person. Unlike pagan slavery, as practiced by the non-Christian, the Christian slave master could not kill or harm a person because only God had that authority. Under paganism, the *whole* person was considered to be property; under biblical slavery, only property in the *labor* of the individual was owned.

In the Old Testament, the Hebrew laws on slavery from Leviticus Chapter 25 were often quoted as proof of God's regulation of the institution. In the New Testament in Paul's letter to Philemon, Paul begs a Christian slave master to accept the return of a runaway slave who has converted to Christianity. In this letter Paul makes no demands for emancipation of the slave nor does he condemn the institution of slavery.[9] Thus, said the antebellum Churchmen, the Bible does not condemn slavery; it condemns sinful acts by both slave and slave master.

Both of the Davis brothers were very progressive in their views of slavery and did as much as any men of the Old South to improve the lot of the slave population. This care was greatly repaid by those

---

8   Kennedy & Kennedy, *The South Was Right!* 3rd edition, (1991, 1994, Columbia, SC: Shotwell Publishing, 2020), 120.

9   J. Steve Wilkins and Douglas Wilson, *Southern Slavery as It Was* (Moscow, IA: Canon Press, 1996), 14-20.

servants who had the good fortune to live on either of the Davis plantations. Joseph Davis believed that people always responded in a positive manner to being treated well and rewarded for jobs well done. He did his utmost to follow this pattern of management on his plantation, and Jefferson followed his brother's example.[10] Among the innovations established by Joseph Davis, and copied by Jefferson Davis, were (1) providing a slave system of justice, where slaves sat as jurors against offenders of the law of the plantation and where no slave could be punished except when found guilty by a jury; (2) limiting the arbitrary authority of an overseer, preventing an overseer from punishing a slave unless conviction had been obtained by a jury; (3) allowing slaves appellate rights to their master in cases when conflicts with an overseer arose; (4) providing technical training in trades and crafts to improve slave productivity and to improve their skills allowing slaves to keep any money above the value of their daily work; (5) encouraging slaves to grow crops and raise various livestock for sale and allowing them to keep the profits; (6) giving of gifts to each person on special days, such as birthdays, weddings, and other special occasions.

The general idea of the Davis brothers was to induce people (slaves) to improve their own lot while at the same time providing the labor force needed for maintaining a large plantation system. The Davis brothers believed that in this effort they were assisting the black race to equip itself for eventual freedom and competition with white people. Of the system of Southern slavery, Jefferson Davis would state upon the floor of the United States Senate that it would have "for its end the preparation of that race for civil liberty and social enjoyment .... When the time shall arrive at which emancipation is proper, those most interested will be most anxious to effect it."[11]

The mutual trust and faith between the Davis brothers and their slaves were demonstrated when Jefferson Davis armed his slaves in order to defend the Davis property from an assembly of white brigands. Of this incident, Davis wrote, "I presume I was the only person in the Confederacy who had ever armed and led Negroes

---

10 Hermann, 54.

11 Jefferson Davis, as cited in McElroy, I, 104.

against white men, they were the slaves of my Brother and myself and the movement was against a band who were paid and employed secretly to make a cut off behind our plantations."[12] Because of their liberal attitude about slavery, the Davises were known throughout Mississippi as "friends to the Negroes."[13]

After the war, when the Davis family fortunes were bleak, Joseph and Jefferson Davis sold their plantations to one of their former slaves. Joseph had two offers of purchase for the two plantations, one from a wealthy Northerner and the other from their former slave and friend, Ben Montgomery. Even though they received less money for their property, Joseph and Jefferson Davis preferred doing business with an old friend and former slave than with a Yankee. The respect and affection that the Montgomery family had for the Davis family were displayed as late as 1889 at Jefferson Davis's funeral.

At home at Briarfield, Jefferson Davis's life was full of work and political conversation. At his brother's and other local Democrats' insistence, Jefferson Davis offered himself as a candidate for the Mississippi legislature. The Whig party controlled politics in Warren County; therefore, Davis was a long shot for victory. Although Davis narrowed the gap between the Whigs and Democrats as no one had done up until that time, he was defeated. For the most part, this campaign should have passed into history as a "non-event." But, because of the action of the state of Mississippi in relation to the repudiation of certain bonds at or near that time, many historians have charged Davis with culpability in fraud. Even Theodore Roosevelt felt compelled to slander the name of Jefferson Davis. In his book on the life of Thomas Benton, Roosevelt stated:

> Before Jefferson Davis took his place among the arch-traitors in our annals, he had already long been known as one of the chief repudiators. It was not

---

12 Jefferson Davis, as cited in Hermann, 64.

13 Hudson Strode, *Jefferson Davis, Tragic Hero* (New York: Harcourt, Brace, and World, 1964), 400.

unnatural that to dishonesty towards the creditors of the public he should afterwards add treachery towards the public itself.[14]

When Jefferson Davis read of this slander, he made an attempt to explain that he never was a member of the Mississippi state government and therefore had no dealings with the "repudiation" scheme. Not only did Davis not have anything to do with the "repudiation" scheme but he also spoke out in opposition to any such move by the state. The only reply that Davis ever received was from Theodore Roosevelt's secretary: "Mr. Theodore Roosevelt declines to have any correspondence with Mr. Jefferson Davis."[15] After the death of Davis, Roosevelt, in 1907, spoke to an overflow crowd at the courthouse square in Vicksburg, Mississippi. At that time Roosevelt atoned for his earlier remark by praising the valor of both the Confederate soldiers and Jefferson Davis.[16]

In 1843, while visiting W. B. Howell, a friend in Natchez, Joseph Davis invited Howell's sixteen-year-old daughter, Varina, to visit him and his wife at Hurricane upriver near Vicksburg. Varina had to complete her study in Latin and English before her parents would allow her to accept the invitation. By December of the same year, preparations were completed, and Varina boarded a steamboat in Natchez for the trip upriver. At the landing, she was met by thirty-six-year-old Jefferson Davis with instructions to escort her party to Hurricane. Varina's first impression of Jefferson has been preserved in a letter she wrote to her mother shortly after arriving at Joseph Davis's home:

> To-day Uncle Joe sent, by his younger brother (did you know he had one?), an urgent invitation to me to go at once to "The Hurricane." I do not know whether this Mr. Jefferson Davis is young or old. He looks

---

14 Theodore Roosevelt, Strode, 51.

15 *Ibid.*

16 Gordon A. Cotton, *The Old Court House* (Raymond, MS: Keith Printing Company, Inc., 1982), 66.

both at times; but I believe he is old, for from what I hear he is only two years younger than you are. He impresses me as a remarkable kind of man, but of uncertain temper, and has a way of taking for granted that everybody agrees with him when he expresses an opinion, which offends me; yet he is most agreeable and has a peculiarly sweet voice and a winning manner of asserting himself. The fact is, he is the kind of person I should expect to rescue one from a mad dog at any risk, but to insist upon a stoical indifference to the fright afterward. I do not think I shall ever like him as I do his brother Joe. Would you believe it, he is refined and cultivated, and yet he is a Democrat![17]

In January 1844, Jefferson Davis, a "Democrat," became engaged to the daughter of a Natchez "Whig" family. On February 26, 1845, on a two-hundred-foot-high bluff overlooking the Mississippi River in Natchez, Mississippi, at Varina's family home The Briars, Jefferson Davis and Varina Howell were married.

Summary

Jefferson Davis's life as a planter began with his marriage to Sarah Knox Taylor in 1835 and essentially ended with his marriage to Varina Howell in 1845. Between those dates, Davis had undergone the tragic loss of his first wife; been introduced to many Washington, D.C., insiders; established a successful plantation; and been introduced to the world of local politics. In the spring of 1845, Davis met Zachary Taylor for the first time since his marriage to the general's daughter. A complete reconciliation between the two gentlemen took place. General Taylor was on his way to the Texas frontier, a fact that would have many repercussions for Davis and for America. No matter where he would go after these years, Briarfield, his home with its slaves and crops, would always have its influence upon Jefferson Davis, the planter.

---

17 Varina Howell Davis, I, 191-92.

Chapter 7

JEFFERSON DAVIS: THE STATESMAN

AT THE AGE OF THIRTY-FIVE, Jefferson Davis, encouraged by his brother Joseph, made his first move into the political arena. In the early 1800s there were two major political parties in Mississippi, the Whigs and the Democrats. The Davis brothers were avid supporters of the Democratic party in Mississippi and held to the strong State's Rights view of strict construction constitutionalism.[1] The Whig party was the dominant party in the planter society of Vicksburg and Natchez. Although Joseph and Jefferson Davis were included in this class, they remained loyal to the Democratic party.[2] During the election of 1843, Jefferson Davis was asked to place his name on the ballot for state representative from Warren County. With only one week left in the election, the Democrats withdrew their original candidate and Jefferson Davis filled the vacancy.

In the election, the Whigs were highly favored to win. Nevertheless, when Democrat Davis announced his candidacy, the Whigs responded by introducing Mississippi's most renowned public orator, Sergent S. Prentiss, into the contest to assist Davis's Whig opponent. Even though Prentiss was not Davis's opponent, Davis accepted a challenge to debate this renowned orator during the election. Although losing the election, Davis and the Democrats

---

[1] Janet S. Hermann, *Joseph E. Davis, Pioneer Patriarch* (Jackson, MS: University Press of Mississippi, 1990), 71.

[2] Ibid., 85.

were pleased by the increase in the Democratic vote. With only one week left to campaign, Davis had closed the gap between the Whigs and Democrats to within a few hundred votes. This exposure served to propel him into Mississippi Democratic politics and led the way for his upcoming election to the United States Congress.[3] The only other notable event attributable to this election was that it gave future political enemies of Davis the excuse for falsely charging him with being a "repudiator." A repudiator was an individual who desired to repudiate the bonded indebtedness that the state of Mississippi had contracted. Jefferson Davis was an opponent of this move and therefore was not a repudiator.

The Twenty-Ninth Congress

The national election of 1844 offered Jefferson Davis another chance to display his political skills. Qualifying as an elector for the Democratic ticket led by James K. Polk, Davis proceeded to campaign for Polk. Canvassing the state, Davis made many public speeches throughout Mississippi for Polk and the Democratic ticket. The resulting election victory for the Democrats was also a personal boost for Davis political fortune. The election offered him a chance to become known throughout the state and greatly increased his popularity at home. In 1845, the same year he married Varina Howell, Jefferson Davis was elected to the United States House of Representatives from Mississippi. Davis took his seat in the Twenty-Ninth Congress, the first session of Congress under the newly elected Democratic president, James K. Polk.

The major diplomatic issues before the nation at the time of the Twenty-Ninth Congress were (1) dealing with the joint claim by the United States and Great Britain of the Oregon Territory and (2) managing the hostilities between the United States and Mexico growing out of the Texas issue.

---

3 J. William Jones, *A Memorial Volume of Jefferson Davis* (1889, Harrisonburg, VA: Sprinkle Publications, 1993), 68.

In dealing with the Oregon Territory question, Representative Davis was in favor of continuing the joint occupancy of the territory by both powers until a final settlement could be negotiated. Unlike many Northern representatives who desired incorporating the Oregon Territory into the Union, an event Davis feared was destined to cause war, Davis preferred negotiation with Britain. Even as Northern representatives were pushing for a resolution that would lead to war, Davis cautioned his countrymen, "War, sir, is a dread alternative and should be the last resort."[4] Davis had a soldier's understanding of America's unpreparedness for a war with a world power like Great Britain. At this first session of the Twenty-Ninth Congress, Jefferson Davis talent as an orator so impressed former president John Q. Adams (ex-president Adams was a representative from Massachusetts in 1846) that Adams remarked to a colleague, "That young man, gentlemen, is no ordinary man. Mind me, he will make his mark yet. He will go far."[5]

Davis was convinced that the most pressing diplomatic problem facing the new administration was the friction between the United States and Mexico. Texas, with more than just a little support of the United States, had won its independence from Mexico (a very successful secession movement) and subsequently had petitioned and been admitted into the federal union on December 19, 1845. The act of union having been achieved; Mexico began to build up its military along the disputed border with the United States. Mexico claimed the Nueces River as the border of Texas, whereas Texas, and therefore the United States, claimed the Rio Grande River. Jefferson Davis supported the claim by Texas that the Rio Grande River was its southern border. This claim ultimately led to a clash of arms and war between the two nations.

On May 8 and 9, 1846, Gen. Zachary Taylor's army clashed with the Mexican Army north of the Rio Grande River. This conflict cost the lives of forty-nine Americans and an estimated one thousand Mexicans. This was clearly an act of war. Prior to this event, while

---

4   Jefferson Davis, as cited in Hudson Strode, *Jefferson Davis, American Patriot* (New York: Harcourt, Brace, and Company, 1955), 149.

5   John Q. Adams, as cited in Jones, 104.

the Mexican Army was north of the Rio Grande River, President Polk issued a message in which he declared that war already existed between Mexico and the United States. At this announcement, two men, one in the Senate and the other in the House of Representatives, rose to challenge the presidential declaration. In the Senate, John C. Calhoun of South Carolina, and in the House of Representatives, Jefferson Davis of Mississippi, both made the same argument against the president. Both men, without the knowledge oi the other's action, made the point that, while the president could inform Congress of hostilities with a foreign power, it was only Congress that had been delegated, by the states, the right to declare a state of war. To the modern mind, this may seem a trivial matter, but to those who believe in maintaining the spirit of the constitutional compact, it was pivotal. If no one is willing to check the abuses of power by an agent of the United States government, how long would the Constitutional Union, as established by the Founding Fathers, last? Davis understood that no true lover of the Union would allow it to be destroyed by the act of political usurpation, even if that usurpation was in the service of a worthy objective. The Constitution defines and limits the powers delegated to the United States government by the states. To preserve the Union, the United States government must abide by the limitations imposed upon it. For Davis, the glory of the Union resided in the principles of sound constitutional government as expounded by the Founding Fathers—not territory; not land mass, not empire.

While working with other representatives on the Oregon Territory question, Davis availed himself of an opportunity to express his loyalty to the Union as established by the common efforts of all Americans and his fear of the spirit of sectionalism.

> If envy and jealousy and sectional strife are eating like rust into the bonds which our fathers expected to bind us, they come from causes which our Southern atmosphere has never furnished. As we [Southerners] have shared in the toils, so we have gloried in the triumphs of our country. In our hearts, as in our history, are mingled the names of Concord, and Camden,

and Saratoga, and Lexington, and Plattsburg, and Chippewa, and Erie, and Moultrie, and New Orleans, and Yorktown, and Bunker Hill. Grouped all together, they form a record of the triumphs of our cause, a monument of the common glory of our Union. What Southern man would wish it less by one of the Northern names of which it is composed? Or where is he who, gazing on the obelisk that rises from the ground made sacred by the blood of Warren, would feel his patriot's pride suppressed by local jealousy?[6]

This early statement by Davis demonstrated the willingness of Davis and the South to recognize that the Union, as established by the founders, offered benefits of protection and common glory for all members. The knowledge of this common good motivated Jefferson Davis always to be ready to defend the Constitution. Davis made it plain that Mississippi and the South stood ready to defend the Oregon Territory or any Northern state from any enemy.

Davis's view, and the traditional Southern view, of the Constitution maintained that only by strictly adhering to the principles established by the Constitution could the Union be maintained. Davis understood that the Union was an association of sovereign states where republican institutions ruled. The Constitution contained the "by-laws" of that association. No party of the association could break the "by-laws" without destroying the association (i.e., the Union). Thus, we see Davis in Congress reminding Americans of the need to forego policies of sectional aggrandizement and pursue the common good. This theme is seen in Davis's work as a statesman, even in his farewell address to the Senate in 1861. After the defeat of the South and while defending the South's correctness in its cause, Davis would remind his fellow Southerners of the need to defend the common good of all Americans.[7]

---

6   Jefferson Davis, as cited in Varina Howell Davis, *Jefferson Davis, A Memoir by His Wife* (New York: Belford Company, Publishers, 1890), I, 234.

7   Jefferson Davis, *The Rise and Fall of the Confederate Government* (New York: D. Appleton and Company, 1881), I, viii.

The integrity of Davis's character was displayed at his debut as a congressman. The arch (political) enemy of John C. Calhoun and therefore of the South, Daniel Webster, was under investigation by the House of Representatives when Davis became a member of the House. Webster, at that time, was accused of defrauding the government of several thousand dollars. A committee, composed of mostly Northern Democratic representatives and Jefferson Davis, was authorized with investigating the charge. Many Northern Democrats had hoped that Davis, a Southerner, would lead the attack upon Webster, a Whig. Yet, Davis was motivated not by sectional or party spirit but by his commitment to Justice. Davis stood by the facts in the case against Webster and wrote a "minority" report of the investigation which was accepted by the House, exonerating Webster from all guilt. After studying the evidence in the case, Davis stated that "he [Webster] was acquitted of every charge that was made against him, and it was equally my pride and my pleasure to vindicate him in every form which lay within my power."[8] Davis's actions in vindicating Webster display his devotion to truth, honesty, and the American system of justice. After the failure of the Confederate cause, this, no doubt, was one reason he felt so secure in demanding a public trial for charges brought against him.

Daniel Webster was so impressed with the forthright courage and integrity displayed by Jefferson Davis that he made a formal call on Davis to thank him personally for his action. Later during that session of Congress, Senator Webster and his wife called upon Mr. and Mrs. Davis at their residence and invited the Mississippi couple to visit them at Marshfield, Massachusetts. It should be noted here that both the Whig and the Democratic parties were national parties, unlike the soon-to-be-formed Republican party. As long as the two sections, North and South, could work within mutual political parties, the American Union was secure. With the advent of a purely sectional (i.e., Republican) party determined to use the power of the federal government for its (i.e., Northern) advantage, the tragic clash between North and South was inevitable. Also, when one contrasts the way in which Davis dealt with his political

---

8 Jefferson Davis, as cited in Robert McElroy, Jefferson Davis, *The Unreal and the Real* (New York: Harper and Brothers Publishers, 1937), I, 73.

opponent and the shocking lack of integrity, as displayed by many modern American politicians, it makes for a sad commentary on modern American politics.

Jefferson Davis's reputation among Washington's power brokers began increasing daily. Very few freshmen congressmen come to Washington with the recognition that Davis held. Once, as Jefferson and Varina were viewing the displays at the National Exhibition of 1845, they chanced upon former president John Tyler. The former president remembered Davis from the trip Davis made to Washington in 1835 and invited the young congressman and his wife to sit and take refreshments with him. After their departure, Varina noted, "I never saw him [Tyler] again until he came on the arm of his beautiful wife to visit us in the Mansion [Confederate White House], at Richmond, sixteen years afterward, and two years before my sister became his grand-daughter-in-law."[9] Not only did Jefferson Davis have as his brother-in-law Richard Taylor (a Confederate general), the son of a former United States president, but also his wife's sister was married to the grandson of another former United States president. During his lifetime, Jefferson Davis was a personal friend of three United States presidents: John Tyler, Zachary Taylor, and Franklin Pierce. Also, he worked with and was recognized by two other United States presidents, Martin Van Buren and James Buchanan. How many Americans can match such a record?

When Congress received President Polk's message requesting a declaration of war against Mexico, Jefferson Davis was among the supporters of the declaration. The Mexican-American war would play a major role in Davis's life. Davis's was held in high regard by President Polk; therefore, it was no surprise when the president offered Davis's a commission as a general officer of the volunteer army then being raised. Davis's, having been informed of being the choice for colonel of the First Regiment of Mississippi Volunteers, and believing that only the states had the right to appoint officers of the militia, refused the president's offer. It must be kept in mind what a sacrifice this refusal was for a man trained as a soldier, but

---

9   Varina Howell Davis, I, 258.

Davis's remained loyal to his faith in State's Rights.[10] Returning from the war as a wounded hero, Davis, once again, would turn down the same offer from the president. Davis's faith in sound constitutional theory left him no other option but to refuse what in his view would be an unconstitutional promotion. Davis always believed that if the states had not delegated a power to the United States government, then that power did not lawfully exist.

First Term as Senator

The statesman's life was put on hold as Davis shouldered the responsibility of colonel of Mississippi troops. In his short tenure in the House of Representatives, Davis had proven his skills as a statesman and his dedication to high principles of honor, duty, and constitutional government. After the war, Davis returned to Washington as a wounded hero. On August 10, 1847, while Davis was recuperating from battle wounds, the governor of Mississippi wrote to Davis and informed him of his election to fulfill the term of the late United States senator from Mississippi, General Speight.[11] On December 6, 1847, Davis, walking with the assistance of crutches and still suffering from a painful wound to his foot, took the oath of office of senator from Mississippi. Also taking the oath of office that day were John P. Hale of New Hampshire, an advocate of the more radical brand of abolitionism, and Stephen A. Douglas of Illinois, an advocate of squatter's sovereignty.[12] These men were destined to oppose each other from time to time on the floor of the Senate.

At the very time that Davis and other Southerners were fighting the nation's battles, Northern sectionalism was injected into the scene of American politics. With the prospect of the United States gaining vast amounts of new territory from Mexico, radical Northern elements conspired to prevent this new territory from becoming new states that would be friendly to the South. The cry went up for "free soil" and "free states," meaning states that would be free from both slavery and the

---

10   *Ibid.*, I.

11   Strode, *Jefferson Davis, American Patriot*, 190.

12   Varina Howell Davis, I, 362.

Negro. While discussing the issue of who would occupy the Western lands then in the hands of Native Americans, William H. Seward in 1858 said, "The white man needs this continent to labor in and must have it."[13] This attitude permeated most of the Northern element then demanding "free soil." As these men knew only too well, if Southerners were allowed in the territories, the Negro, free and slave, would surely become part of the population. Even during the War for Southern Independence such men as Gen. William T. Sherman noted their dislike for black people as when in a letter Sherman stated that he was fighting for a government strong enough for "vindicating its just and rightful authority, independent of *niggers*, cotton, money, or any earthly interest" [emphasis added].[14]

For all practical purposes, the effect of keeping Southern institutions (i.e., slavery), out of the territory resulted in predominantly non-Southern emigrants moving into the newly acquired territories of the West. Slavery played a small but important role in Southern emigration. In the South, only approximately 5 percent of Southerners owned slaves and fewer than one-third were even members of a slave-owning family.[15] Although only a very small proportion of Southerners were slave holders, non-slave-holding Southern emigrants followed slave-holding families into new territories. A classic example is the settlement of North Central Louisiana. The largest segment of early settlers who moved into this area followed trails that had been explored and carved out of the wilderness by white and black pioneers. As in the case of James W. Nicholson's family, one white family and a slave family moved into and settled the wilderness.[16] The slave holders were followed by non-slave-holders who would make up the largest

---

13 William Seward, as cited in Mildred L. Rutherford, Truths of History (Athens, GA: M. L. Rutherford, Publisher, 1907), 92.

14 William Sherman, as cited in Kennedy & Kennedy, *The South Was Right!* 3rd edition, (1991, 1994, Columbia, SC: Shotwell Publishing, 2020), 395.

15 Grady McWhiney, *Cracker Culture, Celtic Ways in the Old South* (Tuscaloosa, AL: University of Alabama Press, 1988), 51

16 James W. Nicholson, *Stories of Dixie* (Baton Rouge, LA: Claitor's Publishing Division, 1915), 11-19.

portion of the population. If the slave holders were not allowed into the territory, it was less likely that non-slave-holding Southerners would move there. This is exactly what the Northern Radicals desired.

By keeping Southerners out of the new territory, new Southern states would not be formed; therefore, Southern influence in Congress would continue to diminish. With the South no longer a menace in Congress, the industrial and commercial interests of the North would have dominant power over legislation. The North, then, could use the power of the United States government to its advantage, while taxing the South to pay the cost of government. It should also be noted that this movement of black and white people was often, as in the case cited, the migration of two families, one black the other white, living and working as a team. This contribution to the settlement of the American South by the slave population has often been overlooked by modern historians. This contribution could never have happened if the stereotypical view of slavery, propagated by Radical Abolitionists, was really the whole truth about Southern slavery. As so often is the case when issues are raised surrounding slavery, only the negative aspects of the subject are discussed.

As has been noted, during the Mexican-American war, while Southern blood was being spilled in defense of the flag and nation, a sectional bombshell exploded in the Congress of the United States. David Wilmot, a representative from Pennsylvania, introduced a provision (Wilmot Proviso) to an appropriation bill that would prohibit the introduction of the institution of slavery in any territory acquired from Mexico. The South viewed this provision as more than an attack upon its "peculiar" institution; it was a continuation of the ongoing sectional aggression by the North against the South. The South would be denied equal access to new lands gained from Mexico, even though more Southern men had volunteered for military service and more Southerners had died securing the new territory. More tariffs were being demanded to protect Northern manufactured goods, and more money was being collected in the South by the federal government and used for "internal improvements" in the North. From the beginning of the nation, the sharp divide between the two sections, even before slavery became an issue, had progressed to the point where many Southerners were beginning to say, "enough is enough!" The struggle touched off by the Wilmot Proviso led in 1848 to the movement of unity among Southern states to protect their rights within the Union if possible, out of the Union if necessary.[17] As always, Jefferson Davis advocated maintaining the Constitutional Union in a non-sectional spirit.[18] In response to an attack upon Southerners by Senator Hale of New Hampshire, Davis said:

> We, of the South, stand now, as we have always stood, upon the defensive .... I know the temper of those whom I represent, and they require no prompting to resist aggression or insult .... It is well and deeply taken, and will be shown when the crisis comes. They make no threats against anyone, and least of all against the Union for which they have made such heavy and such continued sacrifices. They know their rights while they feel their wrongs ... the Union without the Constitution they hold to be a curse. With the Constitution, they will never abandon it.[19]

In Davis's response to the attack on the South by a Northern senator, he chided and reprimanded those in the North who would, with little concern for the *general* welfare of the Union, scandalize a purely sectional issue to the point of rupturing the Union. Davis noted that Northern politicians had "raised a storm which they cannot control ... invoked a spirit which they cannot allay and dare not confront."[20] Yet, his love for the Union of the founders of the republic would not allow him to believe that all Northerners wished the South ill:

---

17 Thelma Jennings, *The Nashville Convention: Southern Movement for Unity, 1848-1850* (Memphis, TN: Memphis State University Press, 1980), v, 105-6.

18 Jefferson Davis, *Rise and Fall of Confederate Government*, I, 18-19.

19 Jefferson Davis, as cited in Varina Howell Davis, I, 433-34.

20 *Ibid.*, I.

> I believe that the descendants of the Franklins, the Hancocks, and the Adamses, if they saw our institutions about to be destroyed by a mean and captious exercise of the power of demagogues to press to a fatal extremity aggressions upon our rights by the North, would rise up in their strength and would enforce the justice and obligations of the Constitution.[21]

Yet, Davis did not stop at merely beseeching the North to relent in its attacks upon the South; he warned of dire consequences if it continued its assault:

> If, on the other hand, the spirit of hostility to the South, that thirst for political dominion over us, which, within two years past, has displayed such increased power and systematic purpose, should prevail .... We shall then have reached a point at which all party measures sink into insignificance under the necessity of self-preservation.[22]

To Davis, the "necessity of self-preservation" would be the cause that would make secession legitimate. Strange as this may sound to modern Americans, this spirit of secession was taught by one of America's foremost Founding Fathers, James Madison. Madison boldly stated that "the safety and happiness of society are the objects at which all political institutions must be sacrificed."[23] For Davis and the South, the institution of the Union was, every day, moving closer to that point in which a judgment must be made: "Is it time to sacrifice the institution in order to maintain our safety and happiness?" Twice before in American history, the American people had made that choice: once in 1776 when the institution of

---

21 *Ibid.*, I, 34-35.

22 Jefferson Davis, as cited in Strode, *Jefferson Davis, American Patriot*, 198-99.

23 James Madison, "Federalist Paper No. 43," as cited in George W. Carey and James McCellan, eds., *The Federalist* (Dubuque, 1A: Kendall/Hunt Publishing Company, 1990), 228.

union with the British government had to be changed, and once in 1787 when the states seceded from the union under the Articles of Confederation. The act of secession may have been radical, but it has never been un-American. During President Zachary Taylor's term, he expressed concern about the abuse of the South by the Northern press and Congress and boldly went on record stating, "[L]et the South act promptly, boldly and decisively, with arms in their hands if necessary, as the Union will in that case be blown to atoms or will be no longer *worth preserving* [emphasis added].[24]

President Taylor, a Whig, was never a great defender of Southern Rights during his term in office; yet, Davis, a Democrat, remained close friends with him and the Taylor family. Taylor's unexpected death in July 1850 would find Jefferson and Varina Davis at the bedside of Davis's former father-in-law, former commander, and friend.[25]

Senator Davis's fame as a defender of constitutional right and his military prowess attracted many people in and around Washington. Davis's fame also caught the attention of General Lopez, a Cuban freedom fighter. General Lopez was a member of a liberation group attempting to free Cuba from Spanish rule. Desiring the assistance of Davis in this effort, General Lopez offered several hundred thousand dollars to Davis if he would lead the Cuban expedition. After some consideration, Davis refused the offer as being inconsistent with his position as a United States senator. Davis did offer to Lopez the name of an officer in whom he believed: "The only man I could indicate to you just now ... [in] whom I have implicit confidence: Robert E. Lee."[26] Varina Davis describes her first meeting with Robert E. Lee a few days later when he came to discuss the Cuban matter with Davis: "I was in the drawing-room when an officer came in, that I thought the handsomest person I had ever seen—his manner, too, was the

---

24 Zachary Taylor, as cited in Strode, *Jefferson Davis, American Patriot*, 205.
25 Hermann, 90.
26 Jefferson Davis, as cited in Varina Howell Davis, I, 412.

impersonation of kindness."[27] No one at that time could have known the impact that these two men were to have upon the history and heritage of America.

The death in 1850 of the South's elder statesman, John C. Calhoun, changed the dynamics not only in the Senate but also in the life of Jefferson Davis. Although Davis and Calhoun differed on several points, such as the war with Mexico and how the act of nullification should be performed, for the most part, the two men were in agreement on constitutional issues and were the recognized leaders of the South. In an article published in the North American Review just two years before his own death, Davis defended the legacy of a misunderstood Calhoun.

> No public man has been more misunderstood and misrepresented than Mr. Calhoun. Not infrequently he has been described as a "hair-splitting abstractionist," a "sectionist," and a "disunionist." That he was eminently wise and practical, that he was ardently devoted to the Union of the constitution as our Fathers made and construed it, his official acts and published speeches clearly demonstrated.[28]

Davis continued, in the above-quoted article, to defend Calhoun's effort to prevent sectional division in the United States. Neither Calhoun nor Davis were "fire brands" of secession, but rather, they were devoted to the *Union as established by the founders*. Unfortunately for both men, the Union created by the Founding Fathers was replaced by the Union of the Northern majority—creating the Yankee Empire. Thus, the South, and now the nation, had to learn to live under a constitution that meant only what the majority said it meant. The South had been warned, in 1829, about the danger of the tyranny of the majority by men such as John Randolph of Roanoke: "I would not live under King Numbers. I would not be his

---

27 Varina Howell Davis, I, 412.

28 Jefferson Davis, "Life and Character of the Hon. John Caldwell Calhoun," *North American Review* (1887, New York: AMS Press, Inc., 1965), v, 145, 246.

steward, nor make him my taskmaster."²⁹ As understood by Calhoun and Davis, the written Constitution stood as a barrier between the caprice of the majority against the rights of the minority in a federal republic. When republican rule was surrendered to mob rule (i.e., majority rule), the rights of the minority group could exist only as long as the majority deemed it appropriate. Seen in this light, it is easy to understand why Davis spoke of Calhoun as a supporter of the Union. In the *Union as established by the Founding Fathers*, the rights of the minority of states were protected by a strict construction of the Constitution.

In the *North American Review*, Davis concluded his defense of the character and legacy of Calhoun by quoting from Calhoun's political but not personal enemy, Daniel Webster:

> [Calhoun] had the basis, the indispensable basis of all high character, and that was unspotted integrity—unimpeached honor and character. If he had aspirations, they were high, and honorable, and noble. There was nothing groveling, or low, or meanly selfish that came near the head or the heart of Calhoun ... we shall carry with us a deep sense of his genius and character, his honor and integrity, his amiable deportment in private life, and the purity of his exalted patriotism.³⁰

A modern authority on Calhoun also notes the efforts of Calhoun to defend the American Union and its republican institutions: "His goal always was to enhance the success of the American experiment in federal republicanism by harmonizing its potentially conflicting parts."³¹ Rather than being a "disunionist" as charged by his enemies, Calhoun and later Davis were the American Unionists!

---

29 John Randolph of Roanoke, as cited in Russell Kirk, *John Randolph of Roanoke, A Study in American Politics* (Indianapolis, IN: Liberty Press, 1978), 567.

30 Jefferson Davis, *North American Review*, 260.

31 Clyde N. Wilson, *The Essential Calhoun* (New Brunswick, NJ: Transaction Publishers, 1992), xx.

In 1850, Jefferson Davis was elected to a fill the 1851-57 term as one of Mississippi's senators. This term would be cut short by his being drafted by the state Democratic convention as its candidate for governor. Davis was called upon in a forlorn hope when it became obvious that the original Democratic candidate would be defeated. As he had done in 1845, he narrowed the gap of defeat to within a few thousand votes; nevertheless, Davis was defeated. Having resigned from his office as senator to run for governor and having been defeated in this bid, Davis retired to a tranquil lifestyle on his plantations.

The planting and improving of his lands coupled with the responsibility of caring for his servants during his political retirement were described as happy and peaceful pursuits for Davis and his wife. Although he was no longer an elected official, Davis political life was far from over. During the 1852 presidential campaign, he worked for the election of his friend and fellow Democrat from New Hampshire, Franklin Pierce. With the election of Pierce, Davis was offered a cabinet position in the Pierce administration. Varina was much pleased to have her husband at home and healthy and did not wish to go back to Washington, Davis, therefore, refused the offer. Not to be outdone, the president-elect wrote Davis and requested that he at least attend the inauguration. When Davis accepted the invitation, Varina knew they would be staying in Washington.

Secretary of War

President Pierce used all of his persuasive talent to convince Davis that he and the nation needed Jefferson Davis at the head of the War Department. Thus, Franklin Pierce secured for himself and the nation the services of Jefferson Davis as secretary of war.

Davis's training at West Point, his experiences on the field of battle, and his tenure in Congress made him an ideal choice for the post. With these qualifications, is it any wonder that president-elect Franklin Pierce desired the services of Jefferson Davis? Yet, it was more than mere ability; Davis had the respect of Pierce. This respect would last throughout their lifetime. After the defeat of the Confederacy, when Davis and his family were without means of support, it was Pierce, his New England friend, who visited Davis in prison. After Davis's release from prison, Pierce offered the use of a small home in New Hampshire to the homeless Davis family. To his credit, Pierce never allowed sectional strife to destroy the friendship between these two great Americans.

President Pierce presented his nominees for cabinet positions to Congress on March 7, 1853. Of those in Pierce's cabinet, Davis of Mississippi, secretary of war; William L. Marcy of New York, secretary of state; and Caleb Cushing of Massachusetts, attorney general; were the strong men in Pierce's administration. A unique friendship was established between Cushing of Massachusetts and Davis of Mississippi. Through the coming years of sectional strife, these two men would use their friendship to mollify tensions between the North and South. All in all, Pierce's cabinet was rather balanced along sectional lines with four Northern members and three Southern members.

Only a few months after his inauguration as president, Pierce, escorted by cabinet members Davis, Cushing, and Guthrie, made a tour of several states: Delaware, Pennsylvania, New Jersey, and New York. Davis was called upon to make speeches for the president on numerous occasions. A unique feature of Davis speeches was that in each state he would make a speech that complimented the local or state service of that state while pointing out the need of addressing the common good of America. In his speeches, he pointed to the need to adhere strictly to the Constitution to prevent the dangers of "consolidation, centralization, and the re-establishment of despotism upon the liberties of the people."[32] Davis spoke in favor of building a transcontinental railroad to connect the Pacific territory to the East. This proposal was warmly received in Pennsylvania, the center of American iron production at that time. As secretary of war, Davis understood the need for rapid transportation of troops and supplies from the populous East to the West in case of invasion from a maritime power (Britain) on the Pacific coast. Speaking in New York before an audience of business, professional, and foreign delegates, Davis advocated the Democratic position of free trade. Davis even spoke on the positive international effect for peace and

---

32 Jefferson Davis, as cited in Strode, *Jefferson Davis, American Patriot*, 254.

international understanding that free trade offered. Davis asserted, "[I]t is for the comfort, peace and salvation of the civilized earth, that there shall be untrammeled, unbroken free trade."[33] At every stop where Davis spoke, he was enthusiastically received. Upon his return from the tour with the president, Davis's political star was bright indeed. His name was often mentioned as a future president.

Davis's overriding political philosophy was of the Jeffersonian strict construction constitutional theory. Although of the strict construction school, Davis also believed that, as a member of the national administration, his duty was to promote the general welfare of the states by providing the states with the best defense system possible. To do so his first task was to improve the nation's ability to defend itself. When Davis assumed leadership at the War Department, the United States Army had an aggregate strength of just over ten thousand men. Not only did these men have to defend both northern and southern borders, with both Britain and Mexico at that time considered as possible threats, but also it had to defend citizens from Indian attacks at far-removed posts in Florida, Michigan, Texas, California, and points in between.

Many innovations in the disposition, organization, and training of troops were undertaken by Davis. The United States Army had for many years attempted to keep many small posts scattered over an immense territory. These small posts were often the object of attacks by hostile Indian tribes and were the source of tedium and boredom for the troops stationed within them. The latter problem resulted in poor morale, a high desertion rate, and few reenlistments. Davis suggested the establishment of larger posts that could not be overwhelmed by hostile Indian forces and that would offer better duty stations for the troops. Davis also sought and obtained increases in pay and a system to reward longevity of service. To modern Americans, this "pay increase" for military personnel will seem to be a common fact, but by the standards of the nineteenth century it was highly unusual. Davis was going against tradition in

---

33 *Ibid.*

asking for an increase in pay for the military. The pay for officers of the United States Army had been fixed some forty years earlier and had not been increased.[34]

During his term as secretary of war, Davis was responsible for a 50 percent increase in the standing army, a dramatic drop in the desertion rate, and an increase in recruitment. This success served to make Davis a very popular secretary of war with the officers and the rank and file of the army.[35] But more than just organizational changes were made by Davis. He ushered in, as a standard weapon, the rifle and a standard system of drill for the use of "Rifle and Light Infantry Tactics." Of historical note here is the fact that one of the men most commonly associated with this system of drill that Davis introduced was a United States Army officer, Bvt. Lt. Col. William J. Hardee. "Hardee's Tactics" was destined to be taught and used by several hundred thousand men, both North and South, during the War for Southern Independence. Lieutenant Colonel Hardee, U.S.A., would follow the fortunes of his home state of Georgia and become known as Lieutenant General Hardee, C.S.A.

Davis's department recommended fortifying numerous exposed positions along the Pacific and Northern borders, improving military roads in Minnesota and supporting efforts for the maintenance of strong state militia. One of the most far-sighted of Davis's proposals was the building of a railroad to connect cites along the Mississippi River with the Pacific coast. As a result of Davis's efforts, several routes were surveyed for this rail system. Much of the credit for the completion of America's first transcontinental railroad system is due to the efforts of America's secretary of war, Jefferson Davis.

After the secession of the Southern states, a common slur made against Jefferson Davis was that he used the office of secretary of war to advance the military capabilities of the South. Yet, when one looks at Davis's record as secretary of war, it is clear that he was a consistent nationalist. As always, Davis was motivated by principle, not by political expedience. For those accustomed to the politics

---

34 Varina Howell Davis, I, 497.

35 Jones, 132.

of expedience, it is hard to believe that the future president of the Confederate States of America would not use this office for the peculiar benefit of the South. Yet, Davis was a man of principle and a man dedicated to the common good, not the sectional good, of these United States. Davis's fidelity to the national cause was illustrated by Gen. Caleb Cushing of Massachusetts, who in 1860 stated:

> [I] n these United States we had examples, and illustrious ones, of the fact that men, eminent in their places in Congress, abandoned their stations and their honors to go among fellow-citizens of their own States, and raise troops with which to vindicate the honor and the flag of their country. Of such men was Jefferson Davis.[36]

Former postmaster general during President Pierce's administration, Judge James Cambell of Pennsylvania also related his high regard of his fellow cabinet member, Jefferson Davis:

> I believe Davis was a conscientious, earnest man. I am sure that he always meant to be right .... He was very quiet and domestic in his habits and correct in his private life, and was exceedingly temperate both in eating and drinking.[37]

After the national crisis of 1861, many falsehoods were circulated about the former secretary of war with respect to his appointment of officers of the new regiment created during his tenure in office. It was stated that Davis used his position to fill the ranks of the United States Army with Southern men and therefore deprive the North of men of that ability when the war ensued. This statement is clearly shown as the falsehood it is by looking at the roster of officers of the new regiments formed under his supervision. Those officers appointed to the new regiments would, during the upcoming war,

---

36 Caleb Cushing, as cited in *Ibid.*, 163.

37 James Cambell, *Ibid.*, 137.

provide the United States government with eighteen general officers, twelve field and staff officers, and an inspector general, for a total of thirty-one officers. The officers appointed to the new regiments would, likewise, furnish the Confederate cause the following officers: twenty-two general officers and two field officers for a total of twenty-four officers.[38] In looking at the officers drawn from the newly established regiments, it is obvious that thirty-one (United States) is larger than twenty-four (Confederate States); therefore, the charge that Davis used his office as secretary of war to assist the pending war effort of the South is clearly false.

Davis, both as secretary of war and as Confederate president, was often charged with being too partial to graduates of West Point over those who had "come up through the ranks." Davis's loyalty to his alma mater was demonstrated on the floor of the House of Representatives on the eve of the war with Mexico. In commenting on the effect of military tactics as taught at West Point, Davis noted that military science, like any other science, had to be taught and practiced before it could be perfected.[39] The results of the efforts against Mexico, led by men trained at West Point, would prove Davis correct. During the War for Southern Independence, the same institution, West Point, provided both belligerents with their most famed generals.

Far from showing partisanship, under Davis's leadership, appointments to positions within the War Department were made on an appraisal of ability, not on partisan concepts. This was, and still is, unique in American history. Early in Davis's tenure, a delegation of Democratic congressmen paid a visit to the newly appointed secretary of war to complain about the appointment of a Whig to a position within the War Department. Secretary Davis replied that the man "had been appointed neither as a Whig nor a Democrat, but merely as the fittest candidate for the place. ... I further gave them to understand that the same principle of selection would be followed in similar cases, so far as my authority extended .... [T]

---

38 *Ibid.*, 133.
39 Varina Howell Davis, I, 244.

he visitors withdrew, dissatisfied with the results of the interview. Thenceforward, however, I was but little troubled with any pressure for political appointments in the department."[40]

One point in Davis's character that was obvious to many in the War Department was his sensitivity to the needs of those less fortunate than himself. An invalid sat close to the entrance of the office of secretary of war where Davis had to pass daily. Each day Davis would send a message to the individual with a small sum of money. Davis even had Varina make a cushion for the comfort of the man. Many people in the department noted that Davis was always moved by the plight of the less fortunate. His chief clerk and friend, Archibald Campbell, would often warn Davis that some people would take advantage of his good will. Campbell noted that his warnings would go unheeded because once left alone, Davis "grieves over their suffering, and it wears him very much."[41]

The fastidious care with which Davis managed public funds is demonstrated by his unwillingness to use his official position even in the most nebulous of matters. He never used his office to send flowers from the congressional greenhouse to anyone, never used official stationery for family correspondence, and, even when his father-in-law requested a small memento from Congress, Davis gave his father-in-law an article given to Davis, and refused to have it replaced at government expense.[42] According to one of Davis's biographers, George B. McClellan remarked that Davis's stewardship of the War Department proved that Davis "was the best Secretary of War—and I use best in its widest sense—I have ever had anything to do with."[43] His integrity in office stands in sharp contrast to the actions of many of today's politicians and bureaucrats who view their position as a chance to plunder the public treasury and enjoy the spoils of political victory.

---

40   Jefferson Davis, as cited in Jones, 140-41.
41   Archibald Campbell, as cited in Varina Howell Davis, I, 567.
42   *Ibid.*, I, 572.
43   George B. McClellan, as cited in McElroy, I, 173.

Throughout the administration of Franklin Pierce, Davis remained a trusted friend and confidant of the president, and the feelings were reciprocated by Davis. Of President Pierce Davis stated, "Chivalrous, generous, amiable, true to his friends and to his faith, frank and bold in the declaration of his opinions, he never deceived anyone."[44] The president's opinion of Davis was very similar. On March 4, 1857, Davis held his last interview with the president as secretary of war. That morning, after four years of service to president and country, Jefferson Davis handed the president his resignation. In accepting the resignation, Pierce, shaking Davis's hand, said, "I can scarcely bear the parting from you, who have been strength and solace to me for four anxious years and never failed me."[45] That afternoon, Davis was sworn in as a senator from Mississippi.

President Pierce's confidence in and respect for Davis was displayed in Pierce's letters to Davis before the inauguration in 1853, in his choice of Davis as secretary of war, in his reliance on Davis to speak for the administration, in his warm parting words to Davis in 1857, in his willingness to face ridicule in 1865 by visiting the "prisoner of state" in Fortress Monroe, and, after the war, by his offer to a homeless Davis of the use of his second home in New England. The close relationship between these two prominent Americans, a New England Yankee and a Deep South Southerner, should offer hope, in the minds of fair-minded people, for a just settlement of disputes between the North and South. This warm relationship also refutes the charge made against Davis that the Southern secession movement, of which he was the ultimate leader, was based in hatred of the North. With his service to his country, both military and political, and his many friends from the North, Davis was a confirmed nationalist in the truest American sense. Davis, the constitutionalist, never doubted the right of a state to secede but always sought to avoid, at all cost *except* the loss of constitutional rights, the implementation of the act of secession. In a letter dated August 22, 1852, Davis stated his true feelings about

---

44 Jefferson Davis, *Rise and Fall of Confederate Government*, I, 25.

45 Franklin Pierce, as cited in McElroy, I, 174.

the right of secession: "After my return to Mississippi in 1851 I took ground against the policy of secession and ... declared that secession was the last alternative, the final remedy, and should not be resorted to under existing [1851] circumstances."[46]

Second Term In the Senate

On March 4, 1857, Jefferson Davis began his second and last term as a United States senator from Mississippi. Within twenty-four hours of his being sworn in as senator, Davis and the nation would witness the explosion of the sectional controversy that was destined to engulf America. The United States Supreme Court, with Justice Roger Brooke Taney of Maryland speaking for the majority, declared the Missouri Compromise to be unconstitutional in the celebrated Dred Scott decision. The court stated that Congress could not assume a power, even in the service of a worthy objective, that the states had not delegated to it in the Constitution. The determination of the court was, "No word can be found in the Constitution which gives Congress a greater power over slave property, or which entitles property of that kind to less protection than property of any other description. The only power coffered is the power, coupled with the duty, of guarding and protecting the owner in his rights."[47] Davis, who had always opposed the Missouri Compromise because of its unconstitutional nature, felt justified as a result of the court's decision.

The Missouri Compromise, the brainchild of Henry Clay, effectively partitioned the territory of the Louisiana Purchase into two districts. These two districts would be formed by a line drawn from Missouri at the level of the border of Virginia and Kentucky at the latitude of 36' X 36'. Above this line was a district where slavery would not be allowed, and below the stated line was a district where slavery would be allowed; any state that prohibited slavery could be admitted to the Union from that district. The "compromise" brought all new states above the line into the Union under the influence of Northern interest and allowed the North to take as many states as possible from Southern control south of the line.

---

46 Jefferson Davis in a letter to James A. Pearce of Maryland, as cited in Jones, 144.
47 Dred Scott decision, as cited in McElroy, I, 175.

This type of compromise was condemned by many in the South as a ruse, wherein the North won much and lost little and the South lost much and won little. But Davis had greater concerns about the compromise. Davis often stated that, pursuant to the Constitution, only sovereign states could prohibit slavery. Nowhere could Davis find in the Constitution a congressional delegation of such power to allow Congress to discriminate on the type of property taken from a state into the common territory. Davis's position that only states could abolish slavery was not something unique to Davis or the South. Oliver Ellsworth of Connecticut, one of America's Founding Fathers, believed that only the states should legislate in the matter of abolition of slavery. Ellsworth, a New Englander, stated, "The morality or wisdom of slavery are considerations belonging to the States themselves .... [T]he States are the best judges of their particular interest .... Let us not intermeddle."[48]

The Radical element of the North reacted to the Dred Scott decision by devising and carrying out even more virulent attacks upon the South. They even demanded wholesale defiance of the Supreme Court. Screaming that the Supreme Court had "recognized" slavery, Radicals in the North shrieked that the "slaveocracy" would force slavery upon the whole nation. The truth is that the court only repeated what the Constitution in many places had said since 1787. In Article IV, Section 2, Paragraph 3, the so-called fugitive slave section of the Constitution, the right of a master to his slave property is recognized. This section of the Constitution was written by the Founding Fathers, both North and South, and then given authority by the unanimous actions of all the states adopting the Constitution. The fugitive slave section of the United States Constitution is not something "thought up by Southerners," but rather a continuation of an act passed by the New England states in the mid-1600s. The very first fugitive slave act enacted in America can be traced to the Articles of Confederation of the United Colonies of New England, May 19, 1643. New York historian George H. Moore states, "The original of the Fugitive Slave Law provision in the Federal Constitution is to be traced to this [New England] Confederacy, in

---

48 Oliver Ellsworth, as cited in M. E. Bradford, *Founding Fathers* (Lawrence KS: University Press of Kansas, 1994), 33.

which Massachusetts was the ruling colony."[49] As Davis and other Southerners were continually pointing out, as long as slavery was useful to the North, it was maintained and protected. It was the Northern (white) workers' fear of competition from slave workers that caused slavery to be ended and the free black people gradually removed from the North. John Adams of Massachusetts stated that slavery in the North was not abolished for moral or ethical reasons, but because Northern white workers refused to compete with black workers. Adams stated, "Argument might have some weight in the abolition of slavery in Massachusetts, but the real cause was the multiplication of laboring white people, who would no longer suffer the rich to employ these sable rivals so much to their injury. ... If the gentlemen had been permitted by law to hold slaves, the common white people would have put the slaves to death, and their masters too perhaps."[50] Therefore, the whine of the Radicals of the North, who pronounce the North as morally superior to the South and that the South must be punished because of slavery, should be seen in its proper light (i.e., as nothing less than hypocrisy and self-serving political slander).

The court in the Died Scott decision never interfered with the right of a state to prohibit slavery within its domain. Neither did the court thwart the privilege of the states to amend the Constitution and thus end slavery. The court merely restated the constitutional principle that the United States government could act only where it had been delegated the privilege to do so.

Finding themselves hemmed in by the plain words of the Constitution, the Radicals turned to the subterfuge and the sophistry of "higher law." Among the leaders of the "higher law" theory was William Seward.

---

49 George H. Moore, *Notes on the History of Slavery in Massachusetts* (New York: D. Appleton and Company, 1866), 27.

50 John Adams, as cited in Lorenzo Johnston Green, *The Negro in Colonial New England 1620-1776* (Port Washington, NY: Kennikat Press, Inc., 1966), 113,322.

Seward, a Northern Radical and political foe of Davis, was, nevertheless, a friend of the Davis family. Seward proved his friendship one winter during Davis's tenure as secretary of war. Having just given birth to their second son, Varina became ill and was thought to be near death. A violent snowstorm fell upon Washington, and movement about the city was almost impossible. Upon hearing that Varina was near death and that her nurse could not be brought to her assistance, Seward had his own horses hitched to a sleigh and with much effort and great hazard to life and property he brought Varina's nurse to her. Even after years of conflict and war, Varina wrote of Seward, "[A]fter all those long years of bitter feuds, I thank him as sincerely as my husband did to the last hour of his life."[51] The Davises and Sewards became friends after this incident and remained so until the outbreak of war.

The relationship between Davis and Seward must seem strange from today's perspective. Without surrendering their respective views, they maintained, while in Washington, a close friendship. Early in his second term as senator, Davis began to suffer from an eye infection. He always believed that this problem began while he was posted in the Northwest Territory during his army service in the 1830s. In 1858, because of the infection and severe pain, Davis was confined to a dark room for two months and many believed he would lose his eye. During this time, he had many visitors from all sections and both political parties. One daily visitor was William Seward. He would read to Davis and tell Davis what was happening in Congress. Davis was much amused at Seward as he would relate who "got the best" of which speaker in Congress, "your man, or, our man." Upon hearing that Davis may have to have his eye removed, Seward, with tears in his eyes told Varina, "I could not bear to see him maimed or disfigured, he is a splendid embodiment of manhood."[52] Fortunately, Davis did not lose his eye but would suffer with eye problems all his life.

It was during one of these visits by Seward that Varina and Jefferson discovered something very disturbing about Seward's character. In a conversation between the two men, Davis had noted

---

51 Varina Howell Davis, I, 571.

52 *Ibid.*, I, 580.

that he would lose his thoughts if an audience was inattentive. Seward then stated that he would rather speak to an empty room and let the newspapers report what he wanted the people to hear. Seward told Davis, "I speak to the papers, they have larger audience than I, and can repeat a thousand times if need be what I want to impress upon the multitude."[53] Davis then questioned Seward as to how he could make statements against the South that he must know were false. Seward said that anything he said was done only to "affect the rank and file of the North."[54] Being somewhat shocked at Seward's statements, Davis asked Seward if he ever spoke from a sense of conviction. Whereupon, Seward replied, "Nev-er." Dismayed, Davis, pulling himself up from his reclining position and removing his blindfold asserted, "As God is my judge, I never spoke from any other motive."[55] Varina recalled that "Mr. Seward put his arm about him [Davis] and gently laid down his head, saying, with great tenderness 'I know you do not—I am always sure of it.'"[56] It must have been obvious to Davis that more separated these friends than place of birth. Varina noted that Seward "was thoroughly sympathetic with human suffering, and .... [h]e frankly avowed that truth should be held always subsidiary to an end, and if some other statement could subserve that end he made it ... political strife was a state of war, and in war all stratagems were fair."[57]

Thus, we see displayed the nature of the man by whom the doctrine of "higher law" was most profoundly advocated. Seward's philosophy can be summed up as "the ends justify the means." This is and has always been the battle cry of the terrorist, regardless of the name, John Brown, Hezbola, Unibomber, ISIS, BLM, or Antifa. Davis intuitively understood what type of government these United States would have if "all stratagems were fair." An elected official could say anything, true or false, if it would advance his cause. A

---

53 Ibid., I.

54 Ibid., I, 581.

55 Ibid., I.

56 Ibid.

57 Ibid., I, 583.

president could be elected by saying whatever he needed to say to get elected. Under those circumstances, how could the people respect and believe their leaders?

The advocates of the "higher law" theory would never allow a passage in the Bible or an article in the Constitution to stand in the way of what they considered their duty to "higher law." The "higher law" cult demanded that laws be passed and other laws be ignored according to their definition of what the "higher law" demanded. These same people condemned the Constitution as "a compact with hell." Davis had little use for men of such caliber. In speaking out against these "higher law" advocates, Davis said:

> They say, it is true the Constitution dictates this, the Bible inculcates that, but there is a higher law than those; and they call upon you to obey that higher law of which they are the inspired givers. Men who are traitors to the compact of their fathers—men who have perjured the oaths they have themselves taken—they who wish to steep their hands in the blood of their brothers; these are the moral law-givers who proclaim a higher law than the Bible or the Constitution, and the laws of the land .... What security have you for your own safety if every man of vile temper, of low instincts, of base purpose, can find in his own heart a law higher than that which is the rule of society, the Constitution and the Bible?[58]

It was not long before the "higher law" advocates began to take the law into their own hands. In faraway Kansas at a place called Pottawatomie, John Brown led his fellow believers in "higher law" in an orgy of murder. Brown, with the support of Radical elements in the North known as the "secret six," was putting into action in Kansas the principle enunciated by Seward that "in war all stratagems are fair." In the service of the abolition of slavery, Brown was willing to appeal to a law higher than "Thou shall not kill" or any restraints

---

58 Jefferson Davis, as cited in McElroy, I, 187-88.

imposed by a constitution; after all, he had a "higher law." Cloaked in darkness, with a cry of "The Northern Army is upon you,"[59] John Brown's terrorists invaded peaceful homes and pulled unarmed men and boys from their beds and with sabers slashed open the heads of their victims. At Pottawatomie, Brown and his men hacked to death and mutilated the bodies of five men. This "higher law" zealot, fighting to end slavery, murdered five men that night. Of the five men slain by the Abolitionist zealots, none owned slaves; their guilt consisted not in owning slaves but in being Southerners! This hideous crime was committed by men who had never before committed such an outrage. As sickening as these and other crimes were, there was another fact that would outrage and worry the South. Although the names of the perpetrators were well known, none was ever brought to justice for these and other such crimes.[60] But worse yet, Brown was supported by influential men of the North, and few were those who spoke out against the conspirators. One biographer of John Brown notes that those men who supported Brown were "contemptible men who hired an assassin, armed a murderer, supported secret crime in the name of compassion and dealt their country a terrible blow while claiming the motives of angels."[61]

The people of the South could not understand how "in the name of compassion" the North could support those responsible for such hideous crimes. How compassionate is it to break into the home of a family and systematically butcher all its male members? How compassionate is it to incite the slave population to assist in this bloody work throughout the South? In the name of instant abolition of slavery, a compassionate idea, certain elements in the North were willing to commit any act because they felt justified by "higher law." The concept of "higher law" that Seward, Brown, and other Radical elements in the North advocated must be distinguished from the term commonly used by modern evangelicals. To modern evangelicals, the term usually indicates a belief that all law flows from God and

---

59 Otto Scott, *The Secret Six, John Brown and the Abolitionist Movement* (Murphys, CA: Uncommon Books, 1993), 8.

60 *Ibid.*, 9.

61 *Ibid.*, 4.

nothing in man's law can negate this "higher law." As Davis pointed out, the Radicals in the North believed in the supremacy of "higher law" not only in constitutional arguments but also in biblical issues. This belief marks the proponents of "higher law" as advocating a pagan system where man, the chief magistrate of government, is the supreme lawgiver. The pagan system of Egypt and Rome had as its pharaohs or emperors men who were considered gods, the source of a law higher than any other. This pagan system is very similar to the system advocated by the Unitarian and secular humanist advocates of "higher law" in the late 1850s, and the trend continues today.

At last, the non-slave-holding South understood that the actions of the Radicals in the North would not be limited to slave holders, but would encompass all Southerners. The people of the North who were deluded by the concept of "higher law" found it easy to forego all recognition of conventional morality and support a maniacal fiend such as John Brown. If one is not limited by the teaching of the Holy Bible or by the plain words of the written Constitution, but limited only by that which is deemed "higher law," then any act can and will be justifiable. Attila the Hun, Adolph Hitler, or Joseph Stalin could not have asked for a better system of morality to justify their actions than this system of "higher law" as advocated by Radical, anti-Southern Abolitionists of the North.

The South, led by men such as Randolph of Roanoke, Lee, and Davis, had been the consistent advocate of gradual emancipation of the slaves. The North, even as late as 1850, was still gradually emancipating slaves. New Jersey, for example, had more than two hundred slaves within its borders as late as 1850.[62] From the beginning of slavery in the North in 1643 until the passage of the Thirteenth Amendment, the North always chose gradual emancipation as the method of ending slavery. Yet, by 1858, the Northern Radical element was now demanding immediate elimination of slavery in the South. The Radicals of the North were not willing to allow the South, with many more slaves to free than the North, the privilege they had exercised (i.e., gradual emancipation).

---

62 R. L. Dabney, *A Defense of Virginia and the South* (1867, Harrisonburg, VA: Sprinkle Publications, 1977), 85.

Seward, the Radical's Radical, speaking at Rochester, New York, shocked Southerners by his statements that either the states having free labor or the states having slave labor must disappear.[63] Seward's statements were as hypocritical as they were shocking. As Davis would point out, "Though the defense of African slavery is left to the South, the North are jointly benefitted by it. Deduct from their trade and manufactures all which is dependent upon the products of slave labor, their prosperity would fall."[64] While castigating Southerners for making money from slave-grown cotton and other goods, Northerners felt it their right to do the same thing without any reproach. Thus, at the outbreak of the war, Northern newspapers bemoaned the loss of revenue from Southern goods. The *New York Times* warned about the loss of profits from slave-grown goods: "The commercial bearing of the question has acted upon the North .... We were divided and confused until our pockets were touched."[65] Merchants from New Hampshire bemoaned the loss of profits from slave-grown goods: "The Southern Confederacy will not employ our ships or buy our goods. What is our shipping without it? The transportation of [slave-grown] cotton and its fabrics employs more ships than all other trade."[66] The hypocrisy is obvious. If it is evil for Southerners to make money from slave-grown goods, then it is just as evil for Northerners to make money on the same slave-grown goods.

With an anti-South, Northern majority in control of the United States government, surrounded by supporters of terrorists, and the continuing target of Northern scorn, the South began to display something akin to siege mentality. Davis, on the floor of the Senate, chided the North for its actions against the South and asked, "You have made it a political war. We are on the defensive. How far are you

---

63 McElroy, I, 189.

64 Jefferson Davis, as cited in *Ibid.*, I, 331.

65 "The Great Question," *The New York Times*, March 30, 1861, 1.

66 "Let Them Go!" *Union Democrat* (Manchester, NH), February 19, 1861.

to push us?"⁶⁷ The North would continue to push the South until the South felt compelled to secede. Then the North, with self-righteous arrogance, would damn the South for "disunionist" sentiments.

NORTHERN VACATION SUMMER OF 1858

Davis, still suffering from eye problems and general weakness, was advised by his physician to retire to a more Northern climate for a short rest. Being so advised, Jefferson, Varina, and their two children, Margaret and Jefferson, left Washington for Portland, Maine. With no little apprehension, Davis took his family into the heart of Northern opposition to the South. Expecting a cool reception from the people of the North, Davis was delighted to be proven wrong. Of his New England visit, Davis stated, "[C]ourtesy and kindness met me on my first landing, and attended me to the time of my departure."⁶⁸

Serenading Davis and his family at their residence, the citizens of Portland, on July 9, offered music and cheers for their distinguished guest. At the close of the music, Davis was invited to speak to the large crowd. Davis, although still in frail health, spoke to the assembled crowd, praising the country's unity of spirit and of purpose. He received the cheers of the crowd not for himself but "as the medium through which Maine tenders an expression of regard to her sister, Mississippi."⁶⁹ He reminded the crowd that Americans were safe anywhere in the world because the world knew that Americans were united in the cause of self-protection.

> United as we now are, were a citizen of the United States, as an act of hostility to our country, imprisoned or slain in any quarter of the world, whether on land or sea, the people of each and every State of the Union,

---

67 Jefferson Davis, as cited in McElroy, I, 176.

68 *Ibid.*, I, 179.

69 Jefferson Davis, as cited in Jones, 154.

with one heart and with one voice would demand redress, and woe be to him against whom a brother's blood cried to us from the ground.[70]

This speech cheered the New Englanders who, as America's merchants to the world, understood the danger to merchants far removed from their native land. Warning of the dangers of unbridled sectionalism, Davis reminded his audience that the common benefit and well-being of all Americans were the source of America's greatness. Once again, Davis took the opportunity to remind Americans that what held the Union together was its common benefits, "national sentiment and fraternity which made us and which alone can keep us, one people."[71] Here, Davis was repeating the sense of national unity he had been taught at West Point in James Kent's Commentaries on American Law. Kent, a native of New York, in his textbook on the Constitution states, "[F]or on the concurrence and good will of the parts, the stability of the whole depends."[72] The warmth with which Davis was received and cheered on many such occasions served to stir him to greater efforts in maintaining the Union as given to America by the Founding Fathers. In August, Davis received an honorary LL.D, degree from Bowdin College, Maine, and again spoke for national unity by adhering to the limits imposed upon the United States government by the Constitution.

From Maine, the Davis family traveled to Boston with the intent of staying only a day, but, because of the sudden illness of Davis's son Jeff, their stay was prolonged. Varina made note of the attention and care given by so many sympathetic people in Boston when they discovered that the Davis child was critically ill. In later years, she would write, "These reminiscences of Boston to this day soften all the asperities developed by our bloody war."[73] The leading men of the Democratic party requested that Davis speak to a gathering of

---

70   *Ibid.*

71   *Ibid.*

72   James Kent, *Commentaries on American Law* (1826, New York: Da Capo Press, 1971), I, 369.

73   Varina Howell Davis, I, 594.

party faithful. Among those requesting Davis's appearance was a Boston Democrat by the name of Benjamin F. Butler, later to become infamous throughout the South, and especially in New Orleans, as "Beast Butler."

On October 10, 1858, Davis gave an address to a large crowd at Faneuil Hall in Boston. This hall had been used on several occasions by Radical Abolitionists to attack the South and slavery. Of some historical note, Faneuil Hall was named in honor of a famous Boston merchant, Peter Faneuil. It was from this hall that the famous Boston Tea Party originated. What most people don't know is that Peter Faneuil was a major backer in a slaving mission to Africa. Faneuil was, among other things, a slave trader. Think of the hypocrisy of Radical Abolitionists screaming denunciations against the South while standing in a hall named in honor of a Yankee who participated in the hideous African slave trade; of meeting in a hall located in Massachusetts where the first law instituting slavery in America was enacted, where the first slave ship in America, the *Desire*, and the last slave ship, the *Nightingale*, were built, and from which the first American fugitive slave law was enacted. The hypocrisy could not be greater!

At Faneuil Hall, Davis was introduced by Caleb Cushing of Boston, a friend and fellow cabinet member in President Franklin Pierce's administration. As Davis stood to take the stand to speak, he was welcomed by "three cheers" and a standing ovation. As he had always done while traveling throughout the country, Davis found ways to praise the attributes of the state he was then visiting. Davis, therefore, praised the people of Massachusetts for their efforts during the war for American independence. He related how the people of the Union were bound by *common* interest and for *common* good had united their efforts. As always, he was received with much fanfare and warm applause. Davis reminded his Northern friends of how they were, at one time, the prime defenders of State's Rights, so much so that when the first president of the United States, George Washington, visited Boston while John Hancock was governor, "Hancock refused to call upon the President, because he contended that any man who came within the limits of Massachusetts must yield rank and precedence to the Governor of the State."[74] In his eloquent manner, Davis continued his defense of the foundational concept of American liberty. Davis, the son of an American Revolutionary War soldier, reminded the assembled crowd of America's basis for independence: "Our fathers asserted the great principle—the right of the people to choose their own government and that government rested upon the consent of the governed."[75]

In Portland, Maine; Boston, Massachusetts; and New York, New York, Davis appealed to the sense of state pride to promote the common welfare and the mutual benefit of all citizens. The words of Davis stand in sharp contrast to the caustic and vengeful harangues of the Radical Abolitionists who were daily pushing the country toward disunion and war. Returning to Washington, Davis prepared for the opening session of the Thirty-Sixth Congress.

THE THIRTY-SIXTH CONGRESS

A few weeks before the opening of the Thirty-Sixth Congress, John Brown, the Abolitionist zealot, attacked the United States arsenal at Harper's Ferry, Virginia. Brown led a force of twenty-one armed men. With the support and assistance of several prominent Northern men, Brown was able to bring into Virginia several wagons loaded with weapons. With the assistance of his Radical Northern conspirators, Brown secured two hundred Sharp's carbines, two hundred revolvers, adequate ammunition, and one thousand pikes. These weapons were to be used to arm slaves whom Brown foolishly thought would fly to his cause. If African servitude in the South had been as horrible as the Yankee Abolitionists' propaganda pretended it to be, Brown would have had his "insurrection" slave army. Brown violated the first rule of a deceitful propagandist: "Never believe your own propaganda."

These disciples of "higher law" purported to be advocates of freedom for black Southerners; yet, the first victim of Brown's raid to end slavery was a free black citizen of Harper's Ferry. Before the

---

74 Jefferson Davis, as cited in Jones, 175.

75 *Ibid.*, 176.

attack was over, twenty-one men were dead: seventeen raiders, four citizens of Harper's Ferry, and one United States Marine. The South was shocked at Brown's intentions of leading a slave insurrection. In the aftermath of the raid, the South would obtain even more shocking intelligence. Northern newspaper editors and intellectuals were slowly turning a murderous zealot into a national hero. Utilizing the idea of "higher law," the North began to focus upon Brown's intention (i.e., freeing the slaves) and to overlook his immoral methods (i.e., the slaying of innocent men, women, and children). The South began to understand that the North saw no evil in "the idea of killing innocent people ... in an effort to achieve a greater good."[76] Conceiving his actions as progress in the service of a "greater good," John Brown, reflecting the attitude of the Radical element in the North, would never admit that what he had done was evil. "The North started to play down the extent of the violence and the significance of twenty-two deaths, and stress the glorious goals of John Brown."[77]

At a congressional hearing into the Brown raid, it was shown that William Seward had given money to and otherwise assisted John Brown. Seward, of course, pleaded that he had no idea that Brown intended to commit such an act. This is the same Seward who had told Jefferson and Varina Davis that any act that promoted his cause was ethical. Was Seward telling the congressional committee the truth, or was he just saying that which would advance his idea of the "higher law" imperative? President James Buchanan noted that Seward had the uncanny ability to say that which was "calculated both to inflame the ardor of his anti-slavery friends and to exasperate his pro-slavery opponents .... He thus aroused passions, probably without so intending, which it was beyond his power to control."[78] Thus began America's flirtation with the political zealot, a type of person who had the "right" (power) to do as he pleased provided enough "right" people agreed with his intentions. Regardless of how horrendous the act, one could commit any deed provided he had

---

76 Scott, 295.

77 *Ibid.*, 296.

78 James Buchanan, as cited in Varina Howell Davis, I, 652.

the right attitude or was pursuing a desirable end. No restriction of conventional morality would be allowed to stand in the way of the "higher law" concept of a virtuous society. In reflecting upon what John Brown and the advocates of "higher law" were doing to America, President Buchanan stated,

> But even admitting slavery to be a sin, have the adherents of John Brown never reflected that the attempt by one people to pass beyond their jurisdiction, and to extirpate by force of arms whatever they may deem sinful among another people, would involve the nations of the earth in perpetual hostilities? We Christians are thoroughly convinced that Mahomet was a false prophet—shall we, therefore, make war upon the Turkish Empire to destroy Islamism? If we would preserve the peace of the world and avoid much greater evils than we desire to destroy, we must act upon the wise principles of international law, and leave each people to decide domestic questions for themselves.[79]

While America was immersed in the struggle into which John Brown and his cohorts had plunged the nation, Hilton Helper wrote a book entitled The Impending Crisis. Of this book, President Buchanan stated, "No book could be better calculated for the purpose of intensifying the mutual hatred between North and South."[80] The book was written as an appeal to white workers in the South to join the Abolitionist movement and overthrow the slaveholding Southern establishment. Non-slave-holding Southerners were insulted by this attempt to pit Southerner against Southerner and rejected the book's intention. Yet, in the North the book was sold and given out by Radical Abolitionists to encourage Northerners to be bolder in their attacks upon the South.

---

79 *Ibid.*, I, 677.
80 *Ibid.*, I.

It was during the Thirty-Sixth Congress that the Democratic party finally succumbed to sectional tension. The consequence of the Democratic split would be realized in 1860 by the election of America's first purely sectional political party's candidate, Abraham Lincoln. Stephen Douglas, the leader of the Northern Democrats, advocated what was commonly known as "squatter sovereignty." This view advanced the idea that the people of a territory could decide for themselves if slavery would be allowed in a territory. Jefferson Davis, as leader of the Southern Democrats, countered that any citizen should be allowed in the commonly held territory, regardless of the property he owned. Davis held that only a sovereign state could limit the type of property held within its boundaries. He noted that, if the citizens of a territory could decide for themselves what type of institutions were and were not allowed, then Mormons had every right to establish polygamy in their territory. Davis's assertion was consistent with his view that Congress was bound to protect the property of citizens of all states and that only when citizens were formed into sovereign states could they make alterations in such matters as slavery.

It should be noted that Jefferson Davis and the Southern men in Congress never attempted to foist the system of slavery upon any people; rather, they held that the people and only the people of a sovereign state could restrict slavery. Because of the limitation on crops that could be grown in the Western territories, it was always doubtful that many states would be formed that allowed the institution of slavery in that area of the nation. What the South demanded was an equal right to go into the commonly held territories and settle there. It is hard to believe that Colorado, Idaho, or Nevada could have ever been slave states. Nevertheless, the North had no intention of allowing the South even this this nebulous chance of gaining "new" Southern states. The North, by 1860, had "monopolized to herself more than three-fourths of all that had been added to the domain of the United States since the Declaration of Independence."[81] Thus, the debate, against the backdrop of Radical Abolitionist theatrics, proceeded along the course that led to the final rupture of the Democratic party and consequently the Union.

---

81 Jefferson Davis, *Rise and Fall of Confederate Government*, I, 52.

Davis did not allow the sectional dispute to keep his attention away from minding the "general welfare" of the nation. He maintained his efforts to get the transcontinental railroad off the drawing board. Davis advocated a Southern Pacific route for the railroad that would start in Memphis, Tennessee. He had been instrumental in having several routes surveyed during his term as secretary of war, and one of these would eventually become the first route.

On April 23, 1860, the Democratic party met in Charleston, South Carolina, to nominate its candidate for president. The convention was doomed from the outset. Neither faction, Northern or Southern, was willing to forego its objective of securing its interests. This determined resistance by each faction led to the rupture of the Democratic party. The result was an election in November of 1860 in which four major parties offered candidates.

Throughout the history of America, from Washington to Buchanan, political parties had recognized the divergent interests in the nation by always offering a candidate for president from the North or South and a candidate for vice president from the opposite section of the country. If a Northerner was president, a Southerner was vice president, and vice versa.

In 1860, the Northern Democrats nominated Stephen Douglas of Illinois for president and Benjamin Fitzpatrick of Alabama as vice president; the Southern Democrats nominated John C. Breckinridge of Kentucky for president and Joseph Lane of Oregon for vice president; a gathering of Whigs and disheartened Democrats nominated John Bell of Tennessee for president and Edward Everett of Massachusetts for vice president; the Republicans nominated Abraham Lincoln of Illinois for president and Hannibal Hamlin of Maine for vice president. Note that three out of four parties had a balanced ticket (i.e., one Northern man and one Southern man). Even the "Northern" and "Southern" Democrats adhered to this principle. Only the Republican Party offered a purely *sectional* ticket.

With a divided opposition, Lincoln, with only 39 percent of the popular vote and as a nominee of the nation's first purely sectional party, was elected president. The South, which at best never had more than bare parity with the North, began to wonder what would remain of its constitutional rights once the party dedicated to the destruction of the South came into power. The House of Representatives had long since passed from Southern control; the Senate, now that no new Southern states would be formed from the territories, moved inexorably into the hands of its foes, and now the chief executive of the republic was elected from a sectional party that backed men such as John Brown. Throughout the South, hope for the Union of the Founding Fathers was fading fast. Of Lincoln and his party, Varina Davis spoke for the entire South:

> To the South he [Lincoln] represented nothing but the embodiment of the enmity of his party. He was the candidate of a part only of the people of the United States, elected with the express understanding that he would rule in hostility over the minority, while ostensibly acting as the guardian of the whole country.[82]

SECESSION BEGINS

With the election of an avowed enemy of the South to the chief executive position of the republic, the legislature of South Carolina called for a convention of the people of the state to consider her relationship with the federal Union. South Carolina's two senators resigned their positions in the Senate and returned home. Accepting the fact that secession was a right of the states, but hoping to the last for some form of reconciliation, Davis cautioned Gov. John J. Pettus of Mississippi about radical action. So cautious was Davis in the secession movement that many Mississippians considered him to be against secession or entirely "too slow"[83] in efforts for secession. In December 1860, Governor Pettus called a conference in Jackson, Mississippi, with the state's congressional delegation, to discuss Mississippi's response to South Carolina's act of secession.

---

82 Varina Howell Davis, I, 685.
83 Jefferson Davis, *Rise and Fall of Confederate Government*, I, 58.

O. R. Singleton, a member at the conference, noted that Davis was indeed not a secession extremist. Singleton expressed the view that many members of the Mississippi conference held of Davis:

> After the conference was ended, several of its members were dissatisfied with the course of Mr. Davis, believing that he was entirely opposed to secession, and was seeking to delay action upon the part of Mississippi, with the hope that it might be entirely averted.[84]

This, and the reports of many others who knew Davis during that time, refutes the claim of those who accuse Davis of fomenting the secession movement in the South. In the view of Gen. C. Irvine Walker of Charleston, South Carolina, Davis did not seek the leadership of the new government but was drafted by the Southern people as their leader. Walker, in an article published in 1908, stated that "we should ever remember that he was placed at its head by its people and against his wishes. He did not seek to govern us, but we called him to direct the destinies of our new nation."[85]

Davis had always viewed secession as a sacred right of the people of a sovereign state, but as a right that should only be resorted to as the very last alternative in the defense of liberty. This lifelong view of secession is clearly demonstrated in both his military and political life; yet, to this day, his enemies persist in the slander of calling Davis a disunionist and a radical secessionist.

With the secession sentiment in the Deep South running white hot, Davis returned to Washington and, with the cooperation of many Northern Democrats, including Democratic rival Stephen Douglas of Illinois, attempted one last time to save the Union. Senator John J. Crittenden of Kentucky, one of the oldest and most respected men in the Senate at that time, was in the forefront of efforts to reconcile the various sections of the Union. Around the middle of December 1860, Davis was appointed a member of a committee of Congress

---

84 O.R. Singleton, as cited in Jones, 211.

85 C. Irwine Walker, "Correct Estimate of Jefferson Davis," *Confederate Veteran*, Oct., 1908, Vol. XVI, No. 10, 496.

to propose appropriate compromises to maintain the Union. The Southern Democrats, Northern Democrats, and Senator Crittenden, a Whig, were all willing to compromise to save the Union. Yet, every compromise was defeated by the Republicans on the committee. In desperation, Senator Douglas of Illinois challenged the Republicans to offer some suggestion that they would be willing to abide by in order to save the Union.[86] The Republicans sat in silence, having nothing to say in response to Senator Douglas. Obviously, the Radical Republicans had an agenda that did not include maintaining the original Republic of Sovereign States.

Senator Davis took the floor of the Senate and reminded the members, "This Union is dear to me as a Union of fraternal States. It would lose its value if I had to regard it as a Union held together by physical force."[87] He noted that the people of the South were convinced "that hostility, and not fraternity, now exists in the hearts of the people, that they are looking to their reserved rights."[88] At last, Davis threw down the gauntlet to the Northern majority: "Upon you ... it depends to restore peace and perpetuate the Union of equal States."[89] Every idea and suggestion for a compromise made by Northern or Southern men was defeated by the Republican Party and its Northern majority.

On January 9, 1861, Mississippi joined South Carolina in recalling her delegated rights to the United States government. Upon this act, Mississippi became an independent state. With official notification of Mississippi's secession, Davis prepared to take his leave of the capital city where he had served for so long. In an emotion-packed letter to his friend, former president Franklin Pierce of New Hampshire, Davis wrote:

---

86 Jefferson Davis, *Rise and Fall of Confederate Government*, I, 69.

87 *Ibid.*, I, 68.

88 *Ibid.*, I.

89 *Ibid.*

> I have often and sadly turned my thoughts to you during the troublous limes through which we have been passing ... for the independence and union of which my father toiled, and in the service of which I have sought to emulate the example he set for my guidance. Mississippi, not as a matter of choice, but of necessity, has resolved to enter on the trial of secession. Those who have driven her to this alternative threaten to deprive her of the right to require that her government shall rest on the consent of the governed ... to reduce a State to the condition from which the colony rose.[90]

Davis's devotion to the Union, as established by the Founding Fathers, is seen in his remarks to President Pierce. Davis's father was a Revolutionary War veteran, and he felt the close kinship to the liberty his father had fought to secure. Jefferson Davis was also a wounded veteran of one of America's wars and had served in both Congress and the cabinet of President Franklin Pierce; the act of removing himself from such a connection was not taken lightly by Davis. Yet, notice that Davis stated that his state seceded not out of a vain desire to cause harm but of the necessity of self-defense. The deed (i.e., secession) having been done, Davis prepared to make his final statement to the United States Senate. On January 21, 1861, Jefferson Davis addressed the Senate. Word that Davis was to make this address spread rapidly across the city. As early as seven o'clock on the twenty-first, people began to take whatever seating was available. By nine o'clock, every seat had been taken, and there was standing room only in the chamber and balcony. Davis, showing all the effects of his chronic ill health, arose from his seat. Every eye was fastened upon the figure known for his eloquence of speech and profound understanding of constitutional theory. Davis "glanced over the Senate with the reluctant look, the dying cast on those upon

---

90 Jefferson Davis, as cited in Jones, 216.

whom they gaze for the last time."⁹¹ Varina, witnessing the farewell address from the Senate gallery, recounted the mood of Davis and his audience:

> He was listened to in profound silence, broken only by repeated applause, which his face revealed he deprecated before the Vice-President called the audience to order. The orator was too grief-stricken and too terribly in earnest to think of the impression he might create upon others. Had he been bending over his bleeding father, needlessly slain by his countrymen, he could not have been more pathetic or inconsolable.⁹²

After customary remarks, Davis informed the Senate that he had received official notification from Mississippi that she had withdrawn from the Union. Upon that notification, Davis was making his appeal to the Senate and the nation. Davis made several points during his speech. He called attention to the difference between nullification and secession.

> Secession belongs to a different class of remedies. It is to be justified upon the basis that the States are sovereign. There was a time when none denied it. I hope the time may come again when a better comprehension of the theory of our Government, and the inalienable rights of the people of the States, will prevent anyone from denying that each State is sovereign, and thus may reclaim the grants which it has made to any agent whomsoever.⁹³

Davis reminded his colleagues in the Senate of a time when Massachusetts was under attack for not abiding by a constitutional mandate. Even though Davis disagreed with what Massachusetts was doing, he refused to advocate "one dollar nor one man to coerce

---

91 Varina Howell Davis, I, 697.

92 *Ibid.*, I, 698.

93 Jefferson Davis, as cited in *Ibid.*, I, 690.

her back."⁹⁴ By this, Davis sought to overthrow the logic of those who stated that Davis sought a special privilege for the South in secession. Davis reminded his audience that in the Declaration of Independence the colonies had condemned Great Britain for attempting a servile insurrection among the colonies: something the North was at that very time doing to the South. This very act of instigating a servile insurrection was so heinous that it was "enumerated among the high crimes which caused the colonies to sever their connection with the mother country."⁹⁵

Davis then set forth the foundation on which secession is based and why secession was correct for any American state:

> Then, Senators, we recur to the principles upon which our Government was founded; and when you deny them, and when you deny to us the right to withdraw from a Government which, thus perverted, threatens to be destructive to our rights, we but tread in the path of our fathers when we proclaim our independence and take the hazard. This is done, not in hostility to others, not to injure any section of the country, not even for our own pecuniary benefit, but from the high and solemn motive of defending and protecting the rights we inherited, and which it is our duty to transmit unshorn to our children.⁹⁶

Feeling the full weight of the events happening throughout the country he loved so, Davis reached out in an emotional appeal to his fellow senators one last time:

> In the course of my service here, associated at different times with a great variety of Senators, I see now around me some with whom I have served long;

---

94   Ibid., I.
95   Ibid., I, 693.
96   Ibid., I, 694.

there have been points of collision, but, whatever of offence there has been to me, I leave here. I carry' with me no hostile remembrance. Whatever offence I have given which has not been redressed, or for which satisfaction has not been demanded, I have, Senators, in this hour of our parting, to offer you my apology for any pain which, in the heat of discussion, I have inflicted. I go hence unencumbered by the remembrance of any injury received, and having discharged the duty of making the only reparation in my power for any injury offered. Mr. President and Senators, having made the announcement which the occasion seemed to me to require, it only remains for me to bid you a final *adieu*.[97]

The gallery of the Senate chamber erupted in a loud and sustained ovation for Davis. In order to regain senatorial decorum, the president of the Senate threatened to have the sergeant-at-arms remove loud and boisterous persons. Davis sank into his chair with his head in his hands as one hiding his crying face from the public. Saddened, emotionally spent, and with little hope of a restoration of the Union, Davis left the Senate. That night, he had little sleep and Varina would hear him often repeat the prayer, "May God have us in His holy keeping, and grant that before it is too late peaceful councils may prevail."[98] His prayer was to be answered by massed bayonets in the hands of blue-clad troops invading the South.

President, Confederate States of America

"Deeply depressed and supremely anxious" is the manner in which Varina Davis described the feelings of the Davis family as they left Washington for Mississippi. Washington had been home to the Davises for more than fifteen years. Friends of all political persuasions and sections would now be separated, to meet again

---

97 *Ibid.*, I,

98 *Ibid.*, I, 699.

perhaps only on a field of battle. Davis, the consistent advocate of the national good, feared only one thing more than the end of the Union: that was the end of constitutional liberty. As a true advocate of state sovereignty, he placed his faith in a union of common interests and good will, not a union where the majority of states would subject a minority of states to a condition of servitude.

Upon arriving in Mississippi, he was offered and accepted the office of commander in chief of the Mississippi volunteer army. Longing for peace, he nevertheless understood the need to prepare for a defense of Mississippi. Davis was one of very few members of Mississippi's government who actually expected war as a result of Mississippi's act of secession. Most Southerners could not accept the idea that Northerners, in total disregard of the sovereign nature of the states, would approve the unconstitutional act of invading a sovereign state. Yet, Davis insisted that not only would the United States government invade the South but, he also insisted that the coming war would be long and bloody. When Davis informed Governor Pettus of Mississippi of the need for more than seventy thousand rifles, Pettus remarked, "General, you overrate the risk."[99] Events would soon prove Davis's estimation correct. After his return to Mississippi, Davis made preparations for his people at Briarfield. He had several meetings with the older slaves and saw to the special needs of the older servants. To one of the oldest couples at Briarfield, Bob and his wife Rhinah, he gave extra blankets and furniture that they would need during the coming winter months. When the Yankee Empire's troops invaded the area in 1863, they sacked the "slave quarters" of Davis's plantation and stole all the articles given to "Old Bob" and his wife.[100] Such were the tender mercies of the Yankee liberators! While Davis was busy placing everything in good order in case of his early departure, he made a very revealing and succinct comment to Varina about the future of slavery: "I think that our slave property will be lost eventually."[101]

---

99 Governor John J. Pettus, as cited in *Ibid.*, II, 8.

100 *Ibid.*, II, 11.

101 *Ibid.*, I, 12.

Davis's strongest desire at this time was to take an active part in the military defense of his state and the South. When the call came from the Southern delegates in Montgomery, Alabama, for Davis to serve as the first president of the Confederacy, Davis reluctantly consented to their request.[102]

The new union of six Southern states, with its capital in Montgomery, Alabama, was to be known as the Confederate States of America. On February 18, 1861, Jefferson Davis was sworn in as the provisional president of the Confederate States of America. In his inaugural address, Davis spoke of the South fighting for the principles of the American colonists: "[W]e hope to perpetuate the principles of our revolutionary fathers."[103] Davis made special note of the fact that the actions of the states of the South had been done with the complete support of the people and not by secret or violent methods. "Actuated solely by the desire to preserve our own rights, and promote our own welfare, the separation by the Confederate States has been marked by no aggression upon others, and followed by no domestic convulsion."[104] The complete address was a grand defense of the American right of self-government. In closing, Davis took the opportunity to point out that the new nation would be guided by a constitution only slightly different from the original constitution of 1787:

> We have changed the constituent parts, but not the system of government. The Constitution framed by our fathers is that of these Confederate States. In their exposition of it, and in the judicial construction it has received, we have a light which reveals its true meaning.[105]

---

[102] Jones, 301.

[103] Jefferson Davis, Inaugural Address, as cited in Jefferson Davis, *Rise and Fall of Confederate Government*, I, 232.

[104] Davis, 235.

[105] *Ibid.*, 236.

The provisional constitution was little different from the one established by the American patriots of 1787. Indeed, in many ways, the new Confederacy was nothing but a remake of the original Constitutional Republic of America. This affinity for the founding document of the United States by the Confederate States has been noted by many scholars. Marshall L. DeRosa notes, "The Southerners did not abandon constitutional government; to the contrary, they reaffirmed their commitment to constitutional government under the auspices of the Confederate Constitution."[106] In explaining the foundational basis for the Confederate Constitution, DeRosa states, "In light of the principles of limited government and the consent of the governed, there is much to be learned from the theories that gave life and death to this American constitution."[107]

Davis's strong faith in strict construction constitutional theory did not terminate with his election as president. The very first veto Dads issued as president of the Confederacy was in defense of the Confederate Constitution's abolition of the African slave trade. When the Confederate Congress attempted to pass a law authorizing the sale of slaves captured on the high seas or otherwise illegally imported into the Confederacy, Davis vetoed the bill. In his veto message to the Confederate Congress, Davis stated,

> The Constitution (section 7, article I.) provides that the importation of African negroes from any foreign country other than slave-holding States of the United States is hereby forbidden, and Congress is required to pass such laws as shall effectually prevent the same. The rule herein given is emphatic, and distinctly directs the legislation which shall effectually prevent the importation of African negroes .... This provision [bill just vetoed] seems to me to be in opposition to the policy declared

---

106 Marshall L. DeRosa, *The Confederate Constitution of 1861* (Columbia, MO: University of Missouri Press, 1991), 1.

107 *Ibid.*, 134.

in the Constitution—the prohibition of the importation of African negroes—and in derogation of its mandate to legislate for the effectuation of that object.[108]

Jefferson Davis's first veto as president of the Confederate States demonstrates his abiding faith in strict construction constitutionalism. Davis's words, spoken in defense of the prohibition against importation of African slaves and the very words of the Confederate Constitution, clearly demonstrate the error of those who maintain that the South was a "slaveholders' Confederacy," established only for the expansion of slavery. The Northern argument that the South seceded in order to promote slavery in America is obviously ridiculous because, when the Southern States seceded, they surrendered all claims to any territory outside of the South. It should also be remembered that even Lincoln stated that the institution of slavery would not be disturbed "in those states where it now exists." Even the so-called Emancipation Proclamation offered security for the system of slavery if the slave states would return to the Union. In a letter to Abolitionist Horace Greeley on August 25, 1862, Lincoln clearly stated his view about "freeing the slaves." In his letter to Greeley, Lincoln noted, "My paramount object in this struggle is to save the Union, and is not either to save or to destroy slavery. If I could save the Union without freeing any slave, I would do it; and if I could save it by freeing all the slaves, I would do it; and if I could save it by freeing some and leaving others alone, I would do that. *What I do about slavery and the colored race, I do because I believe it helps to save this Union*" [emphasis added].[109] For Lincoln, the Negro and the issue of slavery were just another convenient weapon to use against the South. Unlike Davis and the South, who were fighting for the maintenance of constitutional rights, Lincoln's prime objective was the maintenance of governmental authority, North and South, with or without the "consent of the governed."

---

108 Jefferson Davis, Veto Message, February 28, 1861, as cited in Kennedy & Kennedy, *The South Was Right!* 2nd edition, (Gretna, LA: Pelican Publishing Co., 1994), 332.

109 Abraham Lincoln, as cited in the *New York Tribune*, August 25, 1862, Vol. 22, 4.

The most pressing problem at hand for the newly elected government of the Confederacy was how to deal with issues relating to the United States. The South, unprepared for war, did not seek a conflict with the United States. The very first action of the Confederate government was to declare the desire to settle all accounts resulting from the disruption of the relationship it recently had with the Union. The Confederate government on February 25, 1861, sent agents to the United States government to negotiate equitable adjustments on any disputes between the two sections. These agents were rebuffed by the Yankee Empire's new government and, at best, they could only speak through second parties to the Yankee Empire's government. Virginia, led by her eminent native son, former president John Tyler, along with the other "border" states, initiated its own peace effort. All efforts on the part of Virginia and moderate elements in Congress were a dismal failure. The warlike intentions of the Lincoln government were becoming clear. Speaking for many extreme Republicans of the Lincoln administration, Zack Chandler of Michigan stated, "[W]ithout a little blood-letting this Union will not, in my estimation, be worth a rush."[110] While Radicals gleefully anticipated a "little blood-letting," Northern and Southern conservative elements in Washington launched one last effort to avoid hostilities.

United States Supreme Court Justice John A. Campbell, acting as the "go-between" for the Southern agents and Secretary of State Seward, inaugurated discussions to defuse the potentially hostile situation. The most pressing problem was the removal of troops from Fort Pickens in Florida and Maj. Robert Anderson's troops from Fort Sumter, South Carolina. Even Northern men such as Stephen Douglas of Illinois voiced the hope that troops would be withdrawn from the South. Douglas, in the Senate, demanded the "withdrawal of the garrisons from all forts within the limits of the States which had seceded."[111] Yet, while conservative elements in and out of Congress worked to reduce the threat of war, the Lincoln government was making plans for coercion. Major Anderson's secret

---

110 Zack Chandler, as cited in Jones, 307.

111 Stephen A. Douglas, as cited in Varina Howell Davis, II, 53.

removal of his troops from Fort Moultrie to Fort Sumter was made in violation of a tacit agreement between the governor of South Carolina and President James Buchanan. This move, with the destruction of the guns and property at Fort Moultrie by Anderson, heightened the feelings of hostility throughout the seceded states. Also, at Fort Pickens in Pensacola, Florida, the clandestine reinforcement of Fort Pickens by the Federal government was the source of another violation of an agreement between the governments of the North and South.[112] It was now becoming clear, even to the most ardent pacifist, that the new administration in Washington was pursuing a course of coercion and domination against the seceded states. The South was witnessing the birth of the Yankee Empire. It would become an empire that, as General Robert E. Lee predicted after the war, it would become "aggressive abroad and despotic at home."[113]

In a last-ditch effort to prevent hostilities, South Carolina sent a commissioner, I. W. Hayne, to Washington to obtain an amicable solution to the problems surrounding Fort Sumter. Every effort by Hayne was met with evasion and contempt. Secretary of State Seward assured the South that Sumter would be evacuated; he promised "Faith as to Sumter fully kept. Wait and see."[114] This assurance was made two weeks after Seward had promised the evacuation of Fort Sumter and ten days after his assurance that the delay in the evacuation was "accidental."[115]

While these negotiations were ongoing, clandestine efforts were underway by the United States government to re-enforce Fort Sumter. While the South was offering peace, the Radicals in the North were making plans to force the hand of the South and thus instigate war. The plan for the relief of Fort Sumter was an open secret in Washington, and it was becoming obvious to everyone

---

112 John S. Tilley, *Lincoln Takes Command* (1941, Nashville, TN: Bill Coats, Ltd., 1991), 70.

113 Kennedy & Kennedy, *Yankee Empire: Aggressive Abroad and Despotic at Home* (Columbia, SC: Shotwell Publishing, 2018).

114 William Seward, as cited in *Jefferson Davis, Rise and Fall of Confederate Government*, I, 273.

115 Davis, 272.

that Lincoln's government was not negotiating in good faith; rather, it was merely stalling for time. On April 8, one day after the final assurance by Seward of the evacuation of Sumter, notice was given to the governor of South Carolina of the *resupply* of Fort Sumter by peaceful means or by force, if necessary. A United States naval force was already forming off the cost of Charleston, South Carolina, when the state received the message from the United States government. The Confederacy was now faced with a hostile force within it harbor and a naval force with the capability of landing troops waiting off its coast. With the combined efforts of the guns of Fort Sumter and the guns of the *USS Pawnee*, the *USS Harriet Lane*, the *USS Pocahontas*, and the troops on board the transport vessel Baltic, the Confederates were in imminent danger of defeat at Charleston. For this reason, Davis and the Confederate government recommended to Gen. Pierre Gustave Toutant Beauregard to demand Major Anderson's surrender of Fort Sumter.

The action taken by the Confederates, as a result of the combined forces arrayed against them, has often been criticized by the intellectually shallow as causing the war. "You fired the first shot" is a retort that has been heard by Southerners from the beginning of the war to the present day. Yet, as Davis was taught at West Point Military Academy (Lincoln, having never had the benefit of a good education, in some ways could be forgiven for his ignorance), "Every nation has an undoubted right to provide for its own safety, and to take due precautions against distant as well as impending danger."[116] If an armed thief were breaking into a home and threatening violence to the occupants, would the homeowner be required to wait until the thief fired the "first shot" before he defended his family? How ridiculous! Henry Hallam stated the case well when he said, "[T]he aggressor in a war (that is, he who begins it), is not the first who uses

---

[116] Kent, I, 23. For several years, James Kent was an examiner of students studying constitutional law at West Point Military Academy. Kent's Commentaries were used as the textbook for constitutional and international law at West Point from 1826 until after the War for Southern Independence.

force, but the first who renders force necessary."¹¹⁷ Lincoln and the Radicals of the North were the ones who rendered force necessary at Charleston, South Carolina, not Davis and the South.

Many have speculated as to why Lincoln would force the South to fire on Fort Sumter. In Lincoln's view, the effort to provision Fort Sumter had its desired effect. It ended all hope of peaceful secession and silenced the influential pro-Southern voices in the North. Appealing to the patriotic sentiment with the call of "defending the flag," Lincoln was able to rally the various elements in the North in an effort to defend the "national honor." In a revealing letter, Lincoln noted the true reasons for the effort to re-enforce Fort Sumter: "You and I both anticipated that the cause of the country would be advanced by making the attempt to provision Fort Sumter, even if it should fail; and it is no small consolation now to feel that our anticipation is justified by the results."¹¹⁸ The letter was signed, "Very truly, your friend, A. Lincoln."

Lincoln's response to the events at Fort Sumter resulted in two divergent consequences. First, the North rallied to the call for the overthrow of the seceded states; and the border states initiated the second round of secession. The "Cotton" states of the lower South would be joined by the states of the upper South, including Kentucky and Missouri. Swift and illegal action by both the Lincoln administration and Northern Democrats (i.e., Generals George McClellan and John A. Dix) prevented Maryland from joining the Confederacy.¹¹⁹ In a secret meeting, Lincoln, Frederick Seward (son of Secretary of State William Seward), Gen. Nathaniel Banks (commander of the military forces in the western region of Maryland), and General Dix (commander of the military forces in the eastern region of Maryland) made plans for the arrest of "secessionist"

---

117 Henry Hallam, as cited in Alexander H. Stephens, *The War Between the States* (1870, Harrisonburg, VA: Sprinkle Publications, 1994), II, 35. This passage is cited by Stephens from Hallam's work *Constitutional History of England*, II, 219.

118 Abraham Lincoln, as cited in Tilley, 267.

119 Mark E. Neely, Jr., *The Fate of Liberty, Abraham Lincoln and Civil Liberties* (New York: Oxford University Press, 1991), 15, 16.

members of the Maryland state legislature.[120] Note that no court action or violation of law is asserted as the reasons for these arrests. These men, in violation of every constitutional principle supposedly held sacred by all Americans, were arrested simply because they held political views the Northern majority held in contempt.

The South's fear of a sectional party using the power of the United States government to abuse the rights of the minority of the states was realized soon after Lincoln's inauguration. The new administration's total disregard for the right of the people of Maryland to govern themselves freely was proof positive for Southerners that the North intended to govern in hostility. (See Addendum IV).

Lincoln moved quickly. Without the consent of Congress, he suspended the writ of habeas corpus and proceeded to jail "secessionist" members of Maryland's legislature. All these acts were committed in flagrant violation of the Constitution and Bill of Rights. Only during the days of the Alien and Sedition Acts have Americans' civil liberties been so *totally* disregarded. The arrest of one prominent Marylander in particular should cause a blush of shame on the face of every American who stands at attention when the national anthem is played. The Marylander's name is Francis Key Howard, the grandson of Francis Scott Key.

As a prisoner on board a British man-of-war, a Southerner from Maryland, Francis Scott Key, wrote "The Star Spangled Banner." Francis Scott Key's grandson, Francis Key Howard, was thrown in prison by the Lincoln administration because he advocated the right of the people of Maryland to live under a government established by their consent (what a radical idea!). Francis Scott Key's grandson was imprisoned for fourteen months for advocating the Jeffersonian idea of "government by the consent of the governed." Francis Key Howard stated that the reason he and other Southerners of Maryland were imprisoned was because they insisted that "the people of the State had the right to decide their own destiny for themselves."[121]

---

120 *Ibid.*

121 Francis Key Howard, as cited in Neely, 263.

Not only did Maryland suffer under the unconstitutional acts of the Lincoln administration but all Americans were subjected to these acts. During his administration, Lincoln unconstitutionally suspended the writ of habeas corpus (see Addendum V), closed down newspapers that were unsympathetic to his administration, and acquiesced in the imprisonment of civilians by military tribunals. The new administration in Washington even allowed the military to suspend the writ of habeas corpus,[122] an act resorted to by military dictators. Lincoln's un-American activities were not limited to the South. Many civilian editors, politicians, and elected officials in Northern states were arrested by the Yankee Empire's military for demanding peace with the South. For example, in the states of Ohio, Indiana, and Illinois, Gen. Ambrose Burnside, a military/political commissar, was in command and routinely excluded from the mail newspapers such as the *New York Herald* and *Chicago Times* because of their anti-war sentiments. Burnside even threatened civilians who dared oppose the Northern war policy. In Ohio, the Yankee Empire's military at 2:00 A.M. broke into the home of Representative Clement L. Vallandigham and arrested him. This civilian-elected official of Ohio was then taken before a military court, tried, and banished from the Yankee Empire![123] If the biblical injunction of "by their fruit ye shall know them" means anything today, the fruit of Lincoln's America must leave a bitter taste in the mouths of Americans who love liberty.

While the Lincoln administration was attempting to repress resistance to its action in the North, Jefferson Davis embarked upon his career as leader of the Confederate States of America. The role of president was one he never sought and wished to avoid, but he was the one man respected above all other Southerners as being capable of pulling the divergent parts of the Confederacy together. The following four years and the aftermath would secure for Davis a place of fame and infamy in the annals of American history. Very few men in America could have done as much for the Southern cause as Davis; none could have done more. Nowhere in

---

122 *Ibid.*, 10.

123 Charles L. C. Minor, *The Real Lincoln* (1904, Harrisonburg, VA: Sprinkle Publications, 1992), 170.

the South could one find a man better qualified for the position he was to occupy for four years. To his credit, even though his country was being invaded by enemy troops, Davis never closed down any newspaper that spoke out against his administration. Even critics within the Confederate government had no fear of midnight arrest or *banishment* at the hands of their own government. Davis's secretary of state, unlike Lincoln's secretary of state, Seward, never had a bell on his desk that he could ring and send any citizen to jail.[124] The most frightful aspect of Seward's bell is that it was used on non-Southerners—it was used against Northern subjects of the newly created Yankee Empire. Thus, the 2022 attack on free speech had its origins in Lincoln's newly created Yankee Empire. It was the beginning of the death of the original Constitution, Bill of Rights, and the guarantee of free speech!

In May 1861, the capital of the Confederacy was moved to Richmond, Virginia. Davis and the Confederate government made Richmond their home for the following four years. On February 22, 1862, Davis took the oath of office as the president of the Confederate States of America. Until that time, the government was styled "provisional." The new Confederate Constitution and government, like its predecessor, was a reflection of early American conservative constitutionalism. In his inaugural address Davis again stressed the proper role of government and the reasons for the formation of the Confederate States of America:

> The people of the States now confederated became convinced that the government of the United States had fallen into the hands of a sectional majority, who would pervert the most sacred of all trusts to the destruction of the rights which it was pledged to protect. They believed that to remain longer in the Union would subject them to a continuance of a disparaging discrimination, submission to which would be inconsistent with their welfare and intolerable to a proud people .... The

---

[124] C. Vann Woodward, ed., Mary Boykin Chesnut, *Mary Chesnut's Civil War* (New Haven, CT: Yale University Press, 1981), 167.

experiment, instituted by our revolutionary fathers, of a voluntary union of sovereign States, for purposes specified in a solemn compact, had been perverted by those who, *feeling power and forgetting right*, were determined to respect no law but their own will [emphasis added].[125]

In the closing remarks of his inaugural address, President Davis, with eyes and hands lifted up to heaven, stated, "With humble gratitude and adoration, acknowledging the Providence which has so visibly protected the Confederacy during its brief, but eventful career, to Thee, O God, I trustingly commit myself, and prayerfully invoke Thy blessing on my country and its cause."[126] Thus, Jefferson Davis embarked upon his career as president of a nation larger than any European nation other than Russia, with a gross domestic product that was the third largest in the civilized world, and a military force that would teach the Yankee Empire many lessons in military science and amaze the world.

In Richmond, as president of the Confederate States of America, Davis would witness the vacillations of the fortunes of his country and his family. Sadness was mixed with joy for the Davis family while living in Richmond. It was in Richmond that the Davises' son Joe was killed when he fell from the porch of the Confederate White House. Yet, many happy hours were spent there by the Davis family. During their stay in the White House, the Davises "adopted" Jim Limber, a young abused black child. In so doing, Jefferson Davis became the first American chief executive to have an integrated household. Jim Limber's story is a touching account of a young black boy who was rescued by Varina and given a home where he was loved and treated as a member of the Davis family.

Jim Limber's status as a free person of color was ensured by Jefferson Davis soon after Jim moved into the Confederate White House. Davis had papers registered in the mayor's office in Richmond

---

125 Jefferson Davis, as cited in Jones, 320.

126 Jefferson Davis, as cited in Varina Howell Davis, II, 182-83.

to validate Jim's status as a free person.[127] Little Jim would become a faithful friend and member of the Davis family for several years. The closeness between Jim and the other Davis children is seen in a letter from Maggie Davis to her brother Jeff in which she stated, "Jim Limber sends his love to you."[128] Unfortunately for Jim and the rest of the family, the war snuffed out their relationship. While trying to escape to Texas after the fall of Richmond, the Davis family was taken prisoner by Yankee Empire's military. The family was horrified by the remarks of several Yankee officers who stated they would take Jim away from the family. Of one such officer, a Captain Hudson, Varina Davis stated that he was "an extremely rude and offensive man, certainly no military gentleman, [who] threatened to take Jim Limber away from us ... and keep him as his own."[129] When Jim learned that he was to be taken away from his family, he engaged in a valiant but futile struggle, clinging to the Davis children, screaming and begging to be left with his "family." The tears of a little boy had no more effect in stopping the madness afoot than the pleas of men of good will, both North and South. Jim was taken away, never to be seen again by the Davis family. For a time, he was put on display in the North as one of "Jeff Davis's slaves." It was asserted that Jim would carry scars on his back all his life that "Jeff" Davis put on him. Yet, Varina Davis denied that Jim was ever beaten by the Davis's and affirmed that the "affection was mutual between us, and we had never punished him."[130] The truth is that the scars on little Jim's back had already been inflicted by the black man who had Jim when the Davis family rescued him.[131] While at the Confederate White House, Jim was always treated as one of the children by the Davis family. Although Davis always loved his family, the ever-present aspect of war kept him occupied.

---

127 *Ibid.*, II, 199.

128 Maggie Davis in a letter to Jeff Davis, Jr., cited in *Southern Partisan*, Second Quarter, 1989, 28.

129 *Ibid.*

130 Varina Howell Davis, II, 646.

131 Chesnut, 568.

When the situation presented itself, President Davis would always go to the field of battle to observe and offer advice to the commanding officers. Reverend J. William Jones wrote of an incident when President Davis and General Lee met on one such battlefield. Reverend Jones stated:

> Early in the day he [Davis] met General Lee near the front, and at once accosted him with "Why general, what are you doing here? You are in too dangerous position for the commander of the army." "I am trying," was the reply, "to find out something about the movements and plans of those people. But you must excuse me, Mr. President, for asking what you are doing here, and for suggesting that this is no proper place for the commander-in-chief of all our armies."
>
> "Oh, I am here on the same mission that you are," replied the President, and they were beginning to consult about the situation when gallant little A. P. Hill galloped up and exclaimed, "This is no place for either of you, and as commander of this part of the field, I order you both to the rear."
>
> "We will obey your orders," was the reply; and they fell back a short distance, but the fire grew hotter, and presently A. P. Hill galloped up to them again and exclaimed: "Did I not tell you to go away from here? And did you not promise to obey my orders? Why, one shell from that battery over yonder may presently deprive the Confederacy of its President and the Army of Northern Virginia of its commander." He finally persuaded the President and General Lee to move back.[132]

---

132 Jones, 438-39.

The following years for Davis centered around names that have been carved deeply into the tablets of history: Shiloh, Chancellorsville, Gettysburg, Vicksburg, Atlanta, Petersburg, and hundreds of other battles that led to the sad events at Appomattox.

Proceeding to St. Paul's Church on April 2, 1865, Davis noticed the clear spring Sunday morning. Regardless of the clear morning sky, a storm was about to break on Richmond and the Confederate States of America. Soon after being seated at church, the president was interrupted by a notification from General Lee's headquarters that Richmond had to be evacuated. After four long, hard years of struggle, the end was near. Nevertheless, Davis proved to be the very last leader of the Confederacy to give up all hope. When informed by the president that Richmond would be evacuated, a lady told Davis, "If the success of the cause requires you to give up Richmond, we are content."[133] Even in this dark hour of defeat, the South could still muster men and women who were defiant in the face of the invaders. As the Confederate government moved South by rail, Davis was cheered by crowds along the way. The cause appeared to be dying; nevertheless, as Davis would often repeat in later years: The cause would not die; only the field of battle would change.

FROM STATESMAN TO PRISONER OF STATE

The devastating news of General Lee's surrender and the determination of Gen. Joseph Johnston to surrender was the death knell for the Confederate cause. Even so, Jefferson Davis determined to make every effort to take the fight for Southern independence to the Trans-Mississippi. During this effort, the presidential party was discovered and captured by United States cavalry near Irwinsville, Georgia. By this time, news of Lincoln's assassination and the accusation of Davis's involvement in it were well known. Throughout the North, children were singing a little ditty, "We'll Hang Jeff Davis From a Sour Apple Tree." News of Davis's capture was embellished with a wild story that Davis was dressed in his wife's clothes. The likely source for this myth was from a report that, when captured, Davis was wearing a female outer garment. This fact was embellished

---

133 Hudson Strode, *Jefferson Davis, Tragic Hero* (Harcourt, Brace, and World, 1964), 168.

and circulated by overzealous Northern journalists. Both Varina and Jefferson Davis denied that he attempted to escape dressed in ladies' clothes. T. H. Peabody, a member of the United States troops who captured Davis, gave his account of Davis's capture as follows:

> Besides the suit of men's clothing worn by Mr. Davis, he had on, when captured, Mrs. Davis's large waterproof cloak or robe, thrown on over his head and shoulders. This shawl and robe were finally deposited in the archives of the War Department at Washington by order of Secretary Stanton. The story of the ' hoop skirt, sun bonnet and calico wrapper" had no real existence, and was started in the fertile brain of the reporters and in the illustrated papers of the day.[134]

America's great nineteenth-century showman, P. T. Barnum, even got into the act by staging skits of Davis being captured in a woman's attire.[135] What Barnum did not show his audiences was Yankee Empire troops stealing ladies' clothes and jewelry, and blue coated soldiers stealing food from the hands of the Davis children and kidnaping Jim Limber. In desperation, Davis protested to the commanding officer, "The worst of all is that I should be captured by a band of thieves and scoundrels."[136] But, as Davis and the entire South were to learn, words could not stop a people whose passion had been spoiled by years of vengeful anti-South propaganda. Davis, his family, and all those in his party were placed under arrest and delivered to United States military authorities. The sorrowful journey from capture to Fortress Monroe remained a bitter and vivid memory for Varina. Even as late as 1890, one year after her husband's death, Varina still found it difficult to describe the "horrors and sufferings" inflicted upon the president's family and companions. Before his incarceration in Fortress Monroe, Davis sent a note to his old friend and Union officer, General Saxton,

---

134 T. H. Peabody, as cited in Jones, 404.

135 Robert Penn Warren, "Jefferson Davis Gets His Citizenship Back," *The New Yorker Magazine*, May 31, 1982, 77.

136 *Ibid.*

with a request for him to look after Jim Limber and see to Jim's education. As has been noted, Jim did not wish to leave and "fought like a tiger" to stay with his family.[137]

As can be imagined, every member of the presidential party was depressed. Postmaster General John A. Reagan being overly depressed, Davis recommended that Reagan read the Sixteenth Psalm. This psalm was one that Davis often looked to during his life and starts with the words, "Preserve me, O God: for in thee do I put my trust."

The conduct of the troops who captured the presidential party was anything but respectful (remember how Chief Black Hawk praised Davis for the fair and humane treatment Davis accorded his defeated foes). The contemptuous actions of Yankee Empire troops were not limited to Davis or to the men of the presidential party but were also felt by the women and children. Denouncing the actions of the United States troops who were responsible for the capture and safety of President Davis, F. R. Lubbock, an aide and friend of the president, wrote,

> The conduct of the captors on that occasion was marked by anything but decency and soldierly bearing. They found no preparation for defense, and encountered no resistance at all. Mr. Davis, Judge Reagan, Colonel William Preston Johnston, Colonel John Taylor Wood, a young gentleman (a Mr. Barnwell of South Carolina), who escaped, and myself constituted the President's party. Colonel Harrison, the private secretary of the President, and a few paroled soldiers, were with Mrs. Davis and party, protecting their little baggage, and Co. Upon taking the camp, they [Yankee Empire troops] plundered and robbed every one of all and every article they could get hold of. They stole the watches, jewelry, money, clothing, and co.[138]

---

137 Strode, *Jefferson Davis, Tragic Hero*, 226.
138 F. R. Lubbock, as cited in Jones, 409.

All that Davis could now do was to await trial and a chance to clear his name and to vindicate the cause of the South. The hope for a public hearing and trial for himself and his cause was uppermost in Davis's mind during the dark days of imprisonment.[139] Even as the guns of the South were stacked in surrender, Davis was far removed from the defeated person that the Northern press ridiculed. For Davis, the struggle would continue, only on a different field of battle and at a different level. During the flight from Richmond, a companion of Davis mentioned to the president that all seemed to be lost for the Southern cause, whereupon, Davis remarked, *"It appears so. But the principle for which we contended is bound to reassert itself though it may be at another time and in another form."*[140]

---

139 Warren, 87.

140 Jefferson Davis, as cited in Edward A. Pollard, *A Southern History of the* War (1866, New York: The Fairfax Press, 1978), 582.

Chapter 8

JEFFERSON DAVIS: THE POLITICAL PRISONER

ON THE TENTH OF MAY 1865, near Irwinsville, Georgia, President Jefferson Davis, his family, and government officials traveling with him were captured and made prisoners of the Yankee Empire. The prisoners were subsequently taken to Savannah, Georgia, and made ready for a sea voyage. During this time, Davis was not only suffering the insulting indignities of his capture, but also the nagging pain of facial neuralgia. This condition, which Davis contracted as a young officer in the Northwest Territory, was a constant source of discomfort when he was under great stress. During the stress of his imprisonment, Davis would suffer from this painful condition as well as other health-related problems.

From the coast of Georgia, President Davis, his wife and children, and members of the Confederate government were taken aboard the U.S.S. Clyde, which steamed north. On May 19, the vessel was anchored in Hampton Roads at Fortress Monroe, Virginia. Inside the massive walls of the fort, two casemates were being fitted to receive Jefferson Davis and Clement Clay,[1] Davis's friend and political ally. The next day, all members of the Davis party were removed from the Clyde with the exception of Davis, Clay, and their families. Two days later, having received no word of what was to become of their families, and with only ten minutes notice, Davis and Clay

---

[1] Clement Clay, an Alabama senator and ardent advocate of secession, was thought by many in the North to be one of the chief leaders of the Confederacy.

were removed from the Clyde and taken to Fortress Monroe. Davis tried to console his wife at their parting, reminding her, "Try not to weep, they will gloat over your grief."[2] Davis's son, Jeff, could not control his emotions; as the Federal soldiers were ushering his father away, he vented his rage, "I'll kill every Yankee in the country when I grow up."[3] The emotional stress of being taken away from his family, not knowing what was to become of them, and suffering from physical illness, would have been enough to destroy the physical and psychological health of any normal man. Yet, although thin, frail, flushed with fever, and suffering from facial neuralgia, Davis would not give up his efforts to secure a fair hearing for his cause.

In a touching account of the incidents surrounding his departure from his family, Davis explains how the emotional torture was the most difficult of all his agonies to withstand:

> Not knowing that the [Yankee Empire's] Government was at war with women and children, I asked that my family might be permitted to leave the ship and go to Richmond or Washington City, or someplace where they had acquaintances; but this was refused. I then requested that they might be permitted to go abroad on one of the vessels lying at the [Hampton] Roads. This was also denied. Finally, I was informed that they must return to Savannah on the vessel by which they came. This was an old transport-ship, hardly seaworthy. My last attempt was to let them the privilege of stopping at Charleston, where they had many personal friends. This also was refused .... Bitter tears have been shed by the gentle, and stern reproaches have been made by the magnanimous, on account of the heavy fetters riveted upon me while in a stone casemate and surrounded by a strong guard;

---

[2] Jefferson Davis, as cited in Burke Davis, *The Long Surrender* (New York: Random House, 1985), 175.

[3] *Ibid.*, 176.

but these were less excruciating than the agony my captors were able to inflict. It was long before I was permitted to hear from my wife and children, and this, and things like this, was the power which education added to savage cruelty.[4]

President Davis was handed over to the not-so-tender care of Gen. Nelson A. Miles. Miles had received orders from Maj. Gen. Henry W. Halleck to ensure the captivity of Davis and Clay. Their imprisonment was accomplished by order of the secretary of war, and Miles was commanded, "No writs or orders of any civil courts will be recognized or obeyed."[5] The spectacle of civilian prisoners being held on orders of the military and said military not being amenable to civil authority is a haunting legacy for all Americans who love liberty.

As Davis stepped from the boat to shore, his arm was seized by Miles while Col. Benjamin D. Pritchard seized Clay's arm. Surrounded by Yankee Empire soldiers, the two prisoners were escorted into the fort. Constructed with masonry walls more than thirty feet high and fifty feet thick in the area of Davis's confinement, Fortress Monroe was surrounded by a moat 125 feet wide. In casemate number two, Davis's "cell," an outer room was prepared for his guards consisting of one officer and two soldiers. The officer was ordered to look in on Davis every fifteen minutes. Off-duty guards were quartered in the casemates on each side of Davis's cell. On the opposite bank of the moat from Davis's cell were posted more guards. Approximately seventy soldiers were posted to guard Davis. To add to the misery' of the prisoner, two guards were posted on either side of his cot and ordered to pace back and forth. No guard, including those pacing to and fro next to his cot, was allowed to speak to Davis or acknowledge anything said by him. A lamp was set at the head of Davis's cot and was to be kept burning all night. Davis was not even allowed the common decency of privacy to attend to personal hygiene or to use

---

4   Jefferson Davis, as cited in Varina Howell Davis, *Jefferson Davis, A Memoir by His Wife* (New York: Belford Company, Publishers, 1890), II, 651-52.

5   *Official Records: War of the Rebellion*, Series II, Vol. 8, 578.

a small portable toilet without the glaring eyes of guards upon him.[6] The North was elated at this final indignity thrust upon its fallen foe. The New York Herald trumpeted, "He [Davis] is literally in a living tomb .... No more will Davis be known among the masses of men .... He is buried alive .... Davis can never escape."

What the enemies of Davis did not understand at that time was that escape was not what Davis wanted. Above all else, Jefferson Davis desired a trial in open court. This was his one last hope for the vindication of the cause of Southern independence. If given the promise of a trial, Davis could have been made secure with just one guard, and that one could have been blind!

Insulated from the world by thick stone walls, iron doors, and window grates, with no one to speak to, forbidden to have any news from his family, not allowed a newspaper, Davis suffered in damp silence in casemate number two. The only article allowed the prisoner was his Bible. Such mundane requests, by the prisoner, as being allowed a prayer book and tobacco, had to be cleared with the authorities in Washington.[7] Yet, General Miles was not content to allow Davis the freedom to move about in his small cell unimpeded. One last insult was left at Miles's command: shackles![8] In solitary' confinement with his Bible in hand, Davis was astonished, when on the morning of May' 23, into his cell walked Capt. Jerome E. Titlow of the Third Pennsylvania Artillery followed by a blacksmith and his assistant, carrying some heavy' shackles. Dr. John J. Craven, Davis's personal physician while Davis was incarcerated, wrote a somewhat melodramatic account of Davis's life in prison. Many historians believe that Dr. Craven was greatly assisted in writing his account of

---

6   Burke Davis, 177.

7   *Ibid.*, 570.

8   Miles attempted to defend his shackling of Davis by stating it was only done while stronger doors could be placed upon Davis's cell. Yet, it is hard to believe that Davis, sick and emaciated, guarded by at least seventy guards, and locked within the virtual tomb of Fortress Monroe, offered any danger of escape. For Miles's response, see *Official Records: War of the Rebellion*, Series II, Vol. 8, 577.

Davis's prison life by a General Halpine.⁹ Although Craven's account has been shown to be more dramatic than one would expect from the rather reserved nature of Jefferson Davis, Craven's account did not do an injustice to what Davis called "the inexcusable privations and tortures which Dr. Craven has but faintly described."¹⁰ Craven gives the following account of Davis's being shackled:

> [Davis] said slowly and with a laboring chest: "My God! You cannot have been sent to iron me?" "Such are my orders, Sir," replied the officer .... These fetters were of heavy iron, probably five-eights of an inch in thickness, and connected together by a chain of like weight. "This is too monstrous," groaned the prisoner, glaring hurriedly round the room .... Can he [General Miles] pretend that such shackles are required to secure the safe custody of a weak old man, so guarded and in such a fort as this?" "It [an appeal to General Miles] could serve no purpose," replied Captain Titlow; "his orders are from Washington."¹¹

General Miles's orders did not command him to shackle Davis; they only gave him permission to do so if he felt it necessary. It is hard to imagine a prisoner, incarcerated as Davis was, needing to be shackled, but Miles, being caught up in the spiteful spirit of the day, gave the order to shackle Davis. As the blacksmith moved toward him, Davis cried out "I tell you the world will ring with this disgrace. The war is over; the South is conquered; I have no longer any country but America, and it is for the honor of America, as for my own honor and life, that I plead against this degradation. Kill me! Kill me! rather than inflict on me, and on my People through

---

9   Felicity Allen, "Martyrdom or Myth-making? Prison Life of Jefferson Davis in a New Light," *Journal of Confederate History*, 1991, No. 6, 5.

10   *Ibid.*, 51.

11   John J. Craven, *The Prison Life of Jefferson Davis* (1866, Biloxi, MS: Beauvoir, The Jefferson Davis Shrine, 1979), 35.

me, this insult worse than death."[12] As the blacksmith attempted to place the shackles on the prisoner, Davis grabbed the man and threw him across the room. More soldiers were ordered into the cell to subdue the weak and emaciated prisoner. Captain Titlow pleaded with Davis not to resist. Davis responded, "[W]hile I have life and strength to resist, for myself and for my people, this thing shall not be done."[13] After a short struggle, Davis was thrown onto his cot, and the blacksmith secured the irons with rivets and a padlock. Dr. Craven describes the ensuing scene:

> Mr. Davis lay for a moment as if in stupor. Then slowly raising himself and turning round, he dropped his shackled feet to the floor. The harsh clank of the striking chains seems first to have recalled him to his situation, and dropping his face into his hands, he burst into a passionate flood of sobbing, rocking to and fro, and muttering at brief intervals: "Oh, the shame, the shame!"[14]

At last, Davis and the entire South were to experience the humiliation spoken of by Chief Black Hawk, years before, when he too was shackled and humiliated by the power of the federal government. Davis's prediction that this act would dishonor the name of America was correct. Both at home and abroad, word of Davis's shackling enraged decent people. Five days later, the irons were ordered removed. Shackled or not, Davis was to live in solitary confinement with no one to talk to. When he asked to be allowed to attend religious services at the fort, permission was denied. How ironic that Jefferson Davis, America's political prisoner, was not allowed to attend religious services; yet, this same Jefferson Davis,

---

12 Craven, 36-37. According to Edward K. Eckert in *Fiction Distorting Fact: The Prison Life, Annotated by Jefferson Davis,* Davis noted that he never made the outcry of "Kill me, kill me" or made any resistance below his station in life. According to Varina and Jefferson Davis his resistance was made in a manly manner and not as "childish ravings." See Allen, 1-52.

13 *Ibid.*, 38.

14 *Ibid.*, 39.

as America's secretary of war, had done much to advance the work of chaplains and religious organizations in the military. Davis's Christian devotion was noticed and noted by his physician, Dr. Craven:

> There were moments, while speaking on religious subjects, in which Mr. Davis impressed me more than any professor of Christianity I had ever heard. There was a vital earnestness in his discourse; a clear, almost passionate grasp in his faith; and the thought would frequently recur, that a belief capable of consoling such sorrows as his, possessed and thereby evidenced, a reality—a substance—which no sophistry of the infidel could discredit.[15]

General Miles may have been forced by public opinion to pursue a somewhat more tolerant policy toward Davis, but his treatment of the families of Davis and Clay never changed. In his reports to his superiors in Washington, he routinely referred to the ladies as "the females." While the Clyde was still at anchor at Fortress Monroe, Varina Davis's sister became ill with a fever. A request was made to General Miles to allow a physician to come aboard to treat the ailing lady; Miles refused the request. When asked by Varina where they would be sent, Miles refused to disclose that information. While in the harbor, small boats and tugs full of mockers issuing forth insults to the ladies and the children were allowed to maneuver around the Clyde. When at last the Clyde left port, she did so under sealed orders which could not be opened until the vessel was well out to sea. Once in Savannah, the Davis family was not given their freedom, but rather placed under what could be called "house arrest." Thus, the families of Jefferson Davis and Clement Clay were treated with no more regard for their liberty than the most profane of prisoners. This treatment brings up an interesting constitutional question. Even if Jefferson Davis and Clement Clay were traitors, the Constitution prohibits the "corruption of blood."[16] In a cryptic

---

15 *Ibid.*, 194.
16 United States Constitution, Article III, Sect. 3, Par. 2.

order from General Halleck, Colonel Pritchard was instructed that "[t]he women, children, and servants are not regarded as prisoners, but will remain on board [the Clyde] till further orders."[17] What are people called who are not free to come and go as they please? These women and children were political prisoners at the mercy and control of the Yankee Empire. According to the United States Constitution, the family of a traitor cannot be punished for the actions of the traitor. James Madison, in The Federalist No. 43, notes this limitation for punishment of treason: "... restraining the Congress, even in punishing it, from extending the consequences of guilt beyond the person of its author."[18] The families of Davis and Clay were held against their will for weeks and never charged with any crime. Once again, the actions of these Federal agents prove that they never regarded the Constitution as being binding upon the Northern majority; this was the very reason the South felt compelled to secede upon the election of Lincoln.

It was Davis's good fortune that General Miles assigned Dr. John Craven as Davis's physician. Dr. Craven, a Union soldier, a Republican, and an Abolitionist, with much consolation and kindness to a fallen foe restored not only Davis's health but assisted in restoring his freedom. Until the arrival of Dr. Craven, the world knew little of the daily living conditions of Davis. When Dr. Craven instructed Davis to spend as little time in bed as possible and to walk for exercise, Davis answered him by showing him his shackled ankles. Davis explained to Dr. Craven,

> It is impossible for me, Doctor; I cannot even stand erect. These shackles are very heavy .... If I try to move, they trip me, and have already abraded broad patches of skin from the parts they touch. Can you devise no means to pad or cushion them, so that

---

17 *Official Records: War of the Rebellion*, Series II, Vol. 8, 566.

18 James Madison, as cited in Carey & McClellan, eds., *The Federalist* (Dubuque, IA: Kendall-Hunt Publishing Company, 1990), 223.

when I try to drag them along they may not chafe me so intolerably? My limbs have so little flesh on them, and that so weak, as to be easily lacerated.[19]

From the moment of his first interview with Davis, Dr. Craven's sympathy for the prisoner was kindled. Dr. Craven, the only man allowed to speak with Davis, other than the commanding officers, spent as much time with Davis as possible and secretly recorded their conversations. In 1866, Dr. Craven would write an account of Davis's prison ordeal titled *The Prison Life of Jefferson Davis*. This account would do much to mold Southern opinion about their fallen leader, Jefferson Davis, and his plight. In the South, the treatment of Davis would make him the idol of millions of Southerners who also were also enduring the Yankee Empire's "loving embrace." The Yankee Empire's "embrace" is also known as Reconstruction. Writing from Gainesville, Alabama, in November 1867, Mrs. Hessie McMahon, upon reading Dr. Craven's book, expressed her feelings about Jefferson Davis and Yankees:

> Have you ever read the Prison Life of Jeff Davis? If you don't want to hate Yankees more than ever, I would advise you not to read it. How I do pity our loved President. I try not to dislike the Yankees. Just think of the wretchedness of putting Davis in irons. They have tried to disgrace him in every way they can. I can't bear to think about the war or anything connected with it because I generally get angry.[20]

Any faults of judgment displayed by Davis during his four years as president of the Confederacy would, after his imprisonment, be gracefully overlooked. Jefferson Davis, prisoner of state, was becoming the co-sufferer of the Southern people. What a supreme irony; the infamous efforts of Northern Radicals to destroy Jefferson Davis made him the idol and beloved leader of his people forever.

---

19 Jefferson Davis as cited in Craven, 50.

20 Hessie McMahon, as cited in Betty Lawrence, *Unrevised History of the War for Southern Independence* (Meridian, MS: Larksdale Publishers, 1995), 3.

On the day that Davis was taken to Fortress Monroe, Varina and the ladies were stripped to their undergarments and searched by two female "detectives." Varina's waterproof raglan that she had thrown around her husband's shoulders on the morning of his capture was taken by Colonel Pritchard. A few hours later another raid was made upon the women and children. During this final raid, the soldiers took most of the ladies' and children's clothes. Finally, the Clyde sailed for Savannah, Georgia, where the women and children were put ashore, attended by their faithful servant and former slave, Robert Brown. There, Varina was instructed that the government would allow her to pay for her room at a hotel but that she would be watched by detectives and not allowed to go beyond the city limits. Such was the treatment accorded the wife and children of the president of the invaded, defeated, and occupied Sovereign nation.

Varina's efforts in behalf of her husband were never ceasing. When her letters to Davis were not delivered, she had her children write him in the hopes that they would elicit the sympathy of his captors. Little Maggie wrote her father, "My Darling Father, the Lord is Your Shepherd, you shall not want." Maggie, showing this letter to her mother, asked, "This letter will not make the Yankees mad, will it? They won't object to the Bible, will they?"[21] But General Miles refused to allow any communication between Davis and the outside world; little Maggie's letter was never delivered.

At the insistence of Robert Brown, her faithful servant, Varina determined to send her children to Canada. In July, Robert Brown, a black nursemaid, the children, and Varina's sister-in-law, Mrs. Howell, were sent by ship to Canada. During this passage, an insolent Yankee made insulting remarks to young Jeff about his father. Robert Brown interposed himself between the two and asked the Yankee if he thought a Negro to be his equal. The Yankee said he did, whereupon Robert replied, "Then take this from your equal," and with a powerful black fist decked the insolent Yankee. With her children in another country and out of harm's way, Varina could turn her full attention to improving her husband's condition. Davis

---

21   Maggie Davis, as cited in Hudson Strode, *Jefferson Davis, Tragic Hero* (New York: Harcourt, Brace, and World, 1964), 257.

made several attempts, from May to August, to write to his wife. Yet, Yankee hatred ruled the day (then as now). They would not allow Davis the privilege of responding to his wife's letters.

With the passage of time, more sober minds in the North began to realize the weakness of the charges being brought against Davis. From both the South and North, fair-minded men offered their services to Davis. In May 1865, one of America's most renowned attorneys, New Yorker Charles O'Conor, offered to defend Davis without charge. By August, O'Conor doubted the government would ever allow Davis to stand trial, predicting, "No trial for treason or any like offense will be had in the civil courts." There were still those in the North who desired to put Davis on trial for treason, an event Davis desired more than his enemies. In preparation for its case against Davis, the War Department presented its evidence to the eminent jurist, Francis Lieber, who, upon reviewing the "evidence," declared, "Davis will not be found guilty and we shall stand there completely beaten."[22] Slowly, the realization dawned that a fair trial of Davis might produce a not-guilty verdict and thereby undo in a courtroom what the Yankee Empire had so cruelly achieved by four years of aggressive, democidal warfare. [Rudolph Rummel used "Democide" as a term to describe "the intentional killing of an unarmed or disarmed person by government agents acting in their authoritative capacity and pursuant to government policy or high command." See Kennedy & Kennedy, *Yankee Empire: Aggressive Abroad and Oppressive at Home*, 125-28]. The Radicals held to one last hope for a conviction. They would play the race card! The grand jury impaneled to indict Davis was composed of an equal number of black and white members, the first time in American history a mixed-race jury had been impaneled.[23] By hook or crook, the Radicals were determined to see Jefferson Davis dangling from the end of their lynch rope.

To make matters worse for the Radicals, many leading men of the North and around the world were beginning to express sympathy for the deposed and incarcerated president. From Milan, Italy, an

---

22 Francis Lieber, as cited in *Ibid.*, 279.
23 "Jury Impaneled to Try Jefferson Davis," *Confederate Veteran*, Vol. XVII, No. 1, 40.

appeal was made to spare Davis's life; Varina Davis had an audience with President Andrew Johnson; Pope Pius IX sent Davis a signed photograph and a Crown of Thorns;[24] and, of course, Dr. Craven's book touched the cords of sympathy in the hearts of many people. Davis was becoming a hero to many even as he suffered in prison at the hands of his cruel and insulting captors.

As sympathy for the incarcerated ex-president mounted, several prominent Northerners, such as Cornelius Vanderbilt, Gerrit Smith, and Horace Greeley, offered to put up whatever money was needed to secure Davis's bail. In Pennsylvania, Davis's niece, Mrs. Brodhead, made contact with the governor of Pennsylvania and Abraham Lincoln's secretary of war, Simon Cameron, in an effort to secure a hearing to set bail for Davis. Varina, as always, was immersed in numerous efforts to secure her husband's release. In Maryland, Varina spoke to the governor, who assisted in her meeting with the prominent John W. Garrett, president of the Baltimore and Ohio Railroad. Secretary of War Edwin M. Stanton was the one man in Washington who stood in the way of Davis's release, and the only man in the country who could move Stanton was his friend John W. Garrett. Through Garrett, a long-time associate of Stanton's and one of his few friends, the secretary of war was persuaded to allow bail for Davis. To secure Garrett's assistance, Varina, dressed in mourner's clothes, made a personal visit to John Garrett. Garrett was so moved by Varina's account of her husband's ordeal that he determined, against the objections of many, to go to his friend and push the case for Davis's release on bond. Acting in concert with many other people North, South, and around the world, Varina obtained her husband's release. Without a doubt, the iron will of Varina was the driving force in the release of Jefferson Davis.

A few weeks before his release on bail, Davis received a visit from his old friend, former United States president Franklin Pierce. Pierce told Davis that he felt the government would never allow

---

24 The photograph and Crown of Thorns, symbolic of the suffering of the innocent, sent to Davis by Pope Pius IX, can be viewed at Confederate Memorial Hall, New Orleans, Louisiana. [There exist questions regarding the origins of the "Crown of Thorns.]

Davis to be tried for treason because it was doubtful a conviction could be obtained. Pierce believed that the spectacle of having a court declare secession a right and not an act of treason would undo all the efforts of the Radicals in Washington; therefore, Davis would never be tried.[25]

The climactic day of liberation of the "caged eagle" was fast approaching. Early in May of 1867, Davis's attorney in New York, Charles O'Conor, informed Burton N. Harrison, Davis's secretary, that a writ of habeas corpus had been secured for Davis. Harrison would need to take the writ to Richmond for the signature of the clerk of court and have it presented to the commander at Fortress Monroe. Harrison obtained the needed signature and, on May 10, the second anniversary of Davis's capture, in the company of a federal marshal, delivered the writ to Gen. Josiah Burton, who had relieved the infamous General Miles as commander of the fort. General Burton displayed all the qualities of an officer and a gentleman, so sorely lacking in General Miles. A warm and lasting friendship between President Davis's family and General Burton's family was established during Burton's tenure as Davis's "prison warden."

It should be noted that it took two years before Jefferson Davis could obtain a court hearing to have charges presented and determine his bail. One reason for this laxity on the part of the court system, as had been noted, is that no such order would be honored by the military. Almost two years before this writ was issued, the military, acting on behalf of the Yankee Empire's government, ordered the commander of Fortress Monroe that "[n]o writs or orders of any civil courts will be recognized or obeyed."[26] What more evidence is needed to prove that the Union "preserved" by Lincoln and the Radicals bore little relationship to the Union established by Jefferson, Adams, Madison, and company! What a chilling effect this order by the military has had upon the idea of true American liberty. The order was never challenged by any civil authority; it was allowed to stand at the discretion of those in control of the Yankee Empire. Although

---

25 Strode, *Jefferson Davis, Tragic Hero*, 306.

26 General H. W. Halleck, as cited in *Official Records: War of the Rebellion*, Series II, Vol. 8, 578.

the infamous order is blatantly unconstitutional, nowhere is there to be found any officer being charged with high crimes against the very Constitution he is sworn to uphold for enforcing this illegal order. The great fear of Jefferson Davis and the South, that a numerical majority, in control of the central government, would not be limited by the words of the Constitution but rather would act only according to the will of "King Numbers," in total disregard for the rights of the minority, is herein displayed. Subsequent history has demonstrated that the South was right to fear an oppressive federal government!

Burton N. Harrison, Davis's personal secretary, later described his feelings as the Davis party ascended the James River for Richmond on the fateful morning of May 13:

> There were very few passengers on the boat, but it had become generally known that the chief was on board, and at every landing was assembled an enthusiastic little group to greet the President. It did my heart good to see the fervent zeal of the good people .... They came aboard, and such kissing and embracing and tears ... employed to manifest their devotion to the leader who was beaten have never been seen out of dear old Virginia.[27]

General Henry S. Burton, obeying the literal command of the writ, on Saturday escorted Davis to Richmond. As Burton N. Harrison noted, Davis was not under guard during this trip, and General Burton and Davis were at their best. On viewing the party going up the James River that day, Harrison said that no one would have "supposed that the quiet gentleman who received his visitors ... was the State prisoner around whose dungeon so many battalions had been marshaled for two years and whose trial for treason against a mighty government was the exciting period of mankind."[28] It seemed as if all of Richmond had turned out to welcome Davis.

---

27 Burton Harrison, as cited in W. O. Hart, "When Jefferson Davis Was Freed," *Confederate Veteran*, June 1923, Vol. XXXI, No. 6, 208.

28 Hart.

Crowds cheered, men stood with hats off, women wept and waved handkerchiefs, flowers were presented, and every effort to assist the deposed president was made by "his people." By chance, Davis was lodged in the very same suite in the Spottswood Hotel that he and Varina occupied when they first came to Richmond in 1861.

After a full afternoon of receiving friends, Davis and his family retired for the night. The next morning, Sunday, the family made a trip to the cemetery where their son Joseph, who had died in a fall at the Confederate White House in 1864, was buried.

Monday morning, as the hour appointed for the arraignment of Davis approached, the counsels for the defense and government filed into the courtroom. Davis's counsels consisted of Charles O'Conor, New York, America's most prominent lawyer at that time; William B. Read, Philadelphia; George Shea, New York; John Randolph Tucker, Richmond, noted constitutional lawyer and former attorney general of Virginia; Robert Quid, Richmond, a distinguished debater of his day; and, James Lyons, prominent lawyer of Virginia. The Yankee Empire was represented by U.S. Attorney General, William M. Evarts, and the District Attorney, W. E. Chandler. Chief Justice Salmon P. Chase was the presiding judge in the court but the heavy-handed Radical judge John C. Underwood conducted the case. First among many Federals judges that the South would learn to hate, Underwood was described as "the notorious John C. Underwood, the *bete noire* of Richmond, a man whom the people had come to regard with unlimited fear and dislike."[29] It was generally feared that the notorious Underwood would avail himself of this opportunity to condemn, castigate, and otherwise punish the South through the agency of its deposed president—Jefferson Davis.

The trial had attracted the attention of some of the most prominent men in America, such as Horace Greeley and Cornelius Vanderbilt. Davis was escorted into the courtroom by General Burton and a federal marshal. As Davis walked in, every eye was upon him, and every man stood in respectful silence. General Burton treated Davis more like a friend than like his prisoner, for the respect between the

---

29 *Ibid.*

two had grown to that quality. George Davis, late attorney general of the Confederacy, noted that if a stranger had witnessed the scene he would have sworn that Davis was the honored judge and Underwood the hideous accused.

Judge Underwood opened the proceeding with several caustic remarks about the nature of the crime the prisoner was accused of committing. He then noted that Davis was no longer under martial law but at the tender mercies of what Judge Underwood called "American Republican Law." [Note: "Republican" as in Republican Party] Considering the fate of the innocents such as Henry Wirz, Mary Surratt, Dr. Samuel Mudd, and the entire South at the hands of "American Republican Law," few in the courtroom were put at ease. Davis's attorney stood and stated the defense was ready and desired immediate trial. The Yankee Empire's attorney general stated that the case could not be tried at the present time, whereupon Judge Underwood declared the case to be bailable. Bail was requested by the defense, and, after Judge Underwood praised the government for its "accommodating" spirit in dealing with the case, bail was set at $100,000. Several prominent Northern men, led by Radical Abolitionist Horace Greeley, signed the bond for Davis's release. At that time, it was announced that Davis was free on bond.

President Jefferson Davis remained incarcerated as the Yankee Empire's political prisoner for two years before his release could be arranged. A strange greeting met the deposed president when he departed the courtroom as a free man. The streets were crowded with people, yet no cheers, no songs, and no weeping were to be heard! For the first time since 1865, from one end of the city to the other, a sound that only Southern men could replicate, the Rebel Yell, was at last heard again.[30] As the carriage in which Davis and his pastor Dr. Charles Minnigerode passed through the crowded streets, people pressed all around extending their good wishes to Davis. Minnigerode noted, "Our carriage passed with difficulty through the crowd of rejoicing Negroes ... shaking and kissing his hand, and

---

30 *Ibid.*

calling out 'God bless Mars [Master] Davis.'"[31] Upon arrival at the hotel, Davis and Minnigerode were met by Varina, George Davis, the former Confederate attorney general, and his family. Jefferson Davis looked to Dr. Minnigerode and asked him if they should not offer prayers of thanksgiving. As they knelt and offered up their prayers, soon it became obvious that all those kneeling in prayer were crying, shedding tears of gratitude and relief. As Dr. Minnigerode stated, "[T]here, in deep-felt prayer and thanksgiving, closed the story of Jefferson Davis's prison life."[32]

The prison life was indeed over, but Davis was far from being a free man. He had been transferred from military to civilian authorities, but he was out on bail, not a free man. He was awaiting his trial for treason and a chance for the vindication of the Southern cause. Davis was always prepared and always eager for the opportunity to take his case to court, but his wait was in vain. As each new trial date approached, the Empire's government determined that it was not yet ready to try the case and would postpone the trial to a more "convenient season." In December 1868, President Andrew Johnson issued a general amnesty that was considered to include Davis. Shortly thereafter, an order was entered in the circuit court of Richmond dismissing all charges of treason against those so indicted by the court. Among those so named were Jefferson Davis and Robert E. Lee.[33] The Yankee Empire had managed to dodge the last bullet an old Confederate had in his gun; Jefferson Davis would die never having a chance to clear his name and the good name of the Southern people in an open court.

Reverend J. Williams Jones summarized the events around the release of Jefferson Davis and the dismissal of charges against him:

> Throughout the Confederacy there was general rejoicing when it was announced that "the caged eagle" was once more free; but this rejoicing was mingled with

---

31 Reverend Dr. Minnigerode, as cited in J. Williams Jones, *A Memorial Volume of Jefferson Davis* (1889, Harrisonburg, VA: Sprinkle Publications, 1993), 422.

32 Jones, 424.

33 Hart, 209.

deep regret that he had not been allowed his coveted opportunity to vindicate the Confederate cause in the courts of the country and in the hearing of the world.[34]

To this day, it is not uncommon to hear the charge of traitor applied to Jefferson Davis and the stigma of treason invoked to discredit him and the descendants of the once free Southern nation. Such slanderous Yankee and Scallywag claims are used to justify the destruction of monuments raised by Southerners to honor their blood relatives who wore the gray in the War for Southern Independence.

It must never be forgotten that it was the Yankee Empire, not Jefferson Davis, who was afraid to give their false charge of treason against President Davis and the South a fair hearing in an open court! Tyranny always censors the truth! Tyrants will never allow the oppressed people a fair hearing in the court of public opinion. Tyrants hate monuments to heroes of the conquered nation. Tyrants pull down monuments hoping the conquered people will forget their past and accept their assigned position on the "stools of everlasting repentance."[35]

---

34 Jones, 426

35 Frank Lawrence Owsley, The Irrepressible Conflict, I'll Take My Stand: The South and the Agrarian Tradition, (1930, LSU Press, Baton Rouge, LA: 1983), 63.

Chapter 9

JEFFERSON DAVIS: THE LAST YEARS

ALTHOUGH RELEASED FROM THE TORMENTS of the Yankee Empire's dungeon in 1867, Jefferson Davis was not a free man. He was still under indictment for treason, had no income to support his family, and had no home of his own. Burton N. Harrison, his private secretary, described Davis's physical condition after release as "very thin and haggard and [he] has very little muscular strength."[1] Two years in the Yankee Empire's Gulag had destroyed Davis's health, but not his spirit of defiance against tyranny.

Demanding his day in court to the end, Davis, by the time of his release on bond, was a sick and weak man. Having lost not only his health but also his political status and his economic independence, he was faced with a bleak future. At the age of sixty, Jefferson Davis, not unlike most Southerners during those traumatic, so-called Reconstruction years, had to start anew building his fortune. Though much had been taken away from him, he still had many loyal friends in the South as well as a few in the North. As soon as his release on bail was announced, Davis received two letters, one from his old friend and fellow Confederate, Robert E. Lee, and one from his good friend, former president Franklin Pierce. Lee wrote Davis, "Your release has lifted a load from my heart which I have not words to tell and my daily prayer to the great Ruler of the World is that he may

---

1   Burton Harrison, as cited in Hudson Strode, *Jefferson Davis, Tragic Hero* (New York: Harcourt, Brace, and World, 1964), 312.

Davis at Beauvoir, Jerry McWilliams artist.

shield you from all future harm, guard you from all evil and give you that peace which the world cannot take away."[2] Former United States president Franklin Pierce wrote Davis offering him the use of one of Pierce's homes in New Hampshire. Pierce wrote Davis, "I need not express how much pleasure I should find in trying to make everything agreeable to you."[3] Pierce had stood by Davis even through the four bloody years of war, thereby incurring the wrath of many anti-Southern bigots in New England. Davis, not wishing to place his friend in more jeopardy, graciously declined.

With his children and many fellow Confederates in Canada, Davis determined to go to Montreal. With the kind assistance of his able attorney, Charles O'Conor of New York, Davis, Varina, and two servants and former slaves, Fredrick Maginnis and his wife Ellen, began the trip from New York to Canada. Davis, fearing for the

---

2   Robert E. Lee, as cited in *Ibid.*, 314.

3   Franklin Pierce, as cited in *Ibid.*

safety of his wife and servants, traveled through New York alone and *incognito*. Nevertheless, many people discovered that Davis was on the North-bound train and gathered along the way to jeer and hoot at the deposed president. Jefferson Davis and the South took notice of the fact that two years of peace had not been enough time to quiet the spirit of Northern hostility against the South.

Responding to an outpouring of support from old friends and local citizens of Canada, Davis's weak and downtrodden spirit began to revive. On a trip from Montreal to Toronto, he was pleasantly surprised by a reception of over one thousand people who cheered him as he stepped from his ship onto the wharf. Many Confederates, availing themselves of Canadian protection from vengeful Yankees, met Davis in Canada. News of the former president of the Confederacy's visit in any Canadian city would bring forth large crowds wherever he went. It was not uncommon for a town's band to serenade the Davis family at night, and all means available to the local citizens were taken to honor their respected guest. Finding the Davis family enduring very modest accommodations in Montreal, John A. Lowell, a prominent member of Canadian society, insisted that the family move into his home while he made arrangements for a more suitable dwelling for them. This gesture by Lowell placed Davis and Varina in the center of Canada's elite society. Although Jefferson's poor health prevented him from much social interaction, Varina, always the "Belle of the Ball," was kept busy entertaining the Lowells' numerous guests.

It was in Montreal, at Varina's insistence, that Davis began writing his account of the war. As he began writing, the pain of his country's defeat and occupation became more than the weary man could tolerate. Unable to cope with the fresh memory of defeat, Davis placed reminders of the tragic lost out of sight saying, "I cannot speak of my dead so soon."[4] It would take ten years before Varina could direct her husband's attention back to the writing his history of the war. At long last in 1881, with Varina's assistance, Jefferson Davis's *The Rise and Fall of the Confederate Government* was published.

---

4   Jefferson Davis, as cited in Varina Howell Davis, *Jefferson Davis, A Memoir by His Wife* (New York: Belford Company, Publishers, 1890), II, 799.

Having been cordially received by many Canadians, Davis, nonetheless, remained somewhat of a recluse while in Montreal. His physical disabilities and his awareness that his every move was being watched and reported back to his enemies were reason enough for him to maintain a low profile. With encouragement from friends, he was persuaded to attend a play conducted to raise money for the Southern Relief Association in Montreal. An account of the event by a local newspaper related how Davis was received by the packed house on the night of the play. As he entered the theater, every eye was upon him; from every section, the crowd rose and cheered the deposed president. One Canadian, caught up in the mood of the moment, cheered and cried out, "We shall live to see the South a nation yet!"[5] Cries for the band to play "Dixie" was followed by wild cheering from the crowd. Davis, sick and weak, gratefully acknowledged the adulation displayed by the cheering throng. The affection for Jefferson Davis and the Southern cause was displayed not only by various leading citizens of Canada but also by the Canadian playmates of Southerner children. Often one could hear young Canadians and young Southerners singing the following song in praise of Jefferson Davis and the Confederacy:

> O! The muskets they may rattle,
>
> And the cannon they may roar,
>
> But we'll fight for you Jeff Davis,
>
> Along the Southern shore,
>
> There goes the Washington Artillery,*
>
> Give 'em a charge of grape!
>
> You should have seen the Yankee
>
> Tryin' to escape.[6]
>
> *[The famous artillery unit from New Orleans. Louisiana]

---

5   Strode, *Jefferson Davis, Tragic Hero*, 319.

6   *Confederate Veteran*, March 1925, Vol. VXXXVII, No. 3, 92.

The Yankee Empire took notice of the display of respect and affection shown Jefferson Davis by his Canadian hosts. Many Northern newspapers wrote scathing editorials condemning the reception shown the "arch-American traitor," Jefferson Davis, by the people of Canada. The imperial proclivity of the new Yankee Empire asserted itself in several editorials suggesting that Canadians could not be expected to "recover their equanimity until they are formally annexed to us."[7] After defeating its Southern neighbors, many Yankee imperialists desired to add even more territory and people under their "benevolent" control. Fortunately for the Canadians, they remained free of direct Yankee domination.

A short visit to the South and several trips to Europe were all attended by much cheering and praise for the leader of the "Lost Cause." While in England, the Davises were guests of Lord and Lady Leigh, of Stoneleigh Abbey. Visiting Parliament in London, Davis was received with much interest and civility. In France, he was offered an audience with the French emperor and empress. At every opportunity, Northern editorials would ridicule those daring to offer courtesy to a man the Yankee Empire wished to portray as a traitor.

The Davis family moved from London to Memphis, after Davis was offered the presidency of an insurance company in Memphis, Tennessee. After the sojourn in Europe, Memphis must have seemed a small town for the Davises. Nevertheless, it soon became home to the Davis family. The love with which Davis was received by the citizens of Memphis was soon reciprocated. Varina's affection for Memphis is illustrated in her comment, "[W]e learned to love the people; and they loved us, and the memory of their cordiality, their sincerity, and ready sympathy will 'hang round my heart forever.'"[8] The love and respect for Jefferson Davis shown by the citizens of Memphis were clearly manifested by the offer of a home as a gift from the people to the Davis family. Declining the offer, Davis remarked that he was still a man "preferring to support himself."[9] Upon assuming the position of president of the Memphis insurance

---

7   *Ibid.*, 92, 320.

8   Varina Howell Davis, II, 812.

9   Jefferson Davis as cited in *Ibid.*

company, he discovered the company to be actuarially unsound. In an effort to save the policyholders from loss, Davis, from his meager estate, invested his own money in the company, all to no avail.

During the following years, Davis struggled to maintain support for his family and himself. Throughout the South, respectful memorials were tendered to him. Several times he was offered homes, land, and other property from Southerners who desired to assist their fallen leader in overcoming his pecuniary adversity. These donations, in most cases, were declined by Davis who noted that he was not alone in suffering privations from war. Jefferson Davis, the consummate defender of the South, was still feeling the burden of defeat as late as 1877 when he wrote to Varina, *"The South, our loved country, is misrepresented, cheated, and the fetters of oppression riveted upon her."*[10]

In February of 1877, Jefferson Davis moved to the Mississippi Gulf Coast, where he rented a cottage at Beauvoir, the spacious residence of Mrs. Sarah A. Dorsey. Mrs. Dorsey, an old schoolmate of Varina, an author, and a lady of no small means, became the benefactor of Jefferson Davis and his family. Varina, although initially unhappy with the arrangements, soon fell in love with the Gulf Coast area and became happily engaged with work on her husband's book. At Mrs. Dorsey's death, Davis became sole proprietor of her estate. It was here at Beauvoir that Davis completed his work on *The Rise and Fall of the Confederate Government*. While Davis was a resident of Beauvoir, his last son died during a yellow fever epidemic in Memphis, Tennessee. During his life, Davis mourned the loss of his first wife and all four of his sons. His only remaining children were Margaret, who later married J. A. Hayes, and little Winnie, the "Daughter of the Confederacy." Winnie would never marry, only Margaret would marry and become a mother to the grandchildren of Jefferson Davis.

By 1877, Reconstruction may have been over, but many in the North were not willing to allow any benefits to flow to former Confederates, especially one by the name of "Jeff" Davis. In 1877,

---

10 Jefferson Davis, as cited in Strode, *Jefferson Davis, Tragic Hero*, 424.

Sen. J. A. Hoar of Massachusetts vehemently opposed granting the hero of Buena Vista, Jefferson Davis, a Mexican War pension. In a laudable defense of Davis, Senator L. Q. C. Lamar of Mississippi gave a noble justification for honoring Davis on the floor of the United States Senate:

> Jefferson Davis stands in precisely the position that I stand in, that every Southern man who believed in the right of a State to secede stands in. The only difference between myself and Jefferson Davis is that his exalted character, his preeminent talents, his reputation as a statesman, as a patriot, and as a soldier, enabled him to take the lead in a cause to which I consecrated myself.[11]

The hero of Buena Vista never received a pension for service to his country. Many Southerners, not just Jefferson Davis, have experienced the ill will of those who prefer viewing the South's struggle as treason rather than a fight to maintain government by the consent of the governed. Yet, Jefferson Davis did everything within his ability to secure a trial for himself on the very charge of treason, but the Yankee Empire, fearful of defeat, never allowed him a day in court to defend his name and cause.

Although a resident of Kentucky for only three years in his early life, Jefferson Davis esteemed the ties of loyalty to the state of his birth. In 1886, he was afforded the unique opportunity of donating the site of his birthplace to the Bethel Baptist Church in Fairview, Kentucky. Knowing the unique nature of the site of their church, its members desired to have the deed to the land presented to the church by Jefferson Davis. Therefore, several men of the congregation bought the land and donated it to Davis who then, in turn, presented

---

11 Senator Lamar, Strode, 440.

the deed to the church.¹² On November 21, 1886, Davis made, in part, the following statement to the congregation at the dedication of their church building:

> I am thankful that I can give you this lot upon which to worship the triune God. It has been asked why I, who am not a Baptist, give this lot to the Baptist church? I am not a Baptist, but my father, who was a belter man than I, was a Baptist. When I see this beautiful church it refills my heart with thanks. It shows the love you bear your creator .... The pioneers of this country, as I have learned from history', were men of plain, simple habits, full of energy and imbued with religious principles .... May the God of heaven bless this community forever, and may the Savior of the world preserve this church to His worship for all times to come.¹³

Having business to attend to at Briarfield, near Vicksburg, Mississippi, Davis departed the Gulf Coast in November of 1889. For a young man in good health, the trip would have offered little danger. But Davis was eighty-one years old and as of yet had not recovered his full strength since his release from prison in 1867. Bundled up in as warm and dry clothes as Varina could find, it was not long into the trip before the elderly gentleman began to suffer from exposure to the elements. Arriving at Briarfield weak, ill, and suffering from exposure, Davis remained bedridden for four days. Davis's refusal to allow his plantation overseer to send for family or physician did little to ameliorate his condition. Without Davis's knowledge, the overseer wired Varina a message providing details of her husband's condition. With encouragement from friends at Briarfield, Davis consented to go downriver to New Orleans and seek medical care there. At Briarfield, Davis was to write his last words.

---

12 Walter L. Fleming, "The Early Days of Jefferson Davis," *University Bulletin*, Louisiana State University, June 1917, Vol. 8, No. 6, 156.

13 Jefferson Davis, as cited in J. William Jones, *A Memorial Volume of Jefferson Davis* (1889, Harrisonburg, VA: Sprinkle Publications, 1993), 44.

Before leaving the plantation, Davis, in response to the request of a little girl, wrote the following tender note of encouragement to the young lady: "May all your paths be peaceful and pleasant, charged with the best fruit, the doing good to others."[14] With his health and stamina declining rapidly, Davis departed for New Orleans.

Arriving at New Orleans by steamer and with Varina now in attendance, Davis was so ill that he was transported by ambulance to the residence of Judge Charles E. Fenner. Several days later on the morning of December 6, 1889, the Picayune reported this account of Jefferson Davis's demise:

> Jefferson Davis closed his eyes in death at fifteen minutes before 1 o'clock this morning, surrounded by all of his friends and relatives who were within call. The handsome and characteristically southern residence of Judge Charles E. Fenner, at the corner of First and Camp streets, is at present an object of interest to every friend of Mr. Jefferson Davis, because it is in the pleasant guest-chamber of this elegant home that the beloved old Confederate chieftain passed away.[15]

News of the death of the former president of the Confederate States of America was flashed from city to city and around the world. Within hours of his death, it became obvious that nothing less than a "state" funeral would satisfy "his people." At three o'clock in the morning, Mayor Joseph Shakespeare of New Orleans issued the following proclamation:

> It is with deepest regret that I announce to the people of the city of New Orleans the departure from this life of Jefferson Davis. He needs no eulogy from me. His life is history and his memory' is enshrined in the

---

14 Alice Desmans, as cited in Strode, *Jefferson Davis, Tragic Hero*, 506.
15 *New Orleans Picayune*, as cited in Jones, 471.

heart of every man, woman and child in this broad South. We all loved him, and we all owe him honor and reverence.[16]

At the same time, the mayor sent telegrams to the governors of the former Confederate states. Each, in turn, issued his own proclamation informing its citizens of the death of Jefferson Davis. In Louisiana, Governor Francis T. Nicholls, a former Confederate general, issued his proclamation:

> It is with profound emotion and heartfelt sorrow that I announce to the people of the State of Louisiana the death of Jefferson Davis, the honored President of the Confederate States. As soldier, statesman and citizen he nobly performed his part. The pages of history will perpetuate his glorious record. The eyes of future generations will turn reverently to that heroic figure whose death the grateful South now mourns. His fame stands impregnable. To it the eulogies of his loving people can add no luster. From it the denunciations of his enemies cannot detract.[17]

Tributes and praise for Davis poured forth from Southern governors and other prominent men of the South. Governor L. S. Ross of Texas said of Davis, in part, "His lofty patriotism, immaculate integrity, and firmness of purpose, which never yielded principle for expediency nor abandoned the right for success, will be held up for emulation by the aspiring youth of Texas."[18] Governor Fitzhugh Lee of Virginia sent this condolence to Mrs. Davis: "The sympathetic cords of the hearts of our peoples are deeply touched at the loss of one we have ever regarded with the greatest affection, and the memory of whose valor and virtue we will ever hold sacred."[19]

---

16 Joseph Shakespeare, as cited in *Ibid.*, 471.
17 Francis Nicholls, as cited in *Ibid.*, 481.
18 L. S. Ross, as cited in *Ibid.*
19 Fitzhugh Lee, as cited in *Ibid.*, 485.

A group of prominent Mississippians in Washington, D.C., led by Federal Supreme Court justice L. Q. C. Lamar, sent a letter that attracted much attention. The letter stated:

> We recall with tender emotion his career as a soldier and civilian, brilliant, eventful, and without parallel in our annals, whether as a soldier pouring out his blood on foreign battlefields, as a statesman in the Cabinet of the nation, as the leader of his party in Congress, as the guiding spirit of the South through the stormiest period of her history, as the vicarious sufferer for us and his people in defeat, he has constantly and fully met the requirements of the most exacting criticism and illustrated in every station and condition the manly courage, the acute intellect, the heroic fortitude, the unfaltering devotion to duty, the constant sacrifice, the conviction that won for him our confidence, admiration, love, and reverence.[20]

Within hours of the news of Jefferson Davis's death, the city of New Orleans went into deep and respectful mourning. Flags were flown at half-staff, businesses closed, the city hall and every building displayed emblems of mourning. New Orleans began to look and feel like a funeral parlor as trains and ships from the North, East, West, and South brought mourners into the city. Clergymen, governors, congressmen, Confederate officers and enlisted men, men of high rank in society, and those of common means, black and white, were all attracted to the city to view Davis lying in state. Many women, widows of the war, alone and dressed in black, also came to show respect and honor the commander in chief of a lost family member. "Many old ladies clad in deep mourning viewed the remains. Most of them sent sons or husbands to the front at the outbreak of the

---

20 Strode, *Jefferson Davis, Tragic Hero*, 515.

war and never saw them again."[21] Various estimates of those viewing the body during the three days of mourning range from 50,000 to 150,000 people

Letters, gifts, and floral tributes poured into the city. From Briarfield, the former slaves of Jefferson Davis sent the following message of condolence: "We, the old servants and tenants of our beloved master, Honorable Jefferson Davis, have cause to mingle our tears over his death, who was always so kind and thoughtful of our peace and happiness. We extend to you our humble sympathy."[22] The son of a slave of Joseph Davis, Thornton Montgomery, a black man whom Jefferson Davis had helped educate, sent the following message from his home in Christine, North Dakota: "I have watched with deep interest and solicitude the illness of Mr. Davis ... and I had hoped that with his great will power to sustain him he would recover .... I appreciate your great loss, and my heart goes out to you in this hour of your deepest affliction .... I beg that you accept my tenderest sympathy and condolence."[23] Many of Davis's former slaves made their way to New Orleans to view the body of their former master. One of them, William Samford, of Vicksburg, Mississippi, wept as he viewed Davis's body. When questioned by reporters, Samford stated, "That I loved him this shows, and I can say that every colored man whom he ever owned loved him. He was a good and kind master."[24]

On December 11, Jefferson Davis was laid to rest in the Tomb of the Army of Northern Virginia, Metairie Cemetery, Metairie, Louisiana. His coffin was draped with a Confederate flag, and upon the flag was placed Davis's sword he had worn at the Battle of Buena Vista. At noon, the bell of First Presbyterian Church in New Orleans began to toll, quickly to be followed by all the church bells in the city and across the South. No one, from Texas to Virginia, needed to ask why the bells were tolling that day. Episcopal bishops Gallager of Louisiana and Thompson of Mississippi led the delegation of

---

21 Jones, 500.

22 *Confederate Veteran*, November-December 1989, 18.

23 Thornton Montgomery, as cited in Varina Howell Davis, II, 934.

24 William Samford, as cited in Jones, 500.

Presbyterian, Baptist, Methodist, Catholic, and Jewish religious leaders in the funeral procession. The procession from city hall to the cemetery was the largest ever seen in the South and possibly anywhere in America at that time. More than two hundred thousand people viewed or participated in the funeral procession, which took over one and one-half hours for the complete procession to pass any given spot along its trek.

On the day of Davis's funeral, far away in Richmond, Virginia, Dr. Charles Minnigerode, rector-emeritus of St. Paul's Episcopal Church and for many years Jefferson Davis's pastor, gave a stirring eulogy of Davis. He stated in part,

> We humbly bow in human sorrow to the Divine Disposer of all things, but lift our hearts in holy hope that, from a life of toil and labor, and martyrdom, he has entered upon the rest in heaven, and obtained a crown brighter than any crown that earth can weave—the crown of glory and eternal life. Of course, he had his faults; he would not have been human without them .... People have misunderstood Mr. Davis very much ... he was no brawler, no demagogue, no friend to violence. It was a sore trouble to him to yield to what appeared to him at last the necessity of secession; and wrath, cruelty, bloodthirstiness were far from him. I went to see him on the subject of confessing Christ. He ... expressed his desire to do so, and unite himself with the church. He spoke very earnestly and most humbly of needing the cleansing blood of Jesus and the power of the Holy Spirit .... He never ceased trying to come up to his baptismal vow and lead a Christian life .... He suffered, but was willing to suffer in the cause of the people who had given him their confidence, and who still loved and admired and wept for the man that so nobly represented the cause which in their hearts

> they considered right and constitutional .... *He loved the truth; he sewed God and his country.* Let us go and do likewise.[25]

After his death and all across the South, eulogies and prayers were said in honor of Jefferson Davis. In New Orleans, Louisiana, Bishop J. C. Kenner of the Methodist Episcopal Church South, speaking on the Christian character of Davis stated,

> It is very delightful for us to realize in our thoughts that his hopes are our hopes, and our hopes his; that he was not merely a public character. A man may be a great man, a magistrate; he may be a great figure in history, and yet when he comes to die he dies like anyone else; he is only a man; [he] has to have the same repentance, the same assurance, the same faith in Christ .... It was my good fortune to know Mr. Davis intimately. He was a sincere believer in the Christian religion. He listened to the Word and to the experiences of the people of God with reverent interest.[26]

The respect accorded Davis by religious leaders of the South was demonstrated by a former president of the Southern Baptist Convention. Dr. Patrick H. Mell led a delegation visiting Davis during Davis's tour of Georgia in 1888. In a news report just one year before Davis's death entitled "Two Striking Figures," a Georgia newspaper related the following account of the lives of these two men:

> When Hon. Jefferson Davis visited Macon last fall the city of Athens sent a delegation to invite him to Northeast Georgia. At the head of that delegation was Dr. P. H. Mell. The venerable Chancellor of the University found the ex-President lying upon a couch, too feeble to rise, but the two men who had so often

---

25 Charles Minnigerode, as cited in *Ibid.*, 416, 418, 421, 424.
26 Bishop J.C. Kenner, as cited in *Ibid.*, 464-65.

heard of each other, had a long and delightful interview .... Both men were old-time heroes. The same strong will and unfailing courage and unfaltering integrity were the trails of each. Those who knew Dr. Mell do not doubt that he would have served a cause with as much fidelity and worn the shackles with as much patience.[27]

It should be noted that Dr. Mell not only was the former president of the Southern Baptist Convention, a noted preacher and chancellor of the University of Georgia, but also was a Confederate veteran. Men of every religious denomination in the South were eager to praise the memory of President Jefferson Davis not only at his death but also during his life.

Few in number have been the funerals where more people, prominent or common, displayed such a heavy burden of grief as was displayed at Davis's funeral. Many Northern newspapers, before his death, had assured their readers that the South no longer believed in Jefferson Davis and his legacy. The outpouring of love and affection for the fallen leader of the Confederacy shocked many in the North. Consumed with the daily task of pursuing material wealth after their victory over the South, most Northerners thought of the South only in terms of market share. Many Northerners found it difficult to understand the South's obsession with "things in the past." In Washington, D.C., no official notice was made of the death of the former war hero, representative, senator, and secretary of war. The usual courtesy, shown to fifty-eight past secretaries of war, of having the flags of the War Department flown at half-staff and an announcement of the death of the former secretary of war read was never given for Jefferson Davis. Most Southerners understood the hatred motivating the official reluctance of Washington politicians to pay homage to Jefferson Davis. Jefferson Davis and, through him, the entire South were still being vilified as "traitors" and "rebels." [And still are being vilified]. Yet, the South, standing at the side of its

---

27 P. H. Mell, Jr., *The Life of Patrick Hues Mell* (1895, Harrisonburg, VA: Sprinkle Publications, 1991), 257-58.

greatest military leader, Lee, would reply to that slur with the very words of Robert E. Lee: "Every brave people who considered their right attacked & their Constitutional liberties invaded, would have done as we did .... The epithets that have been heaped upon us of 'rebels' & 'traitors' have no just meaning, nor are they believed in by those who understand the subject, even in the North."[28]

Giving both a defense of her husband's life and a challenge to his accusers, Varina Davis boldly asserted Jefferson Davis's legacy,

> Does anyone believe that if a warrant could have been found in the Constitution for the epithet of traitor, and if the fear of his entire justification by its provisions had not prevailed, that any felling of mercy or pity would have saved the prisoner from execution, and his name from being one universally execrated both North and South? Instead, he was left to follow his course of dignified seclusion, "by all his country's honors blessed," among his own people, by whom, as well as by many at the North, he was beloved as much as he was esteemed. *Might prevailed, but could not wrest from us the right of secession, or lawfully punish its assertion*"[29] [emphasis added].

The burial of Jefferson Davis in the Tomb of the Army of Northern Virginia in Metairie, Louisiana, from the beginning, was understood to be temporary. Shortly after his interment in Metairie, Louisiana, several states began making requests of Varina to allow them to provide a suitable resting place for the former Confederate president. Kentucky, the place of his birth and early education; Mississippi, the state that he had served so well; and other states such as Georgia and Louisiana all offered to take charge of his final resting place. But for Varina, the one offer that seemed to her as most appropriate was Richmond, Virginia. Richmond, the capital of the Confederacy, was also the resting place of one of the Davis's children and many

---

28   Robert E. Lee, as cited in Strode, *Jefferson Davis, Tragic Hero*, 354.
29   Varina Howell Davis, II, 802.

notable men in the history of the South and the United States. Four years after his death, Jefferson Davis's body was moved to its final resting place in Richmond, Virginia. Once again, the South poured out its emotions in a memorial display. A special train carried the remains from New Orleans to Richmond. The route was marked by large crowds with flowers and flags. All across the South, the train would slow to a respectful pace as the train passed through a city to allow the people to view the coffin containing the body of President Jefferson Davis. In Richmond, Davis was accorded a full military funeral and laid to rest in Hollywood Cemetery. Not far from Davis's grave is the resting place of men such as John Randolph of Roanoke; James Madison; his old friend, President John Tyler; and a host of Confederate soldiers and statesmen.

Thus, cradled in the soil that has given birth to so many of America's great leaders in the cause of constitutional liberty, Jefferson Davis returned to "his people" whom he loved and served so well. Americans in general and Southerners in particular would do well to learn and to emulate the legacy of their great defender of constitutional liberty, Jefferson Davis.

Chapter 10

Conspiracy Allegations

HAVING COMPLETED YOUR INTRODUCTION into the life and character of the accused, you, the jury, must now evaluate the charges and the evidence to support those charges against President Jefferson Davis. As we have demonstrated, several charges were leveled against Davis, and through him, the South, after the defeat of the Confederate States of America. By the time of his capture, Davis was accused of the following "crimes": (1) conspiracy and culpability in the assassination of Abraham Lincoln; (2) conspiracy to cause the deaths of Union POWs at the Andersonville, Georgia, Confederate prisoner of war camp; (3) participating in and attempting to assist in the growth of the system of slavery; and, (4) treason against the United States of America—which, by now, has morphed into the Yankee Empire.

Because of the lack of evidence sufficient to obtain a conviction, all charges against President Davis were eventually dropped. For Davis, having the charges dropped was a great disappointment. Neither he nor his attorneys desired or asked to have the charges dismissed. Davis, along with most Southerners, always desired a fair public hearing in a court of law. It cannot be overly stressed that it was Jefferson Davis's desire to have a fair trial in order to clear his name and through him, the name of the South, against the charge of treason. Although Davis was never tried or convicted on these charges, the very announcement of the charges did have detrimental effects upon his good name. The effects of the first three slanderous charges made against Davis are important because of their impact upon his defense against the charge of treason. If the prosecution is allowed to paint Davis as a loathsome individual, it becomes easier to then transfer that attitude to him as it relates to the primary charge of treason.

Jefferson Davis was eventually indicted and brought before a court in Richmond, Virginia. Yet, he was named and virtually tried *in absentia* in two other notable cases. The so-called Lincoln conspirators, those implicated in the assassination of Abraham Lincoln, were tried from May through July of 1865. The "Lincoln conspirators" trial was the first case in which Jefferson Davis and other Confederates were cited as co-conspirators in a plot against the Yankee Empire. At the end of this first trial, eight defendants were convicted of conspiring with Jefferson Davis and other Confederate leaders to murder President Abraham Lincoln. At least two and perhaps more of those convicted, without a doubt, were innocent civilian victims of this unconstitutional military court. Mary Surratt and Dr. Samuel Mudd are two of the most often noted as being innocent of the charges; their major crime was that of being Southern sympathizers. The second trial in which Jefferson Davis and other Confederates were named as co-conspirators was the famous "Wirz trial" held from August 24 through October 24, 1865. The trial of Maj. Henry Wirz, commander of Andersonville Prison Camp, was held by the same military court system that tried the first-mentioned case. Wirz, along with Jefferson Davis, Robert E. Lee, and other Confederates, was charged with conspiracy to destroy prisoners' lives and the murder of prisoners at the Confederate prisoner of war camp in Andersonville, Georgia.[1] Although cited as a co-conspirator in two of America's most famous court cases, Jefferson Davis was never allowed a day in court to defend his name. It would be almost two years after his capture before Davis would even be allowed in a courtroom. But, even then, the Yankee Empire would not allow Davis's much sought-after trial for treason to begin. We will, therefore, expose the shallow nature of the above charges before we proceed to the most relevant charge which you, the jury, must consider: Was Jefferson Davis a traitor?

---

1 Glen W. LaForce, "The Trial of Major Henry Wirz: A National Disgrace," *Confederate Veteran*, January-February 1989, 27. A reprint of an article published in *The Army Lawyer*, Department of the Army Pamphlet 27-50-186, June 1988, 3.

Davis and the Lincoln Assassination

After the fall of Richmond and while he was resting in Charlotte, North Carolina, news of the assassination of Abraham Lincoln reached President Davis. Upon being informed by Gen. John C. Breckinridge of Lincoln's assassination, Davis stated, "I am sorry to learn it. Mr. Lincoln was a much better man than his successor will be, and it will go harder with our people. It is bad news for us."[2] Although Davis never agreed with Lincoln's political views or his war policy, he nevertheless did regard Lincoln as a man and had no desire to cause him personal harm. While in Charlotte, in reply to a frightened little girl's remark that "old Lincoln's coming and going to kill us all," President Davis allayed the child's fear by stating, "Oh, no, my little lady, you need not fear that. Mr. Lincoln is not such a bad man, he does not want to kill anybody, and certainly not a little girl like you."[3]

On the day after his capture, Davis was to learn that President Andrew Johnson had issued a reward for the arrest of Jefferson Davis and other Confederate government officials as accessories in the murder of Abraham Lincoln. Everyone in the Confederate president's party was shocked by the news of the charge against Davis. Moreover, the effect upon his captors was noted by Varina: "There was a perceptible change in the manner of the soldiers from this time, and the jibes and insults heaped upon us as they passed by … were hard to bear."[4] Davis never believed the account would be credited if a fair hearing was accorded the accused. Yet, he fully understood what was taking place. Davis noted, "[S]uch an accusation must fail at once; it may, however, render these people [Northerners] willing to assassinate me here."[5] Davis, knowing the lack of integrity and the determination of his accusers to implicate him in any heinous crime, assured Varina at their separation at

---

2   Jefferson Davis, as cited in Varina Howell Davis, *Jefferson Davis, A Memoir by His Wife* (New York: Belford Company, Publishers, 1890), II, 629.

3   *Ibid.*, 628.

4   *Ibid.*, II, 642.

5   Jefferson Davis, as cited in *Ibid.*

Fortress Monroe, "No matter what proof is adduced by the North, remember that my dying testimony was to you that I had nothing to do with assassination, or causing any other deed unworthy of a soldier, or of our cause."⁶

The shocking news that Jefferson Davis and the Confederate government had been implicated in the assassination of Lincoln startled the whole continent. These charges flowed from no other than Davis's old senatorial nemesis, Andrew Johnson. Shortly after the death of Lincoln, President Johnson issued a proclamation that in part stated,

> [I]t appears from evidence in the Bureau of Military Justice that the atrocious murder of the late President ... and the attempted assassination of the Secretary of State, were incited, concerted and procured by and between Jefferson Davis ... and other rebels and traitors ... harbored in Canada.⁷

Notice how the Northern victor was, even at this early time, spitefully referring to Davis by the terms "rebel" and "traitor." Johnson's reference to Canada did not go unnoticed by the Canadians. In reply to the announcement of President Johnson, the *Montreal Telegraph*, somewhat tongue-in-cheek, stated,

> That the federal government may have obtained such information is quite probable, and it is only necessary for it to intimate a desire to have Queen Victoria, the Pope, and the Khan of Tartary involved in the same charge to get that evidence also; but we do not believe that there is a word of truth in the assertion. It has no

---

6   Ibid., 704.

7   Andrew Johnson, as cited in Seymour J. Frank, *The Conspiracy Against Jefferson Davis* (1954, Biloxi, MS: The Beauvoir Press, 1987), 15. Originally published as, "The Conspiracy to Implicate the Confederate Leaders in Lincoln's Assassination," *The Mississippi Valley Historical Review* (Bloomington, IN: Indiana University) March, 1954, Vol. XL, No. 4.

doubt been trumped up with the double object of affording an excuse for the murdering of President Davis if caught, and firing the northern heart against Canada.⁸

What was "the evidence in the Bureau of Military Justice" that could have caused such a proclamation to be issued? Actually, there was no such evidence. Johnson had been induced into making the proclamation by Secretary of State Edwin Stanton. Acting under Stanton's direction, Judge Advocate General Joseph Holt provided Johnson with oral records of the testimonies of Richard Montgomery and Dr. James B. Merritt describing a conspiracy by Davis and the Confederate government to murder Lincoln (as many as eight "informers" were later secured by Holt). This testimony had never been put into writing nor was it taken under oath.⁹ Soon it was discovered that the information obtained against Davis was taken from men who were of questionable character and who had been paid for their testimony. Other problems were soon discovered in the testimony of the Yankee Empire's paid witnesses. One such witness, Sanford Conover, alias James Waton Wallace, whose true name was Charles A. Dunham, maintained that he took part in an interview with a Confederate agent, Jacob Thompson, in Montreal in late January or early February of 1865 to plot Lincoln's murder. Yet, Thompson was known to have been absent from Montreal at that time. Other "witnesses" were similarly discredited. William A. Campbell and Joseph Snevel were introduced as witnesses. Campbell's real name was Joseph A. Hoar, and Snevel's real name

New Jersey Democrat, Andrew J. Rogers challenged the Republican Party's attempt to link Davis to Lincoln's assignation.

---

8   Frank, 15.

9   *Ibid.*

was William H. Roberts. Both Hoar and Roberts were employed in New York city and had never been south of Washington, D.C.; yet, both claimed to have been in Richmond, Virginia, and participated in a Confederate planning session for Lincoln's assassination.[10]

Soon it became evident even to the most ardent hater of the South that no real evidence existed to connect Davis or any Confederate government official with the assassination of Abraham Lincoln. Still, Stanton and other Republicans had to have a "fig leaf" to hide behind after circulating the flagrant lies about Davis and other Confederates. The "fig leaf" was provided to Stanton when on April 9, 1866, a committee of the House of Representatives formally demanded all evidence in connection with Lincoln's assassination and Davis's participation in such a conspiracy. For Stanton, this was the out that he and other Republicans in the cabinet needed. The House of Representatives and the House committee charged with the investigation were under the control of the Republicans, and, therefore, an acceptable and sanitized version could be expected. But one thing that Stanton did not expect was the heroic action of a New Jersey Democrat, Andrew J. Rogers. As the "Davis conspiracy" hearing began, Rogers began to ask questions that exposed the whole sordid fabrication against Davis and other former Confederates. As the House committee continued its work, it soon became apparent that some of the "witnesses" would not come before the committee and give a *sworn* deposition. They were willing to give oral testimonies (for pay), but testifying under oath was another matter. One witness before the House committee admitted that his deposition was false. The witness even admitted, under oath, that his earlier testimony had been written by someone else and that he had memorized it. He also admitted that he had committed perjury by doing this and that he had been paid nine hundred dollars total for his "testimony."[11] As this information began to be leaked to the press, the Republicans attempted to close the hearing and to produce a whitewashed report for public consumption. Nevertheless, Representative Rogers

---

10 *Ibid.*, 26.

11 *Ibid.*, 30.

managed to produce a minority report that proved to be the downfall of those attempting to blame President Davis and the Confederate government with Lincoln's assassination.

In "The Conspiracy to Implicate the Confederate Leaders in Lincoln's Assassination," Seymour J. Frank explains why the attempt to railroad Davis and the South in this case should be studied as a warning to all Americans when he states,

> The conspiracy to implicate the Southern leaders in Lincoln's assassination had obviously failed, but the selfish partisan motives behind it and the unscrupulous methods used by its promoters set a pattern which jeopardized the rights of individuals and threatened to undermine the integrity of democratic governmental procedures. That the original idea, conceived in a moment of personal fear and panic, was the brain child of Secretary Stanton can hardly be disputed. It is also clear that when his charges were promulgated through presidential proclamation he had no reliable evidence to support them; and so long as Davis was at large such evidence not essential. But with the capture of Davis while the conspiracy trial was in progress he was placed in an extremely embarrassing position. That he did not intend to have the Confederate President and his "Canadian cabinet" tried for complicity in the murder plot is indicated by his order that the prisoner be taken to Fortress Monroe instead of to Washington. "I do not mean that he shall come here . . he wrote in his instructions of May 15, 1865, to General Henry W. Halleck. "His trial and punishment, if there be any, shall be in Virginia." He [Stanton] could hardly have been ignorant of the fact that the only charge on which Davis could properly be tried in Virginia was that of treason.[12]

---

12 *Ibid.*, 39.

The courageous actions of Representative Andrew J. Rogers of New Jersey in maintaining an honest and correct record about this incident demonstrates that, even with the defeat of the South, many Northerners still understood that the course being pursued by the Republican Party was dangerous to American freedom. In the closing remarks of the minority report of the House committee, Representative Rogers condemned the actions of the Republican majority of the committee and those who perpetrated the "Davis conspiracy scandal." Rogers stated, "[T]he cool turpitude of the whole crew sickened me with shame, and made me sorrow over the fact that such people could claim the name of American."[13] Soon thereafter, the charges of conspiracy to assassinate President Lincoln against Davis and his fellow Confederates were dropped.

Major Wirz was hung due to trumped-up charges and false testimony.

DAVIS, WIRZ, AND ANDERSONVILLE

That the lot of American POWs during the War for Southern Independence was one of unspeakable horror should be evident to all observers. During World War II, for example, the average death rate in a German POW camp was approximately 9 percent. During the War for Southern Independence, the average death rate in a Northern POW camp was approximately 12 percent, and the death rate in Southern POW camps was approximately 15 percent. Many antagonists of the South have pointed to the 3 percent difference in

---

13 Andrew J. Rogers, as cited in *Ibid.*, 40.

the death rates in Southern POW camps as "evidence" to support their charge of Southern cruelty to Northern prisoners. If that is the case, what must be said of the 3 percent difference between that of a Northern POW camp and a German POW camp? In numbers of deaths, according to the Yankee Empire's War Department's own accounting, 26,436 Southerners died in Northern camps as opposed to 22,576 Northerners who died in Southern camps.[14] Yet, while many Americans can readily identify the Southern POW camp of Andersonville, very few have the slightest knowledge of Northern camps such as Elmira, New York, or Camp Douglas, Illinois. These Yankee Empire POW camps had a death rate almost as high as Andersonville in the Confederate states. Although the South was suffering from invasion all across its land and from a naval blockade which caused suffering to all those south of the Mason-Dixon line, the North had food and medicines in abundance; yet the death rates in Northern POW camps were almost as high as in their Southern counterparts. This fact alone should prove that the Confederate States of America was not engaged in an effort to starve Northern POW inmates.

In an attack led by the Republicans in Washington, Confederate major Henry Wirz became an object of scorn after the war. For Yankee Empire's Secretary of War, Edwin Stanton, Wirz became the scapegoat who provided the means of deflecting criticism of his POW policy. It was Stanton who refused to allow any exchange of POWs because, as he believed, the exchange aided the South more than the North. Many returning Northern POWs and their families held Stanton responsible for their suffering to a greater extent than they held Confederate authorities. Thus, by depicting Wirz and Davis as being responsible for the horrors of POW camp life, Stanton protected his standing in the government.

The trial of Major Wirz came as close to a "Star Chamber" proceeding as has ever been seen in an American court. Wirz was charged with causing the deaths of thirteen prisoners; yet no name for any victim was given, nor were any eyewitnesses of any murder provided. When at last an eyewitness was provided, by the name

---

14 LaForce, 30.

of Felix de la Baume, it was subsequently (eleven days *after* Wirz's hanging) discovered that the so-called de la Baume was an imposter.[15] Out of the thousands of men at Andersonville, no one could support the charge of murder against Wirz with an eyewitness account of the murder. Former Andersonville inmate James Madison Page challenges Americans to consider the facts:

> The authorities spent three months in preparation before the trial (if it can be called a trial) began, and it lasted nearly three months, and yet of the thirteen prisoners that Wirz was charged with murdering on his own personal account, not the name of a victim was testified to and not a solitary one of them has been named since that time!
>
> Think of it. Some of the prisoners [those supposedly murdered by Wirz] lived three and four days after the alleged clubbing and shooting by Wirz, and one of the prisoners who was beaten, it was testified to by three or four witnesses, lived six days before he died, and notwithstanding thousands were in and about the prison no one could name them or knew who they were!
>
> The dates of the alleged assaults, the facts down to the most minute particular were testified to with exactness, but in every case the most important thing—the name—was wanting.[16]

To the impartial mind, the fact that so many details could be stated about the deaths of various individuals yet no name of that person could be remembered would be quite out of the ordinary. Are we to believe that none of the alleged thirteen victims of Major Wirz had any friends or comrades who remembered their names? These questions were never explored in the so-called trial.

---

15 Ibid., 29.

16 James Madison Page, *The True Story of Andersonville Prison, A Defense of Major Henry Wirz* (1908, Athens, GA: The Iberian Publishing Co., 1991), 192.

When the defense attempted to call witnesses to disprove the Yankee Empire's claims, the Yankee Empire denied the defense's requests. When Wirz's defense requested to place in evidence the efforts of the Confederate government to relieve the suffering of the POW inmates, that request was denied by the Yankee Empire's military judges. When Wirz's defense requested to be allowed to place evidence before the court showing how the actions of the Yankee Empire actually caused the suffering of the POW inmates, the request was denied by the same military judges. One former POW, Lt. James M. Page, who offered himself as a witness for Wirz, was never issued a subpoena by the Yankee Empire's military court. Lieutenant Page was so enraged by the treatment accorded Major Wirz that he later wrote a book defending the actions of Major Wirz at Andersonville. In the preface of his book, Lieutenant Page stated, "I have finally concluded to write something of my experiences in Southern prisons during the Civil War, not in a spirit of controversy, but in the interest of truth and fair play."[17] Continuing his defense of Major Wirz and his actions at Andersonville, Lieutenant Page declared,

> I shall take the stand not only that … Wirz was unjustly held responsible for the hardship and mortality of Andersonville, but the Federal authorities must share the blame for these things with the Confederates, since they well knew the inability of the Confederates to meet the reasonable wants … and since the Federal authorities failed to exercise a humane policy in the exchange of those captured in battle.[18]

Just three months after the execution of Major Wirz, the Confederate archives, then in safekeeping in Montreal, Canada, were examined for evidence of conspiracy by Davis, Wirz, and other Confederates to cause the deaths of Northern POW inmates. After a review of the records, not only was there no such evidence found to

---

17   *Ibid.*, Preface.
18   *Ibid.*, 11.

implicate the Confederate leaders, but more importantly the records proved that the Confederate government did all within its power to care for its prisoners.[19]

That the trial of Major Wirz was a sordid miscarriage of justice should be evident to anyone who reviews the evidence of the case and the trial. The very fact that a former Union officer (Lt. James M. Page, Company A, Sixth Michigan Cavalry) and a former inmate at Andersonville would write a book defending the honor and name of his former enemy and prison camp warden is virtually unprecedented in the annals of warfare. But the nobility of Wirz and the unscrupulousness of the Yankee Empire's agents cannot be fathomed without the knowledge of Henry Wirz's last days. Forty-eight hours before Wirz was to be hanged, he received a visit from three men who stated that they were representing "powerful men in Congress." [Republicans] The "powerful men" offered Wirz a chance to save himself from the hangman's noose. According to the "powerful men," all Wirz had to do to save himself was to implicate Jefferson Davis in the deaths of prisoners at Andersonville. Wirz, to his credit, refused to give a false statement about Davis in order to save his own life. This offer, made by the representatives of these "powerful men," was made not only to Wirz but also to his attorney, Louis Schade, and in the presence of Wirz's priest, Fr. F. E. Boyle.[20] Wirz's last words about this attempt to induce him to implicate Jefferson Davis in events surrounding Andersonville Prison demonstrates his courage and integrity: "I would not become a traitor against him [Jefferson Davis] or anybody else even to save my life."[21] Louis Schade, attorney for Major Wirz, was so moved by the callous and spiteful manner in which Wirz's trial was handled that in 1867 he addressed a letter to the American people defending his former client, Maj. Henry Wirz (see Addendum VI).

The trial and lynching (the murder of an innocent man cannot be excused by calling it "execution") of Major Wirz served the purpose of deflecting attention away from the true source of the

---

19 Varina Howell Davis, II, 784.

20 LaForce, 31; Page, 210.

21 Henry Wirz, as cited in Page, 210.

deaths at Andersonville—Secretary of War Edwin M. Stanton. The charge against Jefferson Davis of "conspiring to cause the deaths of prisoners at Andersonville" was dropped soon after Wirz's hanging. With all other charges having been publicly proven to be too shallow to support an indictment, only the charge of treason was left to be dealt with. For Davis, this was good news. He could now concentrate on the one pursuit that impelled him forward, the defense of true American constitutional liberty.

JEFFERSON DAVIS: EVIL SLAVE MASTER

As demonstrated throughout this book, Jefferson Davis was far removed from the stereotypical view of the Southern slave holder commonly held in the North. Yet, it is not uncommon, especially today, for the enemies of Davis and the South to wave the "bloody shirt" of slavery whenever they feel they are in danger of losing any argument with defenders of the South's right to be a free and independent nation.

One of the first charges against the South, and therefore against Davis, was that the Southern states were seceding in order to advance the cause of slavery in America. The Confederate States of America are often referred to by their antagonists as the "Slaveholding Confederacy."[22] It has been maintained by many that the South did not have a right to independence because each Confederate state was a slave-holding state. This, of course, overlooks some very important American historical facts. When in 1776 the thirteen original colonies announced their independence, slavery was legal in all thirteen colonies. If the Confederate states did not have the right to independence because of slavery, what does that say about the thirteen slave-holding states of America in 1776? At this point, some will argue that most of the colonies north of Maryland were not greatly involved in slavery; therefore, only the South was truly guilty of slavery. True, the Southern colonies were more involved with slavery than their Northern counterparts, but it must be

---

22 James H. Moore, *Notes on the History of Slavery in Massachusetts* (New York: D. Appleton & Company, 1866), 2.

remembered that the Northern colonies were much more heavily involved in the nefarious slave trade than the Southern colonies; thus, we ask, where is the demand for condemnation of the North?

Modern anti-South partisans will attempt to demean the South as the section of the United States that "protected" slavery. Yet, when we look at the historical record, we find none other than Abraham Lincoln defending the South from the abuse of those who myopically focus upon the issue of radical abolition of slavery. Although opposed to slavery, Lincoln fully understood the dilemma facing the South in regard to the issue of the abolition of slavery. In one of the famous Lincoln-Douglas debates, August 21, 1858, Lincoln expressed his view of Southern slavery and the problems faced by the South in ending the institution. It should be noted how Lincoln's view of Southern slavery differs from the modern politically correct, Woke, view of the same issue. Lincoln stated,

> Before proceeding, let me say I think I have no prejudice against the Southern people. They are just what we would be in their situation. If slavery did not now exist among them, they would not introduce it. If it did now exist among us, we should not instantly give it up. This I believe of the masses North and South. Doubtless there are individuals on both sides who would not hold slaves under any circumstances; and others who would gladly introduce slavery anew, if it were out of existence. We know that some Southern men do free their slaves, go North, and become tip-top Abolitionists; while some Northern ones go South, and become most cruel slave-masters.
>
> When Southern people tell us they are no more responsible for the origin of slavery than we, I acknowledge the fact. When it is said that the institution exists, and that it is very difficult to get rid of it in any satisfactory way, I can understand and appreciate the saying. I surely will not blame them for not doing what I should not know how to do myself.

If all earthly power were given me, I should not know what to do as to the existing institution. My first impulse would be to free all the slaves, and send them to Liberia—to their own native land. But a moment's reflection would convince me that whatever of high hope (as I think there is) there may be in this in the long run, its sudden execution is impossible. If they were all landed there in a day, they would all perish in the next ten days; and there are not surplus shipping and surplus money enough in the world to carry them there in many times ten days. What then? Free them all, and keep them among us as underlings? Is it quite certain that this betters their condition? I think I would not hold one in slavery at any rate; yet the point is not clear enough to me to denounce people upon. What next? Free them, and make them politically and socially our equals? My own feelings will not admit of this; and if mine would, we well know that those of the great mass of white people will not. Whether this feeling accords with justice and sound judgment is not the sole question, if, indeed, it is any part of it. A universal feeling, whether well or ill-fashioned, cannot be safely disregarded. We cannot make them equals. It does seem to me that systems of gradual emancipation might be adopted; but for their tardiness in this, I will not undertake to judge our brethren of the South.

When they remind us of their constitutional rights, I acknowledge them, not grudgingly, but fully and fairly; and I would give them any legislation for the reclaiming of their fugitives, which should not, in its stringency, be more likely to cany a free man into slavery, than our ordinary criminal laws are to hang an innocent one.[23]

In the preceding speech, Lincoln made the very points that Davis and many Southerners had often stated. Lincoln stated that (1) the South was not responsible for the origin of slavery in America; (2) the institution was difficult to abolish; (3) free blacks were not always better off than slaves; (4) the nation, North and South, was not ready to accept blacks as equals; (5) the South had constitutional rights that had to be protected; and (6) the right of reclaiming fugitive slaves was constitutional. Now, consider the response from the liberal establishment when modern Southerners state these facts in defense of the South. In light of Lincoln's view of Southern slavery, how can anyone believe that Southerners such as Jefferson Davis, who desired gradual emancipation, were attempting to expand slavery in the United States?

Secession, rather than expanding the cause of slavery in America actually decreased the territorial expansion of the institution. When the "slave states" seceded from the Union, they surrendered all claims to the commonly held territory from which new "slave states" could have been formed. From the formation of the Confederate States of America, the expansion of slavery in the territory controlled by the United States was a dead issue. How can anyone believe that secession could increase the power of the defenders of slavery in the United States?

When shown these facts, the antagonists of the South wall fall back on the argument that, by seceding, the Southern states were attempting to defend the institution of slavery from those who desired the abolition of slavery. They assert this even though Abraham Lincoln, in his first inaugural address, assured slave holders of America that their slave property would be protected by his administration. Lincoln stated,

---

23 Abraham Lincoln, as cited in Roy Edgar Appleman, ed., *Abraham Lincoln From His Own Words and Contemporary Accounts* (1942, Washington, DC: National Park Service Source Book Two, 1956), 20-21.

> I have no purpose, directly or indirectly, to interfere with the institution of slavery in the States where it exists. I believe I have no lawful right to do so, and I have no inclination to do so.[24]

If Southern slave holders wanted protection for their property, all they had to do, according to Lincoln's inaugural address, was to remain in the Union. There is other evidence that the South, by seceding from the Union, was not seeking the ultimate protection of the institution of slavery. The following historical facts will demonstrate that the South also had a desire to attenuate or end slavery: (1) The first abolition society in America was established in the South, and for many years thereafter most members of abolition societies were Southern men and women. Southerners turned against the abolition movement only after radical cultural bigots in the North captured the movement and proceeded to use it as a weapon against the South. (2) It was a Southern Colony (Virginia), and not a Northern colony, that first demanded the end to the slave trade in America. (3) When the Confederate States of America adopted its constitution, it was the first American constitution to unequivocally abolish the African slave trade. President Jefferson Davis's first veto was issued in support of the spirit of that same constitutional limitation on the African slave trade. From these facts alone, one is forced to conclude that the act of secession was not an act to perpetuate slavery. Furthermore, there are no grounds to support the idea that the existence of slavery in the South should negate the right of a people of American states to form a government by the consent of the governed. An "unalienable" American right boldly proclaimed in the Declaration of Independence of 1776.

Although the opponents of Southern independence would like to use the straw man of slavery as justification for their invasion, conquest, and colonization of the South, the fact remains that the South fought for the same right that colonial Americans fought for in 1776. Without a doubt, slavery was a unique institution in the

---

24 Abraham Lincoln, as cited in Hunter McGuire & George L. Christian, *The Confederate Cause and Conduct of the War Between the States* (1907, Boonton, NJ: Boonton Bookshop, 1994), 66.

South, and it was unique for many good reasons. As many modern investigators have pointed out, it was in the American South that a close and friendly relationship was established between slave and master. This is one reason given for the lack of servile insurrection in the American South as compared to South America and the Caribbean.[25] Even with most of the young men absent during the war and with Yankee armies roaming the land, the vast majority of slaves remained loyal to their masters' families. This fact of black loyalty to white friends was noted by Booker T. Washington when he wrote of "eight millions of Negroes whose habits you know, whose fidelity and love you have tested in days when to have proved treacherous meant the ruin of your firesides."[26] The much sought-after "slave uprising" that the Radical Abolitionists desired never happened. Bill Yopp, a slave and Confederate veteran, when asked why he did not desert his master and go North, answered for many slaves: "I had no inclination to go to the Union side, as I did not know the Union soldiers and the Confederate soldiers I did know, and I believed then as now, tried and true friends are better than friends you do not know."[27]

For many slaves "liberated" by the invader, life was anything but a joyous experience. The Yankee "liberator" brought more than freedom; death was in his wake. The death rate among the "liberated" slaves were so great that President Davis, the Confederate Congress, and the governor of Louisiana all condemned the North for the deplorable fate of many former slaves. In condemning the Northern Army's actions in and around Berwick's Bay in Louisiana, Gov. Thomas A. Moore stated that "more negroes had perished in Louisiana from the cruelty and brutality of the public enemy [the Yankee Empire's Army] than the combined number of white men, in

---

25 Jeffrey Rogers Hummel, *Emancipating Slaves, Enslaving Free Men, A History of the American Civil War* (Chicago: Open Court Trade and Academic Books, 1996), 58.

26 Booker T. Washington, *Up From Slavery* (New York: Doubleday, Page, & Company, 1901), 220.

27 Bill Yopp, as cited in Kennedy & Kennedy, *The South Was Right!* 3rd edition (1991, 1994, Columbia, SC: Shotwell Publishing, 2020), 151-2.

both armies, from the casualties of war."²⁸ Edward Pollard, editor of the *Richmond Examiner* during the war, gave the following account of the fate of the slaves "liberated" by the Northern Army:

> The practice of the enemy in the parts of the Confederacy he had invaded, was to separate the families of the blacks without notice. Governor Moore [Louisiana] officially testified to this practice in Louisiana. The men were driven off like so many cattle to a Yankee camp, and were enlisted in the Yankee army. The women and children were likewise driven off in droves, and put upon what are called "Government plantations"—that is, plantations from which the lawful owners had been forced to fly, and which the Yankees in Louisiana were cultivating.²⁹

Pollard noted that even Northern men noticed the harsh conditions in which the freed slaves existed. According to Pollard, one Massachusetts newspaper published a letter which stated that more than fifty thousand blacks were living in "contraband" camps, in which a death rate of twelve victims per camp per day was common. These unfortunate victims of war had been driven or enticed from their homes by Yankees who sought to use slaves against their former masters and friends. Yet, as Pollard explains, the South never experienced the much sought-after slave revolt that the North hoped would end the war.

> In all the war there had been no servile insurrection in the South—not a single instance of outbreak among the slaves—a conclusive evidence that the negro was not the enemy of his master, but, in his desertion of

---

28 Governor Moore, as cited in Edward A. Pollard., *A Southern History of the War* (1866, New York: The Fairfax Press, 1977), 198. Also see David C. Edmonds, ed., The Conduct of Federal Troops in Louisiana (Lafayette, LA: The Acadiana Press, 1988), 116-19; and Arthur W. Bergeron, Jr., *A History* of the Eighteenth Louisiana Infantry Regiment (Baton Rouge, LA: Arthur W. Bergeron), 131.

29 Pollard, 198.

him, merely the victim of Yankee bribes. Assured, through a thousand channels, as these negroes were, that they were the victims of the most grinding and cruel injustice and oppression; assured of the active assistance of the largest armies of modern times, and of the countenance and sympathy of the rest of the world; assured that such an enterprise would not only be generous and heroic, but eminently successful, our enemies had heretofore failed to excite one solitary instance of insurrection, much less to bring on a servile war.[30]

Jefferson Davis, and many Southerners, would protest the manner in which the Northern invader agitated the race question in the South. Of course, it was to the advantage of the Yankee Empire to drive a wedge between the black population in the South and their white neighbors. But, once agitated, the question would remain for other generations of Americans to resolve. Once again, it must be pointed out that the Yankee Empire's primary purpose, in making this effort, was to weaken the cause of Southern independence—and today to help the Yankee Empire's ruling elite to maintain their control of the South, while also maintaining their control of the political status quo.

That the institution of slavery played a role in the Southern secession movement is undeniable; yet, it was independence that was the goal of the secession movement, not the maintenance of slavery. In 1863, in an editorial published in Jackson, Mississippi, the writer made it clear what the chief desire of the South was when he stated that slavery must not be allowed to cause the Confederacy to lose its "liberty and separate nationality."[31] Even President Jefferson Davis recognized that the institution of slavery was coming to an end, regardless of who was the victor in the war.[32]

---

30 *Ibid.*, 201.

31 Jackson Mississippian, as cited in Hummel, 281.

32 Varina Howell Davis, II, 12.

Apologists for the Yankee Empire's invasion of a sovereign nation, the Confederate States of America, often use the extermination of slavery as a justification for the Yankee Empire's aggression. They claim that slavery would never have been abolished except for the heroic efforts of the Yankee Empire to force the South to end the institution. President Davis addressed this fallacious assertion by declaring:

> War was not necessary to the abolition of slavery. Years before the agitation began at the North and the menacing acts to the institution, there was a growing feeling all over the South for its abolition. But the abolitionists of the North, both by publications and speech, cemented the South and crushed the feeling in favor of emancipation. Slavery could have been blotted out without the sacrifice of brave men and without the strain which revolution always makes upon established forms of government. I see it stated that I uttered the sentiment, or indorsed it, that "slavery is the corner stone of the Confederacy." That is not my utterance.[33]

Confederate general Stephen D. Lee declared that "[i]t is not conceivable that the statesmen of the Union were incompetent to dispose of slavery without war."[34]

Far from being a harsh and evil slave master, Jefferson Davis was one of the South's leading proponents of education for slaves and of gradual emancipation. Davis was so beloved by his slaves that twenty-four years after gaining their freedom, his former slaves were some of the first mourners to display grief at his death. According to one noted Davis historian, Jefferson Davis's love and care for his slaves earned him the contemptuous name of "nigger-lover" by those

---

33 Jefferson Davis, as cited in J. L. M. Curry, *Confederate Military History* (1899, Harrisburg, PA: The Archive Society, 1994), Vol. I, Part 1, 259.

34 Stephen D. Lee, *Ibid.*

who did not agree with his kind treatment of blacks.[35] At Davis's funeral, one former slave told a reporter in New Orleans, "That I loved him this shows, and I can say that every colored man whom he ever owned loved him. He was a good, kind master."[36] While in prison in 1866, Jefferson Davis wrote to Varina about the efforts of Northern agitators who were attempting to instill hate in the freed blacks against their former masters. Davis wrote,

> Like you, I feel sorry' for the negroes. What has been done would gradually and measurably be corrected by the operation of the ordinary laws governing the relation of labor to capital, if they were let alone. But interference by those who have a theory to maintain by the manufacture of facts, must result in evil, evil only and continually .... At every renewal of the assertion that the Southern people hate the negroes, my surprise is renewed; but a hostility, not now or heretofore existing, between the races may be engendered by just such influences.[37]

Jefferson Davis was not the only one who saw the danger of outsiders (i.e., Northerners) asserting "that the Southern people hate the negroes." In 1930, Gora Gillam, a former slave, echoed Davis's prophetic warning about outside influence on race relations in the South, when she stated,

> I'll tell you lady, if the rough element from the North had stayed out of the South the trouble of reconstruction would not have happened .... they tried to excite the colored against their white friends. The white folks was still kind to them what had been their

---

35 Hudson Strode, *Jefferson Davis, Tragic Hero* (New York: Harcourt, Brace, and World, 1964), 276.

36 William Samford, as cited in J. Williams Jones, *A Memorial Volume of Jefferson Davis* (1889, Harrisonburg, VA: Sprinkle Publications, 1993), 500.

37 Jefferson Davis, as cited in Varina Howell Davis, II, 748.

slaves. They would have helped them get started. 1 know that. I always say that if the South could of been left to adjust itself both white and colored would have been better off.[38]

In his book *Up From Slavery*, Booker T. Washington notes how the South, even after the passage of time, still resented outside force, especially from the North. This was important to note because of the effect it would have on race relations in the South. Washington's view of racial cooperation in the South follows the general philosophy of the enlightened slave holders, such as Joseph and Jefferson Davis.

[T]he time will come when the Negro in the South will be accorded all the political rights which his ability, character, and material possessions entitle him to .... Just as soon as the South gets over the old feeling that it is being forced by "foreigners," or "aliens," to do something which it does not want to do, I believe that the change in the direction that I have indicated is going to begin. [In speaking of how well he was treated by white officials at the Atlanta Exposition, Washington asserts that] The Atlanta officials went as far as they did because they felt it to be a pleasure, as well as a duty, to reward what they considered merit in the Negro race.[39]

Booker T. Washington also held to the view that, by self-help and self-improvement, black citizens could earn the respect of those who for years had lived and worked beside them, the white race. In an address to his people in Vicksburg, Mississippi, Washington urged his people to strive to become homeowners and taxpayers:

---

38 Cora Gillam, as cited in *Slave Narratives*, Arkansas, III, 27.
39 Booker T. Washington, 234-35.

> Without moral character ... all count for nothing .... No man has a right to live from year to year in a community, to share the protection and the benefits of that community, who does not become a taxpayer and contribute something to the expense of government .... Blacks might as well make up their minds that the South would be their permanent abode ... [and] cultivate the most friendly and cordial relations with the white man by whose side we live.[40]

The voices of former slaves, former Confederates, and a noted black leader all give evidence that former slaves and slave masters could work for their mutual benefit. This is the same message that Senator Jefferson Davis tried get across to his Northern colleagues during the turbulent years before secession became necessary. Rather than condemn Jefferson Davis as an "evil slave holder," we must consider his efforts to better the life of his slaves and prepare them for eventual freedom.

Jefferson Davis, like the first president of the United States, George Washington, was an enlightened slave holder who looked to the future, not to brute force, for the eventual elimination of the institution of slavery. If the first president of the Confederate States of America is to be condemned for being a slave holder, then what shall we do with the legacy of the first president of the United States?

SUMMARY

In this book, you have read the testimony of those who knew Davis in his early life. At this point you should know that this man, Jefferson Davis, was a man with deep convictions. Politically, he believed that the Constitution of these United States was intended to form a union of sovereign states. We have also demonstrated that Jefferson Davis was no "fair weather" patriot of the Union but had served his country both on the field of battle and in the halls of

---

40 Booker T. Washington, as cited in Gordon Cotton, *The Old Court House* (Raymond, MS: Keith Printing Company, Inc., 1982), 66.

Congress. Now, in the final chapter before considering the charge of treason, we have established that the charges against President Davis of conspiracy in the assassination of Abraham Lincoln, conspiring to cause the deaths of Union POWs at Andersonville, and being an evil slave holder desiring to promote slavery in America were all indeed false. Unable to prove their slanderous charges the Yankee Empire conveniently allowed their charges to fade away. These charges served only to inflame public opinion against Davis and the South and provides the Yankee Empire's modern-day apologists an excuse to continue their efforts to drive a wedge of hatred and mistrust between black and white Southerners.[41] Now that you have heard the facts as to the charges that were made against Jefferson Davis, it is time to proceed to the only charge ever brought before a real court of law, the charge of treason.

---

41 The Yankee Empire's effort to divide the South into warring camps of black vs white continues today. The reason for this effort is as old as empire itself. Empires use the technique of "divide and rule" to make it less expensive for the empire to control a formerly free people. See "divide and rule" in Kennedy & Kennedy, *Punished With Poverty-The Suffering South*, 2nd ed. 13, 56, 73, 93, 135, 149, 152, 231.

*Rawle's Textbook on the Constitution was used at West Point.
It taught the right of secession.*

Chapter 11

THE FEDERAL GOVERNMENT'S TEACHING OF SECESSION AT WEST POINT

THE IDEA OF A STATE SECEDING from the Union is so foreign to today's commonly held view of America that it is difficult to find jurors for Jefferson Davis's trial who are not prejudiced against his case. Modern Americans, schooled by the victors of the War for Southern Independence, find it easy to believe that a man who fought against the "American" government is *ipso facto* a traitor. Yet, as demonstrated throughout this book, there was a time when most Americans would have readily acknowledged the state's right of secession. Secession was seen as the ultimate way in which "We the people" of a sovereign state could defend our rights against the unconstitutional actions of the Federal Government. In other words, at the beginning of the American Republic, the institutions of the Federal Government had to be subservient to the Constitution—a constitution ultimately enforced by "We the people" within our sovereign state(s). One of the Founding Fathers, James Madison, explained that there are fundamental principles that take precedence even over the institution of government: "[T]he safety and happiness of society are the objects at which all political institutions must be sacrificed."¹ As so many Southerners would assert during the tragic years of the war and its aftermath, State's Rights and secession are not Southern ideas, they are essential American political principles.

To illustrate the point that State's Rights and secession were not uniquely Southern ideas, many Southerners pointed to a textbook on the United States Constitution that taught secession as a right of the states. The fact that this textbook was written by a Northerner and used at West Point Military Academy made this defense of the South more creditable. The "secession" textbook was written in 1825 by William Rawle of Philadelphia, Pennsylvania, and was titled *A View of the Constitution of the United States of America*² After studying Rawle's textbook, one is left with the feeling that his book could have been written by John C. Calhoun, Jefferson Davis, or any leader of the Confederate States of America. Indeed, many Southern generals defended their role as Confederates by stating that they had been taught at West Point that secession was a right of the states. Early in the history of these United States, secession, the ultimate "State's Right" of a sovereign state, was viewed as an American, not just a Southern idea. Unfortunately, since Appomattox, this point about secession has been censored, shadow-banned, and otherwise slandered or repressed. To better understand this early American view of State's Rights and secession, a scrutiny of William Rawle, his book *A View of the Constitution*, and the use of this book at West Point Military Academy would be enlightening to any jury trying Jefferson Davis for treason.

William Rawle was born in Philadelphia, Pennsylvania, in 1757. He was educated in colonial Philadelphia and England. After the defeat of the British, Rawle was elected to the Pennsylvania state legislature in 1789. In 1791, President George Washington appointed Rawle as United States attorney for Pennsylvania. During that time,

---

1   James Madison, as cited in George W. Carey and James McClellan, eds., *The Federalist* (Dubuque, IA: Kendall/Hunt Publishing Company, 1990), 228.

2   William Rawle's book was published in two editions, the first in 1825 and the second in 1829. His second edition (1829) has been edited and annotated by Kennedy & Kennedy and republished in 2020 under the title, *A View of the Constitution: Secession as Taught at West Point* (Wake Forest, NC: The Scuppernong Press, 2020).

it became his duty to prosecute the individuals responsible for the Whiskey Rebellion in Western Pennsylvania. While the national government was located at Philadelphia, Rawle became friends with both George Washington and Benjamin Franklin. Rawle was also interested in working for the abolition of slavery and, as such, joined and later became the president of the Maryland Society for the Abolition of Slavery. Note that this abolition society was, as were the majority of such organizations prior to 1820, located in a Southern state. [This was before Maryland was repopulated with leftists, federal employees working for the Deep State in Washington, DC].

The first edition of Rawle's book, one of the earliest definitive texts on the United States Constitution, was published in 1825. St. George Tucker's edition of Blackstone's *Commentaries*, with more than two hundred pages dedicated to an analysis of the United States Constitution, preceded Rawle's work by twenty-two years. Rawle's text was followed by James Kent's *Commentaries on American Law* in 1826 and Joseph Story's *Commentaries on the Constitution of the United States* in 1833; these being the major works of many others on the United States Constitution. Since the defeat of the Confederacy, many Northerners have referred to Rawle's book as a radical and seditious view of the Constitution. Yet, if Rawle's book was laced with radical or seditious (secessionist) views, they were completely overlooked by a review of his work published in 1826. The year after Rawle's book was published, it was reviewed by the eminently respected Boston journal, the *North American Review*. In a full and complete analysis of Rawle's book on the United States Constitution, the reviewer stated that Rawle's book was "a safe and intelligent guide"[3] for understanding the Constitution. In light of the charge of treason leveled against Jefferson Davis, the question that begs to be answered is "why did this eminent New England journal not recognize 'treason' in Rawle's book?" Certainly, this was one of the questions that Jefferson Davis hoped to bring before an American court if the Yankee Empire would allow him to be tried for treason. No doubt, this is why many apologists for the Yankee Empire did not

---

3   *North American Review* (1826, New York: AMS Press, Inc., 1965), XXII, 450.

want to allow Jefferson Davis his "day in court." And modern-day apologists for the Yankee Empire are equally determined to prevent these and other pro-Southern facts from become public knowledge.

Not only was Rawle's book warmly reviewed when it first appeared in print, but also, twenty-eight years later, it was still being recommended. In his book, *On Civil Liberty and Self-Government*, Francis Lieber, LL.D., recommended Rawle's book, among others, to his students and former students as a guide to constitutional issues.[4] Lieber's recommendation was made in 1853, only seven years before South Carolina, acting upon the principle as outlined by Rawle, seceded from the Union.

Rawle's text, blessed by a member of Boston's civic and political orthodoxy and by a noted legal educator some twenty-eight years later, has much to say about the nature of the union created by the by the Sovereign States via the original Constitution. In the introduction of his book, Rawle outlines how and under what circumstances republican institutions were created in America.

As to who has the right to make and unmake a government, Rawle unequivocally states, "A moral power equal to and of the same nature with that which make, alone can destroy .... So the people may, on the same principle, at any time alter or abolish the constitution they have formed."[5] But how can the American people "alter or abolish" a government? Is this to be a great democratic experience of the American nation? Hardly so! The act of altering or abolishing is, according to Rawle, to be done by the same power "which made" the Constitution, that is, the state. "It [ratification of the constitution] was not the act of a homogeneous body of men, either large or small. It was to be the act of many independent states, though in a greater

---

4   Francis Lieber, *On Civil Liberty and Self-Government* (Philadelphia: J. B. Lippincott and Co., 1853), 270.

5   Rawle, Kennedy & Kennedy, ed., *A View of the Constitution: Secession as Taught at West Point*, 6-7.

degree the act of the people set in motion by those states; it was to be the act of the people of each state, and *not of the people at large*"6 [emphasis added].

Throughout his book, Rawle leaves little room to question the fact of who created the Federal Government. He clearly states that each state existed as a free and sovereign entity before and after the ratification of the Constitution.

> Each state was naturally tenacious of its own sovereignty and independence, which has been expressly reserved in their antecedent associations, and of which it was still meant to retain all that it did not become unavoidably necessary to surrender .... [T]he people, formed into one mass, as citizens of the union, yet still remaining distinct, as citizens of different states, created a new government, without destroying those which existed before.7

The act of forming the Federal Government was, as Rawle stated, "the act of many independent states." These views were expressed many times by Jefferson Davis, both as a United States senator and as president of the Confederate States of America. But even more important for the defense of Davis was Rawle's view of the actual act of secession.

Rawle's textbook is a thorough study of the United States Constitution and the powers delegated by the states to the Federal Government. Rawle's investigation of the Constitution is more than just an inquiry into the nature of State's Rights and secession; it is a complete investigation of the nature of republican government. After a careful and precise analysis of the Constitution in the first

---

6   Ibid., 7.

7   Rawle, Kennedy & Kennedy, eds., *A View of the Constitution: Secession as Taught at West Point*, 8.

thirty-one chapters of his book, Rawle, in the final chapter, discusses the nature of the American Union and under what conditions it can be dissolved.

In the opening of the final chapter of his book, Rawle states, "[W]e shall conclude with adverting to the principles of its cohesion, and to the provisions it contains for its own duration and extension."[8] The maintenance of the Union, according to Rawle, is predicated upon the existence of republican institutions within the United States. As Rawle explains the issue, these United States are a republic of federated republics, and, as long as a state remains within the federal Union, it is held accountable to all members of that Union to maintain a republican form of government.

As Rawle notes, when a state withdraws from the Union, it is no longer constrained by the former association. When a state is no longer a part of these United States, it resumes all of its formally delegated rights and may perform any and all acts of sovereignty. Once out of the Union, its will is then unquestioned. But in all cases, the will of the people of the state is supreme, and Rawle explains why this is the case.

> To deny this right [secession from the Union] would be inconsistent with the principle on which all our political system are founded, which is, that the people have in all cases, a right to determine how they will be governed.[9]

This right of determining how a people will be governed is the very principle that Jefferson Davis and his fellow Confederates were fighting to maintain in 1861 and the very point Davis desired to make in a court of law in defense against the charge of treason—if the Yankee Empire would only allow him his day in court.

---

8   *Ibid.*, 251.

9   *Ibid.*, 252.

We find in Rawle's examination of the Constitution his theory of how the people of a state would initiate its secession from the Union. Rawle always recurs to the idea that the people within the sovereign community, that is, the state, have the right to determine their own political destiny.

> The secession of a state from the Union depends on the will of the people of such state. The people alone as we have already seen, hold the power to alter their constitutions .... Still, however, the secession must in such case be distinctly and peremptorily declared to take place on that event .... But in either case the people is the only moving power.[10]

In language that cannot be misunderstood, Rawle instructs his readers not only upon the right of a state to secede from the Union, but also upon the formula for how a state should execute the project of secession. It should be noted, following Rawle's model, the Southern states seceded by action of the people of each state in convention. This "convention" process is the same method recommended and adopted by the representatives of the states for their accession into the Union in 1787. The people of a state seceded from the Union under the Articles of Confederation when they acceded into the Union as established by the Constitution. Those who have the ability to make a compact of union are the only ones who have the power to unmake (secede from) that union. In either case, that is, accession or secession, it is the action of the people of a sovereign state who are giving or withdrawing their consent to be governed. True to his republican principles, Rawle demands that the people, the electors of the state, should have the final voice in the act of withdrawing from the Union, and, true to their belief in republican institutions, the people of the South followed Rawle's model in 1861.

Rather than advocating secession at any cost, Rawle warns his readers of the dangers of such an act. It must be remembered that Rawle was not advocating secession "for the fun of it." Rawle viewed

---

10 *Ibid.*, 256.

secession as an option available to the state in defense of the liberty of its people from an intrusive Federal Government. As Rawle points out, a state must consider whether the wrongs inflicted are sufficient to warrant the loss of the benefits derived from membership in the union before secession is initiated. Jefferson Davis made the same point about the act of secession in his farewell address to the United States Senate in 1861:

> A Stale, finding herself in the condition in which Mississippi has judged she is—in which her safety requires that she should provide for the maintenance of her rights out of the Union—surrenders all the benefits (and they are known to be many), deprives herself of the advantages (and they are known to be great), severs all the ties of affection (and they are close and enduring), which have bound her to the Union; and thus divesting herself of every benefit—taking upon herself every burden... [11]

Thus, Rawle invokes the plea of maintaining the common good as the premise for maintenance of the Union. How many times did Jefferson Davis, as representative, as senator, and as secretary of war, make the same appeal? It is clear from reading Rawle's book that this common good is never sufficient reason to negate the will of the people of the individual state. The appeal he makes is an appeal for sober reasoning when the question of secession arises. Not only Rawle but also Englishmen such as Samuel Rutherford in 1644 have clearly stated the issue of who is to make and unmake a government—"Those who have the power to make have the power to unmake."[12] In the American historical context, it has always been "We the people" of the sovereign states who make and unmake governments. The noble example of self-government given the world by America "ought never to be withdrawn while the means of preserving it

---

11 Jefferson Davis, as cited in Kennedy & Kennedy, *The South Was Right!* 3rd edition (1991, 1994, Columbia, SC: Shotwell Publishing, 2020), 423-29.

12 Samuel Rutherford, *Lex Rex* (1644, Harrisonburg, VA: Sprinkle Publications, 1982), 126.

remains."¹³ This self-government can only be maintained by the good will and intent of the parties of the agreement. Thus, as Burke taught the English, one cannot in the name of self-government destroy another person's right to live under a government by the consent of the governed because "you impair the object by your very endeavors to preserve it. The thing you fought for is not the thing which you recover, but depreciated, sunk, wasted, and consumed in the contest."¹⁴ The independent action of free men is essential for the life of free republican governments. The Union as a free association of sovereign states cannot be enforced at the point of a bloody bayonet because force precludes volition. By using bayonets to "save the Union," America's original Republic of Sovereign States became "consumed in the contest."

The idea that a "secessionist" textbook on the United States Constitution was used at West Point Military Academy has caused much discomfort and embarrassment to the victors of the War for Southern Independence. It has been asserted by some that no such book was ever used at West Point, while others have stated that most of the "Confederate" graduates were taught the right of secession at West Point from Rawle's textbook.

As to the question "was Rawle's textbook ever used at West Point?" a qualified "yes" can be given. In *The Centennial of the United States Military Academy at West Point*, we find the following note in reference to Rawle's textbook:

> The text-book of the law department, from (?) to (?). A copy of this book owned by the Library U.S. Military Academy makes it very probable that it was used as a textbook.¹⁵

---

13 Rawle, Kennedy & Kennedy, ed., *A View of the Constitution: Secession as Taught at West Point*, 260.

14 Edmund Burke, "Speech on Conciliation with the Colonies," as cited in M. H. Abrams, ed. *The Norton Anthology of English Literature* (New York: W. W. Norton & Co., 1974), 2356.

15 *The Centennial of the United States Military Academy at West Point*, New York, 1802-1902 (Washington, D.C.: Government Printing Office, 1904), I, 441.

The journal of Gen. S. P. Heintzelman, which he kept as a cadet at West Point, makes references to "recitation and examination in Rawle on the Constitution."[16] Heintzelman was in the graduating class of 1825, the same class as Confederate general Albert Sidney Johnston. Many Southerners confirm the story of Rawle's textbook being used at West Point. No less a personage than President Jefferson Davis agrees that this text was in use at West Point. President Davis states:

> Rawle on the Constitution was the textbook at West Point, but when the class of which I was a member entered the graduating year Kent's *Commentaries* were introduced.[17]

General Fitzhugh Lee made the following statement about the use of Rawle's textbook:

> My recollection is that Rawle's *View of the Constitution* was the legal text-book at West Point when Generals Lee, Joseph E. Johnston and Stonewall Jackson were cadets there and later on was a textbook when I was a cadet there.[18]

In regard to the use of Rawle's textbook at West Point, Confederate general Dabney H. Maury stated, "It is not probable that any of us ever read the Constitution or any exposition of it except this work of Rawle, which we studied in our graduating year at West Point. I know I did not."[19]

---

16 S. P. Heintzelman, as cited in Edgar S. Dudley, "Was 'Secession' Taught at West Point?" *The Century Magazine* (New York: The Century Co., 1909), LXXVIII, 633.

17 Jefferson Davis, as cited in Dudley.

18 Fitzhugh Lee, as cited in Dudley, 634.

19 Dabney H. Maury, as cited in Dudley.

Colonel Edgar S. Dudley, judge-advocate of the United States Army, reviewed the matter of Rawle's textbook being used at West Point Military Academy. Colonel Dudley made the following report in his findings published in 1909:

> It is undoubtedly true that the question of the right of a State to secede was under discussion by cadets and that Rawle's work was often referred to in these discussions and its views quoted in support of the right of secession .... Rawle's work "A View of the Constitution of the United States" was introduced as a textbook by the professor of geography, history, and ethics for one year only (1826) and was then discontinued.[20]

The fact that Rawle's book was used as a textbook at West Point cannot be realistically denied. The evidence also demonstrates that his textbook was used as a reference work years after it was discontinued as an official textbook. Rawle's textbook was superseded by Kent's *Commentaries on American Law*, which served as a text not only for constitutional law, but also for international law.[21] It should be noted that Kent's textbook does not contradict the principles found in Rawle's textbook. Rather than contradict, Kent and Rawle are in agreement on three major constitutional principles: (1) The people have the right to be the judge of what type of government they are to live under, and the duration of that government. For example, Kent states:

> When the government established over any people becomes incompetent to fulfill its purpose, or destructive to the essential ends for which it was

---

20 Dudley, 633-34.

21 *Centennial of United States Military Academy*, I, 441.

instituted, it is the right of that people ... to throw off such government, and provide new guards for their future security.²²

Both Kent and Rawle see this principle of "government by the consent of the governed" as a basic right of mankind. (2) Both Kent and Rawle express a belief in the "State's Rights" view of American government; that is, the states as sovereign entities acting in their sovereign capacities, were the prime movers in the establishment of the United States. In respect to the sovereign nature of the states, Kent leaves no doubt how he feels: "[T]he state governments would clearly retain all those rights of sovereignty which they had before the adoption of the constitution ... and which were not by that constitution *exclusively delegated to the Union*"²³ [emphasis added]. (3) The maintenance of the Union was to be predicated upon mutual respect among the states and not upon brute force. According to Kent, the manner by which the Union was to be maintained was of vital importance "for on the concurrence and good will of the parts, the stability of the whole depends."²⁴ The "*concurrence* and *good will*," not bayonets, would hold the Union together.

Kent's *Commentaries on American Law* continued in use at West Point until 1880. In 1886, T. M. Cooley's *The General Principles of Constitutional Law in the United States* was substituted as the textbook on constitutional law.²⁵ Cooley had already proven himself to be a loyal advocate of government by centralized power (see T. M. Cooley, *A Treatise on Constitutional Limitations*) and was therefore acceptable to those advocating the policies of the victor of the War for Southern Independence. He was in fact an apologist for the Yankee Empire. It should be noted that only after the defeat of the Confederacy did the views of those advocating federal supremacy begin to be taught at West Point.

---

22 James Kent, *Commentaries on American Law* (1826, New York: Da Capo Press, 1971), I, 195-96.

23 Kent, 363.

24 *Ibid.*, 369.

25 *Centennial of United States Military Academy*, I, 441.

Jefferson Davis and his attorneys were eager to present this information about Rawle's textbook on the United States Constitution and its use at West Point before a jury. A most important aspect about the use of Rawle's textbook is that, even though it contains a pro-secession message, it was never (before 1860) declared a seditionist or treasonous book. A New England journalist in 1825 and one of America's leading jurists in 1853 had both endorsed Rawle's book, without reservations regarding its teaching on secession. It was used as a textbook and a reference book at West Point Military Academy for more than thirty years, yet no one in the Federal Government came forth to declare this book un-American or treasonous. Why? The answer to that question is the very reason Jefferson Davis's accusers feared allowing him to stand trial for treason. The act of secession by a sovereign state is not un-American or treasonous; it is the most American thing a free people of a sovereign American state can do. Many pre-War students at West Point read what Rawle clearly states about secession: "The secession of a state from the Union depends on the will of the people of such state." Jefferson Davis's accusers had hoped that you, the jury, would never read those words.

When faced with such overwhelming evidence that the states do indeed have the right to secede from the Union, many opponents of Southern independence will proclaim, "Yes, but you lost the war!" In effect, this statement concedes to us the points we have always asserted; that is, that Southerners were fighting for rights under the Constitution and were therefore not "traitors." This very point was made by a Confederate veteran in 1900 when he stated:

> Appomattox was not a judicial forum: it was only a battlefield, a test of physical force, where the starving remnant of the Army of Northern Virginia, "wearied with victory," surrendered to "overwhelming numbers and resources." We make no appeal from that judgment, on the issue of force. But when we see the victors in that contest, meeting year by year, and using the superior means at their command, to publish to the world that they were *right* and that we were

wrong in that contest, saying that we were "rebels" and "traitors," in defending our homes and firesides against their cruel invasion, that we had no legal right to withdraw from the Union, when we only asked to be let alone, and that we brought on that war: we say, when these, and other wicked and false charges are brought against us from year to year, and attempt is systematically made to teach our children that these things are true, and therefore, that we do not deserve their sympathy and respect because of our alleged wicked and unjustifiable course in that war and in bringing it on—*then it becomes our duty*, not only to ourselves and our children, but to the thousands of brave men and women who gave their lives a "free-will offering" in defense of the principles for which we fought, to vindicate the justice of our cause, and to do this we have to appeal only to the bar of truth and of justice.[26]

RAWLE ON TREASON

Rawle uses an entire chapter to address the topic of treason. In chapter 11, (1829 edition) titled "Of Treason against the United States," Rawle outlines the factors that make a charge of treason legitimate. Not a single word is mentioned about secession or withdrawing from the Union as being an act of treason. Rebellion in which a group attempt to overthrow the government is discussed but that is entirely distinct from secession as described by Rawle and others.

---

26 Hunter McGuire and George L. Christian, *The Confederate Cause and Conduct in the War Between the States* (1907, Boonton, NJ: Boonton Bookshop, 1994), 138-39.

Summary

You, the jury, now represent the "bar of truth and of justice." It is to you that we offer these facts and make the plea to find Jefferson Davis, and through him the South, innocent of the charge of treason. Jefferson Davis's desire for a fair trial in court and the above quoted elderly Confederate veteran's plea to be heard before "the bar of truth and of justice," must not go unanswered—*if this is truly a nation "with liberty and justice for all."*

Photos

Varina Howell Davis Post-War she became a leading defender of her husband and the South.

Davis family at home at Beauvoir, in Biloxi, Mississippi circa 1885.

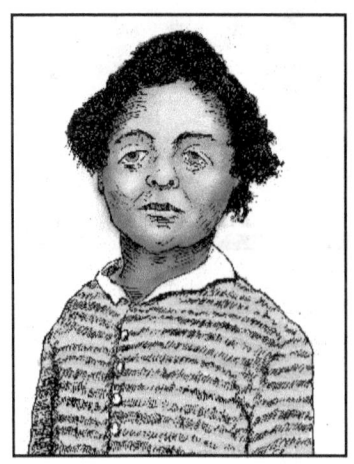

Jim Limber, black orphan adopted by President and Mrs. Davis during the War. Jim was kidnapped by Yankee troops when President Davis was captured and never heard from again.

President Franklin Pierce: Fourteenth president of the U.S.A. He was a life long friend of Jefferson Davis. In 1853 he warned, "The dangers of a concentration of all power in the general government of a confederacy so vast as ours are too obvious to be disregarded."

Sergent Smith Prentiss: A note Mississippi orator. When Davis and his Mississippians came back from the Mexican-American War as heroes, Prentiss was called upon to deliver the homecoming oration to Davis and his troops.

Alexander H. Stephens, former VP Confederate States of America.

Leonidas Polk, Bishop and Confederate General.

First White House of the Confederacy in Montgomery, Alabama.

Warren County Courthouse, Vicksburg, MS: Upon this courthouse square, Jefferson Davis made his debut into politics. From the cupola atop the courthouse in July 1862, three Confederate generals watched the CSS Arkansas take on and defeat the Union blockading fleet.

Sarah Knox Taylor, daughter of President Zachary Taylor and first wife of Jefferson Davis. Sarah is interred in St. Francisville, LA.

General Richard Taylor, son of President Zachary Taylor, brother-inlaw of Jefferson Davis, and Lt. General Confederate States of America.

President Zachary Taylor, hero of Mexican War and 12th president of the United States and close friend to Jefferson and Varina Davis.

Jefferson Davis Memorial Obelisk Fairview, Kentucky located at the site of Jefferson Davis' birth.

Beauvoir Biloxi, Mississippi on the grounds of the Jefferson Davis Presidential Library.

The National Confederate Museum, Columbia, Tennessee, owned and operated by the National Sons of Confederate Veterans. Change to the following: The National Confederate Museum and Headquarters of the Sons of Confederate Veterans, Columbia, TN. Museum owned and operated by the National Sons of Confederate Veterans.

Chapter 12

THE CHARACTER OF PRESIDENT DAVIS'S ACCUSERS

WHO ARE THOSE WHO labeled President Jefferson Davis as a traitor? What type of men were they? What were their motives? These are very important questions that must be answered if you, the jury, are to gain a proper understanding of the allegations made against him. In short, you must analyze and determine the credibility of those who accused President Davis of treason. You must answer for yourself whether their words are worthy of belief. Would such men make believable witnesses in a court of law?

Credibility is that quality in a witness which renders his evidence worthy of belief. A credible person is one who is trustworthy and entitled to be believed. In law and legal proceedings, a credible person is one who is entitled to have his oath or affidavit accepted as reliable, not only on account of his good reputation for veracity, but also on account of his intelligence, knowledge of the circumstances, and disinterested relation to the matter in question.[1] In the previous chapters, you have been given an opportunity to evaluate President Davis's character. It is now time for you to evaluate the character of those who represent the Yankee Empire's anti-secession school—those who believe that President Davis was guilty of the high crime of treason. You must determine if the witnesses for the prosecution possess the required characteristics of a credible witness. You must determine if those who belong to the Yankee Empire's anti-secession

---

1   Black's Law Dictionary.

school (1) have a good reputation for veracity, (2) are intelligent and knowledgeable of the Constitution and the circumstances of its proposal and of its ratification, and (3) are representative of men who have no special (finical, ideological, or political) interest in the controversy at issue. If these witnesses fail to pass the above-mentioned test on any of these accounts, then their testimony and allegations must be viewed with much caution and doubt.

Those who accused President Davis of being a traitor are representative of the Yankee Empire's anti-secessionist school of political thought. They generally described themselves as "unconditional Union men." For our purposes, we will look at two of these men who represent the victorious Yankee Empire, Secretary of War William H. Seward and John L. Motley. In addition, we will look at the two men who at an earlier time established themselves as the spokesmen and advocates of the Yankee Empire's school of centralized, supreme, federalism, United States senator Daniel Webster and Supreme Court justice Joseph Story. We will cite their own words and compare those words with the historical record. From this you, the jury, will be able to assess the credibility of President Davis's accusers.

WILLIAM SEWARD: WORDS AND "HIGHER LAW"

As we have already seen in Chapter 7, Jefferson and Varina Davis became friends with Seward while both men were serving in Congress. The one point that amazed and alarmed them about Seward was the fact that he freely admitted that he would say anything necessary to "affect the rank and file of the North."[2] Varina noted that Seward was the type of individual who held the view that "political strife was a state of war, and in war all stratagems were fair."[3] Here we have a prominent United States political leader who admitted that he used words not to convey truth and to preserve the constitutional balance necessary for the maintenance of the federal Union, but for the impact his words would have on the masses! This willingness to use

---

2   Varina Howell Davis, *Jefferson Davis, A Memoir by His Wife* (Belford Company Publishers, 1890), I, 581.

3   *Ibid.*

words as political tools was shocking to the Davises who disciplined themselves according to the rigid standards of honor and truth. By his own admission, William Seward negated his presumed claim of veracity. He was not too dissimilar from the Northern congressman who, prior to the War for Southern Independence, busied himself with heated speeches against the South at various Abolitionist meetings. After delivering an extremely vicious anti-South speech, he was approached by a friend and asked, "Why do you say such harsh things against the South when you know they are not true?" His response was, "The South will not give us an increase in Tariffs and so we touch them where they feel it the most."[4] Yes, truth or justice in political discourse is not the central theme for all people, as it was for Jefferson Davis. What is important for some is the consequence that unfounded words will have on the mind of the general public. Of course, this impact is calculated to ensure certain politicians will be safe during the next election.

Seward was an advocate of the "higher law" theory of American government. Basically, this theory claimed that the Constitution was not the supreme law of the land regarding political institutions. "Higher law" theorists claimed that if the Constitution stood in the way of some program that they, the advocates of "higher law," viewed as desirable, then they could justify the program on some "higher law" principle and simply ignore the limitations otherwise imposed by the Constitution—today this liberal constitutional theory is often referred to as the doctrine of the "living Constitution." For example, they would claim that the term "created equal" in the Declaration of Independence could be used to justify any law Congress wanted to pass to ensure absolute equality (equality of outcome) even if it violated political limitations imposed on the Federal Government by the Constitution. According to this radical theory, the Constitution should be subservient to any principle based upon a "higher law." It can easily be seen that this "higher law" theory would destroy the constitutional limits placed upon the Federal Government by the Founding Fathers. This was just what the Yankee Empire's political leaders wanted because, before the War and certainly after the War,

---

4 Mildred L. Rutherford, *Truths of History* (Athens, GA: M. L. Rutherford Publisher, 1907), 98.

they were the numerical majority in the Yankee Empire. "Higher law" theories are a direct attack upon the constitutional Republic of Sovereign States as established by the Founding Fathers.

Southerners did not accept this attack upon the handiwork of the Founding Fathers[5] without making strenuous reply. Senator C. C. Clay from Alabama declared that Northerners could not justify ignoring the Constitution until they fabricated their theory of "higher law." He warned that when such people gain control of the United States "the Southern States must elect between independence out of the Union or subordination within it."[6] It is interesting to note that the advocates of "higher law" theories did not attempt to amend the Constitution to reflect their views. They did not attempt to defend, on constitutional grounds, their assertions of this new power and authority over "We the people" of the sovereign states. They simply relied upon their possession of the power of the numerical majority to foist this extra constitutional system of government upon the Southern people. The South, representing the numerical minority and, therefore, not possessing the power in Congress to prevent the "higher law" theorists from conducting their campaign against the legitimately constituted government of the federal Union, saw its rights eroding. By 1861, the South was faced with the choice of remaining in the Union and allowing the liberties of its people to be abused by the Yankee Empire's numerical majority or withdrawing from the Union and establishing a new Union that would be conducive to the maintenance of the government delivered to them from the Founding Fathers.

---

5   When referring to the Founding Fathers, the authors not only include all those who attended the constitutional convention of 1787 in Philadelphia but, also, those writers of *The Federalist Papers* and of *The Anti-Federalist Papers*, and those men who debated the potential ratification of the proposed constitution in the constitutional convention of each sovereign state.

6   C.C. Clay, as cited in Marshall L. DeRosa, *The Confederate Constitution of 1861* (Columbia: University of Missouri Press, 1991), 15.

MOTLEY'S FOLLY

According to Albert T. Bledsoe, author of *Is Davis a Traitor?*, after the end of the War for Southern Independence, John L. Motley played a large role in clothing the Yankee Empire's naked aggression by concocting a pseudo-constitutional justification for the Yankee Empire's invasion of its former sister states. Bledsoe condemned Motley's justification for the invasion and coercion of the sovereign states of the South. Motley's justification for Yankee aggression was published in *The Rebellion Record*.[7] Motley's logic contained nothing new or original. He followed almost word for word the speeches and writings of Daniel Webster and Joseph Story. It will suffice here to quote only the logic given by Motley to justify the Yankee Empire's aggression. In the following text, we will demonstrate his total lack of historical and constitutional accuracy.

The South, as well as every other section in the post-colonial era, maintained that the sovereign states, acting on their own volition and under no compulsion outside of the will and by the consent of "We the people" of each individual state, acceded to the Union by ratifying the Constitution. This small word "accede" creates major problems for those who declare that secession is treason. The plain logic is that "secede" is the constitutional antonym for "accede." Therefore, if a sovereign state accedes to the Constitutional Union, then, as a sovereign state, it has the right to secede from that same Union, unless that right has been clearly and deliberately deposited with the Federal Government.[8] This conclusion is based upon the principle that a sovereign, whether a state, nation, or monarch, has the right to enter into any agreement desired, but the act of entering into an agreement does not encumber the sovereign's right at a later time to modify or withdraw completely from such agreement. We shall see that Northern political leaders used numerous subterfuges

---

7   Albert T. Bledsoe, *Is Davis a Traitor?* (1866, St. Louis: The Advocate Publishing House, 1879), 7.

8   And even it the right to secede had been surrendered to the Federal Government, the act of a prior generation cannot abridge or negate the right of a future generation to follow the example of the Declaration of Independence and "alter or to abolish" existing government and "to institute new government."

to craftily attack and eventually defeat the plain language of the Constitution. In the case of the word "accede," Motley made a simple frontal assault by declaring, "The States never acceded to it [the Constitution], and possess no power to secede from it."[9] Thus, we see one of the leaders of the North denying that states ever acceded to the Constitution; this is the same leadership that would accuse President Davis of treason. We will turn to the historical record relative to this small word "accede" when we look at Webster and Story, but for now, let us look at other statements of this Yankee leader who typifies those who accuse President Davis of treason. Such slanderous words are used today by anti-South Yankees who hate the traditional South as well as our home-grown contemporary Southern Scallywags of both political parties.

Pursuing its aggressive war policy against the Confederate States of America, the Yankee Empire's leadership was often embarrassed by the South's repeated reference to the fact that the Founding Fathers specifically refused to style the Union created by the states' ratification of the Constitution as a "perpetual Union." Motley, writing in the *Rebellion Record*, gave the Northern response for why the Founding Fathers failed to declare the "more perfect Union" to be a perpetual Union. He declared, "How could it do so? ... It would have been puerile for the Constitution to say formally to each State, thou shall not secede."[10] Would it have been *puerile* (i.e., immature or childish) to inform the states that they did not have the right to secede? How can this assertion be maintained in the light of Article I, Section 10, of the Constitution? In that portion of the Constitution, the states had no problems defining the areas in which they would delegate complete power to the Union. Language cannot be clearer: Article I, Section 10, Paragraph 1, unequivocally states, "No State shall ... grant Letters of Marque and Reprisal; coin money ... pass Bill of Attainder"; Paragraph 2 states, "No State shall, without the Consent of Congress, lay any Imposts or Duties on Imports or Exports"; and Paragraph 3 states, "No State shall, without the Consent of Congress ... keep Troops, or Ships of War in time of Peace." If the constitutional

---

9 John Motley, as cited in Bledsoe, 56.
10 Bledsoe, 138.

convention, the Founding Fathers, and the ratifying conventions of the several states did not find Article I, Section 10, to be too "puerile," why should they have balked at inserting a prohibition on secession? After all, the previous constitution that established the union under the Articles of Confederation declared that union to be perpetual. But here, we see Motley's dilemma—despite what was written on the pages of the constitution under the Articles of Confederation, the states did in fact remove themselves from that union, perpetual or not! The sovereign states, under the Articles of Confederation, did exactly what Motley and the Articles of Confederation said they could not do; that is, they seceded from the union even though that union, in numerous places, was branded as being perpetual. Yes, these same states seceded from a union styled perpetual in order to join a union that was not styled/branded perpetual. But following Motley's logic, if it were "puerile" for the Founding Fathers to deny the right of secession in the Constitution in 1787, where did the Yankee Empire acquire this awesome right to do so in 1861? How did the Yankee Empire become possessed of a right that, according to Motley, the Founding Fathers did not dare use? In other words, if Washington, Jefferson, Adams, Hamilton, and company did not, with pens in hand, possess the desire to deny secession, how then could the Yankee Empire in 1861 claim the right to use the moral suasion of bloody bayonets to deny the right of secession?

In another place, Motley denounced the principle of secession because, in his view, "The States never acceded to the Constitution, and have no power to secede from it."[11] (The facts as to who acceded to the Union under the new Constitution will be addressed fully in another portion of this defense of Davis.) Albert Taylor Bledsoe, a noted apologist (i.e., defender of Jefferson Davis and the South) demonstrated how illogical Motley's statements were in the following statement:

> [T]he [constitutional] Convention, in its desire to secede from the old compact [Articles of Confederation], was so greatly embarrassed by the clause declaring that "the

---

11 *Ibid.*, 7.

Union shall be perpetual," that it deliberately removed that obstacle from the path of future legislation: and, whether it was intended by the Convention or not, the legal effect of this was to establish the right of secession under the new compact between the same parties.[12]

From the foregoing narrative, you, the jury, can begin to see an emerging picture of the character of those who would accuse President Davis and the South of treason. You have only begun to see documented examples of the Yankee Empire's apologists who were so wedded to sectional political ideology that they were willing to say anything that might serve their interests or mask their cruel and evil acts. Jefferson Davis, in *The Rise and Fall of the Confederate Government*, took note of Motley's ridiculous views of the Constitution. Davis, after recounting Motley's statement that the Constitution was "ordained and established over the States by a power superior to the States," pointed out that "[i]t would be very hard to condense a more amazing amount of audacious and reckless falsehood in the same space. In all Mr. Motley's array of bold assertions, there is not one single truth."[13] Let us now look at the two men who most nearly incorporate the totality of the ideology used by the Yankee Empire to wage war upon the Constitutional Union.

Senator Daniel Webster and Justice Joseph Story— Advocates of Centralized Federal Power

At the inception of the Union under the new Constitution, there was near parity in the control of the Federal Government between the Northern and Southern sections of the United States. But, by 1861, the Northern numerical majority had claimed the position of supreme leader of, what had become, the Yankee Empire. Yet, there were more elements changing than just population. As time progressed, the political philosophy of the North took a marked turn from the philosophy of the Founding Fathers. This new theory

---

12 *Ibid.*, 139.

13 William M. Coats, ed., Jefferson Davis, *The Rise and Fall of the Confederate Government* (1881, Nashville, TN: Bill Coats, Ltd., 1996), I, 129-30.

taught that the American people were "one people" and therefore the American nation was "indivisible." In other words, this new theory of American government taught that the states were not sovereign but served only as political subdivisions of the larger nation. Therefore, according to this new theory of the Constitution, the states had no more rights relative to the national government than a county has relative to the state government. A word of warning to you, the jury. You have been influenced by the massive pressure of the Yankee Empire's ideology (anti-South slander) as taught in schools, television documentaries, Hollywood, and the mainstream/digital media. You must keep an open mind as we investigate the origins of the modern concept of "one people, one nation indivisible." You may be surprised to discover that the idea of national sovereignty was not held by the majority of the Founding Fathers, neither North nor South. Although this pernicious idea has always been present in American political life, in the early history of America it only had a small following, and only began to take root well after the establishment of the American Republic of Sovereign States. The notion that these United States were established as the result of the action of "one people" rather than the action of sovereign states, so infuriated Jefferson Davis that he referred to those advocating the "one people" theory as "advocates of this mischievous dogma."[14] Since Appomattox, the theory of national sovereignty as opposed to state sovereignty has assumed a stranglehold upon the rights of "We the people" of the sovereign states.[15] It has resulted in the elimination of local self-government.

In order to assure a full understanding of the accusation of treason made against President Davis, we will present the plain words of the historical records relative to the issue of national (supreme Federalism) versus state sovereignty. We will demonstrate to you, the jury, what poor historians Senator Daniel Webster and Justice Joseph Story were. We will demonstrate to you, from the words of the Founding Fathers, that their original intentions were viciously assailed by the emerging Yankee Empire's two premier leaders under

---

14 *Ibid.*, 131.

15 Kennedy & Kennedy, *Yankee Empire: Aggressive Abroad and Despotic at Home* (Columbia, SC: Shotwell Publishing, 2018), 75-90.

this new theory of "one people, one nation indivisible." You will see that it was President Jefferson Davis of the Confederate States of America and the men who wore the gray in the War for Southern Independence who were the true defenders of the principles of the original Constitutional Union! You will see that, at best, Senator Webster and Justice Story misled their own people because of their faulty conclusions drawn from their imperfect understanding of the Constitution or, at worst, they intentionally committed fraud upon the mind of the Northern public.

The States Acceded to the Union Created by the Constitution.

The history of the South, from its earliest point, offers evidence of the type of government its people desired. Francis Butler Simkins, a noted Southern historian, points out that the propensity of the South for limited *decentralized* government has been asserted twice, once against the central government in London and once against the central government in Washington: *"The Southern feeling for state's rights has a Colonial background"*[16] [emphasis added].

As we have noted, the South, from the earliest times of American history, held the position that sovereign states voluntarily acceded to the Union by the specific act of each state ratifying the Constitution proposed in 1787. Northerners such as Webster and Story denied that the states acceded to the Constitution and declared the word "accede" to be an "unconstitutional" word. According to Webster, "This word 'accede,' [is] not found either in the Constitution itself, or in the ratification of it by any one of the States."[17] In his defense of President Davis, Albert T. Bledsoe pointed out that Webster stated that the term "accede" was "out of place," that the South through the office of John C. Calhoun had introduced a "new word" that Webster claimed the people of the United States had never used. As Bledsoe noted, Webster accused the South of using "unconstitutional language."[18] But how stand the facts? Is this really "a new word"?

---

16 Francis Butler Simkins, *A History of the South* (New York: Alfred A. Knopf, 1959), 58.

17 Edwin P. Whipple, ed., *The Great Speeches and Orations of Daniel Webster* (Boston, MA: Little, Brown, & Co., 1894), 276.

18 Bledsoe, 12.

Who is correct, the spokesmen for the emerging Yankee Empire or the spokesmen for the South? Let us look at the record to determine if the spokesmen for the South attempted to inject a "new" and "unconstitutional" word (i.e., "accede") into the debate regarding the legitimate limits of federal powers:

- In the constitutional convention of 1787, James Wilson of Pennsylvania declared that he preferred "a partial Union" of states, "with the door open for the *accession* of the rest."[19]

- Elbert Gerry, a delegate from Massachusetts, was opposed to "a partial confederacy, leaving other States to *accede* or not to *accede*, as had been intimated."[20]

- James Madison used the term "to *accede*" in the convention of 1787, describing the eventual adoption of the proposed "new form of government by the States."[21]

- Governor John Randolph of Virginia reported that "the *accession* of eight States reduced our [Virginia's] deliberations to the single question of Union or no Union."[22]

- Patrick Henry, speaking during Virginia's ratification convention, slated, "If it [the proposed constitution] be amended, every State will *accede* to it."[23]

- William Grayson of Virginia posed this question to the delegates to Virginia's ratification convention who were debating whether to adopt the proposed Constitution: "Does she [Virginia] gain anything from her central position by *acceding* to that paper ... ?"[24]

---

19 James Wilson, as cited in *Ibid.*, 13.
20 Elbert Gerry, *Ibid.*
21 James Madison, *Ibid.*
22 John Randolph, *Ibid.*
23 Patrick Henry, *Ibid.*
24 William Grayson, *Ibid.*, 14.

- Benjamin Franklin stated: "Our new Constitution is now established with eleven States, and the *accession* of a twelfth is soon expected."[25]

- George Washington noted, "If these, with the States eastward and northward of us, should *accede* to the Federal Government. ... "[26]

- Chief Justice John Marshall, in his *Life of Washington*, noted the fact that "North Carolina *accedes* to the Union."[27]

- Justice Joseph Story's own words about the Constitution were that "Rhode Island did not *accede* to it until more than a year after it had been in operation"[28] [emphasis added].

The Southern defenders of the original Constitutional Union, such as Jefferson Davis, understood the Constitution to have been created by the act of sovereign states as they *acceded* to it. Webster and Story denied that the states ever acceded to the Constitution. Webster even declared that the word "accede is wholly out of place." Webster then stated that the South was guilty of introducing "this new word" (accede) into America's political language and that the "States used no such form of expression in establishing the present Government .... It is unconstitutional language." Now, you, the jury, have read the words of the Founding Fathers; you have the allegations of the leaders of the emerging Yankee Empire's school of "one people, one nation indivisible" before you. You must make the determination as to who is correct. You must decide who is the most credible party in this controversy.

The Constitution is a Compact Between Sovereign States.

Both Daniel Webster and Joseph Story attacked the concept of the Constitution as a compact among sovereign states and advocated the concept of the Constitution establishing a system of

---

25 Benjamin Franklin, *Ibid*.
26 George Washington, *Ibid*.
27 John Marshall, *Ibid*.
28 Joseph Story, *Ibid*.

national sovereignty—a supreme Federal Government, a precursor to the emerging Yankee Empire that would eventually be created by Lincoln and the Republican Party. Unfortunately, because of the Yankee Empire's victory in the War for Southern Independence (the victors write the officially accepted and <u>enforced</u> history),[29] most modern-day Americans have accepted the Yankee Empire's view of the Constitution. But it was not until 1833 that prominent Americans would dare to assert that the Constitution of the United States was not a compact among the states. This new doctrine was published by Story in his *Commentaries on the Constitution of the United States*, and by Webster in "the greatest intellectual effort of his life," that is, in his great speech in the Senate on the sixteenth of February, 1833. Until that time, it was an accepted fact of American political life that the Constitution was a compact among sovereign states. Story's Commentaries, written in 1833, stand in direct contradiction not only to commonly held opinion but also to the works of prior constitutional scholars such as James Kent's (New York) *Commentaries on American Law*, published in 1826; William Rawle's (Pennsylvania) *A View of the Constitution of the United States of America*, published in 1825; and St. George Tucker's (Virginia) analysis of the federal constitution in his edition of Blackstone's *Commentaries on the Laws of England*, published in 1803. Story, as a representative of that class of Americans who desired an enlargement in the power of the United States' central government, understood the effect his concept of national sovereignty would have upon the growth of the Federal Government. No doubt, Story understood that the sovereign states would attempt to prevent the Federal Government from usurping the rights of the states. Therefore, Story dedicated himself to the labor of removing this grand American hindrance to centralized federal power. Writing about state sovereignty (i.e., States' Rights theory of federalism) Story scornfully declared, "The obvious deductions which may be, and, indeed, have been, drawn from considering the Constitution a compact between States, are that it operates as a mere treaty or convention between them, and has an obligatory force upon each

---

29 Kennedy & Kennedy, *The South Was Right!* 3rd edition, (1991, 1994, Columbia, SC: Shotwell Publishing, 2020), 21-34.

State no longer, than suits its pleasure or its consent continues ... and that each retains the power to withdraw from the Confederacy and to dissolve the connection, when such shall be its choice."[30] Story's critics claimed that he was such an ardent advocate of increased federal power that he would "find Federal Admiralty jurisdiction over a corn cob floating in a pail of water."[31]

Story acknowledged his departure from accepted constitutional theory in his famous Commentaries when he declared the States' Rights views of St. George Tucker as that view "representing ... the opinions of a large body of statesmen and jurists in different parts of the Union, avowed and acted upon in former times."[32] Thus, the great controversy over secession and treason can be narrowed down to the single question: is the Constitution a compact among the states?

Daniel Webster denied in the strongest language that a constitution is a compact and also that a compact is a constitution. Webster boldly asserted that it is new language to call "the Constitution a compact."[33] In yet another place, Webster charged that Senator John C. Calhoun of South Carolina "introduces a new word of his own, viz., 'compact'... and degrades the Constitution into an insignificant idle epithet attached to compact."[34] Albert T. Bledsoe, writing in defense of President Davis in his famous work of 1866, *Is Davis a Traitor?*, asked, "why the Northern States should wish to get rid of both the idea of a compact and of the word; why the powerful should wish to obliterate and erase from the tablets of their memory every recollection and vestige of the solemn compact or bargain into which they had entered with the weak, but which

---

30 Joseph Story, *Commentaries on the Constitution of the United States* (1833, New York: Da Capo Press, 1970), I, 287-88.

31 "It was said of the late Justice Story, that if a bucket of water were brought into his court with a corn cob floating in it, he would at once extend the admiralty jurisdiction of the United States over it." 37 Am. L. Rev. 911, 916 (1903).

32 Story, I, 287.

33 Whipple, 275.

34 Daniel Webster, Whipple.

they have never observed in good faith."³⁵ Why indeed! The answer is simple. To allow the truth about the constitutional compact to go unchallenged would be to allow a hindrance to stand between them and their dreams of a grand nation—an Empire—controlled by and for the political, social, and commercial benefit of the Northern numerical majority!

According to Webster, "The man is almost untrue to his country who calls the Constitution a compact."³⁶ Now that we have considered the wisdom of the leaders of the Yankee Empire's school of "one people, one nation indivisible," let us move on to compare their wisdom with that of the Founding Fathers. Let us inquire of the historical record to determine if the Founding Fathers considered the proposed constitution to be in any sense a compact. After a careful review of the plain words of history, it should become clear who is correct—who is the more credible witness.

- Gouverneur Morris of Pennsylvania, it is well known, was one of the most celebrated advocates for a strong national government in the convention of 1787; and yet, in that assembly, he stated that he "came here to form a *compact* for the good of America. He was ready to do so with all the States. He hoped and believed that all would enter into such a *compact* .... But as the *compact* was to be voluntary, it is in vain for the Eastern States to insist on what the Southern States will never agree to."³⁷

- Elbert Gerry, the representative of Massachusetts, said, "If nine out of thirteen [states] can dissolve the *compact*, six out of nine will be just as able to dissolve the new one hereafter."³⁸

- James Madison, [in describing the Constitution referred to the Union as] "the *pact*."³⁹

---

35 Bledsoe, 24.
36 Daniel Webster, as cited in Whipple, 278.
37 Gouverneur Morris, as cited in Bledsoe, 24.
38 Elbert Gerry, *Ibid.*
39 James Madison, *Ibid.*

- In the Virginia Resolution of 1798, Madison wrote of "the Federal Government as resulting from the *compact*, to which the States are parties." Again, in his almost equally celebrated letter to Edward Everett, in 1830, he called the Constitution "a *compact* among the States in their highest sovereign capacity." In the same letter, Madison spoke of the states as "the parties to the Constitutional *compact*."[40]

- Even Daniel Webster himself at one time spoke of the Constitution as a compact! Though his memory often failed him in this regard, history records that during the debate on Sen. Henry S. Foote's resolution he referred to "accusations which impute to us a disposition to evade the Constitutional *compact*." Unfortunately for America, his memory[41] failed him just three short years later when he suddenly discovered that there was no compact called the Constitution.

- The first Chief Justice of the Supreme Court, John Jay, though a strong advocate of increased federal power, in the case of *Chisholm v. State of Georgia*, "expressly declares that the Constitution of the United States is a *compact*." [42]

- John Quincy Adams, sixth president of the United States, admitted that "[o]ur Constitution of the United States and all our State Constitutions, have been voluntary *compacts*." [43]

- Edmund Pendleton, president of the ratifying convention of Virginia in 1788, in the course of his argument in favor of the new constitution, said, "This is the only Government founded in real *compact*."[44]

---

40 *Ibid.*, 25.
41 Daniel Webster, *Ibid.*
42 John Jay, *Ibid.*, 26.
43 John Quincy Adams, *Ibid.*
44 Edmund Pendleton, *Ibid.*

- St. George Tucker, in his edition of *Blackstone's Commentaries*, repeatedly called the Constitution "a *compact* .... It is a federal *compact* ... they [the states] will together form a federal republic .... The union is in fact, as well as in theory, an association of states, or, a confederacy."[45]

- Thomas Jefferson specifically noted that "[t]he States entered into a *compact* which is called the Constitution of the United States."[46]

- Daniel Webster's home state of Massachusetts, in its ratification convention, declared that its citizens were "entering into an explicit and solemn *compact* ...."[47]

- James Madison in *The Federalist* No. 39, denoted the Constitution as "the *compact*." Madison, also in *The Federalist* No. 39, reaffirmed the generally accepted view that "[e]ach State in ratifying the Constitution, is considered as a *sovereign* body independent of all others, and only to be bound by its own voluntary act."[48]

- Alexander Hamilton, in *The Federalist* No. 85, described the Constitution as "[t]he *compacts* which are to embrace thirteen distinct States, in a common bond of amity and Union." He also noted that, if any changes were made, said changes "must undergo a new decision of each State." He noted that any constitution for the United States must accommodate "thirteen independent states" ... "to satisfy the parties to the *compact*."[49]

---

[45] St. George Tucker, *Blackstone's Commentaries, With Notes of Reference to the Constitution and Laws of the Federal Government of the United States* (1803, New York: Augustus M. Kelley Publishers, 1969), I, 141.

[46] Thomas Jefferson, as cited in Bledsoe, 26.

[47] Arthur Taylor Prescott, *Drafting the Federal Constitution* (Baton Rouge, LA: Louisiana State University Press, 1941), 170.

[48] James Madison, as cited in George W. Carey and James McClellan, eds., *The Federalist* (Dubuque, IA: Kendall/Hunt Publishing, Co., 1990), 197.

[49] Alexander Hamilton, Carey & McClellan, 452.

- Hamilton also described the constitution of New York as "the *compact* made between the society at large and each individual .... If the community have good reason for abrogating the old *compact* and establishing a new one it undoubtedly had a right to do it; but until the *compact* is dissolved with the same solemnity and certainty with which it was made, the society, as well as individuals, are bound by it." Here, Hamilton was in agreement with Judge William Rawle (as discussed in Chapter 11) that, those who make also have the power to unmake any government.[50]

The principle that "those who have the power to make, also have the power to unmake" is the primary reason the Yankee Empire sought to deny that the states ratified the Constitution. For, if "We the people" of the sovereign states are acknowledged as the ones who created the United States government, then, "We the people" of the sovereign states can unmake that government. To put it bluntly, if sovereign states ratified the compact, then sovereign states have the authority to rescind (unmake), withdraw, or secede from the union formed by that compact; therefore, secession is not treason, and Jefferson Davis must be acquitted of that charge.

Daniel Webster said that the Constitution is "certainly not a compact." He laid great stress on the fact that it does not call itself a compact. We have already demonstrated what a poor logician Webster was, but, with this assertion, we have one more piece of evidence to demonstrate that fact. Webster said that the Constitution is not a compact because it does not call itself a compact. But he either forgot or else he never knew that the old Articles of Confederation did not call itself a compact either; and yet Webster admitted that the Articles of Confederation was "a compact between the States."[51] Webster's sophism, claiming that since the word "compact" is not found in the Constitution and, therefore, the idea of "compact" is alien to our form of government, can be a dangerous line of reasoning. What can be said of other words and ideas not written into the Constitution? For example, can anyone find the word "God"

---

50 Alexander Hamilton, as cited in Bledsoe, 35.

51 Daniel Webster, as cited in Whipple, 288

in the Constitution? Now, using Webster's line of reasoning, one is left with no other conclusion than that the Founding Fathers desired an atheistic system of government. Fortunately, we know that such "logic" is flawed.

President Jefferson Davis noted that John L. Motley's logic was also flawed when Motley claimed that the Constitution was instituted over the states and therefore could not be a compact between the states as the South claimed. Davis noted,

> The language of the final article would have been quite enough: 'The ratification of the conventions of nine States shall be sufficient for the establishment of this Constitution between the States so ratifying the same.' This is not the 'language' of a superior imposing a mandate upon subordinates. The consent of the contracting parties is necessary to its validity, and 'then it becomes not the acceptance and recognition of an authority 'over' them—as Mr. Motley represents—but of a compact between them. The simple word 'between' is incompatible with any other idea than that of a compact by independent parties.[52]

Thus, we see that the advocates for the Yankee Empire's theory of "one people, one nation indivisible" sought to deny that the federal republic was established by a compact calling itself the Constitution. We have shown that the Founding Fathers repeatedly referred to the Constitution as a compact. You, the jury, must decide whether those who accused Jefferson Davis of treason for supporting the sovereign state's right to secede from a compact that they voluntarily acceded to are credible and reliable witnesses. Let the accurate, unbiased, historical record guide your decision.

---

52 Jefferson Davis, *Rise and Fall of the Confederate Government*, I, 140.

The American People Are Not One People

Great stress is placed upon the argument put forth by Joseph Story, and seconded by Daniel Webster, that "We the people" represent one people belonging to one sovereign nation called the United States of America. This centralist theory of "one grand indivisible nation" was adopted and advanced by the Northern majority to the detriment of the Southern minority. Although the advocates of the "one grand indivisible nation" are not so flagrant as to announce these views bluntly, the practical results of advocating national sovereignty over state sovereignty has been the transferal of power from the states to the Yankee Empire's government. The effect of Story's and Webster's political philosophy has been to change the source of political sovereignty from "We the people" within a specific sovereign state to "We the people of the Yankee Empire" in the aggregate. According to this erroneous theory of "one people, one nation indivisible," the point from which legitimate political power originates is no longer considered to be the people at the local level of their respective state but with the people as a general mass of Americans. If this is true, the United States, therefore, has been transformed from its origin as a Republic of Sovereign States, or as the writer in *The Federalist* referred to the new Union, "a compound republic,"[53] into a centrally (Washington, DC) controlled nation. James Madison, in *The Federalist* No. 39, unequivocally refuted those who charged that the new Constitution would create a national (i.e., unitary and supreme) government "which regards the union as a consolidation of the States," rather than a federal government "which regards the union as a confederacy of sovereign States."[54] Madison stated, "The act therefore establishing the Constitution, will not be a national but a federal act .... the act of the people forming so many independent States, not as forming one aggregate nation."[55] In 1825, William Rawle of Philadelphia, Pennsylvania, in his textbook on the Constitution made a similar point about who gave life to the Constitution. According to Rawle, the Constitution

---

53 James Madison, as cited in Carey & McClellan, 268.

54 Carey & McClellan, 196.

55 *Ibid.*

was not ratified as "the simple act of a homogeneous body of men, either large or small. It was to be the act of many independent states, though in a greater degree the act of people set in motion by those states; and not of the people at large."[56] Alexander Hamilton, even though he was an ardent High Federalist who desperately wanted to create a supreme Federal Government, made a similar point in *The Federalist* No. 32:

> An entire consolidation of the States into one complete national sovereignty would imply an entire subordination of the parts; and whatever powers might remain in them would be altogether dependent on the general will. But as the plan of the convention aims only a partial Union or consolidation, the State Governments would clearly retain all the rights of sovereignty which they before had and which were not by that act exclusively delegated to the United States.[57]

Note that Hamilton used the word "exclusively," which he emphasized, when writing of those powers which the states delegated to the Federal Government. William Rawle noted that there are only two constitutional methods by which the sovereignty of a state could be restricted: (1) where specific powers are clearly delegated to the Federal Government, and (2) where a "negative clause" exists in the federal constitution that would restrict the exercise of a power, such as in Article I, Section 10, of the United States Constitution. Please note that nowhere in the Constitution is the right of secession by a state delegated to the United States government, nor is there a "negative clause" found in the Constitution that limits the states from seceding from the Union. Thus, how can anyone find Jefferson Davis guilty of treason?

---

56 Rawle, William, *A View of the Constitution: Secession as Taught at West Point*, Kennedy & Kennedy, editors, 2nd Kennedy edition, (1825, Wake Forest, NC: The Scuppernong Press, 2020), 7.

57 Alexander Hamilton, as cited in Carey & McClellan, 156.

The desire of many in the North to use the power of the central government for sectional aggrandizement led them to embrace the political philosophies of Story and Webster. These men understood that their section could not become the controlling political influence in America as long as "We the people" of the sovereign states of the South possessed a sovereign state to protect them from an abusive Federal Government. Therefore, the North had to destroy the power of the sovereign state. Judge Abel Upshur, in his review of Joseph Story's *Commentaries,* notes how Story incorrectly informed his readers that the colonies were "one people" and that the Declaration of Independence formed a "national government." Upshur states that Story, "Having informed us that, as Colonies, we were for many purposes one people,' and that the Declaration of Independence made us 'a nation de facto,' he now assumes the broad ground that this 'one people,' or nation de facto, formed the Constitution under which we live."[58]

The only justification for this sweeping assertion that Story uses is the language of the preamble to the Constitution. According to Story, an entire people changed the relationship that they had established in 1776, from that of thirteen free, independent, and sovereign states to that of one consolidated unitary state, by the mere act of words in a preamble to the Constitution! "In thus relying on the language of the preamble, Judge Story rejects the lights of history altogether .... It is an admitted rule, that the preamble of a statute may be resorted to in the construction of it .... But the only purpose for which it can be used is to aid in the discovery of the true object and intention of the law, where these would otherwise be doubtful. The preamble can, in no case, be allowed to contradict the law, or to vary the meaning of its plain language. Still less can it be used to change the true character of the law-making power."[59] As Judge Upshur notes, Joseph Story and, following Story's lead, Daniel Webster, is in direct contradiction of Article VII of the Constitution which plainly declares for all to see that the lawmaking power (that is, the authority to make or ratify the Constitution) resides with the

---

58 Abel P. Upshur, *The Federal Government: Its True Nature and Character* (1866, Houston, TX: St. Thomas Press, 1977), 101. Also see Joseph Story, I, 164.

59 Upshur, 102.

states. Article VII of the Constitution states, "The ratification of the conventions of nine states, shall be sufficient for the establishment of this constitution between the states so ratifying the same." Two points are obvious upon reading Article VII: (1) The independent ratification of nine state conventions would give life to the Constitution. No citizen or combinations of citizens from any state could force another state to do that which it did not wish to do. (2) Once nine states ratified the Constitution it would become operative in only those nine states. The idea of majority rule existed only in the state conventions and not with the majority of the states and/or the people at large. Those states not ratifying the Constitution were to be treated as independent and sovereign states (nations). If only nine states had ratified the Constitution, no one would have demanded a "civil war" to force the other four states back into the Union. As Judge Upshur explains the issue, Article VII of the Constitution takes precedence over the preamble of the Constitution.

Nowhere in the words of the text of the Constitution, which is primary and superior to the preamble, will one find even a hint that it was to be ratified by "We the people" in the aggregate acting as "one people, one nation indivisible." Yet, Story and Webster both claim that such was the case and therefore the states have no power to remove themselves from the Union thus created. The Union, we again remind you, was, by their day, fast approaching the point of being completely controlled by the Yankee Empire's numerical majority.

Here is another example of how Daniel Webster was at odds with the Founding Fathers. In 1830 Webster made a speech in which he declared that the Constitution was ordained and established by "the whole people of the United States in their aggregate capacity."[60] What did our Founding Fathers intend when they submitted the Constitution to the states for ratification? Did they intend for the United States to hold a general vote in which the states would be nothing more than polling precincts for a national election to ratify the Constitution? Again, we recur to the words of the Founding Fathers for a true interpretation of the nature and character of the

---

60 Daniel Webster, as cited in Whipple, 271.

ratifying process of the Constitution. Those responsible for writing and adopting the Constitution must be considered better interpreters of who ratified the Constitution than those who took no part in that process.

James Madison, in *The Federalist*, clearly stated who would ratify the Constitution and how the Constitution would be ratified. Madison noted:

> That it [ratification of the Constitution] will be federal and not a national act ... the act of the people as forming so many independent States, not as forming one aggregate nation, is obvious from this single consideration that it is to result neither from the decision of a majority of the people of the Union, nor from that of a majority of the States. It must result from the unanimous assent of the several States that are parties to it, differing no other wise from their ordinary assent than in its being expressed, not by the legislative authority, but by that of the people themselves. Were the people regarded in this transaction as forming one nation, the will of the majority of the whole people of the United States, would bind the minority; in the same manner as the majority in each State must bind the minority; and the will of the majority must be determined either by a comparison of the individual votes; or by considering the will of the majority of the States, as evidence of the will of the majority of the people of the United States. Neither of these rules has been adopted. Each State in ratifying the Constitution, is considered as a sovereign body independent of all others, and only to be bound by its own voluntary act.[61]

---

61   James Madison, as cited in Carey & McClellan, 196-97.

Madison, who is often referred to as the "Father of the Constitution," informs us as to who are the parties to the Constitution: "the States." He also informs us as to the political nature of those states: "Each State ... is considered as a sovereign body independent of all others."

During the ratification debate in Virginia, Madison explained what the words "We the people" in the preamble of the proposed constitution means: "The parties to it were the people, but not the people as composing one great society, but the people as composing thirteen sovereignties."[62] As Madison pointed out, it was the action of "We the people" of the sovereign states who gave life to the Constitution, not the American people in the aggregate.

Daniel Webster was not beyond quoting the Founding Fathers out of context if it furthered the emerging Yankee Empire's theory of "one people, one nation indivisible." Webster, reading from *The Federalist* No. 22, quoted Alexander Hamilton: "The fabric of American empire ought to rest on the solid basis of the consent of the people." Webster then added, "Such is the language, sir, addressed to the people, while they yet had the Constitution under consideration. The powers conferred on the new government were perfectly well understood to be conferred, not by any State, or the people of any State, but by the people of the United States."[63] What Webster did not to tell those hearing him and those reading his thunderous speech later was that Hamilton was speaking of the people giving their consent through their primary constitution-making process of their delegates meeting in each state in a specially called state constitutional convention as opposed to the people giving their consent through their general agent (i.e., the legislatures of each individual state). Hamilton was seeking to avoid the possibility of state legislatures repealing the Constitution by having the Constitution ratified, not by the state legislatures but by the people, in their primary role, electing delegates to their state constitutional convention. This state convention would be called, within each sovereign state, for the specific purpose of ratifying or rejecting the proposed constitution.

---

62 James Madison, as cited in Bledsoe, 84.

63 Daniel Webster, as cited in Whipple, 289.

Said actions of the state convention would be on behalf of "We the people" of that specific sovereign state, unencumbered by the actions of any other state nor would their action be binding upon any other state. The question Hamilton was addressing was entirely different from the issue advanced by Webster; but that did not stop Webster from misusing the quote. Perhaps Webster thought he was safe in misquoting Hamilton since Hamilton was not alive to challenge Webster. But wait; James Madison was still alive in 1833, when Webster made his great speech. What was Madison's reaction to the notion that the Constitution was ratified by "We the people" in the aggregate as one people, one unitary nation as put forth by Webster?

So astonishing were Webster's pronouncements in his Senate speech of 1833 that Madison, then in his old age, wrote a letter to Webster in an attempt to correct Webster's error! See how James Madison, "the Father of the Constitution," takes the wind out of Webster's sails by clearly noting, "it is fortunate when disputed theories can be decided by undisputed facts; and here the undisputed fact is, that the Constitution was made by the people, but as embodied into the several States who were parties to it .... The Constitution of the United States, being established by a competent authority, by that of the sovereign people of the several States, who were parties to it" [emphasis added]. Here, in the words of one of America's premier Founding Fathers, Webster's theory of "one people" is completely debunked.

Bledsoe, in his defense of Davis noted how unfortunate it was for American liberty:

> When those who cling to hitherto undisputed facts are accounted traitors, and visited with a merciless and a measureless vengeance, by those who, having nothing better than disputed theories to stand on, are nevertheless backed by the possession of brute force sufficient to crush their opponents, and silence the voice of truth![64]

---

64 Bledsoe, 76.

Thus, we see from the very words of our Founding Fathers that Webster's and Story's allegation that the Constitution was ratified by one people, the American people in the aggregate, is totally unfounded. The Northern theory of "one people, one nation indivisible" is a pernicious allegation, unfounded in the facts of 1787 but unquestioned in the North in 1861! This pernicious and anti-constitutional theory was forced upon the Southern people at the point of bloody bayonets! So much for the American idea of the "consent of the governed," at least as far as "We the people" of the South is concerned.

Remember, we are assessing the credibility of those who are representative of the best types of Yankee advocates for a strong, centralized, supreme Federal Government—and by implication, the transformation of the original Republic of Sovereign States into the Yankee Empire. Specifically, we are comparing the actual words of Daniel Webster and Joseph Story with the plain record of history. You, the jury, must decide whether these types of men are more likely to be telling the truth than the accused, President Jefferson Davis. With this evidence, you will be better able to decide whether secession in the American political system is an act of treason or an exercise of an inalienable right—the right of self-government as announced in the Declaration of Independence.

The Founding Fathers Did Not Create A Supreme Federal Government

According to the Yankee Empire's school of "one people, one nation indivisible," the Founding Fathers intended to create a supreme national government under the Constitution. This theory alleges that the United States Constitution is the supreme law of the land and, therefore, the government created thereunder exercises supreme authority over the people of the states. Under this theory, enforced by the Yankee Empire since 1861, the states are subservient to the Federal Government.

Daniel Webster, in a speech in the Senate, February 16, 1833, declared, "Indeed if we look into all contemporary history; to the numbers of *The Federalist*; to the debates in the Convention; to the publication of friends and foes, they all agree, that a change had been made from a confederacy of States to a different system; they all agree, that the Convention had formed a constitution for a national government. ... In none of the various productions and publications, did any one intimate that the new Constitution was but another compact between States in their sovereign capacity. I do not find such an opinion advanced in a single instance."[65] As we have already seen, Justice Joseph Story also advocated the theory that the Founding Fathers did in fact create a supreme national government. Now let us, once again, recur to the words of the Fathers of the constitutional, federal, Republic of Sovereign States, and from their words seek the truth. Did they or did they not form a supreme national government?

The first resolution passed by the convention of 1787 declared that "a national government ought to be established."[66] This resolution was passed before the convention was fully assembled and by the vote of only six states, a minority of the whole number. After all the members had arrived at the constitutional convention (Rhode Island being the exception), the resolution in question was reconsidered and rescinded.[67] So, here we see that the convention, by a vote of six states, decided that "a national government ought to be established." But when this resolution was reconsidered, Oliver Ellsworth of Connecticut "objected to the term national government," and it was rejected. The record of the Constitutional Convention states, "The first resolution 'that a national government ought to be established,' being taken up ... Mr. Ellsworth, seconded by Mr. Gorham, of Massachusetts, moved to alter it, so as to run that the government of the United States ought to consist .... This alteration, he said, would drop the word national, and retain the proper title 'the United States.'"[68] The return to this name is important. This is the same title that the country had under the Articles of Confederation and the same title used in the Declaration of Independence. It was

---

65 Daniel Webster, as cited in Whipple, 289.

66 Bledsoe, 19.

67 *Ibid.*

68 *Ibid.*

never considered as a "national" (i.e., supreme) government having dominant authority over the sovereign states during that time. This move was unanimously adopted by the convention. That is, the delegates unanimously *rejected* "the term national government;" yet, both Story and Webster built an argument on this term just as if it had been retained by the convention![69] Look again at the record of the very convention that gave birth to the Constitution. Ellsworth declared, "I propose, and therefore move to expunge the word 'national' in the first resolve, and to place in the room of it government of the United States." Yet, in spite of or in ignorance of recorded history, Justice Story built an argument on the word "national" as used in the first resolution passed by the convention! And to compound the error, Senator Webster, in the written text of his speech, printed that *rescinded* resolution in capital letters![70]

The advocates of the Yankee Empire's theory of "one people, one nation indivisible" desired an all-powerful national government that the Empire's majority could control and use for their particular benefit. James Madison, in *The Federalist*, warned Americans of the danger of a faction gaining control of the Federal Government:

> In a society under the forms of which the stronger faction can readily unite and oppress the weaker, anarchy may as truly be said to reign, as in a state of nature where the weaker individual is not secured against the violence of the stronger."[71]

This was the condition in which the South found itself in 1861 and thus felt driven to the expediency of secession.

By claiming that the United States government was created as a national government, the advocates of a national sovereignty could bypass the argument that the Federal Government is a

---

69 *Ibid.*

70 Whipple, 287. Daniel Webster, in his famous speech, admitted that the term "national government" was eventually removed but insisted that concept of a national government was retained.

71 James Madison, as cited in Carey & McClellan, 269.

constitutionally limited government. In order to preserve the voluntary nature of the Union, this limited Federal Government was required to respect the rights retained by the sovereign states. As a constitutionally limited government, its authority would be supreme only in those areas that were specifically delegated to it *and as long as its acts were "pursuant to the Constitution."* This type of limited government was not what Daniel Webster and Joseph Story were advocating. But, as a matter of historical record, the Federal Government's authority was limited. A few examples will suffice to demonstrate the point.

- During the constitutional convention, several proponents of a national government suggested that the Federal Government be given the authority to veto acts of state legislatures. The proposal for a national veto over the states was soundly rejected.

- During the first Congress under the new Constitution, James Madison, then still a proponent of a strong centralized national government, suggested that the restrictions of the Bill of Rights should be applied to the states. Congress rejected this recommendation.

- In *Chisholm v. Georgia*, the Federal Supreme Court attempted to bring the sovereign state of Georgia into court. The sovereign state of Georgia nullified the federal court's action and declared that any federal official who attempted to enforce the Federal Court order would be "hung by the neck without benefit of clergy"[72] Georgia's action was responsible for the adoption of the Eleventh Amendment to the Constitution—which demonstrated that the constitutional majority of States agreed with Georgia's States' Rights stand. No Yankee armies were raised to "march through Georgia."

- When the Federal Congress passed and the Federal Supreme Court enforced the Alien and Sedition Acts, the states of Kentucky and Virginia passed their famous resolutions of 1798 effectively nullifying these unconstitutional federal acts.

---

72 Bledsoe, 56.

The Alien and Sedition Acts were a brazen violation of the Bill of Rights that threatened the civil liberty of the citizens of the states. But the sovereign states interposed their sovereign authority between their citizens and an abusive United States government and acted as a shield between an abusive government and "We the people" of the sovereign state.

- In 1833, the federal Supreme Court handed down its decision in *Barron v. Baltimore*. In pertinent parts, the decision declared that the Bill of Rights to the Federal Constitution does not limit the power of the states but limits only the power of the United States government. This decision has never been overturned, although it has been conveniently ignored by latter-day activist courts.

These examples demonstrate that the *legitimate* Federal Government created by the Constitution is not a supreme national government. Its authority is not original. Its authority is secondary; it comes from a source other than itself or the people of the nation acting as one people. Its authority is a delegated authority, given to it as a conditional grant from "We the people" of the sovereign states. This grant requires that the Federal Government exercise its limited powers "pursuant" to the limitations imposed upon it by the Constitution. The source of the Federal Government's delegated authority is the sovereign states, the same states who are parties to the constitutional compact that created their agent, the Federal Government. According to the historical record, who were most faithful to the original intentions of the Founding Fathers? Did the Story-Webster school of "one people, one nation indivisible" faithfully adhere to the constitutional limitations imposed upon the Federal Government? Or, did the Southern school that advocated limited federalism and sovereign states within a constitutional Union more closely adhere to the original intentions of the Founding Fathers? Both cannot be right. One must be in violation of the oath required by the Constitution of every United States president: the oath to uphold the Constitution. Who is guilty of treason to the Constitution? You, the jury, will have to weigh the facts and make your determination.

The Sovereign States Are The Only Parties To The Constitution

The above-cited proposition is one that if left standing would utterly destroy the false claim of federal supremacy. If the states are the parties to the Constitution, then the states made the Federal Government and have the right to unmake it. Those who sought to expand the powers of the Federal Government and who became the advocates of "one people, one nation indivisible" knew that they had to destroy the idea that the states created the Federal Government. To promote the view of "one people, one nation, indivisible," the states, as sovereign political entities, had to be removed from the American political equation. Both Joseph Story and Daniel Webster, as we have already seen, advocated the false theory that the Constitution was ratified by the American people in the aggregate. Recall Story's own words previously quoted: "The obvious deductions which may be, and, indeed, have been, drawn from considering the Constitution a compact between States, are that it operates as a mere treaty or convention between them, and has an obligatory force no longer than suits its pleasure or its consent continues." True enough, and that is actually why the apologists of the Yankee Empire labored so long to deny that the sovereign states are the only parties to the Constitution. But once again, let us recur to the words of the Founding Fathers.

- Resolutions unanimously adopted by the constitutional convention of 1787 attest to the fact that each state was acting for itself independent of the acts of other states. "Resolved, That in the opinion of this Convention that as soon as the Convention of nine States shall have ratified this Constitution, the United States in Congress assembled should fix a day on which electors should be appointed by the States which shall have ratified the same."

- James Madison, who at this time was a strong nationalist, introduced a motion which required "a concurrence of a majority of both the States and the people" at large to establish the Constitution; this proposition was rejected by the Convention.[73] Thus, maintaining the supremacy of the sovereign state.

- During the constitutional convention, while discussing the effect of ratification as then required under Article XXI of the proposed constitution, James Wilson of Pennsylvania noted, "As the Constitution stands, the States only which ratify can be bound." Madison, who at the time was a strong nationalist, thought that the ratification of the specified number of states would make the Constitution binding upon all states, even those states that may have rejected it. To resolve the question, Rufus King of Massachusetts, one of the most ardent advocates of a centralized national government at the 1787 convention, introduced the words by which the Constitution would clearly become binding upon only those states that elected to ratify it. He suggested the following words be added to the proposed Article XXI making it binding: "... between the States so ratifying the same."[74]

Justice Story declared that "the States never, in fact did, in their political capacity, as contradistinguished from the people thereof, ratify the Constitution."[75] This is another example of the sophistry that the advocates of centralized, supreme federalism are willing to use to prop up their weak case. Here, we see Story attempting to remove the states from the process of ratification of the Constitution. He would be correct in asserting that the states did not ratify the Constitution if by that he meant that the general agent of the state, the state legislature, did not ratify the Constitution. As we all know, the Constitution was ratified by the people of each individual state through the actions, not of their general agent—their state legislature—but by the action of their special agent—their representatives elected to the state constitutional convention. Each state convention was called, organized, and otherwise empowered to act by the action of the individual state legislature. Each state

---

73 *Ibid.*, 72.

74 *Ibid.*

75 Joseph Story, as cited in Upshur, 108.

convention was held within the actual state that called for the convention for the specific purpose of considering the proposed constitution. But sadly, for Story and his school of "one people, one nation indivisible," he entangles himself in his own illogical net. In his book, *Commentaries on the Constitution of the United States* (1833), he not only admits but also insists that "the State and the people of the State, are equivalent expressions."[76] Again, he insists, "Nay the State by which we mean the people composing the State...."[77] Thus, the same Yankee "authority" who declares that "the States never, in fact did, in their political capacity, as contradistinguished from the people thereof, ratify the Constitution" is the same Yankee "authority" who contradicts himself by writing in his own book that "the State and the people of the State, are equivalent expressions."

Justice Story, true to the necessity of his preconceived theory of "one people, one nation indivisible," attempts to show that in ratifying the Constitution, the states only function was to act as districts of people of the American nation as opposed to sovereign political entities exercising their freedom and independence.[78] If Story's theory is correct, then all the states did was to serve as polling precincts on behalf of the grand American nation. If this is correct, then the votes of all the people of the states in the aggregate should have been considered. Under the Yankee Empire's theory, the ratification of the Constitution would have been a national act, as opposed to a federal act. Each state, or more appropriately, each province or political subdivision of the unitary nation-state, would have been bound by the decision of the majority vote of the "one people, one nation indivisible" But again, how does the Yankee Empire's theory of "one people, one nation indivisible" stand up to inspection in the brilliant light of historical truth?

The clear and undeniable fact of history is that each state, acting under its own laws, executed by its own institutions and governments devised by the people of each sovereign state, exercised its sovereign will by freely choosing to accept or reject the proposed constitution.

---

76   Story, I, 193.

77   *Ibid.*, I, 194.

78   *Ibid.*, I, 195-57.

The people of each state make their decision for themselves and were bound by their act alone. No group of states or combinations of people outside of that specific sovereign state could bind it to the proposed constitution. The authors of *The Federalist* make it very clear that each state was "only to be bound by its own voluntary act."[79] Thus, truth destroys the phantom conjured up by the Websters, Storys, et al, of the emerging Yankee Empire who desired to merge the states into one centralized nation controlled by the Yankee Empire's Northern majority—to the detriment of the Southern minority. "One people, one nation indivisible" is the deadly phantom contrived by those who would eventually wage aggressive war upon the Southern people. With such crafty sophistry and subterfuge, the emerging Yankee Empire turned the Union from its original purpose of preserving American liberties into the instrument of violence, coercion, aggression, and bloody war! A criminal war waged with hideous vengeance against their former countrymen.[80]

"It may be doubted, indeed, if there was ever a more superficial gloss, or a more pitiful subterfuge, than the assertion of Judge Story, that the States adopted the Constitution, not as States, but only 'as districts of people' composing one great State or nation. It is at war with the unanswerable arguments of *The Federalist*. Sad, indeed, must have been the condition to which the great sophist was reduced, when he could stoop to so palpable a gloss on one of the plainest facts in the history of the Constitution!"[81]

Indeed, *The Federalist* so clearly refutes Story's assertion that one wonders how a man, so obviously well educated, could bring himself to pen such an obviously false assertion. Justice Story claims that "the States did not ratify the Constitution as States" but ratified it as part of a national act of all of the American people acting as "one people, one nation indivisible" Yet, the authors of *The Federalist* state that the act of ratification of the proposed constitution was "not a national, but a federal act." The act of ratification was "by the

---

79   James Madison, as cited in Carey & McClellan, 197.

80   See Chapter 7 "Yankee Atrocities" in Kennedy & Kennedy, *The South Was Right!* 3rd edition, 175-204.

81   Bledsoe, 121.

people of America, not as individuals, composing one nation, but as composing the distinct and independent States to which they belong." *The Federalist* describes the Constitution as "the compact" that was ordained by "the States ... as distinct and independent sovereigns." The obvious conclusion drawn from the language of *The Federalist* is that the sovereign states acceded to the Constitution, reserved all powers not specifically delegated, and therefore retained the right to secede from the Constitution "whensoever rights are used against the people" as they were promised in the Tenth Amendment,[82] said amendment being added, as promised, shortly after ratification of the 1787 Constitution.

Perhaps the advocates of "one people, one nation indivisible" would claim that while a state can make a constitution it cannot unmake a constitution. In other words, the people of 1787 who acceded to the Constitution were the only generation of Americans possessing the authority to unmake a constitution (as they did when they seceded from the Articles of Confederation) and the only generation of Americans possessing the authority to make a constitution (as they did when they acceded to the constitution proposed in 1787). But can one generation encumber or destroy the sovereign prerogatives of future generations? According to our American principles of government, the attributes of sovereignty are inherent, God given, and therefore inalienable. No, the Founding Fathers could not and did not monopolize the sovereignty of all succeeding generations of Americans. The actions of unmaking the Articles of Confederation and making the Constitution of 1787 did not extinguish the inalienable rights of the generation of 1861 or any other generation prior to it or any future generation. To deny this truth is to end up in the illogical position of asserting the sovereignty of past generations, while denying the sovereignty of all subsequent generations. Sycophants of the Yankee Empire's school of "one people, one nation indivisible" have placed themselves in the awkward position of defending secession from the union with

---

82 The Tenth Amendment to the U.S. Constitution states, "The powers not delegated to the United States by the Constitution, nor prohibited by it to the States, are reserved to the States respectively, or to the people."

Great Britain in 1776 as an inalienable right[83] and then alienating that same right from all future generations of Americans who find themselves facing an oppressive central government. How can an inalienable right be alienated? To deny the inalienable rights of Americans is to deny the foundational principles upon which the American Republic was founded; to do so is to reject America itself. Yet, this is precisely what the advocates of "one people, one nation indivisible" do when they deny the inalienable right of secession!

You, the jury, must now determine if you think it is likely that Story; Webster, and the advocates of the emerging Yankee Empire's school of "one people, one nation indivisible" were accurate historians and honest politicians when they asserted that the states were not parties to the ratification of the Constitution. Who will you believe, Jefferson Davis who defended the sovereignty of "We the people" of the sovereign states, or the Story-Webster school who asserted the sovereign authority of the American people in the aggregate?

"We The People Of The United States" Means The Same As "We The People Of The Sovereign States"

This phrase taken from the preamble to the Constitution has been a mainstay in the arsenal of the consolidationists (i.e., those wishing to turn the limited Federal Government into a Federal Government of supreme national authority). We have already demonstrated that both Joseph Story and Daniel Webster attempted to use the words "We the people" to disprove the historical fact that the people of the sovereign states independently ratified the Constitution; thus, by sophistry they delivered the Federal Government into the hands of the Northern majority faction and nullified every right reserved to "We the people" of sovereign states by the Ninth and Tenth Amendments. But what did the Founding Fathers mean by the words "We the people?"

Gouverneur Morris certainly wanted the Constitution to be ratified by means other than individual state ratification. He was an advocate of a strong national government and wished all power to emanate from the people of America, thereby creating a

---

83   See Joint Declaration of Independence of the Thirteen American Colonies.

national government. He desired to have the American people in the aggregate regarded as one great nation. But did he accomplish his wish? The convention record shows that "Gouverneur Morris moved that the referred of the plan [the Constitution] be made to one General Convention, chosen and authorized by the people, to consider, amend, and establish the same."[84] If this motion had been adopted, it would indeed have caused the Constitution to be ratified by "the people of the United States in the aggregate," or one nation. But how was this motion received by the convention? Was it approved and passed in the affirmative by that body? No! It was not. *It did not even find a second in the convention of 1787.* This most significant fact is in the record for all to see. The ratification of the Constitution by the people at large was such an unpopular idea that it was deemed out of the question and could not find even the shadow of support from the authors of the Constitution of the United States.[85] But the advocates of "one people, one nation indivisible" allege treason for those who would defend the rights reserved to "We the people" of the sovereign states. Yet, despite the harsh criticism from the defenders (sycophants) of the now well-established Yankee Empire, we shall not be deterred. We shall once again look to the words of the Founding Fathers to determine their true intentions.

The Committee on Style, chaired by none other than Gouverneur Morris, was the committee that changed the wording of the preamble to its present form. Previously, the preamble had contained the names of all thirteen states after the words "We the people," but it soon became obvious that all the states might not accede to the new union. Therefore, the Committee on Style removed all state names. Did the Committee on Style then change the very nature of the American government from a federal republic of sovereign states to a unitary central government? What was Gouverneur Morris's understanding of the phrase "We the people"?

His opinion is very clear and does not lend its support to Yankee sophism. Morris declared, "The Constitution was a compact, not between individuals, but between political societies, the people,

---

84 Bledsoe, 63.

85 *Ibid.*, 62.

not of America, but of the United States, each enjoying sovereign power and of course equal rights."[86] Here, we see the words of the consummate nationalist agreeing not with the Story-Webster school of "one people, one nation indivisible" but with John C. Calhoun, Jefferson Davis, and other defenders of the original Constitution and the Republic of Sovereign States created by the Constitution.

What did the term "We the people of the United States" mean, and what is its significance relative to the debate in the constitutional convention regarding ratification of the Constitution? The answer to this question will once again demonstrate the shallow logic of the advocates of the Yankee Empire's school of "one people, one nation indivisible." "We the people," in the language of the framers of the Constitution, meant precisely the same thing as "We the states." This can be proven by studying the record of the constitutional convention.

When considering the question of by whom and how the Constitution would be ratified, only one question was in doubt in the convention; should the Constitution be ratified by the <u>legislatures</u> of the states or by the people of the states in their sovereign capacity in <u>a state convention</u>? No one doubted that it was to be ratified by the states. This was a settled point. The only question was whether it should be ratified by the states, acting through their legislatures, or by the states acting through conventions elected to represent the people of that specific state for that special purpose. The phrase "We the people," as used and understood by the constitutional convention, meant the people of the several states as opposed to the representatives of the people in their several legislatures. Nowhere in the record of the constitutional convention can it be found where the convention approved a system of ratification by the American people at large. To the Founding Fathers, "We the people" did not mean the people of America in the aggregate, it meant "We the people" in the segregate (i.e., the people of individual, distinct, and sovereign states). The members of the constitutional convention agreed that ratification should be performed by the states. The only debate was regarding the method the various states would use to

---

86   Gouverneur Morris, as cited in *Ibid.*, 64.

ratify or reject the proposed Constitution. Should it be through their state legislatures or via a special state convention called by the legislature of each state especially for the purpose of ratifying or rejecting the proposed constitution?

While debating the proper mode of state ratification, some of the most ardent supporters of state sovereignty (i.e., States' Rights) insisted that ratification should be accomplished by "the people of the United States." They, and every member of the convention, clearly understood that the phrase meant the people of the several states, as distinguished from their legislatures. If, for one moment, they had imagined that their language could have been perverted to mean a ratification of the Constitution by the collective will of the whole people of America (by a majority vote), they would have abandoned the entire enterprise. They dreaded nothing more than the idea of such an immense consolidated democracy. On the contrary, they clung to their states and to their rights as the only reliable defense against the overwhelming and all-devouring flood of a national union of one people, one nation, with supreme authority. They looked with dread upon the tyranny of "King Numbers."[87] Why should ardent supporters of state sovereignty, such as George Mason of Virginia or Robert Yates of New York, see no danger in the use of the phrase "We the people" in the preamble of the proposed constitution? Because they understood it to mean exactly what the convention intended—ratification by "We the people" of each separate state acting in the state's sovereign constitution-making capacity.[88]

Once again, you, the jury, must decide. Who were more accurate and honest in their appraisal of the Constitution; the ones who advocated "one people, one nation indivisible" or Southerners such as President Davis who upheld the rights of "We the people" of the sovereign states? You must determine who were the most reliable defenders of the Founding Father's original intentions.

---

87 Ibid., 70.

88 Ibid., 73.

THE DECLARATION OF INDEPENDENCE DID NOT CREATE ONE SUPREME NATION

The advocates of "one people, one nation indivisible" often use the argument that when the thirteen colonies declared their independence, they also established a national government. Remember that what the advocates of "one people, one nation indivisible" are trying to do is to destroy the position championed by the South in 1861 that the Union is the creature of the sovereign states created under a compact among said states, that compact being the Constitution. The plain language of Article VII of the United States Constitution clearly demonstrates this simple truth of who are the consenting parties: "The ratification of the conventions of nine states, shall be sufficient for the establishment of this constitution *between the states so ratifying the same.*" [Emphasis added] In order to overcome the plain language of the Constitution, the Yankee Empire's apologists appealed to the Declaration of Independence as though it is somehow superior to the Constitution.

Justice Story was so wedded to the theory of one nation indivisible that he attempted to show that the thirteen colonies were actually "one people" during their existence as colonies of Great Britain. Not completely satisfied with his effort to make the colonies "one people" during their colonial period, he then moved on to the revolutionary period. Story declared that, even if Americans were not a nation of one people prior to the Revolutionary War, then, according to his theory, they were certainly made into one by the Declaration of Independence! Justice Story's strained efforts to make the colonies/states into a unitary nation is beginning to tell. If America were one people during its colonial period, why did it need to be made into one people again by the Declaration of Independence? How easy it was for Story to contradict his own ideas! He clearly stated that the union formed in 1776 was formed by the states and not by the people of America: "The union thus formed grew out of the exigencies of the times; and from its nature and objects might be deemed temporary, extending only to the maintenance of the common liberties and independence of the States, and to terminate with the return of peace with Great Britain."[89]

The theory of "one people, one nation indivisible" looks to the Declaration of Independence to justify its claim, as advanced by Lincoln, and endorsed by the Republican Party, that the Union preceded the states.[90] Defenders of the Yankee Empire claim that those who signed the Declaration of Independence did not announce the independence of thirteen colonies but in fact announced the independence of the American people in the aggregate and the formation of the government of the American nation! Even if a person slept through American history in elementary school, he should find this assertion quite shocking. Yet, Story alleges that "[t]he body by which this step was taken constituted the actual government of the nation at the time."[91] Again, he asserts, "The fact that these local or State governments were not formed until a Union of the people of the different colonies for national purposes had already taken place, and until the national power had authorized and recommended their establishment ... shows that no colony, acting separately for itself, dissolved its own allegiance to the British crown, but that this allegiance was dissolved by the supreme authority of the people."[92] According to the theory of "one people, one nation indivisible," the Declaration of Independence was both a document of independence and freedom and at the same time, a document of dependence and submission. According to their theory, the Declaration of Independence codified the act by which the colonies removed themselves from one sovereign (King George III) and then submitted themselves to a higher authority (the sovereign will of the American people in the aggregate)! To accept this perverted theory is to accept that the American people determined to remove

---

89 Joseph Story, *Ibid.*, 105.
90 *Ibid.*, 105.
91 Joseph Story, *Ibid.*, 114.
92 Story, I, 197-98.

themselves from the rule of the central government in London and to submit themselves to a new central government somewhere, yet to be decided, here in America.

As we have come to expect through the previous statements by the advocates of one grand nation, they assume complete ignorance of actual historical facts on the part of those who read their words. The truth is that Virginia seceded from the union with Great Britain prior to the July Fourth joint Declaration of Independence. Of this act, William Wirt Henry, biographer of Patrick Henry states:

> The resolutions as adopted in effect declared Virginia independent, without waiting for the action of Congress, by providing for the immediate framing of a separate Government, which was reported and adopted before Congress declared the Colonies independent.[93]

Those who advance the theory that the Union existed before the states existed must assume that we are not aware of the fact that on the same day that the Declaration of Independence was signed the same people who signed the document appointed a committee for the purpose of forming "a confederation to be entered into between these colonies." This was done *after* instructions from Virginia were given to its delegate, Richard Henry Lee, "[t]hat a plan of confederation be prepared and transmitted to the respective colonies for their consideration."[94]

How could a people remove their allegiance from London and give it to the American nation when no such nation yet existed? The facts speak for themselves. Facts, though, have never stood in the way of the advocates of centralized federalism. How can the agents of "one people, one nation indivisible" explain the fact that on the Fourth of July, 1776, the representatives of one colony refused to sign the Declaration of Independence? If declaring independence was an act

---

93 William Wirt Henry, *Patrick Henry: Life, Correspondence, and Speeches* (1891, Harrisonburg, VA: Sprinkle Publications, 1993), I, 398.

94 Ibid., 401.

of the whole people of America, then the majority of Americans in the aggregate should determine the question for all. Yet, New York's representatives did not sign because they did not have the requisite authority from the people of the state of New York. They signed the Declaration later, but only after receiving instructions from their state to vote for independence. Judge Abel Upshur points out that, although the delegates in Philadelphia acted as a unit, they each acted only for their state. That the delegates acted only for their state is also indicated by the fact that each state had one vote, regardless of how large or how small the state was or how many delegates it sent to Philadelphia. Upshur notes:

> A decisive proof of this is found in the fact that the colonies voted on the adoption of that measure in their separate character, each giving one vote by all its own representatives, who acted in strict obedience to specific instructions from their respective colonies, and the members signed the Declaration in that way.[95]

C.C. Burr, editor of Upshur's review of Joseph Story's *Commentaries*, gives additional proof that the states were considered independent entities, even by the newly seated Congress of the United States: "In October, 1776, Congress directed that every officer should swear that 'I acknowledge the thirteen United States of America, namely: New Hampshire, ... [all thirteen states are then named], to be free, independent and sovereign States."[96] Yet, Story maintains that the states were never independent, only exercising the independence of Americans in general.

Citing the Declaration of Independence, Justice Story declares, "It is the right of the people to alter, or to abolish it [an established government], and to institute a new government, laying its foundation on such principles, and organizing its powers in such forms as to them shall seem most likely to effect their safety and

---

95 Upshur, 80.

96 *Ibid.*, 93.

happiness."⁹⁷ When Story declares that the people have a right, we must be very careful to understand what people he is describing. What he is referring to is the majority of the people, or, in his view the majority of the American people, in the aggregate.⁹⁸ Such a population count would, of course, give the Northern faction the majority and place the South's dearest interests under the rule of those whose interest it would be to oppress the South. The same logic would require the Irish to acknowledge the British Crown as their rightful government, because the British numerical majority could always outvote the Irish numerical minority!

Will anyone contend that "We the people" of the United States (that is, a majority of them) may alter or amend the government of the United States? But if we are one people in a political sense, if "We the people" in the aggregate, compose the American nation, then "We the people" in the aggregate must then possess the sovereign power to alter or abolish the Constitution. This is the only logical conclusion one can draw from the position of both Daniel Webster and Justice Story. According to Story, "The people of the United States have a right to abolish, or alter the Constitution of the United States."⁹⁹ This would be true if "We the people" in the aggregate ratified the Constitution. For it is a well-accepted law of political science that the one who has the authority to make a constitution also possesses the authority to alter or abolish that constitution. In 1644, Samuel Rutherford stated, "Those who have power to make have power to unmake a king."¹⁰⁰ What was true in England when dealing with a monarch is true in a republic of free men.

If the Yankee Empire's constitutional theory that the American people in the aggregate ordained the Constitution is correct, then the American people (that is, a mere majority of the total numbers of the people of the United States) in the aggregate possess absolute authority over the Constitution. Therefore, the majority of the

---

97 Story, I, 300.

98 *Ibid.*, I.

99 Joseph Story, as cited in Upshur, 104.

100 Samuel Rutherford, *Lex Rex* (1644, Harrisonburg, VA: Sprinkle Publications, 1982), 126.

American people possess the sovereign authority to express the national will. The states, under this theory, are but mere subdivisions of people within the greater nation. In this system, the states are to the nation what counties are to the states. Abraham Lincoln put forward this view in one of his first speeches made after his election. But how does this theory comport with constitutional and historical reality? Did the federal Congress authorize a general election after the completion of the Constitution in 1787? Did the American people in the aggregate vote to authorize a national government under the new Constitution? Who among President Davis's accusers can give the tally of such a vote? Let those with accusations of treason in their mouths quiet their slanderous tongues until first they give the number of the American national aggregate vote representing the sovereign will of the American people that was cast to ratify the Constitution! They will not give it, they cannot give it, because it does not exist! Like demons from hell, they would beg to be sent into swine rather than be forced to stand in the presence of truth!

As we have seen, the Yankee Empire's school of "one people, one nation indivisible" rushes from one craftily constructed subterfuge to yet another in an attempt to prop up its weak case for a unitary national authority, i.e., the current supreme Federal Government (the Yankee Empire). The proponents of this philosophy are forever arguing in the alternative, declaring that if thus and such does not prove that the Federal Government possesses the supreme law of the land, then certainly this new theory will prove it! Thus, it is with their theory that the thirteen colonies' joint Declaration of Independence created a unitary, national government with supreme authority over "We the people" of the sovereign states. They purposefully elect to ignore the plain language of the document that declared "these United Colonies are, and of Right ought to be FREE AND INDEPENDENT STATES."[101] Note the use of the plural "states." Also note that at that time the word "state" had the same meaning as "nation."

President Davis and the people of the South understood the significance of this document, and in that spirit as "free, independent, [and sovereign] States" they acted upon the words of the document

---

101 Declaration of Independence.

that declared, "When in the Course of human events, it becomes necessary for one people to dissolve ...." You, the jury, must determine if the South's decision to declare its independence from a union that no longer protected its liberty, but actually endangered its liberty; is tantamount to treason; you must determine, therefore, if President Jefferson Davis is innocent or guilty of treason.

THE GOVERNMENT CREATED BY THE CONSTITUTION IS A CONFEDERACY OF SOVEREIGN STATES

Both Story and Webster agreed that the union formed under the Articles of Confederation was a result of a compact among sovereign states and that it was in fact a confederation. Webster stated that the Constitution had changed the nature of government from that of a confederation under the Articles of Confederation to a national government under the Constitution. Webster, in a speech in the Senate on February 16, 1833, declared:

> Indeed, Sir, if we look into all contemporary history, to the numbers of *The Federalist*, to the debates in the Convention, to the publication of friends and foes, they all agree, that a change had been made from a confederacy of States to a different system; they all agree, that the Convention had formed a Constitution for a national government .... In none of the various productions and publications, did any one intimate that the new Constitution was but another compact between States in their sovereign capacity. I do not find such an opinion advanced in a single instance.[102]

In an exercise that is now all too familiar; let us review the words of the Founding Fathers, words that were well known at the time Webster made these allegations.

---

102 Daniel Webster, as cited in Whipple, 289.

- Alexander Hamilton noted that if the Constitution were adopted it would "still be, in fact and in theory, an association of States or confederacy."[103]

- In *The Federalist* No. 8 Hamilton declared Montesquieu's description of a "CONFEDERATE REPUBLIC" as being "luminous" relative to the principles in favor of the ratification of the proposed constitution.[104]

- In *The Federalist* No. 27 Hamilton while discussing the plan put forth by the constitutional convention described the proposed constitution as "the laws of the Confederacy"..."[105]

- In *The Federalist* No. 80 Hamilton labeled the new union to be created by the Constitution as "the CONFEDERACY." Note that it was Hamilton who placed the word "Confederacy" in all capitals, not some rabid Southern secessionist.[106]

As can be seen from these examples, even an ardent nationalist such as Alexander Hamilton described the government created by the proposed Constitution as an association of states or a "CONFEDERACY." The plain and simple purpose of the Constitution was to "form a more perfect Union" and not to form a consolidated unit out of the thirteen sovereign states. The "more perfect Union" was not a new government with new powers, but as James Madison stated in *The Federalist* No. 45, "If the new Constitution be examined with accuracy and candor, it will be found that the change which it proposes consists much less in the addition of NEW POWERS to the Union, than in the invigoration of its ORIGINAL POWERS" [emphasis in the original]. The confederated nature of the government remained, but what was established was a government "both national and federal."[107] The government was to be national in the sense that the Federal Government would exercise those rights delegated to it

---

103 *The Federalist* No. 9, 41.

104 *The Federalist* No. 8, 40.

105 *The Federalist* No. 27, 138.

106 *The Federalist* No. 80, 411.

107 James Madison, as cited in Carey & McClellan, 197.

by the states on behalf of all the states and, it wouldbe federal in that the states reserved the right to all powers not specifically delegated to their agent, the Federal Government. The actions of the Federal Government were to be supreme in those limited areas delegated to it but only so long as the actions of the Federal Government were *pursuant* to the Constitution. The states, according to *The Federalist* No. 85, retained their sovereign right to "erect barriers against the encroachments of the national authority."[108] A supreme national authority or government is sovereign and therefore does not answer to any other government. The Federal Government was designed by the sovereign states to be their agent, to be amenable to its limitations as established by the states in the Constitution. The Federal Government is not national in the sense of being supreme. It is beholding to the sovereign states for its existence; therefore, ultimate sovereignty belongs not with the creation but with the creators (i.e., "We the people of the sovereign states").

James Kent, author of *Commentaries on American Law*, a textbook used at West Point Military Academy from 1827 until well after the War for Southern Independence, noted that the United States consisted of "national and state sovereignties" forming a "great confederacy of states."[109] This renowned legal scholar from New York understood that most basic aspect of American government; the Union is a confederacy of sovereign states. St. George Tucker of Virginia, in 1803, William Rawle of Pennsylvania, in 1825, and James Kent of New York, in 1827, all agreed that the Federal Government was a system of confederate states that had delegated certain powers to their agent, the Federal Government. Joseph Story published his *Commentaries on the Constitution* in 1833 and, at this late date, "discovered" that the Federal Government was created by "We the people" in the national setting rather than "We the people" of the states. His erroneous departure from accepted historical truth, and Daniel Webster's adoption of this error, would plunge the

---

108 Alexander Hamilton, Carey & McClellan, 453.

109 James Kent, *Commentaries on American Law* (1827, New York: Da Capo Press, 1971), 11,444.

United States into its most bloody conflict and be the death knell of the Original Republic of Sovereign States as envisioned by the Founding Fathers.

As was demonstrated in the beginning of this section, Webster declared that he could not find a single case in which the Founding Fathers even "intimated" that the Constitution was a compact between sovereign states. You, the jury, can compare and contrast the words of Webster and those of Hamilton and Madison. Recall Webster's declaration that "I do not find such an opinion advanced in a single instance." You must decide if Webster's research of the history as documented here earns for him your confidence in his intellectual pursuit of the truth. Remember, he is the man who best represents those who cursed the South for withdrawing from the Union, cried havoc, and loosed the dogs of war upon innocent men, women, and children of the South.[110]

SUMMARY

At the beginning of this chapter, we reminded you of the confession of William H. Seward regarding his use of words in order to elicit a desired effect upon the popular mind. We quoted John L. Motley, the apologist for the Yankee Empire's war of aggression against a sovereign natin, the Confederate States of America, to give you a representative sample of the Yankee Empire's apologists' attitude toward the constitutional compact. Keep in mind that Motley wrote on behalf of the Federal Government that secession was unconstitutional because "the Constitution was not drawn up by the States, it was not promulgated in the name of the States, it was not ratified by the States."[111] Remember that these views were first popularized in the American political system by Yankees such as Justice Joseph Story and Senator Daniel Webster. We offered numerous quotations and citations from *The Federalist* and other documents relative to the state ratification debates and to the

---

110 See, Kennedy & Kennedy, *The South Was Right!* 3rd edition, Chapter 7 "Yankee Atrocities," 175-205.

111 John Motley, as cited in Bledsoe, 54.

writings of the anti-Federalists to prove the complete and abject, if not criminal, error of the Yankee Empire's school of "one people, one nation indivisible."

In this chapter, we have asked you, the jury, to perform that function which falls to the jury in all questions of fact. You are called upon to decide between two mutually exclusive alternatives. You are called upon to judge the guilt or innocence of the deposed president of the Confederate States of America. You must decide whether he was a vicious traitor to his country or a patriot and defender of local self-government who led an unsuccessful defense of the principles of the original constitutional compact. In the first few chapters, we presented to you evidence to support the view of Jefferson Davis as a man of integrity and high moral character. In this chapter, we give you an idea of the character of men who typify those who accused President Jefferson Davis and the Southern people of treason. Both cannot be right. You must decide who is the most credible, the most likely to be telling the truth. You must decide between the Yankee Empire's advocates of "one people, one nation indivisible" and President Jefferson Davis, who defended the principles of the United States' original constitutional compact.

Chapter 13

THE MOTIVES OF PRESIDENT DAVIS'S ACCUSERS

NOW THAT YOU, THE JURY, have a better understanding of the character of President Davis's accusers, let us now inquire into the motives of his accusers. Were these "unconditional Union men" motivated by the emotion of American patriotism? Were their actions against President Jefferson Davis and the Southern people a result of a motive of pure love for the United States? Were the advocates of "one people, one nation indivisible" acting out of a selfless sense of duty to the United States? Or was there another reason for their determination to prevent the Southern states from leaving their Union? In this chapter, we will present to you, the jury, evidence demonstrating a long history of antagonism between the two sections of these United States. We will show you evidence of how dissimilar the North and the South were even at the very beginning of these United States. We will demonstrate to you how the North has always been willing, in some cases eager, to sacrifice the interests of the South if doing so would benefit the emerging Northern financial, industrial, and commercial empire.

TWO DISTINCT PEOPLE WITH TWO DISSIMILAR ECONOMIC INTERESTS

The feelings of distinctiveness and of uniqueness between the people of the North and the people of the South can be observed in some of the debates over the ratification of the Constitution. One Northerner described Southerners as wicked people, worse than "the pirates of Algiers [or] the haughty Spaniard. We shall suffer from joining with them. We shall be slaves to the Southern states."[1] A more honest Northerner asked his fellow Northerners, "Shall we refuse to eat or to drink, or to be united, with those who do not think or act just as we do ... the members of the southern States, like ourselves, have their prejudices."[2] New Englanders distrust of Southerners was reflected by a similar dislike and distrust of New Englanders by Southerners. In South Carolina, as well as in other Southern state constitutional conventions, the Federalists argued that the people of New England were fellow citizens who would never stoop to the low level of oppressing other fellow citizens in the Union. An anti-Federalist from South Carolina was not convinced by the Federalist assurances regarding the honorable disposition of the New England states. With more than just a little hint of sarcasm in his voice, Rawlins Lowndes declared that "our kind friends to the north [were] governed by prejudices and ideas extremely different from ours." He warned that New Englanders should not be trusted to adhere to the strict limitations imposed by the Constitution.[3]

William Grayson, a delegate to the Virginia constitutional convention, saw clearly the difference between the North and the South and declared: "There is a great difference of circumstances between the States. The interests of the carrying States [the North] are strikingly different from those of the productive States [the South]. I mean not to give offence to any part of America, but mankind are governed by interest. The carrying States will assuredly unite and our situation will then be wretched indeed. We ought to be wise enough to guard against the abuse of such a government. Republics, in fact, oppress more than monarchies."[4] Grayson saw

---

1   As cited in M. E. Bradford, *Original Intentions, On the Making and Ratification of the United States Constitution* (Athens, GA: University of Georgia Press, 1993), 48.

2   Ibid.

3   Rawlins Lowndes, as cited in *Ibid.*, 65.

4   William Grayson, as cited in Albert Taylor Bledsoe, *Is Davis a Traitor?* (1866, St. Louis: The Advocate Publishing House, 1879), 262.

no real protection for the liberty of "We the people" of the sovereign states simply because the Constitution established a republic. He knew that "Republics ... oppress more than monarchies."

Patrick Henry of Virginia added his thunderous voice to the call for caution by declaring, "But I am sure, that the dangers of this system are real, when those who have no similar interests with the people of this country [Virginia and the Southern states], are to legislate for us when our dearest interests are to be left in the hands of those whose advantage it will be to infringe them."[5] In opposing the new Constitution, Henry warned his fellow Virginians of dire consequences that would result from a union with the North. Henry stated:

> This government [as proposed in the Constitution] subjects everything to the Northern majority. Is there not then a settled purpose to check Southern interests? We thus put unbounded power over our property in hands not having a common interest with us. How can the Southern members prevent the adoption of the most oppressive mode of taxation in the Southern States, as there is a majority in favor of the Northern States? Sir, this is a picture so horrid, so wretched, so dreadful, that I need no longer dwell upon it.[6]

These words were spoken long before the emergence of those issues that would eventually push the South to secession. Yet, even at this early time, Patrick Henry could foresee the day when the Northern numerical majority would seize control of the United States government and use its taxing powers to enrich the North while impoverishing the South.

George Mason, second only to Patrick Henry among Virginia's anti-Federalists, warned his fellow countrymen that he went on a principle often advanced, and with which he concurred, that

---

5   Patrick Henry, Bledsoe, 261.

6   Patrick Henry, as cited in William Wirt Henry, *Patrick Henry: Life, Correspondence, and Speeches* (1891, Harrisonburg, VA: Sprinkle Publications, 1993), III, 520.

"a majority, when interested, would oppress the minority .... [T]he eight Northern States have an interest different from the five Southern States; and have, in one branch of the Legislature, thirty-six votes against twenty-nine, and in the other in the proportion of eight to three. The Southern States had therefore grounds for their suspicions."[7]

Hugh Williamson of North Carolina warned the people of the South that "[t]he Southern interest must be extremely endangered by the present arrangement. The Northern States are to have a majority in the first instance, with the means of perpetuating it."[8] General Charles Pinckney of South Carolina noted, "[I]f they [the Southern states] are to form so considerable a minority, and the regulation of trade is to be given to the General Government, they [the South] will be nothing more than overseers for the Northern States."[9] Note the concern about the power of the United States government to regulate trade and how this power would be used by the Northern majority against the interests of the Southern minority.

The danger, under the system of government as established by the Constitution, of one faction or section of the United States capturing control of the United States government and using that control to its advantage and to the disadvantage of the smaller section of the Union was observed by noted foreigners as well as by early American patriots. Alexis de Tocqueville, in his historic account of early America, noted how one section of the Union could oppress other sections of the Union.

> If it be supposed that amongst the States which are united by the Federal tie, there are some which exclusively enjoy the principal advantages of union, or whose prosperity depends on the duration of that union, it is unquestionable that they will always be ready to support the central Government in enforcing

---

[7] George Mason, as cited in Bledsoe, 261.
[8] Hugh Williamson, *Ibid.*
[9] Charles Pinckney, *Ibid.*

the obedience of the others. But the Government would then be exerting a force not derived from itself, but from a principle contrary to its nature. States form confederations in order to derive equal advantages from their union; and in the case just alluded to, the Federal Government would derive its power from the unequal distribution of those benefits amongst the States.

If one of the confederate [federal Union] States have acquired a preponderance sufficiently great to enable it to take exclusive possession of the central authority, it will consider the other States as subject provinces, and it will cause its own supremacy to be respected under the borrowed name of the sovereignty of the Union. Great things may then be done in the name of the Federal Government, but *in reality that Government will have ceased to exist*[10] [emphasis added].

De Tocqueville described the North and the South as "more like hostile nations, than rival parties, under one government."[11]

It has now been firmly demonstrated that the North and the South were different people with dissimilar and often conflicting cultural, moral, and economic interests. How did the Founding Fathers hope to bring such a divergent group together under one Federal Government? How did they attempt to balance the interests between these two potential adversaries?

STRUGGLE FOR CONTROL OF THE FEDERAL GOVERNMENT

At the end of the War for American Independence, many Americans believed that the European powers would attempt to seize the newly independent American states. The fear of foreign

---

10 Alexis de Tocqueville, *Democracy in America* (1838, New York: The Classics of Liberty Library, 1992), 368.

11 *Ibid.*, 223.

intrigue was a primary consideration encouraging the states to make an effort to form a union of two such diverse sections. Because the Northern states outnumbered the Southern states, it was felt by many even in the North that to establish a lasting union some consideration had to be given to the concerns expressed by the South. Rufus King of Massachusetts fully believed that the great question "concerning a difference of interest did not lie where it had been hitherto discussed, between the great and the small States, but between the Southern and the Eastern States." For this reason, he had been willing to "yield something, in the proportion of representation, for the security of the Southern [states]." He noted during the Massachusetts constitutional convention that the South deserved "a constitutional power of defense to assure her of protection in the new Union."[12] The South cautiously accepted the offer of union with the North, but only after (1) gaining the assurances of a limited Federal Government and (2) reserving all rights not delegated, even the right to withdraw delegated powers if the Federal Government ever used those rights against the people. Even with these promises, it had been difficult for the Federalists to overcome the reluctance of the anti-Federalists. Indeed, the anti-Federalists initially represented a majority in the constitutional conventions of most states—North and South. The states were very reluctant to put the prosperity and liberty of their citizens at risk, even for the sake of protection against possible foreign tyrants. Each sovereign state was very jealous of its independence.

As we have already seen, each of the original thirteen colonies was independent of any other colony or group of colonies. From the very beginning of these United States, there emerged a struggle between the Eastern colonies (generally referred to as the Northern colonies today) and the Southern colonies. The differences between the North and the South were based on cultural issues[13] as well as

---

12 Rufus King, as cited in *Ibid.*, 257, 230.

13 See Grady McWhiney, *Cracker Culture, Celtic Ways of the Old South* (Tuscaloosa, AL: University of Alabama Press, 1988); David H. Fisher, *Albion's Seed* (Oxford and New York: Oxford University Press, 1989), for a detailed description of the cultural differences between the North and the South; and, Kennedy & Kennedy, *Yankee Empire: Aggressive Abroad and Despotic at Home*, 1-13.

economic issues. The economic differences were the primary factors that provoked the War for Southern Independence. The Northern colonies were more diverse in their economy. They had a mixed economy of industry, agriculture, commerce, and finance. The North's agriculture, in comparison to that of the South's, formed less of its economy. The basis for its economy relied more upon the carrying trade (shipping) and other commercial interests. Later, it would expand to the textile trade. The North's commerce was increasingly dependent on Southern agriculture because the South supplied huge quantities of produce that needed to be transported around the world. As the North diversified into the textile industry, it became more dependent on slave-grown cotton. During the early history of America "Yankee" merchants became infamous for the development of the textile, rum, molasses, and African slave trade. They made regular runs to the Caribbean to pick up molasses, then sailed to New England to drop off the molasses which would be made into rum. Back at home in New England, the thrifty Yankee merchants would pick up textile products and rum to exchange in Africa for slaves, and then begin the "middle passage" in which so many Africans would perish, heading back to the Caribbean with their load of human flesh to trade for more molasses. Of course, the thrifty Yankee merchants would mark up a good profit on each transaction.

The Southern colonies, on the other hand, were land rich. Agriculture was the basis for their economy. They had very little "carrying" business. The "carrying" would be done by Yankee or English ships. The South depended on others to supply the larger part of its manufactured goods, and therefore would be harmed if free trade was interrupted. The North, on the other hand, wanted protective tariffs in order to give its manufactured products a competitive edge in the United States. From this analysis, it can be seen that, if the North controlled the United States government and used that power to protect its peculiar interests, then the South would be forced to pay more for its manufactured products and possibly face trade reprisals in England where a large part of the South's agricultural products were sold. Another factor that is virtually unknown to modern Americans is that in this early period the U.S. did not have an income tax or an Internal Revenue Service. The

Federal Government obtained its revenue primarily via tariffs. This meant that, if a protective tariff was enacted by Congress, then not only would the South pay more for imported goods, it would also face the possibility of trade retaliations from its foreign trading partners. In addition, the Southern people would be paying more monies to the United States treasury than their Northern counterparts! Read the words of Colonel Grayson's letter dated September 29, 1789:

> You will see there is a great disposition here for the advancement of commerce and manufactures in preference to agriculture .... You will easily perceive the ascendancy of the Eastern interest by looking at the molasses, which is reduced to two and one-half cents, while salt continues at six, and with an allowance of a drawback to their fish, etc .... The raising of money by impost has been thought very favorably of throughout America .... Satisfied I am it will be particularly injurious to the southern States, who do not and cannot manufacture, and must, therefore, pay duties on everything they consume. The cry here is, 'raise everything this way;' and to be sure this is good policy with the States east of Maryland.[14]

This is the reason that men such as Patrick Henry and George Mason were alarmed about the possibility of a consolidated Federal Government that would be controlled by the numerical majority of the North. The South, as the minority section among the thirteen original states, stood to lose a great deal if the constitutional limits on federal authority were usurped.

By the mid-1800s, it had become extremely clear to most Southerners that there was little hope of the South ever achieving "a constitutional power of defense to assure her of protection in the new Union." The hoped-for balance of power that the overly optimistic James Madison had dreamed of never occurred. Each generation of Southerners saw their rights more in danger than the

---

14 William Grayson, as cited in William Wirt Henry, II, 447.

previous generation. Madison had hoped that a balance between the Southern and Northern states would provide protection for the liberties and interests of both sections. The dreams of his youth became the South's nightmare of invasion, conquest, coercion, occupation, and economic colonialization. In 1850, Jefferson Davis spoke of the need for a balance of power between the two sections: "The danger is one of our own times, and it is that sectional division of the people which has created the necessity of looking to the question of the balance of power, and which carries with it, when disturbed, the danger of disunion."[15]

The fact is that from the very beginning the South was a minority in the Union. The North possessed the majority, thirty-five to thirty in the House of Representatives and fourteen to twelve in the Senate at the time of the first Congress. The South progressively fell behind the North in representation in the House of Representatives from the first Congress (35-30), through the first United States census (57-49), and the second United States census (77-65).[16] In the House of Representatives in 1790, the North had a majority of four (counting Delaware as a Southern state); by 1850, the Northern majority had grown to fifty-four! In 1787, the South had only a slim hope of gaining equality in the federal Congress, and therefore the Southern states were very reluctant to ratify the proposed constitution. In each state, the vote was barely carried in favor of ratification. Is it reasonable to assume that Southern leaders would have voted for ratification had they known that an aggressive Yankee Empire would hold such a dominating grip upon the reins of the United States government? The decline began at the very inception of the "more perfect Union."

Mississippi River—Case in Point

The conflict between the Northern and Southern states was evident even during the union under the Articles of Confederation. The Northern States wanted to use the government of the union to

---

15 Jefferson Davis, as cited in Bledsoe, 239.

16 St. George Tucker, ed., *Blackstone's Commentaries, With Notes of Reference to the Constitution and Laws of the Federal Government of the United States* (1803, New York: Augustus M. Kelley, Publishers, 1969), I, 190.

negotiate treaties with Spain that would be favorable to Northern commerce. One of Spain's primary objectives was to control the flow of commerce from the Mississippi River by excluding Americans from using the port of New Orleans. The Spanish offered the United States representative in Spain, John Jay from New York, favorable trade concessions in exchange for the United States' agreement to Spanish control of the Mississippi River. From the New England point of view, this was a great deal. But, for the South it would prevent the development of the territory that was destined to become Kentucky, Tennessee, and Mississippi. If the United States government accepted the Spanish offer, it would prevent the development of future Southern states and thereby assure New England the dominant position in the United States. The intrigue, subterfuge, and open dishonesty practiced by the Eastern states to achieve a favorable commercial treaty with Spain served as an early warning to the South regarding the character of the people with whom they were associated. William Wirt Henry in his famous *Life of Patrick Henry* gives the details of this first major conflict between the North and the South.

> Mr. Jay ... was directed to insist on the territorial boundaries and the free navigation of the Mississippi.... The Spaniards professed a willingness to grant liberal commercial advantages, on condition that the right to use the Mississippi was given up. The commercial advantages were to accrue mainly to the Eastern and Middle States, while the occlusion of the Mississippi would not only injure the Southern States, but would prevent the filling up of the valley, and the admission of new States to counteract the weight of the Eastern States in Congress ....Jay proposed to Congress to change his instructions, and to permit him to yield the right to navigate the Mississippi .... This Congress attempted to do in secret session, on August 25, 1786, by vote of seven States to five [under the Articles of Confederation each state had one vote in Congress], revoking at the same time the order to conclude no

treaty' until it was communicated to Congress. As this was in the face of the constitutional provision which required nine States to enter into a treaty, it was justly deemed revolutionary by the minority [the minority' being the Southern states].Jay, however, proceeded to frame an article in accordance with the instructions of the seven Northern States. But it seems that already a disposition had manifested itself in the Eastern States to secede from the Union, which gathered strength from the determination of the Southern States to insist on the free navigation of the Mississippi.[17]

Four important issues emerge from a reading of this historical account:

> 1. The Eastern (that is the Northern) states were willing, even eager, to sacrifice the interests of the Southern people in order to secure commercial advantages for the North. From this, it is clear that profits were more important to the Northern politicians than the principle of good will among the states of the Union.
>
> 2. The Northern states were concerned with keeping their numerical advantage over the Southern states even under the Articles of Confederation. The North recognized that using the treaty with Spain to close off a large section of the South adjacent to the Mississippi River from development was an efficient method of preventing the admission of new Southern states.
>
> 3. The Northern states were not beyond using questionable if not unconstitutional methods to advance their commercial interests.

---

17 William Wirt Henry, II, 290-91.

4. The Northern states were willing to secede if they could not advance their commercial cause and maintain control of the union under the Articles of Confederation.

Governor Patrick Henry of Virginia was informed of the illegal acts perpetrated by the Northern states in Congress in a letter written to him by James Monroe. The letter was dated August 12, 1786, and came from New York, where Congress was in secession. The letter informed Governor Henry of the intrigues of Jay and the Eastern states as they attempted to defeat the plain instruction of Congress regarding the right of navigation of the Mississippi.

> He found he had engaged the eastern states in the intrigue, especially Mass.; that New York, Jersey and Penn, were in favor of it, and either absolutely decided, or so much so to promise little prospect of change .... Since nine states only can give an instruction for the formation of a treaty, to appoint a committee with the powers of nine states was agreed to be a subversion of the government and therefore improper .... It appears manifest they have seven states, and we five, Maryland inclusive with the southern states .... It also appears that they will go on under seven states in the business, and risqué the preservation of the confederacy on it .... This is not the only subject of consequence I have to engage your attention to. Certain it is that committees are held in this town of eastern men, and others of this state [New York] upon the subject of a dismemberment of the states east of the Hudson from the union, and the erection of them into a separate government .... [T]he measure is talked of in Mass, familiarly, and is supposed to have originated there.[18]

---

18   *Ibid.*, II, 296-97.

Notice that James Monroe, future president of the United States, detailed how Massachusetts was the originator of a scheme to dismember states from the Union. Where were the charges of treason against the people of Massachusetts? James Monroe added a postscript to this letter declaring:

> The objective in the occlusion of the Mississippi on the part of these people, so far as it is extended to the interests of their States is to break up so far as this will do it, the settlements on the western waters, prevent any in future, and thereby keep the States southw'd as they now are, or if settlements will take place that they shall be on such principles as to make it the interest of the people to separate from the Confederacy, so as effectually to exclude any new State from it. To throw the weight of population eastward and keep it there.... In short, it is a system of policy which has for its object the keeping the weight of government and population in this quarter [the North], and is proposed by a set of men so flagitious, unprincipled, and determined in their pursuits, as to satisfy me beyond a doubt they have extended their views to the dismemberment of the gov't.[19]

Here we see the scheme of the ancestors of many Northern "unconditional Union men" making secret plans to dismember the government of the Union! Are these Northerners publicly tainted with the tar brush of treason and banished from the society of patriotic Americans? Of course not, but the question remains why it was not treason for the North to scheme secretly to dismember the Union, while the open and public secession of the sovereign states of the South is counted as treason? These Northern schemes to dismember the Union happened long before the 1860s. They happened while America was taking its first steps toward a constitutional federal republic of sovereign states.

---

19 *Ibid.*, II.

Patrick Henry was governor of Virginia during this period. He had been instrumental in rallying the Southern states to the aid of New England during the early days of America's struggle for independence. Time and time again, he had treated with the political leaders of New England, assuming them to be gentlemen worthy of trust. He had reassured his people that New England would be a faithful partner in the American Union. The Jay affair had a marked effect on Governor Henry and changed his attitude toward the South's partners in these United States.

> [N]o one felt the action of the Northern States more keenly than Governor Henry. He had induced Virginia to make common cause with New England in the beginning of the Revolution; had urged the confederation of the States, and the ceding of the northwestern territory to cement it; and when the articles had proved defective, had been the champion of amendments to strengthen the Federal power. That the Northern States, for which Virginia had done so much, should, from a purely selfish policy attempt to barter away the navigation of the Mississippi, so valuable to her, at the risk of losing the all-important Western country and dividing the Union, was a shock to him indeed.[20]

John Marshall wrote to Arthur Lee, March 5, 1787: "Mr. Henry, whose opinions have their usual influence, has been heard to say that he would rather part with the confederation [Union] than relinquish the navigation of the Mississippi." Henry alluded frequently to the subject on the floor of the Virginia convention of 1788, in terms which plainly indicated the distrust of the Northern states that their conduct had engendered in his bosom.[21]

---

20   *Ibid.*, II, 300.

21   *Ibid.*, II, 301.

From the preceding narrative, we can see that early in our history the North was willing to risk the Union in order to increase its commercial empire. The North had a majority in Congress and was not embarrassed by using its political power to advance its special interests regardless of the detrimental effect that action might have upon the Southern states. Indeed, it has been demonstrated that the North desired to restrict the possible growth of the South in order to ensure the North's dominance in Congress.

Assumption Of Revolutionary War Debts By the Federal Government

Each of the thirteen states accumulated considerable debt as a result of the American War for Independence. After the war, many of the states, such as Virginia, had raised enough state revenues to pay off their war debt. But other states had chosen not to bear the burden of the additional taxes needed to pay off their debt. Once the United States government, under the Constitution, acquired the power to raise revenues, many of the states demanded that the war debts be assumed by the United States and thereby relieve the states from the burden. The problem was that this proposal was perceived as unfair to those states that had taxed their citizens to pay off their war debt, and, since most of the United States revenues would be raised by tariff and impost, the greatest burden of taxation would fall on the agricultural states. Eventually, the United States assumed the war debts, and the Southern states paid the larger portion of the taxes necessary to liquidate the debt. Patrick Henry and other anti-Federalists had warned their fellow countrymen about the danger of the United States taxing powers being in the hands of Northern commercial interests; this incident vindicates their warnings.

Conflict Upon Admission Of Louisiana And Texas To The Union

In 1803, the United States purchased the Louisiana territory from France giving the United States complete control of the Mississippi from its source to its outlet a few miles below the port of New Orleans. Instead of being excited about the growth potential for the

United States, members of the New England delegation in Congress actually threatened to secede from the Union! Massachusetts was the leader in the fight to restrict the possible growth of Southern states. In 1803, upon the purchase of the Louisiana territory, Massachusetts passed a resolution: "Resolved, that the annexation of Louisiana to the Union, transcends the Constitutional power of the Government of the United States. It formed a new Confederacy to which the states united by the former compact [note the word "compact" used by Massachusetts' legislature], are not bound to adhere."[22] When Massachusetts saw the possibility of the South gaining equality in Congress and therefore gaining the power to resist the efforts of the North to usurp the power of the Union, then the Union's glory waned in its eyes! Massachusetts even considered the possibility that, as a sovereign state, it and its sister states "are no longer bound to adhere" to the rules of the Union. Again, on the fourteenth of January 1811, Massachusetts representative Josiah Quincy declared that his state would secede if the "mixed race Creoles of Louisiana"[23] were admitted to the Union. What was the source of the North's concern relative to the admission of Louisiana to the Union? Simply, the fact that the addition of any new Southern state threatened the dominance of the North in the government of the United States.

The same conflict arose when Texas was admitted to the Union. Confederate States vice president Alexander Stephens noted that the "Legislature of Massachusetts, in 1844, did, without question, pass a series of Resolutions upon the annexation of Texas, of which the following is a part: 'Resolved, ... That the project of the annexation of Texas, unless arrested on the threshold, may drive these States into dissolution of the Union.'... Resolved, ... as the powers of Legislation granted in the Constitution of the United States to Congress, do not embrace the case of the admission of a foreign State, or foreign territory, by Legislation, into the Union, such an act of admission would have no binding force whatever on the people of Massachusetts.' [These resolutions] ... are not at

---

22 Bledsoe, 200; also see J. L. M. Curry, *Confederate Military History* (1899, Harrisburg, PA: The Archive Society, 1994), Vol. I, Part 1, 155.

23 Kennedy & Kennedy, *The South Was Right!* 3rd edition, 14.

all inconsistent with those said to have been passed on a similar subject in 1803. These Resolutions show clearly the understanding of Massachusetts as late as 1844-45, of the nature of the Compact of our Union. Though she did not see fit to exercise her right to secede or withdraw, she nevertheless unmistakably asserted her right to do so under circumstances then existing, by asserting that she would not be bound by the anticipated action of the General Government in the matter of the annexation of Texas."[24] Again, we see representatives of the Northern States threatening to secede if Texas was allowed to join the Union. Why? Because Texas represented one more Southern state with representatives and senators in Congress who would resist the usurpations of the North.

TARIFF QUESTION

As we have already seen, the question of tariffs was a major (if not the major) point of conflict between the Northern and Southern states. It was well known and understood on both sides that the section that controlled the United States government would be able to use the Federal Government's taxing powers to benefit its section. The desire of the North to use the United States government to force the South to pay a larger percentage of the taxes required by the government was noted by Alexis de Tocqueville in the early 1800s. This impartial foreign observer noted, "The parties that threaten the Union rely not on principles but on material interests. In so vast a land these interests make the provinces into rival nations rather than parties. Thus, recently we have seen the North contending for tariffs and the South taking up arms for free trade, simply because the North is industrial and the South agricultural, so that restrictions would profit the former and harm the latter."[25]

By the year 1828, the misuse of the Federal Government's taxing power had become so great that it led to the first threat to secede by a Southern state. In that year, the United States Congress passed a tariff that was so onerous it was known in the South as the Tariff

---

24 Alexander Stephens, *The War Between the States* (1870, Harrisonburg, VA: Sprinkle Publications, 1994), I, 511.

25 De Tocqueville, 177.

of Abomination! A mere forty-one years had passed since the anti-Federalists in each state had warned about the potential danger of a faction seizing the United States government and using it to promote their particular interests. In 1828, South Carolina began to realize that its minority position in the Union had become an economic liability.

The sovereign state of South Carolina refused to accept the abuse of the federal taxing authority. South Carolina's complaint was not that the federal taxes were too high but that the Federal Government, controlled by the Northern majority, had enacted a discriminatory tariff. The United States Congress had passed a tariff that penalized the South while rewarding the North. As such, it was viewed in the South as an unjust use of governmental powers to take from the productive states for the benefit of the commercial states. The North's only justification for enacting the Tariff of Abomination was the fact that it had the requisite number of votes in the United States Congress to pass any tariff it wanted. According to the Northern view, the South had no choice but to "stand and deliver." The state of South Carolina refused to stand silently by while the legislative highwayman of the North conducted its reign of plunder on "We the people" of the sovereign states.

The state of South Carolina in 1831 passed an act of nullification declaring the Tariff of Abomination to be null and void within its sovereign state. The United States government responded by passing the Force Bill which would have allowed the United States to use military force to enforce the discriminatory tariff. South Carolina responded that it would secede from the Union rather than humbly submit to the threat of military invasion.

The entire episode was resolved in a compromise in which the tariff was gradually reduced. It was the type of compromise that the South would see time and time again over the next thirty years. The South, in good faith and out of a sincere desire to preserve the Union, would surrender something of value. In return, the North would retreat for a while on some point of special interest but would always reserve the right (and the expectation) to bring up the question at some later date.

There is an interesting footnote to the United States threat to use the Force Bill as an excuse to invade a sovereign state. In July 1833, as the crisis over the Tariff of Abomination was waning, the United States government was once again faced with the refusal of sovereign states to abide with federal laws that were contrary to the interests of the state. The states of Alabama and Georgia were ordered by the United States to surrender certain lands within their states to the control of the Native Americans within the limits of their states. The two states refused to obey the federal order. There was even talk of the states seceding if the United States attempted to force the people of these states to abide by federal laws that they perceived as injurious to their interests. President Andrew Jackson was given yet another opportunity to use the Force Bill against sovereign states. What happened? The states of Alabama and Georgia, by refusing to acknowledge federal authority over them in that specific instance, in effect nullified the Federal Government's order. The United States did not attempt to enforce its order.[26] This was a significant victory for the sovereign states over an abusive Federal Government and it was achieved without even a hint of the charge of treason.

THE REPUBLICAN PARTY—
THE CREATION OF A SECTIONAL POLITICAL PARTY

From the very beginning of the United States, there were warnings about the possibility of factions forming that would eventually gain control of the United States government and use its powers to oppress the minority. James Madison, speaking at the Virginia convention in 1788, addressed these concerns by stating that "abuse of power, by the majority trampling on the rights of the minority, [has] produced factions and commotions, which, in republics, have more frequently than any other cause, produced despotism." Writing in *The Federalist*, he warned, "When a majority is included in a faction, the form of popular government, enables it to sacrifice to its ruling passion, or interest, both the public good and

---

26 Forrest McDonald, *A Constitutional History of the United States* (Malabar, FL: Robert E. Krieger Publishing Co., 1982), 109.

the rights of other citizens."[27] At this time, Madison believed that the states were so strong they would prove to be a danger to the Federal Government.[28] Later he would learn that the exact opposite would occur and endanger the liberties of "We the people" of the sovereign states. Recall also the words of Gen. Charles Pinckney of South Carolina who noted, "[I]f they [the Southern states] are to form so considerable a minority, and the regulation of trade is to be given to the General Government, they [the Southern states] will be nothing more than overseers for the Northern States."[29] The South feared the possibility of the development of a partisan Northern faction that would use the United States government as an agent of oppression. Early in American history, the possibility of such a faction forming was considered remote.

President George Washington in his farewell address warned Americans about the dangers of sectional factions developing. He noted that both the North and the South stood to gain from a strong and prosperous Union as long as the sense of mutual respect and good will held the Union together. He warned that all Americans, both North and South, had much to lose if either side yielded to the temptations of sectionalism and the strife such a sectionalism would produce. The South based its optimism on the fact that there were a large number of anti-Federalists in the North. The combination of Northern anti-Federalists and Southern conservatives promised a dominance of the States' Rights school of American politics.

The States' Rights coalition that elected so many American presidents prior to the War for Southern Independence was never a sectional faction. All of the States' Rights presidents were elected with a large majority of Northern electoral votes. Abraham Lincoln, on the other hand, was a sectional candidate who did not receive a single Southern electoral vote and whose name did not even appear on the ballot in many Southern states. The Republican Party was not a legitimate American political party; it was a sectional

---

27 James Madison, as cited in Carey & McClellan, eds., *The Federalist* (Dubuque, IA: Kendall/Hunt Publishing Co., 1990), 46.

28 *Ibid.*, 236.

29 Charles Pinckney, as cited in Bledsoe, 261.

party. Lincoln's Republican Party was an anti-constitutional, anti-republican faction pledged to destroy the last vestige of the original Constitutional Republic of Sovereign States. At the time of the debate over the ratification of the Constitution, the overly optimistic Madison had believed that such a faction as the Republican Party of 1861 would never arise in the proposed "more perfect Union." He admitted that the great object of the Federal Government under the proposed Constitution was "to secure the public good, and private rights, against the danger of such a faction."[30]

Even Madison, who had such high hopes for the "more perfect Union" did not become an idol worshiper at the shrine of Union. By his own words Madison was not "an unconditional Union-man." He declared in *The Federalist* No. 45: "Were the plan of the Convention adverse to the public happiness, my voice would be, Reject the plan. Were the Union itself inconsistent with the public happiness, it would be, *abolish the Union*"[31] [emphasis added]. Here, we see that even James Madison when he was a proponent of a strong Federal Government maintained the right of the people to secede from a union that became "inconsistent with the public happiness."

The sad fact is that by 1860 the North had been captured by a sectional party. It was a party that made no pretenses regarding its hatred of the South or its determination to destroy the South. The Radical Abolitionists had spent a generation poisoning the wells of friendship and mutual respect between the two diverse sections. Madison knew that the Union depended upon "a sufficient amount of sympathy among its population." Yet, by 1860, there appeared to be no sympathy left in the North toward its Southern partner in the Union. Indeed, it appeared that the North was no longer willing to acknowledge the South as "partner" of the North, and the day was fast approaching when the emerging Yankee Empire would claim the South as its conquered territory. The aggressive posture assumed by the North would never have occurred if cool, non-partisan leadership

---

30 James Madison, Bledsoe, 253.

31 James Madison, as cited in Carey & McClellan, 236.

had been in control of the North. Instead of such statesmanship, the North was engulfed in virulent anti-South propaganda, of which the Republican Party was, and still is, a leading advocate.

Wendell Phillips boasted of the success of the Republican Party as a sectional party when he declared, "[N]o man has a right to be surprised at this state of things. It is just what we have attempted to bring about. It is the first sectional party ever organized in this country. It does not know its own face, and calls itself national; but it is not national—it is sectional. The Republican Party is a Party of the North pledged against the South."[32]

It should come as no surprise that the same people who chose to ignore the restraints of a written constitution also chose to ignore the warnings of President George Washington regarding the dangers of a sectional party. In his farewell address to the American people, Washington warned the people of the North and the South about the dangers of factions developing and the formation of political parties based on sectional issues. Washington was concerned for the preservation of the Union. He knew that both sections would, if they maintained *mutual* respect and good will, benefit from the Union. But he also knew that the Union was a delicate balance of diverse interests which would require great effort to maintain. Washington understood that a political party based on a sectional faction would eventually destroy the Constitutional Union.[33]

With the election of Abraham Lincoln, the Republican Party, a purely sectional party, took control of the United States presidency. For the first time in American history, a sectional party was in control of the Federal Government. Lincoln and the Republican Party's attitude toward the South was typical of this long train of abuse we have documented in this chapter. Shortly before the outbreak of the War for Southern Independence, Lincoln was visited by a peace delegation from Virginia. When asked by that delegation

---

32 Wendell Phillips, as cited in Bledsoe, 249.

33 Rawle, William, *A View of the Constitution: Secession as Taught at West Point*, Kennedy & Kennedy, editors, 2nd Kennedy edition, (1825, 1993, Wake Forest, NC: The Scuppernong Press, 2020), 260-2.

to let the seceded states go in peace, while allowing Virginia and the other Southern states still in the Union to negotiate a return to the Union by all seceded states, Lincoln replied, "But what am I to do meantime with those men at Montgomery? Am I to let them go on?" The peace delegates from Virginia replied, 'Yes sir, until they can be peaceably brought back." Whereupon, Lincoln replied, "And open Charleston, etc., as ports of entry, with their ten percent, tariff. *What, then, would become of my tariff?*"[34] Lincoln's attitude about "letting the South go," was similar to the attitudes of other Northern leaders at that time. For example, before the firing on Fort Sumter, the following Northern newspapers also expressed the North's concern about the loss of its Southern revenue source:

> The commercial bearing of the question has acted upon the North .... We now see clearly whither we are tending, and the policy we must adopt. With us it is no longer an abstract question—one of Constitutional construction, or of the reserved or delegated powers of the State or Federal Government, but of material existence and moral position both at home and abroad .... *We were divided and confused till our pockets were touched.*[35] [emphasis added]

> The Southern Confederacy will not employ our ships or buy our goods. What is our shipping without it? Literally nothing .... It is very clear that the South gains by this process, and we lose. No—we MUST NOT "let the South go."[36]

---

34 Abraham Lincoln, as cited in Robert L. Dabney, *Discussions* (1898, Harrisonburg, VA: Sprinkle Publications, 1979), II, 94.

35 "The Great Question," *New York Times*, March 30, 1861, 1.

36 "Let Them Go!" (Manchester, NH) *Union Democrat*, February 19, 1861.

Summary

As Jefferson Davis's jury, it is important for you to know the Motives of those who accused him of treason. In this chapter, we have given you an account of the motivation of the political leaders of the North since the very beginning of the United States. You have seen how the original thirteen colonies were two distinct peoples. You have seen that the population of these United States were not one people but very dissimilar people. You have seen how these United States did not compose one people with a common economic interest. The exact opposite was shown to be the case. These United States were composed of diverse peoples with distinctly different cultural inheritances. They were a people who had economic interests that, in modern-day jargon, represented a "sum zero" dilemma—that is, if one side benefited, the other side lost. If the South had free trade, then the Northern industrialists would be forced to compete against cheaper goods from Europe. If the North had protective tariffs, then the South would be forced to pay more for its goods and face the prospect of a trade war with its European trading partners. From the very beginning, it could be seen that the union of the Northern states with the Southern states was *not* a "marriage made in heaven." Unfortunately for Virginia, her marriage to Uncle Sam would prove to be a very abusive marriage—one from which she was not allowed to escape.

You have also seen that the South has always been the minority section and the North (originally referred to as the Eastern states, commercial states, the carrying or shipping states) has always held the position of the majority section. You have seen how many Southerners were concerned about entering into a union with the Northern states because of the vast differences between these sections and the fact that the North would constitute a majority in the United States Congress.

We have given you vivid examples, taken from historical records, regarding the attempts of the North to use the United States government to benefit itself while harming the South. You have seen examples of how the North was willing to risk the Union itself in order to secure commercial advantages for itself and to ensure continuing Northern control of the United States government. You have seen how the navigation of the Mississippi River by Southerners became one of the early points of conflict between these sections. In this conflict, you saw how the North attempted to give away something very important for the development of the South in exchange for commercial benefits the North would receive from Spain.

We presented to you the evidence of how the threat of secession by the New England states was used in an attempt to prevent the admission of the Southern states of Louisiana and Texas into the Union. We then presented you with the specter of a purely sectional party (the Republican Party) developing in America. We gave you evidence of the Republican Party wedded to the peculiar interests of the North and pledged to work against the interests of the South.

After viewing this evidence, we submit to you, the jury, that those who accused the deposed president of the Confederate States of America of treason did so with tainted motives. They were like the thief who ignites a fire in order to hide his crime. Their motive in accusing President Davis of treason was not a pure motive of an American patriot attempting to bring to justice a nineteenth-century Benedict Arnold. Their motive was to prevent the American people from discovering the fraud they had committed upon all Americans and recognizing the treason they had committed against the original Constitution of these United States of America.

"The first thing I have at heart is American liberty, the second thing is American union," Patrick Henry.

Chapter 14

THE STRUGGLE TO PREVENT A CONSOLIDATED FEDERAL GOVERNMENT

WE WILL NOW LOOK at the efforts of the patriots of early America as they attempted to prevent the development of an abusive, centralized United States government. In this chapter, we will present to you, the jury, information as it relates to the struggle that has continued from the very beginning of these United States. It is a struggle between those forces who desired a strong central government (a supreme Federal Government) and those who desired a small, decentralized government that respects the rights of "We the people" of the sovereign states. At this time, you will be provided with evidence demonstrating that Jefferson Davis and his fellow Southerners were not championing revolutionary ideas by advocating secession in 1861. Indeed, you, the jury, will see that Jefferson Davis and the South were following the same path trodden by American patriots of an earlier era.

The struggle with those who yearned for a strong consolidated government for these United States emerged at the constitutional convention of 1787. Some supporters of consolidation were so intrigued with the idea of a grand national government (a supreme Federal Government) as to advocate the reorganization of the government to include a hereditary upper chamber, similar to the House of Lords, and a chief executive appointed for life. Colonel Alexander Hamilton, a leading Federalist, came to the convention with a proposal that would have stripped the states of all of their attributes of sovereignty. He proposed a system that could best be described as a combination of constitutionalism and monarchism. Under his plan, the nation's chief executive would have the authority to appoint the governor of each state and the authority to veto the legislation of any state legislature.[1] Thomas Jefferson declared that "Hamilton was not only a monarchist, but a monarchist bottomed on corruption."[2] When Hamilton's plan for a strong central government was soundly rejected by the convention, he stormed out and did not return until the convention was nearly over. Even though the monarchist faction was completely beaten in the convention, this did not stop them from scheming to enlarge the powers of the Federal Government. During the convention the monarchist faction tried to limit state authority and enlarge the power of the proposed Federal Government. The monarchists quickly rallied around the Federalist Party. According to Thomas Jefferson, the goal of the Federalists was to establish "a single and splendid government of an aristocracy, founded on banking institutions, and moneyed incorporations under the guise and cloak of their favored branches of manufactures, commerce and navigation, riding and ruling over the plundered ploughman and beggared yeomanry."[3] The possibility of the United States government being seized and used by these powerful groups, or even one section of America, was recognized by the foreign observer Alexis de Tocqueville. De Tocqueville commented that this type of abusive control was always a possibility in a federal government where "the most powerful of the combined states assumed the prerogatives of the federal authority and dominated all the others in its name."[4] Many of the Founding Fathers also feared that a faction would seize the "more perfect Union" created by the Constitution and use its increased powers against "We the people" of the sovereign states.

---

[1] William J. Quirk and R. Randall Bridwell, *Judicial Dictatorship* (New Brunswick, NJ: Transaction Publishers, 1995), 75.

[2] Thomas Jefferson, as cited in Abel Upshur, *The Federal Government: Its True Nature and Character* (1868, Houston, TX: St. Thomas Press, 1977), v.

[3] Thomas Jefferson, as cited in Quirk & Bridwell, 83.

[4] Alexis de Tocqueville, *Democracy in America* (1838, New York: The Classics of Liberty Library, 1992), 137.

During the ratifying process for the Constitution, Americans who were concerned about the potential of abuse in the new Federal Government, and therefore were opposed to ratification of the Constitution, were referred to as anti-Federalists. Those favoring the adoption of the Constitution were referred to as Federalists. The Federalists were often classified as either extreme or moderate. The extreme Federalist faction consisted of those who desired a supreme, centralized, United States government. The moderates, such as George Washington, desired a Federal Government strong enough to protect the United States from foreign invasion or coercion but not so strong that it would destroy the existing system of state governments and local self-government. Alexander Hamilton and James Madison, writing in *The Federalist*, promised the people of the states that the sovereign state instead of being consolidated into one centralized government would be preserved in all of its essential attributes.

The Story-Webster (and later Lincoln and the Republican Party) school of "one people, one nation indivisible" maintains that these United States were originally formed into one central government with the states serving as nothing more than mere political subdivisions of the central government. In a nutshell, the Story-Webster school of political thought alleges that the states do not represent independent, sovereign, political units but are mere provinces of the Federal Government, subservient to the supreme Federal Government's rules, laws, and edicts. This is, of course, the very same "logic" that Abraham Lincoln pursued in the invasion of the South. At this point, we must ask the question, is the Story-Webster-Lincoln school of American government what the Founding Fathers intended? Did the Founding Fathers intend to create a monolithic national government (a supreme Federal Government) to rule over the states? Or, did the Founding Fathers envision a coordinate federal-state governmental system whereby the sovereign states would be preserved?

The following quotations from *The Federalist* will demonstrate how important the sovereign states were to the Founding Fathers:

HAMILTON

- The proposed Constitution, so far from implying an abolition of the State governments, makes them constituent parts of the national sovereignty, by allowing them a direct representation in the Senate, and leaves in their possession certain exclusive and very important portions of sovereign power. This fully corresponds, in every rational import of the terms, with the idea of a federal government.[5]

- The State governments, by their original constitutions, are invested with complete sovereignty .... Everything beyond this must be left to the prudence and firmness of the people; who, as they will hold the scales in their own hands, it is to be hoped, will always take care to preserve the constitutional equilibrium between the general (Federal) and the State governments.[6]

- An entire consolidation of the States into one complete national sovereignty would imply an entire subordination of the parts; and whatever powers might remain in them, would be altogether dependent on the general will. But as the plan of the convention aims only at a partial union or consolidation, the State governments would clearly retain all the rights of sovereignty which they before had, and which were not, by that act, exclusively delegated to the United States.[7]

---

5   Alexander Hamilton, as cited in Carey & McClellan, eds., *The Federalist* (Dubuque, IA: Kendall/Hunt Publishing Co., 1990), 41.

6   Carey & McClellan, 154.

7   *Ibid.*, 156.

MADISON

- Do they require that, in the establishment of the Constitution, the States should be regarded as distinct and independent sovereigns? They are so regarded by the Constitution proposed.[8]

- Having shown that no one of the powers transferred to the federal government is unnecessary or improper, the next question to be considered is, whether the whole mass of them will be dangerous to the portion of authority' left in the several States .... [T]he States will retain, under the proposed Constitution, a very extensive portion of active sovereignty .... The State governments may be regarded as constituent and essential parts of the federal government; whilst the latter [federal government] is nowise essential to the operation or organization of the former [state governments] .... Thus, each of the principal branches of the federal government will owe its existence more or less to the favor of the State governments.[9]

- Many considerations, besides those suggested on a former occasion, seem to place it beyond doubt that the first and most natural attachment of the people will be to the governments of their respective States.[10]

- It has been already proved that the members of the federal [government] will be more dependent on the members of the State governments, than the latter [states] will be on the former [federal].[11]

- In this spirit it may be remarked, that the equal vote allowed to each State is at once a constitutional recognition of the portion of sovereignty remaining in the individual States,

---

8   James Madison, as cited in Carey & McClellan, 203.
9   Carey & McClellan, 235-37.
10 *Ibid.*, 240.
11 *Ibid.*, 241.

and an instrument for preserving that residuary sovereignty. So far the equality ought to be no less acceptable to the large than to the small States; since they are not less solicitous to guard, by every possible expesnt, against an improper consolidation of the States into one simple republic.[12]

Hamilton
[Hamilton's "Assurances vs Actual Experience]

- It is inherent in the nature of sovereignty not to be amenable to the suit of an individual without its consent. This is the general sense and the general practice of mankind; and the exemption, as one of the attributes of sovereignty, is now enjoyed by the government of every' State in the Union. Unless, therefore, there is a surrender of this immunity in the plan of the convention, it will remain with the States, and the danger intimated [by the anti-Federalists] must be merely ideal .... It is evident it could not be done [commanding a state to submit to the authority of the federal court in a suit brought by an individual] without waging war against the contracting States; and to ascribe to the federal courts, by mere implication, and in destruction of a pre-existing right of the State governments, a power which would involve such a consequence, would be altogether forced and unwarrantable.[13] [Forced or not, this is exactly what the federal Supreme Court attempted to do in *Chisholm v. Georgia*, 1793.]

- The principles established in a former paper teach us that the States will retain all pre-existing authorities which may not be exclusively delegated to the federal head.[14]

What were these "pre-existing authorities" that each of the states retained? At the time of the writing of *The Federalist*, the states were in the union created by the Articles of Confederation. Article II of

---

12 *Ibid.*, 320.

13 Alexander Hamilton as cited in Carey & McClellan, 421.

14 Carey & McClellan, 424.

the Articles of Confederation plainly states that "[e]ach State retains its sovereignty, freedom, and independence, and every power, jurisdiction, and right, which is not by this Confederation expressly delegated to the United States in Congress assembled." When the writers of *The Federalist* asserted or implied that the states retained all rights not delegated to the Federal Government, they declared that every right held under the Articles of Confederation remained with the sovereign state unless specifically delegated to the Federal Government. Recall also that under the Articles of Confederation the sovereign states exercised their inalienable right to secede from the "perpetual union" under the Articles of Confederation and then exercised their inalienable right to choose freely whether to accede to the "more perfect Union" created under the Constitution. Nowhere in the Constitution can it be found where the sovereign states renounced any portion of their inalienable right to accede to or secede from the Union. Paraphrasing the Ninth and Tenth Amendments, a right not delegated remains with the states to be exercised or not at the discretion of the sovereign state.

When the Southern states seceded from the Union in 1861, their primary motivation was to remove themselves from the authority of the United States government that had become consolidated into a powerful and abusive government.[15] Thomas Jefferson lamented the Federal Government's "usurpation of the powers retained by the States" and, as late as 1825, solemnly asserted that, though a dissolution of the Union would be a great calamity, submission to a government of unlimited powers would be a greater calamity.[16]

The South was forced to leave the Union because the efforts of the Founding Fathers to establish a limited Federal Government had been defeated by the Yankee Empire's school of "one people, one nation indivisible." To understand why the South felt forced to secede

---

15   For a detailed study of the South's efforts to preserve its rights in 1861 see Kennedy & Kennedy, *The South Was Right!* 3rd edition, (1991, 1994, Columbia, SC: Shotwell Publishing, 2020).

16   J.L.M. Curry, *Confederate Military History* (1899, Harrisburg, PA: The Archive Society, 1994), Vol. I, Part 1, 25.

in 1861, it is necessary to understand why the Founding Fathers desired to limit the Federal Government's power. To determine this, we will once again look to the words of the Founding Fathers.

During the early stages of the constitutional convention, James Madison desired a strong central government. But, as the convention progressed, he became aware of the potential for abuse in an overly strong central government. No doubt, Madison also noted the possibility of the numerical majority of the North gaining complete control of the power of the central government. With this awareness in mind, Madison joined with Thomas Jefferson to become one of America's premier States' Rights proponents. Madison was concerned that any government could and most likely would become a tool used by unscrupulous men. He assessed the potential for men to abuse power and the need to limit the power of any government controlled by men, declaring, "If men were angels no government would be necessary. If angels were to govern men, no controls on government would be necessary."[17] Notice that Madison emphatically declared that because men are not "angels," government by men must be kept under control. Thomas Jefferson also spoke of the danger posed by even good men who control government: "If once they [the people] become inattentive to the public affairs, you and I, and Congress, and Assemblies, judges and governors shall all become wolves." Jefferson was keenly aware of the fact that men could and would use the Federal Government to advance their peculiar interests even if that action caused great harm to their former confederates in other sections of the country. "In every government on earth is some trace of human weakness, some germ of corruption and degeneracy, which cunning will discover, and wickedness insensibly open, cultivate, and improve. Every government degenerates when trusted to the rulers of the people alone. The people themselves therefore are its only safe depositories. And to render even them safe their minds must be improved to a certain degree."[18] From these statements we can see that Jefferson did not trust the unbridled power of government—especially in the hands of uneducated or ideologically brainwashed voters.

---

17 James Madison, as cited in Quirk & Bridwell, xi.

18 Quirk & Bridwell, 11-12.

During the constitutional convention in 1787, the monarchists and the Federalists continually called for a strong national government. They termed such a government an "energetic" government. Thomas Jefferson was not impressed with such governments. Jefferson warned the people that an "energetic" government is always oppressive.[19] Jefferson foresaw the eventual result of establishing an "energetic" Federal Government. He understood human nature well enough to predict what would happen under such a government. The problem with "energetic" governments is that those who believe in them make the arrogant assumption that politicians who devise and pass "energetic" legislation know better than "We the people" what is best for us—"energetic" governments destroy local self-government.[20]

The leaders of the South even at this early time in American history were beginning to fear the possibility of the Northern numerical majority seizing control of the Federal Government and using it to pass legislation that advanced the interests of the North and endangered the interests of the South. James Madison warned, "If a majority be united by a common interest, the rights of the minority will be insecure." Remember, the South was the numerical minority from the very beginning of these United States. Even at this early time, Southern leaders trembled at the possibility of a "majority" faction forming in the North that would use its power against the Southern minority. "In a society, under the forms of which the stronger faction can readily unite and oppress the weaker, anarchy may as truly be said to reign."[21]

---

19 *Ibid.*, 18.

20 See Kennedy, James Ronald, *Freedom Now—A non-violent conservative revolution* (Wake Forest, NC: The Scuppernong Press, 2022).

21 Quirk & Bridwell, 58.

The Founding Fathers' Natural Apprehension of Big Government

The natural apprehension with which the Founding Fathers viewed government was noted by Sir William Holdsworth in his *History of English Law*: "They were not inclined to entrust unfettered powers to a popularly elected legislature; for they recognized that the usurpations of such legislature would lead to tyranny as quickly as usurpations of the Executive. They were not believers in equalitarian theories."[22]

As we have seen, the Founding Fathers did not trust *any* government controlled by men; and, since any human government must, by definition, consist of men, then that government must be controlled. See for yourself the evidence of Thomas Jefferson's apprehension and distrust regarding a consolidated, all-powerful government:

- It should be remembered, as an axiom of eternal truth in politics, that whatever power in any government is independent [with no means by which the people may counteract it], is absolute also; in theory only, at first, while the spirit of the people is up, but in practice, as fast as that relaxes. [Jefferson was seventy-five years old when he wrote this paragraph in a letter to Spencer Roane.][23]

- Sometimes it is said that man cannot be trusted with the government of himself. Can he, then, be trusted with the government of others? Or have we found angels in the forms of kings to govern him? [This quote comes from Jefferson's first inaugural address given in 1801].[24]

---

22 William Holdsworth, as cited in M. E. Bradford, *Original Intentions, On the Making and Ratification of the United States Constitution* (Athens, GA: University of Georgia Press, 1993), 32.

23 Thomas Jefferson, as cited in William B. Parker, ed., *Letters and Addresses of Thomas Jefferson* (Buffalo, NY: National Jefferson Society, 1903), 264.

24 Parker, 137.

- If once they [the people] become inattentive to the public affairs, you and I, and Congress, and Assemblies, judges and governors shall all become wolves.[25]

From these quotes, it is clear that Thomas Jefferson, the early leader of the States' Rights faction, did not trust big government. This natural distrust of government brought the States' Rights faction in direct conflict with those who desired a strong, centralized, Federal Government. Those who wanted a strong central government included initial monarchists united under the Federalist Party banner. Thomas Jefferson noted this fact when, in 1822, he declared of the Federalists, "They see that monarchism is a hopeless wish in this country, and are rallying anew to the next best point, a consolidated government."[26] Three years later, Jefferson, in a letter to William Short, continued his attack upon the monarchist element:

> Monarchy, to be sure, is now defeated, and they wish it should be forgotten that it was ever advocated .... Yet the spirit is not done away. The same party takes now what they deem the next best ground, the consolidation of the government; the giving to the federal member of the government, by unlimited constructions of the Constitution, a control over all the functions of the States, and the concentration of all power ultimately at Washington.[27]

Eventually the Federalist Party would lose so much support that it could no longer offer candidates for president. In other words, the official party of those who wanted a consolidated, supreme, national government was not only defeated at the polls by the States' Rights faction under Thomas Jefferson, but the party of consolidation was also totally destroyed! Such was the American people's disdain for centralized, national government—a supreme Federal Government. But, just like the monarchists who merged their efforts for a strong

---

25 Thomas Jefferson, as cited in Quirk & Bridwell, 1.
26 Quirk & Bridwell, 95.
27 Thomas Jefferson, as cited in Parker, 282.

national government with the efforts of the Federalists, after the defeat of the Federalists by the States' Rights faction, the Federalists merged their efforts with like-minded individuals and continued their efforts to subvert the original intentions of the Founding Fathers.

From the earliest days of our republic, Federalists in high positions used their influence to subvert the sovereign authority of the states. Men such as Supreme Court Justice John Marshall are examples of Federalists who used their offices to promote their concept of a centralized Federal Government. James Madison complained that Marshall's opinion tended "to convert a limited into an unlimited Government."[28] Thomas Jefferson's concern was evident in his letter to Thomas Ritchie written in 1820. Jefferson lamented that the Marshall court was "the germ of dissolution of our federal government ... an irresponsible body [working] like gravity, by day and night, gaining a little today and a little tomorrow, and advancing its noiseless step, like a thief over the fields of jurisdiction, until all shall be usurped from the States, the government of all becoming a consolidated one."[29] Here, we read the words Thomas Jefferson, the author of the Declaration of Independence, and James Madison, the "Father of the Constitution," as they displayed their apprehension about the development of a centralized, all-powerful, Federal Government. If these two Founding Fathers of our republic expressed such concern, can anyone fault Jefferson Davis and the people of the South for acting upon similar, if not identical, concerns?

By 1861, the people of the South were well aware of the trickery, and Machiavellian sophistry used by the Northern majority to expand the role of the Federal Government—to the detriment of Southern interests. The Federal Supreme Court was one of the primary instruments used by the Federalists to expand the Federal Government's powers. Under Chief Justice John Marshall, a Federalist, the court put forward the concept that the Constitution implied that the Federal Court had the right of judicial review. By this tactic, the Federal Government usurped from the sovereign states

---

28 James Madison, as cited in Quirk & Bridwell, 94.

29 Thomas Jefferson, as cited in Quirk & Bridwell, 95.

the power to judge if an act of their agent, the Federal Government, is "pursuant" to the Constitution. In effect, it placed a department of the Federal Government in charge of making sure that the Federal Government respected the limitations imposed upon it by the Constitution! It would be similar to an individual hiring an agent and then allowing the agent to make the final decision regarding disputes about the agent's employment contract. One could be sure that the agent would never lose!

Bishop Hoadly, a seventeenth-century ecclesiastic, warned that whoever has the authority to interpret a document is really more powerful than those who originally wrote the document! He wrote that "[w]hoever hath an absolute authority to interpret any written or spoken laws, it is He who is truly the Law-Giver to all intents and purposes, and not the person who first wrote or spoke them."[30] Early Americans knew that, if the Supreme Court was allowed to be the final judge as to whether an act of the Federal Government is "pursuant" to the Constitution, then the liberty of "We the people" of the sovereign states would be held at the Federal Government's pleasure. A Federal Supreme Court could bend and twist the Constitution to make it say anything the members of the court wanted. In 1810, Thomas Jefferson wrote that the law in the hands of Federalist Justice John Marshall "is nothing more than an ambiguous text, to be explained by his sophistry into any meaning which may subserve his personal malice."[31] He noted that as early as 1810 the Supreme Court had "erected themselves into a political body with the assumed functions of correcting what they deem the errors of the nation."[32]

Chief Justice Charles Evans Hughes, while he was governor of New York, boasted, "We are under the Constitution, but the Constitution is what the judges say it is."[33] Chief Justice Harlan Stone in *U.S. v. Buller* expressed this view of the unlimited powers

---

30   Bishop Hoadly as cited in Thayer, *The Origin and Scope of the American Doctrine of Constitutional Law*, Harvard Law Review 152 (1893).

31   Thomas Jefferson, as cited in Quirk & Bridwell, 3.

32   Quirk & Bridwell, 3.

33   Chief Justice Charles E. Hughes, *Ibid.*, 44.

of the Federal Supreme Court: "[W]hile unconstitutional exercise of power by the executive and legislative branches of the government is subject to judicial restraint, the only check upon our own exercise of power is our own sense of self-restraint."[34] Latter-day Southern scholars have noted the lack of intellectual honesty regarding the interpretation and use of the Constitution by those who desire to use it to justify the creation and maintenance of the supreme Federal Government. Dr. Mel Bradford of Texas accused past and present-day federal judges of using their ignorance as an excuse to create "mischief, judicial and legislative, attempted in the name of 'constitutional principles'—misnomers extrapolated from the 'sacred text' by people who know next to nothing about its origins and have no intention of correcting what they find to be, for their own purposes, a useful ignorance."[35] This "useful ignorance" of the Constitution was used by the Northern numerical majority to nullify the original intentions of the Founding Fathers who established a limited federal republic of sovereign states and helped turn it into a consolidated, supreme, Federal Government. Let us review again the original intentions of the Founding Fathers relative to the establishment of a limited Federal Government that preserved the states as sovereign political entities.

ORIGINAL INTENTIONS FOR A LIMITED FEDERAL GOVERNMENT

The very structure of the Constitution demonstrates that the Founding Fathers intended to establish specific limits to the exercise of power by the Federal Government. Forrest McDonald (1927-2016), a constitutional scholar, described the government under the Constitution as one with numerous limits, restraints, and controls placed upon it by the states. According to McDonald, "The Constitution was designed to bring government under the rule of law, as opposed to achieving any specific purposes .... Fully 20 percent of the text is specification of things that government, state or federal, may not do. Only 11 percent is concerned with positive grants of power. Most of the powers granted had already been vested

---

34 Chief Justice Harlan Slone, *Ibid.*, 45.

35 Bradford, 19.

in the old Confederation Congress, and of the ten new ones, all had previously been exercised by the states .... The main body of the Constitution, more than two-thirds of it, addresses the task of making government act in accordance with law."[36] McDonald's assessment is easily corroborated by the words of the Founding Fathers. John Randolph assured the delegates to Virginia's constitutional convention that they had no intention of giving indefinite powers to the national legislature, declaring that he was entirely opposed to such an inroad on the state jurisdictions and that he did not think any considerations whatever could ever change his determination.[37] Roger Sherman from Connecticut declared that the power being delegated to the Federal Government should be strictly forbidden "to interfere with the government of the individual states in any matters of local police."[38] Hugh Williamson from North Carolina spoke against giving the Federal Government a power that might allow it to restrain the states from regulating their internal police.[39] Colonel Joseph Varnum, an anti-Federalist from Massachusetts, was sure that under the United States government established by the Constitution the government would have "no right to alter the internal relations of the states."[40] According to Charles Pinckney from South Carolina, "[N]o powers could be executed, or assumed [by the Federal Government] but such as were expressly delegated."[41]

As reassuring as these statements are, some Federalists desired the new government to have the extraordinary power to nullify acts passed by state legislatures. This would have been something never before allowed within the thirteen former colonies. Gouverneur Morris of Pennsylvania described the proposed power to allow a federal negative over state legislation as "terrible to the states."[42] From the words of the Founding Fathers, as cited here, it can be seen

---

36   Forrest McDonald, Bradford, xii.

37   Bradford, 8.

38   Roger Sherman, as cited in *Ibid.*, 10.

39   Hugh Williamson, as cited in *Ibid.*, 10.

40   Joseph Varnum, as cited in *Ibid.*, 40.

41   Charles Pinckney, as cited in *Ibid.*, 65.

42   Gouverneur Morris, as cited in *Ibid.*, 10.

that the people of the states did not create a national government having dominant authority over "We the people" of the sovereign states; but, they intended to, and did in fact, create a limited Federal Government to serve the states as their agent. Now that we have established the fact that the original intention of the Founding Fathers was the creation of a limited Federal Government, let us look at the role the Founding Fathers intended to leave for the states under the new Union.

THE SOVEREIGN STATE—
THE ULTIMATE DEFENDER OF PERSONAL LIBERTY

In *The Federalist* No. 85, Alexander Hamilton assured the people of the states that they had nothing to fear from the proposed Federal Government under the Constitution. He promised the people of the states that if they ratified the Constitution their liberty would always be secure because the sovereign state would always retain the right and power to "erect appropriate barriers"[43] between an abusive Federal Government and the people of the states. The right and duty of the state to protect its citizens from an abusive Federal Government were celebrated by President Thomas Jefferson in his first inaugural address when he said:

> [W]hat I deem the essential principles of our government ... the support of state governments in all their rights, as the most competent administrations for our domestic concerns and the surest bulwarks against anti-republican tendencies ... what more is necessary to make us a happy and prosperous people? Still one thing more, fellow citizens, a wise and frugal government, which shall restrain men from injuring one another, which shall leave them otherwise free to regulate their own pursuits of industry and

---

43 Alexander Hamilton, as cited in Carey & McClellan, 453. For a full discussion of the right of the state to protect its citizens from an abusive Federal Government in modern times, see Kennedy & Kennedy, *The South Was Right!* 3rd edition, (Columbia, SC: Shotwell Publishing, 2020).

improvement, and shall not take from the mouth of labor the bread it has earned. This is the sum of good government.[44]

William Samuel Johnson from Connecticut declared that the states needed some way to defend themselves against the new powers given to the Federal Government. He said of the states that "the states do exist as political societies—[they] must be armed with some power of self-defense."[45] Most of the Founding Fathers agreed with Patrick Henry of Virginia and Rawlins Lowndes of South Carolina that their primary concern was to establish a system of government that would protect the liberty of the states from foreign dangers while maintaining the liberty and independence of each state to negotiate within itself to determine the values it would affirm. The sovereign states, within their sphere and according to the authority they specifically reserved unto themselves, would be supreme.

Even Federalists admitted, on all hands, that the Federal Government was given no powers but those specifically and expressly granted to it by the Constitution and that all rights not expressly delegated to the Federal Government were reserved by the several states. The following is only a partial listing of America's Founding Fathers who believed and publicly affirmed the general attitude that "all powers not expressly delegated to Congress are reserved to the several states, to be by them exercised."[46]

- Samuel Adams from Massachusetts

- James Wilson from Pennsylvania (see his State House Yard Speech of October 6, 1787)

- General William R. Davis of North Carolina

- Justice James Iredell of North Carolina

---

44 Thomas Jefferson, as cited in Parker, 138.
45 William Samuel Johnson, as cited in Bradford, 9.
46 Samuel Adams, as cited in Bradford, 40-41.

- James Madison of Virginia • Edmund Pendleton of Virginia
- John Lansing of New York

The concept of a limited Federal Government and a union of sovereign states was the generally held conviction of most Federalists at the dawn of the Constitutional Federal Republic. (Federalists were those who wanted a strong or vigorous Federal Government—remember that James Madison was numbered among this group early in the debate between limited and consolidated government.) State sovereignty was an accepted and acknowledged fact in the beginning of the republic, even among Federalists.

The following quotations from the writings of Alexander Hamilton and James Madison in *The Federalist* demonstrate the fact that our Founding Fathers acceded to the Union only because they felt that their rights could be protected by their sovereign states. Two important points are clear: (1) even extreme Federalists such as Hamilton and moderate Federalists such as Madison agreed that the sovereign state would have means at its disposal to counteract an intrusive or oppressive Federal Government; and (2) the Federalists were overly optimistic, or even naive, about the ability of the states to resist the Federal Government's unconstitutional acts. It should be remembered that, when the Constitution was submitted to the states for consideration, the anti-Federalists held a slight majority in most states. The only way the Federalists could gain ratification of the proposed Constitution was by assuring the moderate anti-Federalists that their states would always have means "to erect appropriate barriers against the encroachments of the national authority,"[47] plus the promise of a Bill of Rights limiting federal authority, and the acceptance of *conditional* ratification whereby some states specifically reserved the right to withdraw their delegated authority; that is, they reserved the right to secede from the United States. These quotations demonstrate the fact that the Founding Fathers intended for the sovereign states to serve as a defense against an abusive Federal Government:

---

47 Alexander Hamilton, as cited in Carey & McClellan, 453.

Hamilton

- It may safely be received as an axiom in our political system, that the State governments will, in all possible contingencies, afford complete security against invasions of the public liberty by the national authority .... If the federal army should be able to quell the resistance of one State, the distant States would have it in their power to make head with fresh forces. The advantages obtained in one place must be abandoned to subdue the opposition in other; and the moment the part which had been reduced to submission was left to itself, its efforts would be renewed, and its resistance revive.[48]

- But it will not follow from this doctrine that acts of the larger society [the Federal Government] which are *not pursuant* to its constitutional powers, but which are invasions of the residuary authorities of the smaller societies [the state governments], will become the supreme law of the land. These will be merely acts of usurpation, and will deserve to be treated as such. Hence we perceive that the clause which declares the supremacy of the laws of the Union, like the one we have just before considered, only declares a truth, which flows immediately and necessarily from the institution of a federal government. It will not, I presume, have escaped observation, that it *expressly* confines this supremacy to laws made *pursuant to the Constitution*; which I mention merely as an instance of caution in the convention; since that limitation would have been to be understood, though it had not been expressed.[49]

---

[48] Carey & McClellan, 141.

[49] *Ibid.*, 161.

Madison

- [C]ompare the militia officers of three millions of people with the [United States] military and marine officers of any establishment which is within the compass of probability, or, I may add, of possibility, and in this view alone, we may pronounce the advantage of the States to be decisive.[50]

- On the other hand, should an unwarrantable measure of the federal government be unpopular in particular States, ... the means of opposition to it are powerful and at hand. The disquietude of the people; their repugnance and. perhaps, refusal to co-operate with the officers of the Union; the frowns of the executive magistracy of the State; the embarrassments created by legislative devices, which would oppose, in any State, difficulties not be despised; would form, in a large State, very serious impediments; and where the sentiments of several adjoining States happened to be in unison, would present obstructions which the federal government would hardly be willing to encounter .... Extravagant as the supposition is, let it however be made. Let a regular army, fully equal to the resources of the country, be formed; and let it be entirely at the devotion of the federal government; still, it would not be going too far to say, that the State governments, with the people on their side, would be able to repel the danger.[51]

- [T]he considerations stated in this and the last paper, they seem to amount to the most convincing evidence, that the powers proposed to be lodged in the federal government are as little formidable to those reserved to the individual States, as they are indispensably necessary to accomplish the purposes of the Union; and that all those alarms which have been sounded, of the meditated and consequential annihilation of the State governments, must, on the most favorable interpretation, be ascribed to the chimerical fears

---

50 James Madison, *Ibid.*, 238.

51 *Ibid.*, 242-43.

of the authors of them.⁵² [The Yankee Empire's invasion and conquest of Sovereign States in 1861-5 proves that it was not a "chimerical" fear!]

- [I]t has, on another occasion, been shown that the federal legislature will not only be restrained by its dependence on the people, as other legislative bodies are, but that it will be, moreover, watched and controlled by the several collateral legislatures, which other legislative bodies are not.⁵³

- I am unable to conceive that the State legislatures, which must feel so many motives to watch, and which possess so many means of counteracting the federal legislature, would fail either to detect or to defeat a conspiracy of the latter against the liberties of their common constituents.⁵⁴

Hamilton

- We may safely rely on the disposition of the State legislatures to erect barriers against the encroachments of the national authority.⁵⁵

The Federalists eventually overcame the reluctance of the anti-Federalists to enter into a union that the anti-Federalists feared could be used against the people of the sovereign states. The Federalists did so by assuring the moderate anti-Federalists that "the State governments will, in all possible contingencies, afford complete security against invasions of the public liberty by the national authority,"⁵⁶ and other such hollow promises. When the Southern states seceded in 1861, they were merely acting upon the assurances given to their generation and all other generations of Americans by the Founding Fathers.

---

52 *Ibid.*, 245.
53 *Ibid.*, 276.
54 *Ibid.*, 288.
55 Alexander Hamilton, as cited in *Ibid.*, 453.
56 Carey & McClellan, 141.

The unconstitutional change from a limited constitutional republic to a consolidated, supreme Federal Government occurred under the direction of the political leaders of the Northern numerical majority—the emerging Yankee Empire. This change in the nature of the government of these United States was accomplished by denying that the Constitution was a compact among sovereign states and by calling upon a "higher law" that would, according to the Northern majority, supersede the Constitution. This "higher law" gave the Northern numerical majority an excuse for voiding and nullifying the Constitution. This "higher law" theory provided the Northern majority an excuse for ignoring the limitations placed upon the Federal Government by the Constitution, and allowed them to use the Federal Government's military power to force the numerical minority of the nation (i.e., the South) to accept a government harmful to its interests and oppressive of the rights of "We the people" of each sovereign state—a government that violates the unalienable American right of a government based upon the consent of the governed.

In the beginning of the struggle for a consolidated national government, the sovereign states were able to rebuff the efforts of those who yearned to unconstitutionally expand the Federal Government's powers. At first, the proponents of federal supremacy were not able to induce the states to surrender their reserved rights. As long as the advocates of federal supremacy "played by the rules" (that is, they respected the authority of the constitutional compact), the sovereign states were capable of defending the rights and liberties of their citizens. It was not until the advocates of federal supremacy changed their tactics that they began to subdue the sovereign states. The following are examples of conflicts between the Federal Government and the sovereign states in which the states were able to defeat unauthorized encroachments of States' Rights by the federal government.

- *Chisholm v. Georgia*: The states had been assured by the writings of the Federalists that they need not fear that the sovereign state would ever be commanded to appear and defend itself in a suit brought by an individual in a federal court.⁵⁷ Yet, in 1793, the Federal Supreme Court attempted to bring the sovereign state of Georgia into court in a suit brought by an individual from another state. The Georgia legislature gave a reply that demonstrated the view of that state regarding the proper role of a sovereign state within the United States. It passed a resolution declaring that any federal official who attempted to enforce the federal court order would be "hung by the neck without benefit of clergy."⁵⁸

- As a result of the federal court's attempt to infringe upon the sovereignty of the state of Georgia, the states ratified the Eleventh Amendment which prohibits the federal court from hearing such suits. Here, we see that the very first amendment to the United States Constitution was passed by the states to ensure state sovereignty.

- In 1798, the states of Kentucky and Virginia passed their famous resolutions which had the effect of nullifying the unconstitutional Alien and Sedition Acts passed by the United States Congress. These resolutions were authored by Thomas Jefferson and James Madison and were a response to the Federal Government's violation of the Bill of Rights. According to these unconstitutional federal laws, it was a crime to criticize publicly a federal officer, or to publish anything critical of the Federal Government. Numerous political enemies of the Federalist president John Adams were harassed, arrested, and jailed under these federal laws! The states of Kentucky and Virginia protected their citizens from the dangers of an oppressive Federal Government by passing these acts. These resolutions declared that the states entered into a "compact" under the Constitution, and, as with all compacts between equals, each party (each state) has the right to "judge for itself" if the acts of its mutual agent are in accordance to the compact. If a party determines that the compact is not being adhered to, then that party, according to the States' Rights principle as established by our

---

57 Bradford, 421.

58 Kennedy and Kennedy, *The South Was Right!,* 3rd edition, 14.

Founding Fathers, has the "right to judge for itself, as well of infractions, as of the mode and measure of redress." In other words, the remedy for the violation of the Constitution is to be determined and enforced by "We the people" of the sovereign state(s). The oppressive acts of the Federalists during John Adams's tenure as president were so displeasing to the American people that in the next election they elected Thomas Jefferson, a firm States' Rights man, as president. Again, the efforts of those who desired a supreme Federal Government were defeated by the States' Rights faction who relied upon the constitutional authority of the sovereign states to nullify the Federal Government's unconstitutional acts.

- The Tariff of Abomination was passed by the Northern-controlled Congress in 1828. The South by this time had seen the dreadful predictions of the anti-Federalists of 1787 come to pass. The Northern majority assumed their dominance in Congress gave them the right to tax the South and use the revenues raised to enrich the North. South Carolina saw the tariffs of 1828 and 1832 as a death sentence on its economy. As a sovereign state South Carolina decided to nullify the tax and if necessarily withdraw from an oppressive union. By this time, the advocates of "one people, one nation indivisible" were in control of the federal legislature. They used their control of the legislature of the Union as a means of aggrandizement for the Northern industrial and commercial empire. The South had become a major source of revenue for that empire, and for the first time there were hints that the North would use military force to maintain its empire. South Carolina stood its ground, and eventually a compromise was reached that allowed the crisis to wane. This crisis brought into sharp conflict the president, Andrew Jackson, and his vice president, John C. Calhoun. Vice President Calhoun was so alarmed by the federal government's threat to use force against a sovereign state that he resigned his office. As far as Calhoun was concerned, the Union was very important but not as important as American liberties.

We have seen in the foregoing examples how the sovereign states were initially assured that, under the union formed by the Constitution, the states would always have the power to erect appropriate barriers between a potentially abusive Federal Government and "We the people" of the sovereign states. We have seen numerous examples of how the sovereign state did in fact interpose its sovereign authority between its citizens and an abusive Federal Government. We have also seen that, as long as those who desired a supreme federal government "played by the rules" of the Constitution, the sovereign states were able to defend their reserved rights. It was not until the advocates of a supreme Federal Government adopted the extra-constitutional ideology of "one people, one nation indivisible" that they began to make inroads upon the rights legitimately belonging to "We the people" of the sovereign states.

It should be evident by now that early in American history the people of the South in particular and of these United States in general believed in and adhered to the principles of States' Rights. These principles were completely interwoven in the fabric of early American politics. Most observers of the American political system agree that the Kentucky and Virginia Resolutions penned by Thomas Jefferson and James Madison mark the first use of States' Rights by two or more states to halt unauthorized federal intrusion into the states' reserved rights. It should be emphasized, once again, that the States' Rights principle belongs to all of America, not just to the South. In ratifying the federal Constitution in 1787, Massachusetts's very first recommendation was the addition of an amendment to the Constitution as follows:

> That it be explicitly declared that all Powers not expressly delegated by the aforesaid Constitution are reserved to the several States to be by them exercised.[59]

---

59 Arthur T. Prescott, *Drafting the Federal Constitution* (Baton Rouge, LA: Louisiana State University Press, 1941), 171.

Not even Jefferson Davis, or any other defender of the rights of the Southern states, could provide a better defense of the Union as a compact between sovereign states than the people of Massachusetts did when they acceded to the Union in 1787—unfortunately, by 1861, their adherence to constitutional principles vanished when their profits were at risk!

STATES' RIGHTS—
THE ULTIMATE CHALLENGE TO FEDERAL USURPATIONS

The Kentucky and Virginia Resolutions of 1798 were passed just eleven years after the Constitution was proposed. It formed the creed of the States' Rights party in the United States. These resolves penned by Thomas Jefferson and James Madison were accepted as legitimate, mainline American political opinions. They spoke of the Constitution as a compact and declared that the sovereign states were free to judge for themselves whether an act of their agent, the Federal Government, was pursuant to the Constitution. Therefore, the state could not be legally constrained by any federal court, congress, president, or any power other than the will of the people of that particular sovereign state. In addition, those resolves declared that the state had the right to determine and implement the most appropriate "mode and measure of redress."[60] What these resolutions said and what they demonstrated was that the individual state had the right to decide how it would respond to a violation of its reserved rights. It could respond by a simple resolution passed by the state legislature appealing to its sister states for assistance in resisting unwarranted federal intrusions, an act of nullification; or, if necessary, the sovereign state could elect to withdraw its delegated authority from the Federal Government by means of secession. Did anyone in 1798 dare accuse James Madison or Thomas Jefferson of treason for advocating the States' right to exercise its reserved rights?

The States' Rights philosophy that developed as a reaction to the centralizing efforts of the Federalist Party was America's primary political idea immediately following the ratification of

---

60 Bledsoe, 207.

the Constitution. Evidence of the popular support for the States' Rights political philosophy can be seen in the following account of presidential election results from 1800 through 1820:

It can be seen by a brief review of the chart that from the time of the passage of the 1798 Kentucky and Virginia Resolutions, the States' Rights candidate always soundly defeated the Federalist party' candidate. The Federalists were so completely defeated and their ideas so discredited that the party disbanded! Yet, today's advocates of "one people, one nation indivisible" would have the world believe that the principles of the States' Rights faction, as announced in the Kentucky and Virginia Resolutions, are tantamount to treason. The truth is just the opposite! The truth is that it was not until the invasion of the Confederate States of America by the Yankee Empire that the very nature of the original government was radically and unconstitutionally changed.

There were Northerners who recognized the fact that the major consequence of the War for Southern Independence was to transform the United States from a limited government to an unlimited one. Governor Richard Yates of Illinois in a message to his state assembly on January 2, 1865, declared that the war had "tended, more than any other event in the history of the country, to militate against the Jeffersonian idea that the best government is that which governs least."[61] Here we see a Northern governor several months before the end of the war acknowledging the rapid, anti-Republican change in the Federal Government's power. Thus, we see how the enemies of state sovereignty have used the South's defeat as a means to destroy state sovereignty. A Constitutional Federal Republic cannot exist without sovereign states. This is why our Founding Fathers sought to defend the concept of state sovereignty. This is the principle that Jefferson Davis and his fellow Southerners were fighting to preserve for "We the people" of the South.

---

61   Governor Richard Yates, as cited in Professor Thomas J. DiLorenzo, "Letters to the Editor," *The Wall Street Journal*, February 17, 1997.

Summary

You, the jury, will be called upon to determine if Jefferson Davis and his fellow Southerners were justified in their fear of unbridled Federalism. You must determine if the people of the South were justified in asking Jefferson Davis to be their president, to lead them away from an oppressive union, and to help them establish a better union among people having common ancestry, heritage, interests and moral values. We have demonstrated that the actions of Jefferson Davis and the Southern people were the acts of those attempting

Year	State's Rights Candidate	Electoral Vote	Federalist Candidate	Electoral Vote
1800	Thomas Jefferson	73	John Adams	65
1804	Thomas Jefferson	162	Charles Pinckney	14
1808	James Madison	122	Charles Pinckney	47
1812	James Madison	128	De Witt Clinton	89
1816	James Monroe	183	Rufus King	34
1820	James Monroe	231	John Quincy Adams	13

to re-establish the political principles of constitutional government as originally delivered to all Americans from the Founding Fathers. As we have seen, the struggle to defend the original Constitutional Federal Republic began even before the Constitution was ratified by the states. In defense of President Davis, we have demonstrated that the great constitutional struggle has always been between (1) those desiring a strong, all-powerful, and supreme national government—a supreme Federal Government controlled by elites of the Yankee Empire, and (2) those desiring to maintain local self-government within the boundaries of a constitutionally limited Republic of Sovereign States. The people of the South heeded Thomas Jefferson's warning that "when all government, domestic and foreign, in little as in great things, shall be drawn to Washington as the center of all power, it will render powerless the checks provided of one government on another, and will become as venial and oppressive as the government from which we separated."[62] In our day, we have witnessed the supreme Federal Government that has fulfilled General

---

62 J.L.M. Curry, *Confederate Military History* (1899, Harrisburg, PA: The Archive Society, 1994), Vol. I, Part 1, 84.

Robert E. Lee's prophecy of a nation that is "aggressive abroad and despotic at home."[63] If the people of the South were correct in their belief that the North intended to ignore the limitations imposed by the original Constitution and to substitute, by the force of bloody bayonets, a new and harmful form of government, then you must vote to approve the stand taken by President Jefferson Davis. Yes, you must find President Davis not guilty of treason for acting upon the inalienable American right of secession!

---

63 General Lee as cited in Kennedy & Kennedy, *Yankee Empire: Aggressive Abroad and Despotic at Home* (Columbia, SC: Shotwell Publishing, 2018).

James Madison declared, that the permanence or perpetuity of a government is based upon two factors, "the safety and happiness of society are the objects at which all political institutions must be sacrificed." Following Patrick Henry's and James Madison's advocacy of liberty over union, the sovereign states of the South seceded from the emerging Yankee Empire which placed union over liberty.

Chapter 15

A Perpetual or Conditional Union

PRESIDENT ABRAHAM LINCOLN declared that the government of the United States would last forever. He stated, "[P]erpetuity is implied, if not expressed, in the fundamental law of all national governments."[1] Contrast the difference between the ways Lincoln and James Madison viewed government. Madison stated, "[T]he safety and happiness of society are the objects at which all political institutions must be sacrificed."[2] Madison, the "Father of the Constitution," viewed the institution of government as subservient to the "safely and happiness of society." From Lincoln's statement, it appears that he viewed government as having some form of everlasting life. Adolph Hitler predicted a mere one thousand year duration for his Third Reich; Abraham Lincoln, on the other hand, contemplated his government lasting forever. Of course, Lincoln's statement was directed at the question of secession. He implied that the Southern states could not legally secede from the Union because the government of the United States was "perpetual." Even Alexander Hamilton, the foremost nationalist of the Founding Fathers, writing in *The Federalist* acknowledged that the government of the United States is not perpetual. Hamilton admitted that the states had the power to destroy the government! "It is certainly true that

---

1 Abraham Lincoln, as cited in Forrest McDonald, *A Constitutional History of the United States* (Malabar, FL: Robert E. Krieger Publishing Co., 1982), 125.

2 James Madison, as cited in Carey & McClellan, eds., *The Federalist* (Dubuque, IA: Kendall/Hunt Publishing Co., 1990), 228.

State legislatures, by forbearing the appointment of senators, may destroy the national government."³ The clear answer to Lincoln is that, even if one accepts the absurd claim that the government of these United States is destined to last forever, the mere fact that the South seceded from the Union in no way lessens the existence of the United States. The United States government continued after the secession of the Southern states. Not only did the government continue, but it grew far more powerful than it had ever been under the original Constitution—with Lincoln and the Republican Party's help it morphed into the Yankee Empire. Lincoln's above-quoted statement is just another example of the sophistry that continues to be practiced by the Yankee Empire's school of consolidation and supreme Federalism. With this statement Lincoln was seeking a legal pretext to serve as a screen behind which the Yankee Empire could hide its naked aggression against a sovereign nation—the Confederate States of America. Lincoln's idea of a perpetual union (government or Reich) is not new to America or the world.

The hope for a perpetual and indivisible union was expressed no less than five times in the Articles of Confederation, which preceded the Constitution. The dream of sovereign states joining together in an indivisible union was based upon the presumption that perpetual peace, good faith, and mutual respect would remain among the states. This was James Madison's vision for an American federal republic.

Many other Founding Fathers, such as George Mason and Patrick Henry, did not share Madison's early optimism. They foresaw the approaching calamity for the South under the proposed constitution. Their fear was not based upon a dislike for the language of the Constitution. They knew that a mere parchment barricade would prove to be a weak defense against a determined and unprincipled adversary. They did not trust the people of any section, especially of New England, to remain loyal to the limitations imposed by the Constitution if said limitations became onerous to their section and if they possessed the numbers in Congress necessary to control the Federal Government. Mason

---

3   Alexander Hamilton, as cited in Carey & McClellan, 307.

and Henry predicted that an aggressive and greedy North, armed with a majority in Congress, would seize the new government and use it for the benefit of its commercial empire. Madison criticized such speculations as being uncharitable and unfounded. The record of Southern history bears evidence as to whose view was correct. Instead of being mean-spirited and judgmental, Mason and Henry were prophets whereas Madison, instead of being kind and charitable, was naive. Madison, early in his political life, could not imagine that people from other sections of these United States would one day become as tyrannical as King George III. He did not believe that Americans were capable of using force to coerce their fellow Americans into accepting a government detrimental to their own wellbeing. For Madison, the union proposed under the Constitution would never be used for such vile purposes. As he understood it, the union was an association of sovereign states held together by *mutual* self-interest and respect. The nature of a union is unique. The marriage union offers an example of this uniqueness. A marriage union is not held together by force or violence; it is held together by *mutual* love and respect. The talons of a hawk grasping the breast of a dove does not form a union. A true union in the context of marriage or the American political setting must be formed and maintained on the basis of voluntary association for mutual benefit. Anything other than a voluntary association changes the character of the association from voluntary to coercive. As every military person knows, volunteers and conscripts all wear the same type of uniform, but their motive for wearing it is vastly different. In like manner, an individual may perform public service out of a sense of duty and charity toward his community, or the same work can be done by the forced labor of convicts. While the work accomplished is the same, the motivation and the volition of the actors are vastly different. A union that is pinned together by the force of bloody bayonets is no longer a union—for the conquered people (those forced to remain in an onerous union against their will), it is captivity. American states voluntarily uniting for their mutual benefit form a union whereas states forced together at the point of bloody bayonets form an empire. Regardless of how gilded the federal prison may be, it is, nonetheless, a prison. In this federal prison, volition is denied, and government is no longer ordered upon the free and unfettered consent of the governed. Thus, the end result is the denial of secession. As Albert Bledsoe points out, "[I]f the right of secession be denied ... and the denial enforced by the sword of coercion; the nature of the polity is changed, and freedom is at an end. It is no longer a government by consent, but a government of force. Conquest is substituted for compact, and the dream of liberty is over."[4]

In order to maintain that secession is treason and not a right reserved by the states under the Ninth and Tenth Amendments,[5] it is necessary to demonstrate that the Constitution sanctions the use of force to coerce a state to remain in the Union. If the right of secession was not reserved by the states, then it must be shown to have been delegated to the Federal Government by the Constitution or a negative clause must be found in the Constitution prohibiting secession. A right, federal or state, cannot exist without a remedy for its violation. Where then in the Constitution is the Federal Government given the power to remedy a state's act of secession? If the Founding Fathers had intended for the "more perfect Union" to be perpetual, they would certainly have provided some clear, unambiguous, and specific means for the Federal Government to ensure its perpetual existence in the face of secession. Even the extreme nationalist Alexander Hamilton rejected the notion that force could be used against the sovereign states. "To coerce the States was one of the maddest projects ever devised."[6] Here, we see the very idea of coercing a sovereign state described by one of the Founding Fathers as "the maddest projects ever devised." Unfortunately for President Jefferson Davis and the South, the Yankee Empire's advocates of "one people, one nation indivisible" had a very short and convenient memory of constitutional history.

---

4   Albert Taylor Bledsoe, *Is Davis a Traitor?* (1866, St. Louis: The Advocate Publishing House, 1879), 183-85.

5   Well before the 9th & 10th Amendments, the Declaration of Independence announced to the world that people have an unalienable right to remove oppressive government and to institute a new one that will protect the rights of the people. This was America's first secession document.

6   Alexander Hamilton, as cited in J.L.M. Curry, *Confederate Military History* (1899, Harrisburg, PA: The Archive Society, 1994), Vol. I, Part 1, 50.

The simple fact is that coercion is a moral wrong, it is a civil wrong, it is a social wrong; but more to the point, it is unconstitutional. The "right" to coerce a state cannot be found in the Constitution. The reason it cannot be found is that when a faction stoops to coercion, that faction, and not those states seceding from an abusive union, is responsible for destroying the most fundamental principle of America, the right of living under a "government by the consent of the governed." The anti-secession faction places itself in league with King George III who refused to recognize the right of the thirteen American colonies to secede from his empire. King George III, just like Lincoln and the Republican Party, considered his empire to be indivisible. The anti-secession faction places itself in direct opposition to the God-given and therefore inalienable right of self-determination. By embracing the tyrant's right of coercion, the anti-secession faction wages war upon the people of free, independent, and sovereign states. On the other hand, those who support the right of secession assert the right of self-determination, the right of local self-government, and the right to maintain and deliver to their children free, independent, and sovereign states.

In his book *Democracy in America*, Alexis de Tocqueville noted that these United States were a voluntary grouping of states and that the government established by them possessed no legal authority to force a state to remain in the union thus formed. "The Union was formed by the voluntary agreement of the States; and in uniting together they have not forfeited their nationality, nor have they been reduced to the condition of one and the same people. If one of the States choose to withdraw from the compact, it would be difficult to disprove its right of doing so, and the Federal Government would have no means of maintaining its claims directly either by force or right."[7]

As we have noted, the Articles of Confederation contain no less than five references attesting to the fact that the states were forming a "perpetual union." The Constitution, on the other hand which formed "a more perfect Union" makes no claim that the "more perfect Union"

---

7   Alexis de Tocqueville, *Democracy in America* (1838, New York: The Classics of Liberty Library, 1992), 368.

being formed was to be perpetual. The Founding Fathers attempted to create a perpetual union under the Articles of Confederation. When it was found necessary to create a new government and therefore a new union, the Founding Fathers were in the embarrassing position of advocating the death of their heretofore "perpetual union." The death of the erstwhile "perpetual union" was accomplished by the accession to yet another union formed by the Constitution. How could the Founding Fathers advocate the death of one "perpetual union" and at the same time claim that they were creating a new and even more "perpetual union"? The simple logic is that they did not intend to repeat the mistake of declaring a human creation to be perpetual. They certainly hoped that this "more perfect Union" would be perpetual, but the endurance of the new union would not be guaranteed in writing. The new union was designed to last only as long as there existed a sense of mutual trust among the contracting parties. The Founding Fathers knew that the new union would last only if the stipulations of the compact of the Constitution were faithfully observed by all parties. Men such as Lincoln, Webster, and Story, who denied the right of secession, are guilty of forcing into the Constitution something that the Founding Fathers specifically left out—a guarantee for the existence of a perpetual Union. Consider the statement of the "Father of the Constitution," James Madison, when he spoke of the "safety and happiness of a society." Would the "Father of the Constitution" demand loyalty to the union regardless of how dysfunctional or abusive of its powers the new government became?

Thus, we see the fact that the Founding Fathers specifically refused to style their new union as perpetual is a strong indication that they did not rule out that, one day, it would be necessary to do to their new creation what they had done to their union with Great Britain and their union under the Articles of Confederation. As we have seen, under the Articles of Confederation, each sovereign state withdrew from that union, and those who freely chose to do so, acceded to the new union under the Constitution. Under the "more perfect Union," the sovereign states delegated more power to their agent, the Federal Government, but they did not create a "perpetual" government binding each state forever nor did they surrender the right to withdraw from the "more perfect Union" if it became necessary.

A little known fact in American history is that the death of the so-called perpetual union under the Articles of Confederation was not the first such casualty in America. In 1643, during the English Civil War, the colonies of Massachusetts, Plymouth, Connecticut, and New-Haven formed a union they declared to be "perpetual."[8] This union was named the United Colonies of New England. This "perpetual" union lasted for forty-three years before it came to an end. With such a record of "perpetual" unions not being perpetual, is it any wonder that the Founding Fathers opted not to style the union under the Constitution as perpetual?

Those indoctrinated by the teachings of the Yankee Empire's theory of "one people, one nation indivisible" often become confused by the concept of powers delegated by the state to the Federal Government. The act of delegation of powers has nothing to do with the question of where sovereign authority resides. In the American setting, no government is sovereign. Governments, both state and federal, are agents of a higher authority. Governments receive their legitimacy, their authority, their right to rule from the source of sovereign (political as opposed to divine)[9] authority— "We the people." In the American setting the states receive their authority directly from the people, more precisely the qualified electors residing within their respective state. The Federal Government, as distinguished from the state government, receives its authority from the states. In both cases, federal and state, the governments created are subordinate to a higher authority. The states, as creatures of "We the people" of the respective state, are subordinate to the people of that state through elected representatives who meet in that state's legislature or in the state's constitutional convention. The Federal Government, as a creature of "We the people" of the respective sovereign states, is ultimately subordinate to "We the people" acting through their agent, the state. The distinguishing factor is that in either case "We the people" of

---

8   James Kent, *Commentaries on American Law* (1826, New York: Da Capo Press, 1971), 190.

9   The Founding Fathers, with their Biblical world new, were very much aware of the source of all legitimate authority. For more information of this subject see Kennedy & Kennedy, *Why Not Freedom! America's Revolt Against Big Government* (Gretna, LA: Pelican Publishing Company, 1995), 169-81.

the respective state are the ultimate source of sovereign political authority. The ultimate sovereign authority is determined by asking, "Within a particular political system, who has the final authority to make, modify, and unmake constitutions and governments?" Governments may be said to be sovereign, but they possess only delegated sovereignty, not original or inherent sovereignty (this is the premise upon which all republican governments exist). The sovereignty of a government is derived from without; it has an external source, and, therefore, is not inherent. Instead of being supreme, government depends upon a power greater than itself *if it is to be legitimate*. Sovereignty and the power/authority arising thereof, as exercised by government, is divisible and may be divided among different governments or agents of the supreme power. This stands in contrast to the sovereign power of an American state or more precisely the power of "We the people" of a respective state. This power is inherent, original, supreme, indivisible, and inalienable.[10] As can be seen from the preceding narrative, the very act of delegating certain powers demonstrates where the supreme authority originates. Thus, William Rawle, in his textbook on the United States Constitution, noted that the very words of Article I, Section 1, of the Constitution, "all legislative powers herein granted," demonstrate that a limited government is being formed, and that it is being formed by a higher authority than itself.[11]

The fact that the states by ratifying the Constitution delegated specific sovereign authority to the Federal Government has nothing to do with whether these states have the right to secede from the union created by the Constitution. The power to make is also the power to unmake. This is why the Yankee Empire's theory of "one people, one nation indivisible" is so dangerous to constitutional liberties. Using their false, unconstitutional, and un-American theory, the Yankee Empire's school has altered the source of sovereign authority in the American political system. They have used an unconstitutional theory, backed by the immoral

---

10 Bledsoe, 131.

11 Rawle, William, *A View of the Constitution: Secession as Taught at West Point*, Kennedy & Kennedy, editors, 2nd Kennedy edition, (1825, Wake Forest, NC: The Scuppernong Press, 2020), 19.

suasion of bloody bayonets, to change the government from one of a constitutionally limited Federal Government composed of sovereign states to a government of "one people, one nation indivisible" exercising supreme control over the people of each state. The once sovereign state has been reduced to a mere subdivision of the Yankee Empire, no more than a province whose legislation is now subject to the Empire's veto. This radical change was accomplished without constitutional authorization; in other words, it occurred without the free and unfettered consent of "We the people" of the sovereign states. This new, unconstitutional, and revolutionary government may rule *de facto*, but it is void of *de jure* legitimacy!

Often, those who believe in a perpetual union will ask, "Where is it written in the Constitution that a state has the right to secede?" This is the question that the proponents of "one people, one nation indivisible" trot out as their ultimate champion—a Goliath who will surely force the advocates of constitutional federalism into meek submission. But, for every Goliath defending falsehood, there is a David willing to risk all in order to allow the solid rock of truth to seek its target. The question itself displays considerable confusion and insufficient understanding as to the role of the Constitution vis-à-vis the states. States' Rights are not derived from the Constitution. The states entered into the constitutional union as "free, sovereign, and independent states."[12] The states came to the Constitution in full possession of all rights including the right to accede or secede from any agreement, including the proposed constitution. They had previously exercised this exact right when they first acceded to the Articles of Confederation and then, as they ratified the proposed constitution, by seceding from the so-called perpetual union created by the Articles of Confederation.

The doctrine of inherent States' Rights is set forth in *The Federalist* "The principles established in a former paper teach us, that the States will retain all preexisting authorities which may not be exclusively delegated to the federal head."[13] In another of *The*

---

12 The Articles of Confederation, Article II.

13 Alexander Hamilton, as cited in Carey & McClellan, 434.

Federalist Papers, this doctrine is echoed: "All authorities, of which the States are not explicitly divested in favor of the Union, remain with them in full vigor." John Marshall, later to become Chief Justice of the United States Supreme Court, during the ratification debate in the Virginia convention, declared, "The state government did not derive their powers from the general government .... [D]oes not a power remain till it was given away?"[14] Here, we see two men known for their high Federalist (i.e., consolidationists) tendencies, Alexander Hamilton writing in *The Federalist* and John Marshall speaking during the Virginia debates on ratification, both admitting that the states possess original sovereignty and cannot be bound without their individual consent. For consent to have validity, it must be given freely and under no compulsion other than the workings of the parties' own will. Consent extracted at the point of a bloody bayonet is a nullity! For this reason, we have in other places demonstrated that the Federal Government used unconstitutional force to compel "We the people" of the sovereign states to submit to a government that does not govern with the consent of the governed. Therefore, this same Federal Government does not have the moral authority to charge President Jefferson Davis with treason.[15]

Now, some will argue that this is but the opinion of James Madison and Alexander Hamilton; therefore, it cannot express the opinion of the sovereign will of the American people (i.e., "one people, one nation indivisible"), that great phantom dreamed up by the advocates of centralized federalism. How speaks the record of history? When the people of Massachusetts, speaking through their specific agent, their constitutional convention, ratified the proposed constitution, they warned that:

> As it is the opinion of this Convention, that certain amendments and alterations in the said Constitution would remove the fears & quiet the apprehension of

---

14 John Marshall, as cited in Bledsoe, 125.

15 Kennedy & Kennedy, *The South Was Right!* 3rd edition, (1991, 1994, Columbia, SC: Shotwell Publishing, 2020), 209-54: Also see Kennedy & Kennedy, *Why Not Freedom! America's Revolt Against Big Government* (Gretna, LA: Pelican Publishing Company, 1995), 23-32.

many of the good people of this Commonwealth & more effectually guard against an undue administration of the Federal Government, The Convention do therefore recommend that the following alterations & provisions be introduced into the said Constitution. [Then there were listed nine proposed amendments to the constitution, the very first stated]: That it be explicitly declared that all powers not expressly delegated by the aforesaid Constitution, are reserved to the several States, to be by them exercised.[16]

So, we see that the historical record demonstrates that the state of Massachusetts (whence came America's two greatest advocates of "one people, one nation indivisible," Daniel Webster and Joseph Story), also provides us with the warning of a potentially abusive Federal Government if the states fail to make it clear that "all powers not expressly delegated ... are reserved to the several States." Another example of a state's jealously guarding its sovereignty, of many that could be cited, is the constitutional convention statement of Pennsylvania: "All the rights of sovereignty, which are not by the said Constitution expressly and plainly vested in Congress, shall be deemed to remain with, and shall be exercised by the several States in the Union."[17] The people of Virginia recommended that a "Declaration or Bill of Rights asserting and securing from encroachment the essential and unalienable Right of the People"[18] be incorporated into the proposed constitution. In the third item recommended by the people of Virginia, they asserted "[t]hat Government ought to be instituted for the common benefit, protection and security of the People; and that *the doctrine of non-resistance against arbitrary power and oppression is absurd, slavish, and destructive of the good and happiness of mankind.*"[19] [Emphasis added]

---

16 Arthur Taylor Prescott, *Drafting the Federal Constitution* (Baton Rouge, LA: Louisiana State University Press, 1941), 170-71.
17 Bledsoe, 127.
18 Prescott, 174.
19 *Ibid.*, 174.

The Founding Fathers, speaking at the constitutional convention in 1787, writing in *The Federalist*, and debating in each state convention, all understood and attempted to make it clear to those who would come after them that, if the states did not voluntarily delegate a specific right, then that right remained with the state to be exercised at its pleasure. Numbered among those rights not delegated to the Federal Government nor denied to the states by a negative clause in the Constitution but reserved to each sovereign state is the inalienable right of "We the people" of the sovereign states to withdraw our consent from any government. In the words of the joint Declaration of Independence, "That whenever any Form of Government becomes destructive of these ends, it is the Right of the People to alter or to abolish it, and to institute new Government ...."

In response to the unlearned question, "Where is it written in the Constitution that a state has the right to secede from the Union?" we must respond with the constitutionally accurate question, "Where has the sovereign right of a state to recall any power it has delegated been surrendered or prohibited by the Constitution?" Those arrogant and elitist politicians who worship at the altar marked "one people, one nation indivisible" may rage, cut their flesh, and flail their bodies in worthless sacrifice to their false god, but the fire of truth will not fall from heaven to sanctify their evil cause!

Both Joseph Story and Daniel Webster admitted that when the states entered the Union they emerged from the Articles of Confederation as "free, sovereign, and independent states." Where in the compact of the Constitution is it clearly and unequivocally declared that these sovereign states renounced their sovereign authority to recall or resume the powers which they delegated to their mutual agent, the Federal Government? In short, where is it written that a sovereign state cannot secede from the Union? Let the advocates of "one people, one nation indivisible" point to the place in the Constitution where this great attribute of a sovereign state is surrendered. Let them show where the states are explicitly divested of this most necessary right. Let them show where the sovereign states surrendered this right to the Union. It cannot be shown, and therefore it remains in full vigor where it always resided—within the power of each sovereign state to be exercised if necessary to protect the rights of its citizens.

> Ignorance, or passion or patriotism may 'veil this right;' but, nevertheless, the question is, where is this right given away in the compact of the Constitution? If it be not given away there it still exists with the States in all the plentitude of its power. The stars do not cease to shine, or to exist, because they are concealed from view by exhalations from the earth, or by the blaze of the noon.[20]

The clear fact of history is that the union established by the Constitution is a conditional union. It was the voluntary association of "free, independent, and sovereign" states. These states joined the Union only after receiving assurances that the Union would be based upon a good-faith effort by all parties and sections to abide by the strict limitations imposed upon the Federal Government by the Constitution. These assurances were not enough to allay the fears of the vocal anti-Federalists. They insisted upon the added assurances of the first ten amendments to the Constitution now known as the Bill of Rights. Conditions upon conditions were demanded and agreed upon prior to the acceptance of the Constitution. Even with the assurance that the only laws the Federal Government could enforce were those that were "pursuant" to the Constitution,[21] some states were still not satisfied. The state of Rhode Island, which, along with North Carolina, refused to join the Union until after the government had been organized, declared in its ratification document that "the powers of government may be resumed by the people, whenever it shall become necessary to their happiness."[22] Did this fine Yankee state consider itself to be entering into a perpetual or a conditional union? What greater condition can be placed upon a compact

---

20 Bledsoe, 128.

21 Alexander Hamilton, as cited in Carey & McClellan, 161.

22 Curry, Vol. I, Part 1, 18.

than the right to withdraw any or all powers delegated to it? Did the government of these United States have any problem accepting this conditional ratification of the Constitution? Was Rhode Island accused of encouraging rebellion and treason by asserting its right to recall its delegated powers?

The government of the United States could not reject Rhode Island's conditional ratification because other states had already entered the Union under similar conditions. The state of New York was very explicit in its conditional ratification of the Constitution:

> That the powers of government maybe resumed by the people whenever it should become necessary to their happiness, that every power, jurisdiction and right which is not by the said Constitution clearly delegated to the Congress of the United States or the departments of the government thereof, remains to the people of the several States, or to their respective State governments, to whom they may have granted the same; and that those clauses in the said Constitution, which declare that Congress shall not have or exercise certain powers, do not imply that Congress is entitled to any powers not given by the said Constitution; but such clauses are to be construed either as exceptions to certain specified powers or as inserted merely for greater caution.[23]

What greater caution could be expressed than the act of the sovereign state of New York reserving for itself the right to withdraw those powers it freely delegated to the government of the United States? New York's condition for entering the Union was that it could and did reserve the right to recall delegated powers—in other words, it reserved the right to secede from the very Union it was acceding to, if it became necessary.

---

23 *Ibid.*, Vol. I, Part 1, 17-18.

Virginia, in its ratification document, also reserved the right to recall its delegated powers. "The delegates do, in the name and in behalf of the people of Virginia, declare and make known that the powers granted under the Constitution, being derived from the people of the United States, may be resumed by them whensoever the same shall be perverted to their injury or oppression, and that every power not granted thereby remains with them and at their will."[24] "Every power" remains with "We the people" of the sovereign state of Virginia. Even the right to secede if the powers delegated to the Union are "perverted to their injury!" From the ratification document of these sovereign states, it can be seen that the preservation of the Union was conditioned upon the strict adherence to the limitations of the Constitution, good faith, and mutual respect for the rights and interests of each state. If the conditions were not met, then the states were free to take whatever actions they deemed necessary to procure (in the words of James Madison) the "safety and happiness" of the people of their sovereign state.

When the Constitution was submitted to the states for ratification, not everyone agreed with the idea of a conditional ratification. Some advocates of the Constitution desired a "take it or leave it" ratification. If this mode had been adopted, it would have eliminated all conditions except those specified in the Constitution itself, such as the pledge that the Federal Government would act only "pursuant" to the limitations of the Constitution. Madison desired to prevent a conditional ratification of the Constitution. He went so far as to declare that a conditional ratification would be tantamount to no ratification at all. Yet, when his native state of Virginia, as well as other states, passed a conditional ratification, he changed his opinion and accepted Virginia's conditional ratification. The conditions established by Virginia were clearly a forethought of the possibility of secession. After Virginia passed its conditional ratification, Madison declared that the conditions laid down by the people of Virginia in convention contained "some plain and general truths, that do not impair the validity of the act."[25] Here, in Madison's

---

24 Prescott, 173.

25 James Madison, as cited in Bledsoe, 175.

own words, we see the right of "We the people" of a sovereign state to withdraw delegated rights when those rights are used against the people; that is, the right of a state to secede from the Union if necessary to protect the rights and liberty of its people. According to Madison, this right is declared to be a "plain and general truth."

SUMMARY

Those who oppose the right of "We the people" of the sovereign state to recall our delegated authority from our agent, the Federal Government, claim that Americans have lost that most precious and inalienable right because the union established by the Founding Fathers is perpetual, not conditional. They have taken the government of these United States and have created of it an idol to be worshiped. Their god can do no wrong, their god is all powerful, their god rules as supreme lawgiver, their god is everlasting, their god commands, and the subjects of their god must obey. This is not the vision of the Founding Fathers for the government of a free people, nor was it the vision that Jefferson Davis and the South held dear in 1861.

> They [the Founding Fathers] regarded the Union as conditional, an 'experiment' in George Washington's terms, and knew that it would require work and minor revision if the fundamental law was to operate as they hoped—but not too much revision or too often. Nevertheless, they meant for their form of government to last, and most of them were confident that it would, so long as it was not manipulated out of shape by ideology' or human selfishness.[26]

You, the jury, must now decide whether the Constitution was meant to establish a union of perpetual bondage from which the states, upon entering, could never escape, or whether the Constitution established a conditional union from which the states were free to withdraw. Ask yourself, "Would I enter a marriage if that union was

---

26 M. E. Bradford, Founding Fathers (Lawrence, KS: University Press of Kansas, 1994), xx.

to be perpetual regardless of how abusive my spouse was to me and regardless of how much my spouse dishonored the marriage vows?" If you would not enter such a marriage, do you think. our Founding Fathers would have entered a potentially abusive union with no means of escape?

If the Story-Webster-Lincoln school of thought is correct, then President Jefferson Davis and the entire South were guilty of waging an unsuccessful revolt against the legitimate authority of the Union. If, on the other hand, you find evidence that the Founding Fathers laid down certain specific and clear conditions regarding their willingness to allow the Federal Government to exercise those powers delegated to it, then President Jefferson Davis and the South were guilty of nothing more than exercising an inalienable right. As President Davis stated at his first inauguration, "The experiment instituted by our revolutionary fathers, of a voluntary Union of sovereign States for purpose specified in a solemn compact, had been perverted by those who, feeling power and forgetting right, were determined to respect no law but their own will."[27]

---

27 President Jefferson Davis, as cited in Kennedy & Kennedy, *The South Was Right!* 2nd edition, (Gretna, LA: Pelican Publishing Company, 1994), 328. Also found at Jefferson Davis's Second Inaugural Address, The Papers of Jefferson Davis, Rice University, https://bit.ly/3Sf7ZZ5 (Accessed 6/16/2022).

Chapter 16

SECESSION AS AN AMERICAN POLITICAL PRINCIPLE

AS WE HAVE ALREADY EXPLAINED, if President Jefferson Davis is judged a traitor, then the condemnation must also fall upon every Southerner who wore the gray during the War for Southern Independence. If President Davis is judged a traitor, then it means that virtually every Southerner today has within his veins the blood of treason!

In this chapter, we will demonstrate to you, the jury, the fact that Jefferson Davis and his fellow Southerners prior to, during, and after the war maintained that they were fighting for honorable principles. Yet, few people today realize that the principle of secession has a long, extensive, and honorable legacy in America. President Davis and his Southern contemporaries were well aware of this legacy. This knowledge provided the basis for their ethical motivation to support secession from the emerging Yankee Empire. Indeed, this information represents evidence critical to the defense of President Davis and his fellow Southerners. This is the reason why the victors in the War for Southern Independence have use every method available to them to suppress public knowledge of this evidence![1]

---

1   Kennedy & Kennedy, *The South Was Right!* 3rd edition, (1991, 1994, Columbia, SC: Shotwell Publishing, 2020), 21-34.

President Davis, the son of a Revolutionary War veteran, was well aware of the history of America's colonial period. He and his generation of Southerners accepted the fact that the individual colonies, acting on their own initiative, freely dissolved their bonds to the central government in London and asserted their right of self-determination. The words of the joint Declaration of Independence spoke clearly to this issue: "When in the Course of human events, it becomes necessary for one people to dissolve the political bands which have connected them with another, and to assume among the powers of the earth, the separate and equal station to which the Laws of Nature and of Nature's God entitle them..." Even the very name chosen to represent the independent colonies, "Thirteen United States of America," spoke clearly to Davis's generation: "United" not consolidated, "States" in the plural, not "State" in the singular. If the Declaration of Independence had used the word "State" in the singular, it would have denoted one large, centralized nation-state, based upon the European model. Davis's generation, and all the generations of Americans prior to his generation, were taught that these United States were formed by thirteen free, independent, and sovereign states united in the joint defense of their independence. For President Davis's generation, it was apparent that the colonies had seceded from their union with Great Britain. An unbiased reading of history led them to understand secession, not as a negative and evil political movement, but as a legitimate remedy available to an oppressed people.

During the American Revolutionary War, the American states determined to establish a formal Federal Government to replace the Continental Congress. Each state was extremely jealous of its independence, but each desired to join together in some limited fashion with the other states of America. The primary concern was to establish a Federal Government with only those powers necessary to carry out functions that the individual states could not efficiently accomplish. The Articles of Confederation were the result of the states' first effort to create a Federal Government.

Article II of the Articles of Confederation makes it very clear that the states possessed independence and sovereignty prior to the adoption of the Constitution and the establishment of the new "more perfect Union." Article II also demonstrates that the sovereign states considered their states' sovereignty as an essential element for the maintenance of liberty. Article II of the Articles of Confederation is irrefutable evidence that the states were determined to defend the rights that the mother country had been forced to acknowledge in the Treaty of Paris. The Treaty of Paris was signed by Great Britain acknowledging the fact that the thirteen individual American states, formerly colonies, were in fact free and independent states. In this treaty, each of the thirteen states is individually named and declared to be independent. From this it can be seen that States' Rights preceded the Union! Actually, the right of secession as exercised by the colonies not only preceded the Union, but secession preceded these United States. [The term "state" as used in the founding of the U.S.A. and until 1861 was internationally recognized as meaning the same term as "nation."]

COLONIAL SECESSION FROM THE UNION WITH GREAT BRITAIN

Each of the thirteen American colonies was established as a separate colonial entity. Each colony owed allegiance directly to Great Britain. There were no formal ties between the colonies other than their mutual attachment to their common mother country. As colonies, each of the thirteen American colonies stood in the same political relation to each other as they did to any other British colony in the world. After many years of efforts to remedy violations of the "rights of Englishmen," the thirteen American colonies became convinced of the need to withdraw from the union with Great Britain. In May 1776, more than a month before the famous July Fourth joint Declaration of Independence, the colony of Virginia seceded from the union with Great Britain making the following statement in its secession document: "Resolved, That the *union* that has hitherto subsisted between Great Britain and the American colonies is thereby *totally dissolved*, and that the inhabitants of this colony are discharged from any allegiance to the crown of Great Britain."[2] [Emphasis added].

---

2   William Wirt Henry, *Patrick Henry: Life, Correspondence, and Speeches* (1891, Harrisonburg, VA: Sprinkle Publications, 1993), I, 396.

Note the use of the words "union" and "dissolved." It is also very important to note that this act of secession occurred before the joint Declaration of Independence. Virginia acted on its own volition. It was not required to wait for the approval of the other colonies. Virginia was at that moment a free, independent, and sovereign state.

Virginia's decision to assert the right of self-determination was made by the legislature of Virginia on behalf of the people of that colony. Thus, Virginia, in May 1776, became an independent and sovereign nation. The joint Declaration of Independence worked the same political transformation with each of the individual thirteen colonies. It should be noted that each delegate sent to Philadelphia carried instructions from his respective state giving him permission to vote for independence. For example, on April 5, 1776, the delegates from Georgia were *empowered* to vote for independence by the congress of the state of Georgia.[3] As another example of a state's delegation being controlled by its state government that famous July, look to the actions of the delegates from New York. The New York delegation could not sign the famous July Fourth document until they received permission/instructions to do so from their state. For this reason, New York did not officially sign the Declaration of Independence until well after the famous date of July 4, 1776.

The moment the thirteen colonies officially signed the Declaration of Independence, they threw off the shackles of colonies and assumed the mantle of free, independent, and sovereign states. The July Fourth Declaration of Independence is a collective statement of the independence of thirteen individual states. This is why these sovereign states insisted that Article II of the Articles of Confederation spoke so clearly regarding their "independence" and "sovereignty."[4] The people of the states were very jealous of their hard-earned freedom and did not wish to hazard it, even in the hands of a presumed, friendly Federal Government.

---

3   Francis B. Simkins, *A History of the South* (New York: Alfred A. Knopf, 1959), 85.

4   Article II of the Articles of Confederation reads as follows: "Each state retains its sovereignty, freedom, and independence, and every power, jurisdiction, and right, which is not by this confederation expressly delegated to the United States in congress

From this it can be seen that, in 1776, the thirteen American colonies withdrew from their union with Great Britain. It is important to note the similarity of the secession movement in 1776 with the South's secession in 1861. In 1776, colonies, which originally owed their allegiance to Great Britain, withdrew that allegiance and established a new government more likely to protect their special interests. In 1776, every colony that seceded from the central government in London had laws that sanctioned African slavery, and large segments of the Northern commercial section were actively engaged in the slave trade! How often have we heard an apologist for the Yankee Empire's invasion of the South claim that secession in the South was wrong because of slavery. Yet, the same charge is never heard regarding the 1776 secession of the American colonies from their union with Great Britain.

STATES RESERVE THE RIGHT TO RECALL THEIR DELEGATED POWERS

As we pointed out in Chapter 15, numerous states placed conditions on their ratification of the Constitution. These conditions plainly declared that the states reserved the right to withdraw any or all of their delegated powers from the Federal Government, if those powers were ever used against their people. The fact that these states placed this requirement on their accession to the Constitution indicates that there was substantial concern that the day would come when secession would be necessary. This reservation of the state's right to recall delegated powers was necessary because the ratification was done prior to the passage of the Bill of Rights which included the Ninth and Tenth Amendments. The language of these amendments makes it clear that the states reserved all rights not specifically denied to the states by the plain language of the Constitution. These amendments reserved to the sovereign states the right to recall delegated powers or the right to secede. The actions of states such as Rhode Island, New York, and Virginia make it clear that the states looked upon secession as a possible means of escape from federal tyranny. Even before

---

assembled."

the union under the Constitution was created, the possibility of a sovereign state withdrawing from the union was clearly defined and acknowledged by the Founding Fathers.

Northern Threats To Secede Related To the Mississippi River

As we have already documented in Chapter 13, the Northern states threatened to secede if they were not allowed to exchange navigation rights on the Mississippi River for favorable trade agreements with Spain. Recall the letter sent to Gov. Patrick Henry of Virginia by James Monroe detailing the Northern secession conspiracy: "It appears manifest they have seven states, and we five, Maryland inclusive with the Southern states .... It also appears that they will go on under seven states in the business, and risque the preservation of the confederacy on it .... Certain it is that committees are held in this town of eastern men, and others of this state [New York] upon the subject of a dismemberment of the states east of the Hudson from the union, and the erection of them into a separate government."[5] Nothing more need be said on the subject except to add that no one attempted to bring these gentlemen of New England and New York up on charges of treason just because they believed in and were willing to exercise the right of secession.

Massachusetts Threatens to Secede

In 1803, during the debate over the purchase of the Louisiana territory, a representative of Massachusetts declared that his state would secede if this great territory was added to the United States. Of course, as we have already demonstrated, the primary concern was that the new territory might add states to the Union which were friendly to the South. Our point here is to call attention to the fact that it was not tantamount to treason for Rep. Josiah Quincy to threaten secession in the halls of Congress. When Louisiana petitioned for admission to the Union, Quincy again gave vent to the secession sentiments that were widely held in the North by

---

5   William Wirt Henry, II, 291-96.

declaring, "If this bill passes, it is my deliberate opinion that it is virtually a dissolution of this Union; that it will free the States from their moral obligation, and, as it will be the right of all, so it will be the duty of some, definitely to prepare for a separation, amicably if they can, violently if they must."[6] Again, we stress the point that Representative Quincy was not charged with treason for advocating the right of secession.

NEW ENGLAND'S FIRST SECESSION CONSPIRACY

New England begrudgingly accepted the purchase of the Louisiana Territory, but former United States secretary of state, Timothy Pickering, attempted to form a secession movement among the New England states in reaction to the Louisiana Purchase. The details of this movement are veiled in mystery, but it appears that Pickering gained some support in New England. His scheme included the five New England states and New York. There is reason to believe that Pickering gained support from Vice President Aaron Burr. The plan was aborted when Burr failed to win the governorship of New York.[7] Even though this effort did not succeed, it demonstrates the fact that the right of secession was a commonly held belief in the United States prior to 1861.

NEW ENGLAND'S HARTFORD SECESSION CONVENTION

The War of 1812, with its disruption of normal commerce wreaked havoc on the economy of New England. Even though the United States was locked in a war with Great Britain, the New England states wanted an end to the war in order to secure a return to their profit-making commerce. Thus, New Englanders decided to take matters into their own hands by initiating a secret New England secession movement. The following account is taken from the Journal of the Hartford Convention, January 4, 1815.

---

6   Josiah Quincy, as cited in J.L.M. Curry, *Confederate Military History* (1899, Harrisburg, PA: The Archive Society, 1994), Vol. I, Part 1, 173-74.

7   Forrest McDonald, *A Constitutional History of the United States* (Malabar, FL: Robert E. Krieger Publishing Co., 1982), 97-98.

Events may prove that the causes of our calamities are deep and permanent. They may be found to proceed, not merely from blindness of prejudice, pride of opinion, violence of party spirit, or the confusion of the times; but they may be traced to implacable combinations of individuals, or of States, to monopolize power and office, and to trample without remorse upon the rights and interests of the commercial sections of the Union .... Whenever it shall appear that these causes are radical and permanent, a separation by equitable arrangement, will be preferable to an alliance by constraint, among nominal friends, but real enemies, inflamed by mutual hatred and jealousies, and inviting, by intestine divisions, contempt and aggressions from abroad .... That acts of Congress in violation of the Constitution are absolutely void, is an undeniable position. ... In cases of deliberate, dangerous, and palpable infractions of the Constitution, Affecting the Sovereignty of the State, and liberties of the people; it is not only the right, but *the duty, of such State to interpose its authority* for their protection, in the manner best calculated to secure that end .... *States, which have no common umpire, must be their own judges, and execute their own decisions.*[8] [Emphasis added to show the similarity to the Resolutions of Kentucky and Virginia of 1798].

If anything, the Hartford Convention held in 1815 was even stronger than the Virginia and Kentucky Resolutions of 1798! Thus spoke New England regarding the right of secession when it felt its interests (i.e., profits) were endangered by remaining in the Union.

---

8   Albert T. Bledsoe, *Is Davis A Traitor?* (1866, St. Louis: The Advocate Publishing House, 1879), 194-96.

No less than former president John Quincy Adams admitted that the purpose of the New England states meeting in convention at Hartford was to secede from the Union. "That their object was and had been for several years, a dissolution of the Union, and the establishment of a separate Confederation, he knew from unequivocal evidence, although not provable in a court of law; and that in case of a civil war, the aid of Great Britain to effect that purpose would be assuredly resorted to, as it would be indispensably necessary to their design."[9] Former president James Buchanan also noted "that this body [the Hartford Convention] manifested their purpose to dissolve the Union, should Congress refuse to redress the grievances of which they complained."[10]

So, here we see the home state of Joseph Story and Daniel Webster, America's future exponents of the Yankee Empire's school of "one people, one nation indivisible," holding a secret meeting to plot secession! Were the citizens of that state accused of treason? Was their leader seized, held without bail, chained and manacled? Has their leader been denounced by press and pulpit? No, there appears to be two standards of punishment for secessionists in America: one applied gently, if at all, to the North, and the other applied with vengeance against the South.

UNITED STATES RECOGNIZES LEGITIMACY OF TEXAS' SECESSION FROM MEXICO

When the people of Texas seceded from the central government of Mexico, they were following the example of the thirteen colonies which had seceded from Great Britain in 1776. The gallant people of Texas, fighting against overwhelming odds, won their independence. Thus, the Republic of Texas was born. If secession is tantamount to high crime and treason, then the United States government was guilty of being an accessory to the crime. If secession is illegal, then it would be illegal to assist a seceding state or to recognize it after it has "illegally" broken away from its central government. The United States government recognized the legitimacy of Texas's secession

---

9 John Quincy Adams, as cited in *Ibid.*, 198.

10 James Buchanan, *Ibid.*, 198.

by first officially recognizing the Republic of Texas and then by accepting its petition for admission to the Union. Again, we see just how important the American political principle of secession has been to the United States.

New England's Radical Abolitionists Advocate Secession

Some of the most vocal advocates for a genocidal war against the South in 1861 were the militant Abolitionists. Yet, when we look into their history, we find that they too were at one-point advocates of secession. Again, this proves just how widespread the American doctrine of the right of secession existed in pre-1861 America.

William Lloyd Garrison, the North's leading advocate of radical abolition, announced his views on secession at an annual meeting of the Anti-Slavery Society of America. Garrison's views were subsequently published in the *Anti-Slavery Examiner* in 1844. These views regarding the right of secession, as advocated by Abolitionists, demonstrate that even they believed in this grand American principle of secession.

> Our motto is, no Union with slave-holders, either religious or political .... In withdrawing from the American Union, we have the God of justice with us .... Circulate a declaration of disunion from slave-holders throughout the country .... No honest use can be made of it [the Constitution] in opposition to the plain intention of its framers, except to declare the contract at an end, and to refuse to serve under it .... It is the duty of the friends of freedom to deny the binding authority of them all, and to *secede* from all, we distinctly affirm.[11] [Emphasis added]

---

11 William Lloyd Garrison, *Ibid.*, 146-47.

Educated and well-established Yankees such as Wendell Phillips, who served as secretary of this society, subscribed to the right of secession. This same society passed a resolution declaring, in part, "Resolved, That secession from the United States Government is the duty of every Abolitionist .... Resolved, That the Abolitionists of this country should make it one of the primary objects of this agitation to dissolve the American Union .... "[12]

Once the South made its escape from the bondage of the emerging Yankee Empire, these very same men became the most vocal advocates of war and revenge against the Southern people who would dare to rend the "perpetual union" of "one people, one nation indivisible!"

FEDERAL MILITARY SCHOOL AT WEST POINT TAUGHT SECESSION

This subject was covered in Chapter 11. Suffice it to say that the United States government used a textbook to instruct United States military cadets on the Constitution and that the textbook taught the right of a state to secede from the Union; these facts represent one of the most amazing pieces of evidence supporting the right of secession within the American political system. Judge William Rawle's text, *A View of the Constitution*, was accepted and praised by people of the North and the South. In Chapter 32 of his text (1829 edition), Rawle provided his readers with the formula that a state should use if it became necessary for it to secede from the Union! Many future generals of both the United States and the Confederate States armies studied from this text while under the instruction of the United States Military Academy. To our knowledge, no one has ever accused Judge Rawle of encouraging revolt against lawful authority or encouraging his students to participate in treason against the Union.

---

12   *Ibid.*, 148.

SECESSION AS AN ATTRIBUTE OF STATE SOVEREIGNTY

The thirteen original American states boldly proclaimed their separate "freedom, independence, and sovereignty" in the Articles of Confederation. At least up to this point, it is clear, despite the sophism of men such as Story, Webster and Lincoln, that the states were sovereign. If there was any change in this status, then it could only have occurred with the accession of each sovereign state into the union created by the Constitution. The point is that, if the states are sovereign, then as sovereign powers they retain the inalienable right to withdraw their consent from their agent, the Federal Government. It is certain that the states were sovereign under the Articles of Confederation. Did they renounce that sovereignty when they ratified the Constitution? Again, let us look at their very words as recorded in the historical record, as it pertains to state sovereignty and the Constitution.

Did the states, especially the states of the North, understand the fact that they were entering into a union while maintaining their own sovereignty? To answer this question let's look at the historical record of Massachusetts. Massachusetts declared in its 1780 constitution, "The people of this commonwealth have the sole and exclusive right of governing themselves, as a free, sovereign and independent State; and do, and forever hereafter shall exercise, and enjoy every power, jurisdiction, and right, which is not, or may not hereafter, be by them expressly delegated to the United States of America, in Congress assembled."[13] Now, this is the expression of New England as announced by Massachusetts seven years before the New England states acceded to the new union under the Constitution. Twelve years later another New England state, New Hampshire, incorporated almost identical language into its constitution. Thus, after the "more perfect Union" was formed under the Constitution, this New England state declared to all the world that while it was a faithful partner in the "more perfect Union" it still retained its status

---

13 Constitution of the state of Massachusetts, as cited in *The American's Guide to the Constitutions of the United States of America* (Trenton, NJ: Moore and Lake, 1813), 70.

as a "free, sovereign and independent State."[14] So, we can see from this that even the New England states insisted upon maintaining their claim to state sovereignty.

SECESSION: AN AMERICAN POLITICAL PRINCIPLE

The American principle of secession is based upon two concepts. First, the Constitution is a compact freely entered into among sovereign states; second, a sovereign state, as a party to the compact creating the union, is free to withdraw from said compact. If secession is treasonable or an act of sedition, then it must also be treasonable or seditious to assert, promote, and advance the idea that the Constitution is a compact among sovereign states. A reading of the speeches of President Jefferson Davis, while holding public office in his country's service, demonstrates clearly that he supported the proposition that the Constitution is a compact between sovereign states. Not only President Davis but virtually all elected Southerners prior to the War for Southern Independence held this belief. Were they guilty of promoting and encouraging treason? Were they ever censured by the federal authorities for advocating the "seditious" notion that the Constitution was a compact between sovereign states? Were Davis and his fellow Southerners ever called to order in Congress and voted out of order for advocating these principles? No! And even more striking, when Massachusetts representative Josiah Quincy declared on the fourteenth of January 1811, that his state would secede if Louisiana were admitted to the Union, his statement caused an uproar, and Quincy was called "out of order"; but, by a vote of the House of Representatives then in session, Quincy was voted to be "*in* order" and allowed to continue speaking![15] Let us review again the words of this Massachusetts official to see if they are different from the words and ideas as advanced in 1861 by President Jefferson Davis. Quincy stated, "If this bill passes it is my deliberate opinion that it is virtually a dissolution of the Union; that it will free the States from their moral obligation and, as it will be the right of all, so it will

---

14 Constitution of the state of New Hampshire, *The American's Guide to the Constitutions of the United States of America*, 39.

15 Bledsoe, 201.

be the duty of some, definitely to prepare for separation, amicably if they can, violently if they must."[16] If Representative Quincy's threat of New England's secession was not treason, certainly defending secession as a right under the constitutional compact could not be considered treason. Indeed, this same Yankee state of Massachusetts in 1803, upon the purchase of the Louisiana Territory, passed a legislative resolution declaring, "Resolved, that the annexation of Louisiana to the Union, transcends the Constitutional power of the Government of the United States. It formed a new Confederacy to which the States united by the former compact, are not bound to adhere."[17] Yet, this same state of Massachusetts visited upon the South war, rapine, pillage, and the infamous rule of its favorite son, Gen. Benjamin "Beast" Butler, for acting upon what Massachusetts had proclaimed so insistently to be its right!

When urging the people of the states to ratify the proposed constitution, the authors of *The Federalist* did not hesitate to call the constitution "the compact" to which "the states as distinct and independent sovereigns" were parties. Did the writers of *The Federalist* commit treason? Both Alexander Hamilton and James Madison urged the people to accept the new government as a union created by "the compact between thirteen sovereign and independent States." Were these men promoting treason? Daniel Webster and the emerging Yankee Empire's school of "one people, one nation indivisible" alleged that those who held dear to the idea of a constitutional compact "are untrue to their country." But we must question who was untrue—those who understood historical truth and acted accordingly, or those who were possessed by the passion of sectional politics and acted upon it? Is it treason to understand the Constitution the same way that the Founding Fathers understood it? As sad as the result of the War for Southern Independence may have been for "We the people" of the South, it is sadder still for all Americans who, knowingly or not, now reside in a land where historical truth is counted as treason.

---

16 Josiah Quincy, as cited in Curry, Vol. I, Part 1, 173-74.

17 Bledsoe, 200.

We find it a remarkable fact that in 1861, when the sovereign states of the South exercised their inalienable right to be free, the states of the North cried havoc and eagerly let loose the dogs of war. Yet, in 1798 when the states of Kentucky and Virginia passed their famous resolutions declaring the Union to be a compact among sovereign states, not a single Northern state dared to question this great American principle. These resolves were published and sent to each state legislature. The reply made by Webster's and Story's own state of Massachusetts contained not one word questioning the fact that the states formed a confederacy or that the Constitution was a compact among sovereign states![18] In its reply to the Kentucky and Virginia Resolutions of 1798, Massachusetts declared its desire to "co-operate with its Confederate States; that solemn compact which is declared to be the supreme law of the land."[19] If the Union was not formed under the compact of the Constitution, then why did this Yankee state call it a "compact?" If the Union was not a voluntary association of sovereign states, then why did this most Yankee of all New England states refer to the Union as the "Confederate States?" If secession was considered to be an act of treason, why, in 1798, did no one in the North think of issuing a warning to the "erring" brothers in the South? Why indeed did it take the emerging Yankee Empire from 1798 to 1861 to discover the grand, but otherwise unknown, constitutional provision declaring the inalienable right of secession to be a nullity in these United States? And most amazing of all—where did the gentlemen of the North hide this grand and secret constitutional clause, before they suddenly and conveniently found it? Perhaps they hid it so well that they could not, after the War, find it themselves—at least not in time to present it in evidence against President Jefferson Davis at his trial for treason.

---

18 *Ibid.*, 191.

19 *Ibid.*, 192.

SUMMARY

These United States of America were born as a result of a successful secession movement. The right of a people to secede from an abusive central government is enshrined in the joint Declaration of Independence adopted on July 4, 1776. The Declaration boldly declares this right to be inalienable because it is a God given human right. Prior to the secession of the sovereign states of the South in 1861, numerous threats of secession were made by Northern states. Prior to the invasion of the South during the War for Southern Independence, secession, although at times considered imprudent or unwise, was not condemned as "treason." The warnings issued by various Americans against the act of secession reflected the desire to maintain the Union, as delivered to the nation by the Founding Fathers, by seeking mutually acceptable compromises on divisive issues. The idea of the right of secession by an American state was so commonly held in early American history that the use of a textbook at West Point Military Academy which taught secession as a reserved right of the states was never questioned. William Rawle, author of the "secessionist" textbook, and friend of both George Washington and Benjamin Franklin, was never ridiculed as an evil promoter of treason.

In this chapter, you, the jury, have been presented with a sampling of the overwhelming body of historical evidence which clearly demonstrates that secession was an accepted, mainstream, American, political idea. In pursuing independence in 1861, President Jefferson Davis and the people of the South did not betray their American political heritage, they bravely defended that heritage. A man so brave and so principled as Jefferson Davis deserves your vote of not guilty to the slanderous charge of treason. After all, Davis and "his people," that is, the South, were defending not only their right to live as free men—but our right to freedom as well!

Chapter 17

THE FINAL ARGUMENT

WHEN ALL OTHER ARGUMENTS against the right of secession have been disproved, the opponents of Southern independence will then retreat to their last arguments—utility, practicality, and blind fanaticism. Needless to say, these arguments are not points upon which the charge of treason should be judged. Moral, ethical, and constitutional issues should never be judged by materialistic or emotional standards. In a truly impartial court of law, where only facts related to the charge are considered, the injection of utility, practicality, and fanaticism in a trial for treason would not be allowed. Nevertheless, considering that for more than a century-and-a-half the victor's negative view of Southern independence has been publicly enforced, the defense, in the service of a balanced perspective, offers the following facts. These facts are presented to counter the prejudicial views about secession, and Southern independence, which the Yankee Empire has consistently advocated and enforced since its unprincipled invasion, conquest, occupation, and colonization[1] of the Confederate States of America.

In one form or another, the charge is often leveled against Southern secession, and Southern independence, that "the South was (and is) too small, too weak, and too poor to be an independent nation." The hidden message here is that, even if the South had a right to secede, Jefferson Davis and company were leading the South

---

1 See, Kennedy & Kennedy, *Punished With Poverty-the Suffering South*.

to destruction; therefore, the Yankee Empire's invasion and conquest were (and are) beneficial to the people of the South. This message is usually stated in the following manner, "You know, Southerners are really better off as a result of losing the Civil War."

Let us consider the question, "Is the South too small to be an independent nation?" In a letter to the British government, President Davis, responding to a perceived slur against the Confederacy by the use of the term "so-called" in reference to the Confederate States by Lord Russell, noted that the "so-called" Confederate States were "a nation comprising a population of more than twelve millions, occupying a territory many times larger than the United Kingdom."[2] Certainly, as President Davis noted, the Confederacy was not some small fiefdom; rather, it was one of the largest nations on earth at that time.

As to the charge that the South was too weak to remain an independent nation, one must only look at what it accomplished while defending itself against an invader. The South provided itself with a government, an army, and a navy. It was able to equip and maintain the second largest army on the face of the earth at that time. No nation, other than the Yankee Empire and Great Britain, had a navy with more modern ships and equipment than did the Confederate States of America. In the production of ironclads, steam ocean raiders, pioneering submarine warfare, torpedoes (mines), and naval ordnance, the Confederate States of America was one of the world's leaders. The Confederate States produced military leaders who were on a par with recognized military leaders anywhere in the world, and the military' prowess of the Confederate armies was recognized by the civilized world. From a military perspective, the South was among the world's top five nations of the mid-nineteenth century. Because it was defeated by the world's number one military power in 1865 does not demean the South's role as a powerful nation. It cannot be maintained that from a military point of view the South was too weak to have the right to be an independent nation. If one maintains that the South was militarily too weak to have the right of

---

2 Jefferson Davis, as cited in Hudson Strode, *Jefferson Davis, Tragic Hero* (New York: Harcourt, Brace, and World, 1964), 27.

independence, then what must be said about the rest of the world's independent nations at that time? Few people will doubt that, if any nation, other than the Yankee Empire or Great Britain, had invaded the Confederate States of America in 1861, the invader would have been defeated.

Others have argued that the South was too poor to maintain its independence. It is true that, in comparison to the Northeast section of the Yankee Empire, the South was "poorer." Yet, when the Southern states are compared with the states west of Pennsylvania, they look much better. According to Nobel Prize-winning economist Robert W. Fogel, per capita income for Southerners in 1860 was higher than per capita income for people in the twelve North Central states of the Yankee Empire.[3] According to this study, the people of the South were not on the bottom of America's economic ladder; rather, they were in the middle. At this point of the discussion, many opponents of secession will assert that this high income was reflective of a minority of Southerners who were slave holders and does not reflect the well-being of the average Southerner. We must respond with the words of noted Southern historian, Dr. Grady McWhiney:

> Neither slavery nor the plantation system was as distinctively southern as the raising of livestock, especially hogs and cattle, on the open range. In 1860 two-thirds of the nation's hogs were grown in the Old South, and hogs and other southern livestock were worth half a billion dollars—more than twice the value of that year's cotton crop and approximately equal to the value of all southern crops combined.[4]

---

[3] Robert W. Fogel and S. L. Engerman, *Time on the Cross* (Boston, MA: Little, Brown and Company, 1974), 248-49.

[4] Grady McWhiney, *Cracker Culture, Celtic Ways in the Old South* (Tuscaloosa, AL: University of Alabama Press, 1988), 52.

As McWhiney explains, the vast majority of Southerners were neither rich nor poor; they were in the comfortable middle class. This condition is far removed from the typical Yankee view of the South as a wretched mass of "poor whites" suffering under the rule of rich plantation aristocrats.

The average Southerner was a middle-class American in 1861, but where did he stand on the international economic scale? First, let us compare per capita income. With the South as an independent nation, comparing it to the world's nine other leading industrial nations (American and European) at that time, the South would rank number three in per capita income.[5] In other words, the average Southerner in 1861 would have had an income greater than all other people in the world other than those in Great Britain and in the Yankee Empire. In his work, Fogel gives other economic indicators of where the Southern nation in 1861 would rank on an international scale. The Southern nation would have been number two in per capita railroad mileage, number six in per capita textile production, and number six in per capita pig iron production worldwide.[6] The anti-secession argument that the South was too small, too weak, and too poor to be an independent nation in 1861 is herein demonstrated to be false. Such claims are pure, slanderous, anti-South, Yankee propaganda promoted by the victor to hide his heinous crimes against "We the people" of the South.

Since you, the jury, are not living in the nineteenth century but at the commencement of the twenty-first century, you may be inclined to think, "That was then, what about today?"

In order to demonstrate that secession, even today, would not cause the untoward effects the anti-secessionists predict, the utility and practicality of secession in this century will be discussed.

To present a balanced view of what an independent South would look like in this century, we will compare the following states (eleven out of the original thirteen) of the Confederate States of America as one nation. The states considered will be South Carolina,

---

5   Fogel & Engerman, 250.

6   *Ibid.*, 256.

Mississippi, Florida, Alabama, Georgia, Louisiana, Texas, Virginia, Arkansas, Tennessee, and North Carolina. We will consider how these "Confederate" states would rank among the nations of the world today in the following areas: (1) population, (2) gross domestic product, and (3) governance of a Confederate Congress as opposed to governance under the Yankee Empire's Congress.

As of 1997, the United Nations had 185 member nations. They range in population from 1.3 billion in Communist China to 17,000 in Palau. In order to provide you, the jury, a point of reference to consider if the Confederate states are of sufficient size and strength to be an independent nation, let us examine the following facts. According to world population data, obtained in 1993, China ranks number one, India number two, the Yankee Empire number three, Russia number six, Great Britain number eighteen, France number twenty, and Canada (with Quebec as part of its union) number thirty-two. Therefore, if the Confederate states were considered as a separate nation, it would rank number thirteen in world population just behind Germany and ahead of every other European nation. Even with the loss of 74 million people to the Confederate states today, the Yankee Empire would drop only from number three to number four in world population, just behind Indonesia. What is even more startling is the fact that, if only five of the Deep South states were to form an independent nation, it would have a population of 22 million people and rank number 43 out of 185 nations in world population, only a few million behind Canada.

By comparing the gross domestic product of a modern Confederate States of America with other nations of today's world, we may get an idea of the economic viability of an independent South. A top-ten list of nations according to their gross domestic product would read as follows: (1) Yankee Empire, (2) Japan, (3) Germany, (4) France, (5) Italy, (6) United Kingdom, (7) Russia, (8) Canada, (9) Spain, (10) Brazil. [Note: This list is from 1998 data—today (2022) China would be challenging the Yankee Empire]. If the eleven Confederate states were withdrawn from the Yankee Empire, the United States would still be in first place, with the Confederate States bumping France for the number four position, placing the Confederacy ahead of every European country except Germany.

This would put the Confederate States in the top 3 percent of the earth's economic powers. Not bad for a "poor" country! And again, if only five of the Deep South states were in a confederacy, it would rank number eleven in gross domestic product, ahead of China (the world's other "superpower"), Australia, The Netherlands, Sweden, South Korea, and 169 other nations.

By contrasting the voting patterns of the Yankee Empire's Congress at large with the patterns of the delegations of the eleven Southern states, we may be able to discern the nature of a Confederate Congress. When looking at the voting patterns of the Yankee Empire's Congress, regardless of whether we look to the Senate or to the House of Representatives, a clear conservative voting trend is seen in Southern members of either house. From this perspective, we may deduct that a Confederate government would likely be more conservative in fiscal, social, and foreign policy matters. Here are some examples of the voting pattern contrasts between the Yankee Empire's Congress and its Southern delegates: (1) 1990 act to increase legal immigration, Yankee Empire 31% no; Southern delegates 53% no (the act passed, over the objections of the South); (2) 1994 assault weapons ban, Yankee Empire 49% no; Southern delegates 66% no (the bill passed, over the objections of the South); (3) 1985 bill to restrict the federal court's involvement in school prayer issues, Yankee Empire 63% against restricting court; Southern delegates 72% in favor of restricting court (opponents of restriction won, overriding the votes of the South); (4) vote to ban forced busing, Yankee Empire 68% against banning forced busing; Southern delegates 76% in favor of banning forced busing (the bill failed, over the objections of the South); (5) aid to anti-communist rebels in Nicaragua, Yankee Empire 48% yes; Southern delegates 66% yes (the bill failed, over the objections of the South). The preceding is a sampling of the voting dissimilarities between the Yankee Empire's Congress in the aggregate and the delegates from the South, demonstrating the profound differences in political philosophies between the two nations that exist even to this day! It is clear that there exists an irreconcilable ideological divide between "We the people" of the South and the Yankee Empire's ruling elites.[7]

The review of the congressional voting record demonstrates the that the people of the South, as a result of the Yankee Empire's invasion, conquest, and occupation, have been denied the right to live under a government ordered upon the consent of the governed! The astounding fact is that since 1865 the people of the South have been forced to live under a government that does not represent their interests and values. And in 2022 the Yankee Empire is deliberately exterminating the remaining fragments of the conquered South's honorable heritage. The Yankee Empire coerced the people of the South into accepting government rules, edicts, and court orders that Southerners would have never voluntarily inflicted upon themselves. As Jefferson Davis said, "The only alternative to secession is coercion."[8]

Another misguided, contemporary argument used against the principle of secession is that it is "unpatriotic" because it violates the principles enshrined in the "Pledge of Allegiance." Specifically, secession violates the idea that the original United States is "one nation … indivisible." It is unfortunate when constitutional principles are forced to take second place to a ritual of questionable origins having nothing to do with the constitutional principles of American government.

The Story-Webster-Lincoln idea of the United States as a unitary and indivisible nation became ingrained into American national life through the efforts of American socialist Francis Bellamy.[9] Bellamy, a defrocked Baptist minister, wrote the now famous Pledge of Allegiance. With the assistance of the Woman's Relief Corps on Patriotic Teaching, the women's auxiliary of the Union veterans

---

7   Kennedy, James Ronald, *Freedom Now: A non-violent conservative revolution* (Wake Forest, NC: The Scuppernong Press, 2022), 6-7.

8   William Coats, ed., *Jefferson Davis, The Rise and Fall of the Confederate Government* (1881, Nashville, TN: Bill Coats, Ltd., 1996), Vol. I, p. 177.

9   Margarete S. Miller, *Twenty-Three Words* (Portsmouth, VA: Printcraft Press, Inc., 1976), 49.

organization of the Grand Army of the Republic (G.A.R.), Bellamy succeeded in having his pledge adopted by America's public school systems. Bellamy believed that the defining event in American history had been the "Civil War," and he admitted that he desired that his pledge would reenforce everything that the arguments of "Hamilton, the Webster-Hayne debate, the speeches of Seward and Lincoln, [and] the Civil War"[10] had accomplished.

Francis Bellamy's cousin, Edward Bellamy, was the author of the socialist-utopian novel *Looking Backward*. Both were utopian dreamers who dedicated their lives to various socialist causes. Francis was an advocate of "Christian Socialism." Christian socialist rejection of orthodox Christian views resulted in Francis's removal from the Baptist ministry. Bellamy's family were all New England Yankees. A short stay in the South was enough to convince him that the South was hopelessly tied to religious orthodoxy even to point of rejecting such modern and progressive theories as evolution.[11] Bellamy's hostility to the "puritanical" and "cracker" nature of Southern churches prompted his rejection of biblical Christianity altogether. Bellamy rejected the belief in Christ's divinity and resurrection. He was openly critical and scornful of Southerners who faithfully adhered to biblical Christian doctrines.[12]

Senator Jefferson Davis, in his 1858 Senate speech, warned Americans of the danger of following the disciples of "higher law" because of their faith in man's reason rather than faith in the Bible. Francis Bellamy's rejection of biblical Christianity and his adoption of the Story-Webster-Lincoln premise of "one people, one nation indivisible" is positive proof that Davis's warning was on target. With the help of unsuspecting but otherwise patriotic Americans, the socialist author of the now famous Pledge of Allegiance was able to enshrine in the hearts of American school children the unconstitutional principles of a unitary, nationalist, and supreme Federal Government—without realizing it, school children are pledging allegiance, not to America's constitutional Republic, but

---

10 Francis Bellamy, Miller, 121.

11 Miller, 351.

12 *Ibid.*, 354.

to the Yankee Empire. If patriotism is defined as love of liberty, constitutional government, and adherence to the principles of the original Constitution, then Francis Bellamy's socialist utopian pledge to an all-powerful, "one nation indivisible," central government does not meet the standard of American patriotism! Yet, those who would deny the inalienable right of secession are quick to accuse secessionists of being un-American and unpatriotic because we refuse to blindly worship at the altar inscribed "one nation indivisible." Never forget: Only empires are indivisible."[13]

SUMMARY

From what we have demonstrated in the preceding pages, it is clear that the often-heard anti-secession "truism" that the South is too small, too weak, or too poor to have been an independent nation in 1861 or to be independent today cannot be maintained by facts. In an 1862 speech at Newcastle, England, William E. Gladstone, British chancellor of the exchequer, asserted, "There is no doubt that Jefferson Davis and other leaders of the South have made an army. They are making, it appears, a navy. And they have made what is more than either; they have made a nation."[14] Therefore, we implore you, the jury, not to allow such biased notions of Southern poverty and weakness or fanatical reasoning to prejudice your opinion in this case. By now, it should be obvious that these anti-secession arguments are utilized by desperate ideologues who cannot otherwise maintain their illogical premise. Let us move from such unsound, unethical, and fanatical ground and judge President Davis and the Southern people upon the sound foundation of historical fact. In doing so, there is no choice but to find President Jefferson Davis and the people of the South, not guilty of treason.

---

13 Kennedy & Kennedy, *The South Was Right!* 3rd edition, Chapter 10, "Only Empires are Indivisible," 259-66.

14 William E. Gladstone, as cited in *Journal of Confederate History*, 1991, 6.

Chapter 18

Your Verdict - Your Decision - Your Future

YOU ARE NOW A PART of the jury that must decide whether or not Jefferson Davis is guilty of treason. But judge carefully because your decision not only impacts Jefferson Davis's legacy, it also impacts your future and the future of Southern generations yet unborn. The impact does not end in the South. Its impact extends to all Americans. If Jefferson Davis is guilty, then everything the current left-of-center, Deep State, supreme Federal Government does is legitimate. But if Jefferson Davis is innocent, then the current supreme Federal Government is an *illegitimate* government (the Yankee Empire) that has no right to rule over the people of the Confederate States of America! And its rule over the rest of America is therefore *illegitimate*. As Confederate Vice President Alexander Stephens declared after the War, "The cause of the South is now the cause of all [Americans.]"

We have documented the life of Jefferson Davis, his attitude toward slavery, his dedication to the original, Constitutionally-limited Republic of Sovereign States, and his effort to preserve the union of Sovereign States as originally established by the Founding Fathers. We have documented the character of greedy Northern radicals who sought to use their political power in the Federal Congress to exploit the South for the benefit of Northern commerce. We have exposed and documented the political sophistry (intellectual dishonesty) used by those championing the Yankee Empire's right to invade, conquer, and impoverish a peaceful, democratically elected, sovereign nation—the Confederate States of America.

The question before you, the jury, is: "Was Jefferson Davis an evil traitor seeking to preserve slavery forever and seeking to destroy the United States, or was he an American patriot seeking to preserve for the people of the South those ancient rights belonging to all Americans?" We, his defense, maintain that he and his fellow Southerners were seeking to secure for themselves and their descendants those ancient rights inherited from England, ancient rights announced by the Sovereign States in their July 4, 1776, Declaration of Independence. These ancient rights were codified by the Founding Fathers in the proposed Constitution of 1787 and subsequently given political life on the North American continent when, and only when, the thirteen Sovereign States individually ratified the original Constitution.

The question of Jefferson Davis's status of traitor or patriot hangs on the answer to the following points:

- Did the ratification of the original Constitution in 1787-8 by the Sovereign States create a *conditional* union by establishing a constitutionally-limited Federal Government while reserving the vast majority of rights, including the right of secession, to "we the people" of the sovereign states?

- Was secession, in the original American system of government and before Lincoln and the Republican Party, an accepted American political principle?

- Is secession one of those "unalienable Rights" described in the Declaration of Independence signed by each Sovereign State in 1776?

If the answer to any one of the three questions above is "yes," then you, the jury, must vote not guilty on the charge of treason. The evidence in favor of Jefferson Davis and the South is overwhelming. It is only with the power of bloody bayonets that the Yankee Empire can maintain their claim that Jefferson Davis and, therefore, the South was guilty of treason. And never forget whose blood is dripping from the tips of those bloody Yankee bayonets.

It is now your hour of decision. Will you judge him guilty and continue your unquestioning allegiance to the current indivisible supreme Federal Government, or will you judge him innocent? If innocent, then what will you do about your current condition as a stateless person—a political slave to the indivisible, unconstitutional, supreme Federal Government?

We the people are a stateless people— we are the ruling elites' political slaves.

No conservative organization, Southern heritage organization, or the "conservative" Republican Party has ever developed a strategic plan to defeat America's neo-Marxist enemies. None of these organizations can define what the ultimate victory would look like, much less how to achieve that victory. Conservatives go from one dismal political defeat to another, thinking: "well, we will do better the next time." At the rate we are going as a nation, we are fast approaching the moment when there will not be another time.

We must recognize that Southerners and non-Southerners in Red State and Red County America are a stateless people. We have no government that will actively protect and (more importantly) actively promote our interests. As stateless people, we are, in reality, political slaves to the country's ruling elites. Here are two examples of Americans as stateless people: (1) the people of California passed a statewide ballot initiative that the definition of marriage would be between one man and one woman, but the Federal Government nullified the will of the people. (2) The people of Mississippi voted in a statewide ballot initiative to keep their traditional state flag but the Republican governor and Republican legislature, following the instructions of their Deep State masters, met in a rump session and overruled the will of the people. We are the political slaves of America's leftist ruling elites—regardless of which national political party is in control.

A strategic plan to defeat America's Woke, politically correct ruling elite is outlined in *Dixie Rising-Rules for Rebels*.[1] The book explains how to conduct irregular political warfare. It also documents five occupied nations that used irregular political warfare to gain their independence or, at least, they forced their central government to respect their heritage and natural rights. Constitutional government can be reclaimed—it can be done if we have the courage and audacity to implement this plan. The plan centers around the establishment of Provisional Governments in every Southern County and State; using the Provisional Government organized at the county level to support the lobbying efforts in the state legislature; and forcing Congress to submit to the States the Sovereign State Amendment, which acknowledges the Sovereign State's rights of nullification and secession.

The key to "jump-starting" this movement is to elect one of our own to a statewide office—someone who will use that office as a Bully Pulpit to promote the establishment of Provisional Governments across the South and Red State Red County America. The Bully Pulpit must be held by one of our own—NOT a "good" conservative politician. He must be someone with a plan and who is dedicated to the movement of reclaiming America's original Constitutionally limited Republic of Sovereign States—the original American government that Lincoln and the Republican Party destroyed.

This is a choice between liberty or continued political slavery. If we keep doing what we always do, we will find ourselves—in the words of John Randolph of Roanoke, Virginia, "When the little on which we now subsite will be taken for us." The choice is yours—but remember time is running out!

DEO VINDICE

---

1   Kennedy, James Ronald, *Dixie Rising-Rules for Rebels,* 2nd edition (Columbia, SC: Shotwell Publishing, 2021).

Addendum I

KENTUCKY AND VIRGINIA RESOLUTIONS OF 1798

A VERY SHORT ELEVEN YEARS after the Constitution was drafted, President John Adams, a Federalist, with the assistance of a Federalist dominated Congress, for the first time in American history assaulted the civil liberties of the American people. This attack demonstrated how easy it is for a faction to take control of the Federal Government and oppress the rights and liberties of "We the people" of the sovereign states. In the spring of 1798, Federalist president John Adams and the Federalist-dominated Congress passed the Alien and Sedition Acts. The Sedition Act made it a crime to criticize the government! The Federalist-dominated Supreme Court enforced this act and convicted and imprisoned numerous anti-Federalists (then known as Republicans who were led by Thomas Jefferson). It took the United States Supreme Court more than 160 years to declare this act an unconstitutional violation of the Bill of Rights!

The sovereign states of Kentucky and Virginia responded to this unconstitutional act by passing their famous Resolutions of 1798. These resolutions became the fundamental statements of the States' Rights party in American politics. The famous Kentucky and Virginia Resolutions are credited to Thomas Jefferson (Kentucky) and James Madison (Virginia). As you may recall, James Madison had originally been in favor of a strong central government. But after realizing the dangers posed by the spirit of sectional factionalism in the (Yankee) commercial states, he altered his opinion and embraced the States' Rights doctrine.

Even though these resolutions were authored by two different individuals and were then submitted to the actions of two different state legislatures, they still speak of the same principles. The tone and tenor of these resolutions are of limited federalism, States' Rights, and the ultimate right and duty of the sovereign state to judge for itself whether or not an act of the Federal Government is *pursuant* to the Constitution. Then, as a sovereign state, that state has the duty to take whatever action is required to protect the liberty of its citizens—the ultimate expression of local self-government!

The following **selections** from these resolutions demonstrates the conditional nature of the Union and establishes that the sovereign state is the *ultimate guardian* of the liberties of "We the people" of the state(s).

Kentucky Resolution, November 10, 1798

1. Resolved, That the several states composing the United States of America, are not united on the principle of unlimited submission to their general government; but that by compact, under the style and title of a Constitution for the United States, and of amendments thereto, they constituted a general government for special purposes, delegated to that government certain definite powers, reserving, each state to itself, the residuary mass of right to their own self-government; and that whensoever the general government assumes undelegated powers, its acts are un-authoritative, void, and of no force: That to this compact each state acceded as a state, and is an integral party, its co-states forming as to itself, the other party: That the government created by this compact was not made the exclusive or final *judge* of the extent of the powers delegated to itself; since that would have made its discretion, and not the Constitution, the measure of its powers; but that, as in all other cases of compact among parties having no common judge, each party has an equal right to judge for itself, as well of infractions, as of the mode and measure of redress.

2. *Resolved*, That the Constitution of the United States having delegated to Congress a power to punish treason, counterfeiting the securities and current coin of the United States, piracies and felonies committed on the high seas, and offences against the laws of nations, and no other crimes whatever, ... all other [of] their acts which assume to create, define, or punish crimes other than those enumerated in the Constitution, are altogether void, and of no force, and that the power to create, define, and punish such other crimes is reserved, and of right appertains, solely and exclusively, to the respective states, each within its own territory.

3. *Resolved*, That it is true as a general principle, and is also expressly declared by one of the amendments to the Constitution, that "the powers not delegated to the United States by the Constitution, nor prohibited by it to the states, are reserved to the states respectively, or to the people"; and that no power over the freedom of religion, freedom of speech, or freedom of the press, being delegated to the United States by the Constitution, nor prohibited by it to the states, all lawful powers respecting the same did of right remain, and were reserved to the states, or to the people; that thus was manifested their determination to retain to themselves the right of judging how far the licentiousness of speech and of the press may be abridged without lessening their useful freedom, and how far those abuses which cannot be separated from their use, should be tolerated rather than the use be destroyed; and thus also they guarded against all abridgment by the United States of the freedom or religious opinions and exercises, and retained to themselves the right of protecting the same, as this state by a law passed on the general demand of its citizens, had already protected them from all human restraint or interference: and that in addition to this general principle and express declaration, another and more special provision has been made by one of the amendments to the Constitution, which expressly declares, that "Congress shall make no law respecting an establishment of religion, or prohibiting the free exercise thereof, or abridging the freedom of speech, or of the press," thereby guarding in the same sentence, and under the same words, the freedom of religion, of speech, and of the press, insomuch, that whatever violates either, throws down the sanctuary which covers the others, and that libels, falsehoods, and defamations, equally

with heresy and false religion, are withheld from the cognizance of federal tribunals: that therefore the act of the Congress of the United States, passed on the 14th day of July, 1798, entitled, "an act in addition to the act for the punishment of certain crimes against the United States," which does abridge the freedom of the press, is not law, but is altogether void and of no effect.

4. *Resolved*, That alien-friends are under the jurisdiction and protection of the laws of the state wherein they are; that no power over them has been delegated to the United States, nor prohibited to the individual states distinct from their power over citizens; and it being true as a general principle, and one of the amendments to the Constitution having also declared, that "the powers not delegated to the United States by the Constitution, nor prohibited by it to the states, are reserved to the states respectively, or to the people," that act of Congress of the United States, passed on the 22nd day of June, 1798, entitled "an act concerning aliens," which assumes power over alien-friends not delegated by the Constitution, is not law, but is altogether void and of no force ....

6. *Resolved*, That the imprisonment of a person under the protection of the laws of this commonwealth, on his failure to obey the simple *order* of the President, to depart out of the United States, as is undertaken by the said act, entitled "an act concerning aliens," is contrary to the Constitution, one amendment to which has provided, that "no person shall be deprived of liberty without due process of law," and that another having provided, "that in all criminal prosecutions, the accused shall enjoy the right to a public trial by an impartial jury, to be informed of the nature and cause of the accusation, to be confronted with the witnesses against him, to have compulsory process for obtaining witnesses in his favor, and to have the assistance of counsel for his defense," the same act undertaking to authorize the President to remove a person out of the United States, who is under the protection of the law, on his own suspicion, without accusation, without jury, without public trial, without confrontation of the witnesses against him, without having witnesses in his favor, without defense, without counsel, is contrary to these provisions, also, of the Constitution, is therefore not law, but utterly void and of no force.

That transferring the power of judging any person who is under the protection of the laws, from the courts to the President of the United States, as is undertaken by the same act, concerning aliens, is against the article of the Constitution which provides, that "the judicial power of the United States shall be vested in courts, the judges of which shall hold their offices during good behavior ...."

Virginia Resolution, December 21, 1798

1. *Resolved*, That the General Assembly of Virginia doth unequivocally express a firm resolution to maintain and defend the Constitution of the United States, and the Constitution of this State, against every aggression, either foreign or domestic, and that it will support the government of the United States in all measures warranted by the former ....

3. That this Assembly doth explicitly and peremptorily declare that it views the powers of the Federal Government as resulting from the compact to which the States are parties, as limited by the plain sense and intention of the instrument constituting that compact; as no further valid than they are authorized by the grants enumerated in that compact; and that in case of a deliberate, palpable, and dangerous exercise of other powers not granted by the said compact, the States, who are the parties thereto, have the right, and are in duty bound, to interpose for arresting the progress of the evil, and liberties appertaining to them.

4. That the General Assembly doth also express its deep regret that a spirit has in sundry instances been manifested by the Federal Government, to enlarge its powers by forced constructions of the constitutional charter which defines them; and that indications have appeared of a design to expound certain general phrases (which, having been copied from the very limited grant of powers in the former articles of confederation, were the less liable to be misconstrued), so as to destroy the meaning and effect of the particular enumeration, which necessarily explains and limits the general phrases, and so as to consolidate the States by degrees into

one sovereignty, the obvious tendency and inevitable result of which would be to transform the present republican system of the United States into an absolute, or at best, a mixed monarchy.

5. That the General Assembly doth particularly protest against the palpable and alarming infractions of the Constitution, in the two late cases of the "alien and sedition acts," passed at the last session of Congress, the first of which exercises a power nowhere delegated to the Federal Government; and which by uniting legislative and judicial powers to those of executive, subverts the general principles of free government, as well as the particular organization and positive provisions of the federal Constitution; and the other of which acts exercises in like manner a power not delegated by the Constitution, but on the contrary' expressly and positively forbidden by one of the amendments thereto: a power which more than any other ought to produce universal alarm, because it is leveled against that right of freely examining public characters and measures, and of free communication among the people thereon, which has ever been justly deemed the only effectual guardian of every other right.

6. That this State having by its convention which ratified the federal Constitution, expressly declared, "that among other essential rights, the liberty of conscience and of the press cannot be canceled, abridged, restrained, or modified by any authority of the United States," and from its extreme anxiety to guard these rights from every possible attack of sophistry of ambition, having with other States recommended an amendment for that purpose, which amendment was in due time annexed to the Constitution, it would mark a reproachful inconsistency and criminal degeneracy, if an indifference were now shown to the most palpable violation of one of the rights thus declared and secured, and to the establishment of a precedent which may be fatal to the other.

Addendum II

Sovereign States Defy the Federal Government's Unconstitutional Acts

THE APOLOGISTS FOR THE NORTHERN IDEA of "one people, one nation indivisible" either ignore the Kentucky and Virginia Resolutions of 1798 or treat them as insignificant historical oddities. These resolutions are absolutely damning to the concept of a supreme Federal Government and the United States as "one nation indivisible." The apologists for the Yankee Empire's invasion of the Confederate States of America would prefer that these resolutions be viewed as an oddity of Southern politics that were forgotten shortly after they appeared. The following citations, mostly from Northern state legislatures, will demonstrate just how important and widely accepted the idea of States' Rights was in the early history of these United States. The language and intent of each of these citations are similar to, if not exactly the same, the language and intent of the Resolutions of 1798. Each addresses the Federal Government as an agent of a conditional union. They all speak of an America composed of sovereign states competent to judge for themselves whether the United States government was infringing upon the rights reserved to "We the people" of the sovereign states. They all speak of sovereign states that were competent to judge for themselves whether or not their agent, the Federal Government, was conducting itself "pursuant to the Constitution." They all speak of the authority of "We the people" of the sovereign state to interpose the state between its citizens and an abusive Federal Government;

or, by implication, they all speak of the inalienable right of "We the people" of the sovereign state to recall any or all of the authority delegated to the government of these United States.

New Hampshire Resolution 1795

Can the rage for annihilating all the power of the States, and reducing this extensive and flourishing country to one domination make the administrators blind to the danger of violating all the principles of our former government, to the hazard of convulsions, in endeavoring to eradicate every trace of State power, except in the resentment of the people....

Forced by events, the Legislature of New Hampshire have made the foregoing statements; and while they cheerfully acknowledge the power of Congress in cases arising under the Constitution, they equally resolve not to submit the laws made before the existence of the present government by this (then independent State) to the adjudication of any power on earth, while the freedom of the Federal Government shall afford any constitutional means of redress. Impressed with the singular merits of the present case, and deprecating the many and complicated evils which must be the necessary consequence of establishing the power claimed by the courts of the United States, and its tendency to produce disaffection to our government, the Legislature of New Hampshire rest assured that a speedy and just decision will be had, and that the right of State Governments and the interests of their citizens will be secured against the exercise of a power of a court, or any body of men under Congress, of carrying into effect an unconstitutional decree of a court instituted by a former Congress, and which in its effects, would unsettle property and tear up the laws of the several States.[1]

Pennsylvania Resolves 1809

And whereas the causes and reasons which have produced this conflict between the general and State government should be made known, not only that the State may be justified to her sister States,

---

1 James J. Kilpatrick, *The Sovereign States* (Chicago: Henry Regnery Co., 1957), 108.

who are equally interested in the preservation of the State rights; but to evince to the Government of the United States that the Legislature, in resisting encroachments on their rights, are not acting in a spirit of hostility to the legitimate powers of the United States courts; but are actuated by a disposition to compromise, and to guard against future collisions of power, by an amendment to the Constitution; and that, whilst they are contending for the rights of the State, that it will be attributed to a desire for preserving the Federal government itself, the best features of which must depend upon keeping up a just balance between the general and State governments, as guaranteed by the Constitution....

Although the Legislature reverence the Constitution of the United States and its lawful authorities, yet there is a respect due to the solemn and public acts, and to the honor and dignity of our own State, and the unvarying assertion of her right, for a period of thirty years, which right ought not to be relinquished....

... Whilst they yield to this authority, when exercised within Constitutional limits, they trust they will not be considered as acting hostile to the General Government, when as guardians of the State rights, they cannot permit an infringement of those rights by an unconstitutional exercise of power in the United States courts....

Resolved, that should the independence of the States as secured by the Constitution, be destroyed, the liberties of the people in so extensive a country cannot long survive. To suffer the United States courts to decide on STATE RIGHTS will, from a bias *in favor of power*, necessarily destroy the FEDERAL PART of our Government: And whenever the government of the United States becomes consolidated, we may learn from the history of nations what will be the event.[2]

---

2 *Ibid.*, 114-16.

MASSACHUSETTS RESOLVES OF 1809

While this State maintains its sovereignty and independence, all the citizens can find protection against outrage and injustice in the strong arm of the State government.... [therefore the Federal embargo is] ... not legally binding on the citizens of this State.³

MASSACHUSETTS RESOLVE, 1814

A power to regulate commerce is abused, when employed to destroy it; *and a manifest and voluntary abuse of power sanctions the right of resistance, as much as a direct and palpable usurpation.* The sovereignty reserved to the States, was reserved to protect the citizens from acts of violence by the United States, as well as for purposes of domestic regulation. We spurn the idea that the free, sovereign and independent State of Massachusetts is reduced to a mere municipal corporation, without power to protect its people, and to defend them from oppression, from whatever quarter it comes. Whenever the national compact is violated, and the citizens of this State are oppressed by cruel and unauthorized laws, this Legislature is bound to interpose its power, and wrest from the oppressor his victim.

This is the spirit of our Union ....⁴

CONNECTICUT RESOLVE, 1809

The General Assembly are decided in the opinion, and do Resolve, that the acts aforesaid are ... grievous to the good people of this State, dangerous to their common liberties, incompatible with the Constitution of the United States, and encroaching upon the immunities of this State....

Resolved, that to preserve the Union, and support the Constitution of the United States, it becomes the duty of the legislatures of the States, in such a crisis of affairs, vigilantly to watch over, and

---

3   *Ibid.,* 130.

4   *Ibid.,* 137.

vigorously to maintain, the powers not delegated to the United States, but reserved to the States respectively, or to the people; and that a due regard to this duty, will not permit this Assembly to assist, or concur in giving effect to the aforesaid unconstitutional act, passed, to enforce the embargo.[5]

CONNECTICUT RESOLVE, 1812

The people of this State were among the first to adopt that Constitution. ... They have a deep interest in its preservation, and are still disposed to yield a willing and prompt obedience to all the legitimate requirements of the Constitution of the United States.

But it must not be forgotten, that the State of Connecticut is a FREE, SOVEREIGN AND INDEPENDENT STATE; that the United States are a confederacy of States; that we are a *confederated* and not a consolidated Republic. The Governor of this State is under a high and solemn obligation, "to maintain the lawful rights and privileges thereof, as a sovereign, free and independent State," as he is "to support the Constitution of the United States," and the obligation to support the latter imposes an additional obligation to support the former. The building cannot stand, if the pillars upon which it rests, are impaired or destroyed.[6]

RHODE ISLAND RESOLVE 1809

[Rhode Island claims the sovereign authority] to interpose for the purpose of protecting them [its citizens] from the ruinous inflictions of usurped and unconstitutional power.[7]

---

5   *Ibid.*, 131.

6   *Ibid.*, 134.

7   *Ibid.*, 131.

OHIO RESOLVE, 1820-21

The committee are aware of the doctrine, that the Federal courts are exclusively vested with jurisdiction to declare, in the last resort, the true interpretation of the Constitution of the United States. To this doctrine, in the latitude of contended for, they [Ohio's legislatures] never can give their assent....

Addendum III

President Franklin Pierce Defends States' Rights

> All that the South has ever desired was that the Union, as established by our forefathers, should be preserved; and that the government, as originally organized, should be administered in purity and truth.
>
> Robert E. Lee, January 1866

THE MAJOR CONSEQUENCE of Lincoln's and the Republican Party's revolution was to foist upon America a supreme Federal Government that the Founding Fathers had specifically rejected. As pointed out in this defense of Jefferson Davis, the Story-Webster-Lincoln and Republican Party' view of American government maintains that the Federal Government is sovereign (supreme) and that the states must submit to Federal domination. Yet, as we have demonstrated, this view was not advocated by the Founding Fathers during the ratifying process for the federal Constitution. What may be more shocking to modern Americans is that Jefferson Davis's and the South's view of States' Rights and American government was advocated by prominent Northern political leaders such as Franklin Pierce, the fourteenth president of the United States. President Pierce of New Hampshire did not formulate his States' Rights doctrine in a political vacuum. Early in the history of the United States, the people of New England were among the strongest advocates of States'

Rights. In its 1792 constitution, New Hampshire boldly proclaimed not only its independence and sovereignty but also its authority to recall a right delegated to any government.

> The people of this state have the sole and exclusive right to governing themselves as a free, sovereign, and independent state; and do, and forever hereafter shall, exercise and enjoy every power, jurisdiction, and right, pertaining thereto, which is not, or may not hereafter be, by them expressly delegated to the United States of America in congress assembled.
>
> Article VII, New Hampshire State Constitution, 1792
>
> Government being instituted for the common benefit, protection, and security, of the whole community, and not for the private interest or emolument of any one man, family, or class of men; therefore, whenever the ends of government are perverted, or public redress are ineffectual, the people may, and of right ought to, reform the old, *or establish a new government* [emphasis added]. The doctrine of non-resistance against arbitrary power, and oppression, is absurd, slavish, and destructive of the good and happiness of mankind.
>
> Article X, New Hampshire State Constitution, 1792

Sixty-one years after the adoption of New Hampshire's 1792 constitution its favorite son, Franklin Pierce, took the oath of office as president of the United States of America. In his March 4, 1853, inaugural address, Pierce articulated several points that are central to the States' Rights view of American government and, in retrospect, his inaugural address makes a perfect defense for President Jefferson Davis and the right of the South to be a free and independent nation. The following examples, taken from Pierce's inaugural address, demonstrate his high estimation of the American political doctrine of state sovereignty.

1. In total disregard for Daniel Webster's allegation that the States never acceded to the Union, Pierce quoted President George Washington's statement that a state had indeed acceded to the Union. Pierce stated, "Less than sixty-four years ago the Father of his Country made the *'recent accession* of the important State of North Carolina to the Constitution of the United States' one of the subjects of his special congratulation" [emphasis added]. Both George Washington and Franklin Pierce understood that "We the people" of the sovereign states created the Federal Government and, therefore, those who make have the right to unmake.

2. In concert with Alexander Hamilton and other Founding Fathers, Pierce noted the special relationship between the sovereign states and their agent, the Federal Government. Pierce even warned Americans of the danger of centralizing all political power in Washington, D.C.:

> The dangers of a concentration of all power in the general government of a confederacy so vast as ours are too obvious to be disregarded. You have a right, therefore, to expect your agents in every department to regard strictly the limits imposed upon them by the Constitution of the United States. The great scheme of our constitutional liberty rests upon *a proper distribution of power between the State and, Federal authorities*, and experience has shown that the harmony and happiness of our people must depend upon a just discrimination between the separate rights and responsibilities of the States and your common right and obligations under the General Government. ... If the Federal Government will confine itself to the exercise of powers clearly granted by the Constitution, it can hardly happen that its action upon any question should endanger the institutions of the States or

interfere with their right to manage matters strictly domestic according to the will of their own people" [emphasis added].

3. During his inaugural address, Pierce referred to the Union as a "confederacy." In referring to the Federal Government and therefore the Union as a "confederacy," Pierce was following in the footsteps of New Yorker Alexander Hamilton (see *The Federalist Papers* No. 9 and No. 18). The term "confederacy," as used by Hamilton and Pierce, flies in the face of the Story-Webster-Lincoln and Republican Party's theory of a centralized, unitary, supreme "one nation indivisible" Federal Government where the states survive as mere dependent political units of the Federal Government.

4. Pierce also noted that member states of the American republic were bound by the Constitution. They could not choose which portions of the Constitution they would obey and which they would ignore. The states were at liberty to amend the Constitution if they desired to change some portion of it, but they were bound by it until such amendment was constitutionally passed. This point was being made by Pierce in response to the radical element in the North who were engaged in a propaganda war against the South over the issue of slavery. Even though not an advocate of slavery, Pierce noted that, according to the Constitution, the states had pledged themselves to uphold the constitutional rights of all states, even those property rights which by that time were mostly unique to the South. Pierce stated, "I believe that involuntary servitude, as it exists in different States [New Jersey had more than two hundred slaves for life within its borders as late as 1850] is recognized by the Constitution. I believe that it stands like any other admitted right, and that the States where it exists are entitled to efficient remedies to enforce the constitutional provisions. . . . I believe that the constituted authorities of this Republic are bound to regard the rights of the South in this respect as they would view any other legal and constitutional right, and that the laws to enforce them should be respected and obeyed."

President Pierce, in the closing paragraph of his inaugural address, warned of the danger of allowing the Union, as delivered to Americans by their Founding Fathers, to be destroyed.

> Let it be impressed upon all hearts that, beautiful as our fabric is, no earthly power or wisdom could ever reunite its broken fragments. Standing, as I do, almost within view of the green slopes of Monticello, and, as it were, within reach of the tomb of Washington, with all the cherished memories of the past gathering around me like so many eloquent voices of exhortation from heaven, I can express no better hope for my country than that the kind Providence which smiled upon our fathers may enable their children to preserve the blessings they have inherited.

Addendum IV

Maryland Resolutions of 1861

THE FOLLOWING TWO RESOLUTIONS passed by the legislature of the state of Maryland demonstrate the general belief, held by Americans as late as 1861, that the Union was composed of the voluntary association of sovereign states. It also gives the modern-day reader an opportunity to sample the thinking of the people of the sovereign state of Maryland at the time of the Yankee Empire's invasion of the Confederate States of America.

The first resolution was passed May 10, 1861, while the peaceful state of Maryland was being occupied by the Yankee Empire's military. The resolution passed the Maryland Senate by a vote of eleven ayes and three nays. The resolution passed in the Maryland House of Representatives by a vote of forty-three ayes and twelve nays. It is interesting to note that the faction favoring immediate secession was in the minority in the Maryland legislature. The conservatives in Maryland's legislature still believed that appeals to the Constitution would provide their people with adequate protection from an abusive Federal Government. Even though the state was not in favor of immediate secession, it nonetheless agreed with the American principles of self-determination and of government by the *consent of the governed*. These resolutions give ample support to Maryland's willing defense of the original Constitution and its state sovereignty.

Maryland's Resolution of May 10, 1861

Whereas, in the judgment of the General Assembly of Maryland, the war now waged by the government of the United States upon the people of the Confederate States is unconstitutional in its origin, purposes and conduct; repugnant to civilization and sound policy; subversive of the free principles upon which the Federal Union was founded, and certain to result in the hopeless and bloody overthrow of our existing institutions; and,

Whereas, the people of Maryland, while recognizing the obligations of their State, as a member of the Union, to submit in good faith to the exercise of all the legal and constitutional powers of the general government, and to join as one man in fighting its authorized battles, do reverence, nevertheless, the great American principle of self-government, and sympathize deeply with their Southern brethren in their noble and manly determination to uphold and defend the same; and,

Whereas, not merely on their own account, and to turn from their own soil the calamities of civil war, but for the blessed sake of humanity and to arrest the wanton shedding of fraternal blood in a miserable contest which can bring nothing with it but sorrow, shame and desolation, the people of Maryland are enlisted with their whole hearts on the side of reconciliation

Now, therefore, it is hereby resolved by the General Assembly of Maryland, that the State of Maryland owes it to her own self-respect and her respect for the Constitution, not less than her deepest and most honorable sympathies, to register this, her solemn protest, against the war which the Federal government has declared against the Confederate States of the South and our sister and neighbor, Virginia, and to announce her resolute determination to have no part or lot, directly or indirectly, in its prosecution.

Resolved, That the State of Maryland earnestly and anxiously desires the restoration of peace between the belligerent sections of the country; and the President, authorities and people of the Confederate States having over and over, officially and unofficially, declared that they seek only peace and self-defense, and to be let alone, and that they are willing to throw down the sword the instant the sword now drawn against them shall be sheathed—The senators and delegates of Maryland do beseech and implore the President of the United States to accept the olive branch which is thus held out to him, and in the name of God and humanity to cease this unholy and most wretched and unprofitable strife, at least until the assembling of the Congress at Washington shall have given time for the prevalence of cool and better counsels.

Resolved, That the State of Maryland desires the peaceful and immediate recognition of the independence of the Confederate States, and hereby gives her cordial consent thereto, as a member of the Union, entertaining the profound conviction that the willing return of the Southern people to their former Federal relations is a thing beyond hope, and that the attempt to coerce them will only add slaughter and hate to impossibility.

Resolved, That the present military occupation of Maryland being for purposes which in the opinion of the legislature are in flagrant violation of the Constitution, the General Assembly of the State in the name of her people does hereby protest against the same and against the arbitrary restrictions and illegalities with which it is attended, calling upon all good citizens at the same time, in the most earnest and authoritative manner, to abstain from all violent and unlawful interference of every sort with the troops in transit through our territory, or quartered among us, and patiently and peacefully leave to time and reason the ultimate and certain re-establishment and vindication of the right.

> Resolved: That under existing circumstances it is inexpedient to call a Sovereign Convention of the State at this time, or to take any measures for the immediate organization or arming of the militia.[1]

The Yankee Empire's responded to Maryland's resolutions by ordering Gen. Benjamin Butler of Massachusetts to seize the city of Baltimore, Maryland, the very night the resolutions were passed.[2] The normal operations of a country's (or sovereign state's) civil laws protecting the liberty of its people are destroyed when that country (or state) is invaded and occupied by a foreign military force. The liberty that Maryland and the other thirteen original colonies had won from Great Britain in 1776 was nullified as soon as the United States moved from a constitutional compact among sovereign states to the Yankee Empire utilizing military coercion to enforce its arbitrary rule.

Of the states remaining in the Union after the Southern states seceded, Maryland became the first to experience the loss of civil liberties that always happens when tyrants seize control of a formerly free country. On May 4, 1861, district judge William F. Giles issued a writ of habeas corpus to Major Morris, the Yankee Empire's military commander at Fort McHenry, for the release of a minor who had illegally enlisted in the army. Major Morris refused to honor the writ from a United States court. The abuse of power and oppression of civil liberties would continue. On May 14, General Butler ordered Yankee Empire troops to arrest Ross Winans, a member of the Maryland legislature. It was widely believed that the arrest was an attempt to terrorize the people of Maryland into submission to the Yankee Empire's authority.

On May 25, the home of John Merryman, a citizen of Baltimore, was invaded by a squad of Yankee Empire soldiers who seized Merryman, claiming to have arrested him. The Yankee Empire's troops offered no warrant or other lawful justification for their

---

[1] Bradley T. Johnson, *Confederate Military History* (1899, Harrisburg, PA: The Archive Society, 1994), II, 30-32.

[2] *Ibid.*, 32.

actions. Yankee Empire's General George Cadwallader, now commanding Fort McHenry, refused a writ of habeas corpus stating that the prisoner had been arrested because he was known or thought to be hostile to the "United States." General Cadwallader stated that he had been authorized by the Yankee Empire's president Abraham Lincoln to suspend the writ of habeas corpus in such cases! This writ of habeas corpus, ignored by the Yankee Empire's military, had been issued by the chief justice of the United States Supreme Court! The United States Supreme Court Chief Justice then issued a contempt order against the general and entered into the record the court's opinion that the alleged suspension of the constitutional right of habeas corpus by President Lincoln was unconstitutional! But appeals to the constraints of the United States Constitution proved to be as useless for the Chief Justice of the United States Supreme Court as it had been proven for the South!

The legislature of Maryland, acting at its adjourned session, passed the following resolution.

Maryland's Resolution of June 22, 1861

The unconstitutional and arbitrary proceedings of the Federal executive have not been confined to violations of the personal rights and liberties of the citizens of Maryland, but have been extended into every department of oppressive illegality, so that the property of no man is safe, the sanctity of no dwelling is respected, and the sacredness of private correspondence no longer exists; and

Whereas, the Senate and House of Delegates of Maryland, recognizing the obligations of the State, as far as in her lies, to protect and defend her people against usurped and arbitrary power, however difficult the fulfillment of that high obligation may be rendered by disastrous circumstances, feel it due to her dignity and independence that history should not record that overthrow of public freedom, for an instant, within her borders, without recording likewise the indignant expression of her resentment and remonstrance:

Now, therefore, be it resolved, That the senate and house of delegates of Maryland, in the name and on behalf of the good people of the State, do accordingly register this their earnest and unqualified protest against the oppressive and tyrannical assertion and exercise of the military jurisdiction within the limits of Maryland, over the persons and property of her citizens, by the government of the United States, and do solemnly declare the same to be subversive of the most sacred guarantees of the Constitution and in flagrant violation of the fundamental and most cherished principles of American free government.[3]

These resolutions demonstrate several important points.

First, they serve as dramatic proof of the exercise of arbitrary and unconstitutional power by the United States—which by this time had morphed into the Yankee Empire—over a people who were not at war with it. Indeed, the people of Maryland were still faithful members of the Union!

Second, the state of Maryland believed it had sovereign authority within the state.

Third, these resolutions demonstrate how useless the claim of constitutional rights are when they are opposed by a faction in possession of unlimited power and the lust to force its views upon a free people. This is a sad lesson that conservatives refuse to accept. The fact remains that the Constitution is not self-enforcing. Without political power to enforce the Constitution—our so-called rights are meaningless.

The conservatives in Maryland's legislature loved the Constitution, they loved the America of old, they desperately clung to a country that no longer existed and appealed to its dead constitution to protect them against the heavy hand of Lincoln's tyranny—all to no avail! Confederate General Bradley T. Johnson of Maryland lamented the futile effort of the conservatives in Maryland's legislature:

---

3   Ibid., 35.

The conservatives never could, never did understand that they were in the midst of a revolution. They stood by constitutional rights. They held on to the claim of constitutional guarantees—to habeas corpus—to trial by jury—to free speech—to law—until they and their constitutional guarantees were landed in Fort Lafayette or the military prisons in New York and Boston. They stood by their faith then and never ceased to protest that they could not be imprisoned without warrant, nor held without bail. They were right in doctrine, but they were imprisoned and held [nonetheless].[4]

Those who refuse to learn this lesson taught the conservatives of Maryland, by an all- powerful Federal Government, whether they intend to or not, end up as apologists for a centralized, tyrannical, government bent on maintaining its empire at the expense of liberty!

---

4   *Ibid.,* II, 30-2.

Addendum V

United States Supreme Court vs. President Abraham Lincoln

FROM THE VERY BEGINNING of the United States, the South had complained of the North's refusal to honor the limitations placed on federal powers by the Constitution. Apologists for the Yankee Empire's aggression have attempted to deflect such criticism by claiming that Southerners, such as Senator John C. Calhoun of South Carolina and Senator Jefferson Davis of Mississippi, were really using the Constitution as a pretext to defend the institution of slavery.

The Yankee Empire's *modus operandi* (m.o.) has been to ignore the Constitution when it stands in the way of the Empire's power and the development of the Empire's commercial profits. When Abraham Lincoln assumed the presidency of the United States, he quickly followed the emerging Yankee Empire's "m.o." of ignoring the plain language of the United States Constitution. The Merryman case is an example of Lincoln's low opinion of such constitutional niceties as due process, constitutional restrictions on the use of federal powers, and rule of law. This case, originating in Maryland, involved a dispute between the United States Supreme Court and the Yankee Empire's president as it relates to the constitutional authority to suspend the writ of habeas corpus. As such, it provides a "smoking gun" that demonstrates Lincoln's and the Yankee Empire's flagrant violation of the United States Constitution. Who could blame the

South for wanting to separate from such capricious, arbitrary, and evil political partners? The following extracts are taken from the text of the Merryman case.

THE MERRYMAN CASE
Decision of Chief Justice Taney
Ex Parte
John Merryman

Before the Chief Justice of the Supreme Court of the United States, at Chambers.

The application in this case for a Writ of *Habeas Corpus* is made to me under the 14th section of the Judiciary Act of 1789, which renders effectual for the citizen the Constitutional Privilege of the Writ of *Habeas Corpus*. That Act gives to the Courts of the United States, as well as to each Justice of the Supreme Court, and to every District Judge, power to grant Writs of *Habeas Corpus* for the purpose of an inquiry into the cause of commitment ....

The petition presents that following case: The petitioner resides in Maryland, in Baltimore County. While peaceably in his own house, with his family, it was at two o'clock on the morning of the 25th of May, 1861, entered by an armed force, professing to act under military orders. He was then compelled to rise from his bed, taken into custody, and conveyed to Fort McHenry, where he is imprisoned by the commanding officer, without warrant from any lawful authority.

The Commander of the Fort, General George Cadwalader, ... does not deny any of the facts alleged in the petition ....

A copy of the warrant or order, under which the prisoner was arrested, was demanded by his counsel, and refused. And it is not alleged in the return that any specific act, constituting any offence against the laws of the United States, has been charged against him upon oath; but he appears to have been arrested upon general charges of treason and rebellion, without proof, and without giving the names of the witnesses, or specifying the acts which, in the judgement of the military officer, constituted these crimes. And having the prisoner thus in custody upon these vague and unsupported accusations, he refuses to obey the Writ of *Habeas Corpus*, upon the ground that he is duly authorized by the President to suspend it ....

As the case comes before me, therefore, I understand that the President [Abraham Lincoln] not only claims the right to suspend the Writ of *Habeas Corpus* himself, at his discretion, but to delegate that discretionary power to a military officer, and to leave it to him to determine whether he will or will not obey Judicial process that may be served upon him.

No official notice has been given to the Courts of Justice, or to the public, by proclamation or otherwise, that the President claimed this power, and had exercised it in the manner stated in the return. And I certainly listened to it with some surprise, for I had supposed it to be one of those points of Constitutional law upon which there was no difference of opinion, and that it was admitted on all hands that the Privilege of the Writ could not be suspended, except by Act of Congress ....

... But being thus officially notified that the Privilege of the Writ has been suspended under the orders, and by the authority, of the President, and believing, as I do, that the President has exercised a power which he does not possess under the Constitution, a proper respect for the high office he fills requires me to state plainly and fully the grounds of my opinion, in order to show that I have not ventured to question the legality of his act without a careful and deliberate examination of the whole subject.

The clause of the Constitution which authorizes the suspension of the Privilege of the Writ of *Habeas Corpus* is in the 9th section of the first article.

This article is devoted to the Legislative Department of the United States, and has not the slightest reference to the Executive Department ....

And even if the Privilege of the Writ of *Habeas Corpus* was suspended by Act of Congress, and a party not subject to the Rules and Articles of war was afterwards arrested and imprisoned by regular Judicial process, he could not be detained in prison or brought to trial before a military tribunal, for the article in the Amendments to the Constitution immediately following the one above referred to—that is the 6th Article—provides that "In all criminal prosecutions, the accused shall enjoy the right to a speedy and public trial, by an impartial jury of the State and district wherein the crime shall have been committed, which district shall have been previously ascertained by law, and to be informed of the nature and cause of the accusation; to be confronted with the witnesses against him; to have compulsory process for obtaining witnesses in his favor, and to have the assistance of counsel for his defense."

And the only power, therefore, which the President possesses, where the "life, liberty or property" of a private citizen is concerned, is the power and duty prescribed in the 3d Section of the 2d Article, which requires "that he shall take care that the laws be faithfully executed." He is not authorized to execute them himself, or through agents or officers, civil or military, appointed by himself, but he is to take care that they be faithfully carried into execution, as they are expounded and adjudged by the Co-ordinate Branch of the Government to which that duty is assigned by the Constitution. It is thus made his duty to come in aid of the Judicial authority, if it shall be resisted by a force too strong to be overcome without the assistance of the Executive arm. But in exercising this power, he acts in subordination to Judicial authority, assisting it to execute its process and enforce its judgments.

With such provisions in the Constitution, expressed in language too clear to be misunderstood by any one, I can see no ground whatever for supposing that the President, in any emergency, or in any state of things, can authorize the suspension of the Privilege of the Writ of *Habeas Corpus*, or arrest a citizen except in aid of the Judicial power. He certainly does not faithfully execute the laws, if he takes upon himself legislative power by suspending the Writ of *Habeas Corpus*, and the Judicial power, also, by arresting and imprisoning a person without due process of law. Nor can any argument be drawn from the nature of Sovereignty, or the necessities of Government, for self-defense in times of tumult and danger. The Government of the United States is one of delegated and limited powers. It derives its existence and authority altogether from the

Constitution, and neither of its Branches, Executive, Legislative or Judicial, can exercise any of the powers of Government beyond those specified and granted. For the 10th Article of the Amendments to the Constitution in express terms provides that "the powers not delegated to the United States by the Constitution, nor prohibited by it to the States, are reserved to the States, respectively, or to the people ...."

The right of the subject to the benefit of the Writ of *Habeas Corpus*, it must be recollected, was one of the great points in controversy during the long struggle in England between arbitrary government and free institutions, and must, therefore, have strongly attracted the attention of the statesmen engaged in framing a new and, as they supposed, a freer Government than the one which they had thrown off by the Revolution.

For, from the earliest history of the Common Law, if a person were imprisoned—no matter by what authority—he had a right to the Writ of *Habeas Corpus*, to bring his case before the King's Bench; and if no specific offence was charged against him in the warrant of commitment, he was entitled to be forthwith discharged ....

To guide me to a right conclusion, I have the Commentaries on the Constitution of the United States of the late Mr. Justice Story ... speaking in his Commentaries of the *Habeas Corpus* clause in the Constitution, says:

> It is obvious that cases of a peculiar emergency may arise, which may justify, nay, even require, the temporary suspension of any right to the Writ. But, as it has frequently happened in foreign countries, and even in England, that the Writ has, upon various pretexts and occasions, been suspended, whereby persons apprehended upon suspicion have suffered a long imprisonment, sometimes from design, and sometimes because they were forgotten, the right to suspend it is expressly confined to cases of rebellion or invasion, where the public safety may require it. A very just and wholesome restraint, which cuts down

at a blow a fruitful means of oppression, capable of being abused in bad times to the worst of purposes. Hitherto no suspension of the Writ has ever been authorized by Congress since the establishment of the Constitution. It would seem, as the power is given to Congress to suspend the Writ of *Habeas Corpus* in cases of rebellion or invasion, that the right to judge whether the exigency had arisen must exclusively belong to that body." *3 Story's Com. On the Constitution, Section 1336.*

And Chief Justice Marshall [stated], in delivering the opinion of the Supreme Court in the case of *ex parte* Bollman and Swartwout ...

If at any time, the public safety should require the suspension of the powers vested by this act in the Courts of the United States, it is for the Legislature to say so. That question depends on political considerations, on which the Legislature is to decide. Until the Legislature will be expressed, this Court can only see its duty, and must obey the law.

I can add nothing to these clear and emphatic words of my great predecessor.

But the documents before me show that the Military authority in this case has gone far beyond the mere suspension of the Privilege of the Writ of *Habeas Corpus*. It has by force of arms, thrust aside the Judicial authorities and officers to whom the Constitution has confided the power and duty of interpreting and administering the laws, and substituted a Military Government in its place, to be administered and executed by military officers.

... For at the time these proceedings were had against John Merryman, the District Judge of Maryland, the Commissioner appointed under the Act of Congress, the District Attorney and the Marshal all resided in the City of Baltimore, a few miles only from the home of the prisoner. Up to that time there had never been the slightest resistance or obstruction to the process of any Court or Judicial officer of the United States in Maryland, except by the Military authority. And if a military officer, or any other person had reason to believe that the prisoner had committed any offence against the laws of the United States, it was his duty to give information of the fact, and the evidence to support it to the District Attorney .... There was no danger of any obstruction or resistance to the action of the Civil authorities, and, therefore, no reason whatever for the interposition of the military.

And yet, under these circumstances a military officer, stationed in Pennsylvania, without giving any information to the District Attorney, and without any application to the Judicial authorities, assumes to himself the Judicial power in the District of Maryland; undertakes to decide what constitutes the crime of treason or rebellion; what evidence (if, indeed, he required any) is sufficient to support the accusation and justify the commitment; and commits the party, without a hearing even before himself, to close custody in a strongly garrisoned Fort, to be there held, it would seem during the pleasure of those who committed him.

The Constitution provides, as I have before said, that "no person shall be deprived of life, liberty, or property, without due process of law." It declares that "the right of the people to be secure in their persons, shall not be violated, and no warrant shall issue, but upon probable cause, supported by oath or affirmation, and particularly describing the place to be searched, and the persons or things to be seized." It provides that the party accused shall be entitled to a speedy trial in a Court of Justice.

And these great and fundamental laws, which Congress itself could not suspend, have been disregarded, and suspended, like the Writ of *Habeas Corpus*, by a military order, supported by force of arms. Such is the case now before me, and I can only say, that if the authority which the Constitution has confided to the Judiciary Department and Judicial officers may thus, upon any pretext or under any circumstances, be usurped by the military power at its discretion, the people of the United States are no longer living under a Government of Laws, but every citizen holds life, liberty and property at the will and pleasure of the Army officer in whose Military District he may happen to be found.

In such a case my duty was too plain to be mistaken, I have exercised all the power which the Constitution and Laws confer upon me, but that power has been resisted by a force too strong for me to overcome. ... I shall, therefore, order all the proceedings in this case, with my opinion to be filed and recorded in the Circuit Court of the United States for the District of Maryland, and direct the Clerk to transmit a copy, under seal, to the President of the United States. It will then remain for that high officer, in fulfillment of his Constitutional obligation, to "take care that the laws be faithfully executed," to determine what measures he will take to cause the civil process of the United States to be respected and enforced.

R. B. Taney,

Chief Justice of the Supreme Court, United States.

Abraham Lincoln's response to the appeals to the Constitution and legal scholarship was to initiate a bloody invasion of a sovereign nation—the Confederate States of America. The purpose of this invasion was to deny the inalienable right of the Southern people to live under a government founded upon the principle of the consent of the governed. Constitutional barriers will always prove an inefficient means of preventing a tyrant from maintaining or expanding his empire. Justice Taney was correct in his assessment of Lincoln's unconstitutional action of suspending the right of writ of habeas corpus. *But citing the Constitution is useless in the face of brute force combined with the lust for power.* The United States Constitution could not protect the citizens remaining in the Union, because those who controlled the Yankee Empire were men who cared not the least for the original intentions of the Founding Fathers. The old America of 1787, the America of limited federalism and constitutional guarantees of liberty, was dead. At last, those who wanted an American empire with a strong central government had won! A new day had dawned. The United States of America was remade anew with a supreme, centralized, Federal Government—a government controlled from Washington, D.C., ruling an America of "one people, one nation indivisible!" The monarchists' view of extreme federalism had won at last!

The apologists for Yankee Empire's aggression will attempt to mask Lincoln's violation of constitutional liberties by suggesting that even though his actions were not authorized by the Constitution, they were necessary as a "war measure." These apologists for "one nation indivisible" imply that had it not been for the outbreak of the war, Lincoln and the Radicals of the North would have never violated the Constitution. Yet, in 1866, well after the war was over, another habeas corpus case came to the attention of the United States Supreme Court. By this time, the advocates of "one people, one nation, indivisible" were in complete control of the Federal Government. The victorious Yankee Empire had imposed radical Reconstruction upon the conquered Southern people. The Yankee Empire imposed Reconstruction on the South even though it had no constitutional authority to do so. But of course, it had no Constitutional authority to invade and conquer the South either. In *ex parte McCardle*,[1] the Supreme Court was asked to issue a writ of habeas corpus for a Southern newspaper editor who had been charged with libel and arrested by the military authorities. Even though the United States Supreme Court no longer had a "radical" Southerner leading it as chief justice (Justice Taney's position had been filled by Lincoln's appointment of S. P. Chase, a Republican, appointed in 1864), the federal Congress was nonetheless afraid that if the court took the McCardle case it would declare Reconstruction unconstitutional! To avoid this possibility, the federal Congress, while the Supreme Court was considering the McCardle case but prior to the court's handing down its decision, passed a law which removed the court's authority to hear the case. The Constitution gives Congress this power. The problem is the motivation that compelled Congress to restrict the Supreme Court's appellate authority. The Constitution requires the president to take an oath affirming his duty to "preserve, protect and defend the Constitution of the United States." Elected members of Congress are sworn in using similar language. Yet, in this case we see the members of Congress, dominated by the Republican Party,

---

1   *Ex parte McCardle*, 74 U.S. 504 (1869).

conspiring to prevent the federal Supreme Court from doing the very thing that it was duty-bound to do, that is, to "preserve, protect and defend the Constitution." Instead of defending the Constitution, the members of the Yankee Empire's Congress voted to prevent the Supreme Court from doing its duty! From this action, it can plainly be seen that the modus operandi of the Yankee Empire, to ignore the Constitution when it interfered with its exercise of power, remained the same in peace as it had during and prior to the war.

Again, we ask, who can blame Jefferson Davis and the people of the South for desiring to remove themselves from such faithless, evil partners, and such a tyrannical regime?

Addendum VI

Appeal for Justice for Major Henry Wirz

Wirz's Attorney's Letter to the American People

AFTER THE ASSASSINATION OF ABRAHAM LINCOLN, the Radicals who controlled the United States government alleged that Confederate captain Henry Wirz and President Jefferson Davis were part of a conspiracy to cause the deaths of Northern prisoners at Andersonville POW Camp. The following letter was written by Wirz's attorney, Louis Schade. It was addressed to the American people and first appeared in a Washington, D.C., newspaper in 1867, two years after Wirz was unjustly executed.

This letter demonstrates several important points relative to the defense of President Jefferson Davis and the South against the charge of treason. First, it again makes clear the lack of credibility of those who charged President Davis with treason; second, it demonstrates the total lack of respect the advocates of "one people, one nation indivisible" had (and still have) for the constitutional requirements of due process; third, it demonstrates the tyrannical nature of the advocates of "one people, one nation indivisible" by again noting their willingness to abandon the Constitution and utilize military courts rather than constitutional and lawful courts; and, fourth, it again demonstrates the fact that the Southern states were correct to attempt to remove themselves from a Union with such faithless and tyrannical partners.

Washington, D.C.

April 4, 1867

To the American Public:

Intending to leave the United States, I feel it my duty before I start to fulfill a promise which, a few hours before his death, I gave to my unfortunate client, Captain Henry Wirz, who was executed at Washington on the 10th of November, 1865. Protesting up to the last moment his innocence of those monstrous crimes with which he was charged, he received my word that, having failed to save him from a felon's doom, I would as long as I lived do everything in my power to clear his memory. I did that the more readily, as I was then already convinced that he suffered wrongfully. Since that time his unfortunate children, both here and in Europe, have constantly implored me to wipe out the terrible stains which now cover the name of their father.

Though the times do not seem propitious for obtaining justice, yet, considering that man is mortal, I will, before entering upon a perilous voyage, perform my duty to those innocent orphans and also to myself. I will now give a brief statement of the causes which led to the arrest and execution of Captain Wirz.

In April, 1865, President Johnson issued a proclamation stating that from evidence in the possession of the Bureau of Military Justice it appeared that Jefferson Davis was implicated in the assassination of Abraham Lincoln, and for that reason the President offered one hundred thousand dollars for the capture of the then fugitive ex-President of the Southern Confederacy. That testimony has since been found to be entirely false and a mere fabrication, and the suborner [one who procures another to commit any crime, particularly to commit perjury], Conover, is now under sentence in the jail in this city, the two perjurers whom he suborner having turned state's evidence against him; whilst the individual by whom Conover was suborned has not yet been brought to justice.

Certain high and influential enemies of Jefferson Davis, either then already aware of the character of the testimony of those witnesses, or not thinking their testimony quite sufficient to hang Mr. Davis, expected to find the wanting material in the terrible mortality of Union prisoners at Andersonville.

Orders were issued accordingly to arrest a subaltern officer, Captain Wirz, a poor, friendless, and wounded prisoner of war (he being included in the surrender of General Johnston) and besides, a foreigner by birth. On the ninth of May he was placed in the Old Capitol prison at Washington, and from that time the greater part of the Northern press was busily engaged in forming the unfortunate man in the eyes of the Northern people into such a monster that it became almost impossible to obtain counsel; even his countryman, the Swiss Consul-General, publicly refused to accept money to defray the expenses of the trial. He was doomed before he was heard, and *even the permission to be heard according to law was denied him.*

To increase the excitement and give eclat to the proceeding and to influence still more the public mind the trial took place under the very dome of the Capitol of the nation.

A military commission, presided over by a despotic general, was formed, and the paroled prisoner of war, his wounds still open, was so feeble that he had to recline during the trial on a sofa. *How that trial was conducted the whole world knows!*

The enemies of generosity and humanity believed it to be a sure thing to get at Jefferson Davis, therefore the first charge was that of conspiracy between Henry Wirz, Jefferson Davis, Howell Cobb, R. B. Winder, R. R. Stevenson, W.J. W. Kerr, and a number of others to *kill the Union prisoners.*

The trial lasted for three months; but fortunately for the bloodthirsty instigators, not a particle of evidence was produced showing the existence of such a conspiracy; yet *Captain Wirz was found guilty of that charge!*

Having thus failed, another effort was made. On the night before the execution of the prisoner (November 9, 1865) a telegram was sent to the Northern press from this city, stating that Wirz had made important disclosures to General L. C. Baker, the well-known detective, implicating Jefferson Davis, and that the confession would probably be given to the public. On the same evening some parties came to the confession of Wirz, Rev. Father Boyle, and also to me, one of them informing me that a high Cabinet official wished to assure Wirz that if he would implicate Jefferson Davis with the atrocities committed at Andersonville, his sentence would be commuted. The messenger requested me to inform Wirz of this. In the presence of Father Boyle, I told Wirz next morning what had happened.

The Captain simply and quietly replied, "Mr. Schade, you know that I have always told you that I do not know anything about Jefferson Davis. He had no connection with me as to what was done at Andersonville. If I knew anything about him, I would not become a traitor against him or anybody else even to save my life."

He likewise denied that he had ever made any statement to General Baker. Thus ended the attempt to suborn Captain Wirz against Jefferson Davis. That alone shows what a man he was. How many of his defamers would have done the same? With his wounded arm in a sling, the poor paroled prisoner mounted the scaffold two hours later. His last words were that he died innocent, and so he did.

The 10th of November, 1865, will indeed be a black stain upon the pages of American history.

To weaken the effect of his declaration of innocence and of the noble manner in which Wirz died, a telegram was manufactured here and sent North stating that on the 27th of October, Mrs. Wirz (who actually on that day was nine hundred miles from Washington) had been prevented by that Stantonian *deus ex machina*, General L. C. Baker, from *poisoning her husband*. Thus at the time when the unfortunate family lost their husband and father, a cowardly and atrocious attempt was made to blacken their character also. On the next day I branded the whole as a lie, and since then I have never heard of it again, though it emanated from a brigadier-general of the United States Army.

All those who were charged with having conspired with Captain Wirz have since been released, except Jefferson Davis. Captain Winder was let off without trial; and if any of the others have been tried, which I do not know, certainly not one of them has been hanged. As Captain Wirz could not conspire alone, nobody will now, in view of that important fact, consider him guilty of that charge.

As to "murder in violation of the laws and customs of war," I do not hesitate to assert that about one hundred and forty-five out of one hundred and sixty witnesses that testified on both sides, declared during the trial *that Captain Wirz never murdered or killed any Union prisoners with his own hands or otherwise.*

Those witnesses, some twelve or fifteen, who testified that they saw Wirz kill prisoners with his own hands or otherwise, swore falsely, abundant proof of that assertion being in existence. The hands of Captain Henry Wirz are clear of the blood of prisoners of war. He would certainly have at least intimated to me a knowledge of the alleged murders with which he was charged. No names of the alleged murdered men could be given, and when it was done no such prisoner could be found or identified.

The terrible scene in court when he was confronted with one of the witnesses, and latter insisting that Wirz was the man who killed a certain Union prisoner which irritated Wirz so much that he nearly fainted, will still be remembered. That witness, Gray, swore falsely, and God alone knows what the poor innocent prisoner must have suffered at that moment. The scene was depicted and illustrated in the Northern newspapers as if Wirz had broken down on account of his guilt.

Seldom has a mortal man suffered more than that friendless and forsaken man.

But who is responsible for the many lives that were lost at Andersonville and in the Southern prisons? That question has not fully been settled, but history will yet tell on whose heads the guilt for those sacrificed hecatombs of human beings is to be placed. It was certainly not the fault of poor Wirz, when in consequence of medicines being declared contraband of war by the North, the

Union prisoners died for the want of the same. How often have we read during the war that ladies going South had been arrested and placed in the Old Capitol Prison by the Union authorities, because quinine and other medicine had been found in their clothing! Our Navy prevented the ingress of medical stores from the seaside and our troops repeatedly destroyed drug stores and even the supplies of private physicians in the South.

Thus the scarcity of medicine became general all over the South.

That provisions in the South were scarce will astonish nobody, when it is remembered how the war was carried on. General Sheridan boasted in his report that in the Shenandoah Valley alone he burned more than two thousand barns filled with wheat and corn and all the mills in the whole tract of country; that he destroyed all factories and killed or drove off every animal, even poultry, that could contribute to human sustenance. And these desolations were repeated in different parts of the South, and so thoroughly that money had to be appropriated to keep the people from starving. The destruction of railroads and other means of transportation by which food could be supplied by abundant district to those without it increased the difficulties in giving sufficient food to our prisoners.

The Confederate authorities, aware of the inability to maintain the prisoners, informed the Northern agents of the great mortality, and urgently requested that the prisoners should be exchanged, even without regard to the surplus, which the Confederates had on the exchange roll from former exchanges—that is, man for man. But our War Department did not consent to an exchange. They did not want to "exchange skeletons for healthy men."

Finally, when all hopes for exchanges were gone, Colonel Ould, the Confederate Commissioner of Exchange, offered early in August, 1864, *to deliver up all sick and wounded* without requiring an equivalent in return, and pledged that the number would amount to ten or fifteen thousand, and if it did not he would make up either number by adding well men. Although this offer was made in August, the transportation was not sent for them until December, although he urged that haste be made. During that very period most of the deaths occurred. It might be well to inquire who these "skeletons" were that Secretary of War Stanton did not want to exchange for healthy men.

A noble and brave soldier never permits his antagonist to be calumniated and trampled upon after an honorable surrender. Besides, notwithstanding the decision of the highest legal tribunal in the land that military commissions are unconstitutional, and earnest and able protestations of President Johnson and the results of military commissions, yet such military commissions are again established by recent legislation of Congress all over the suffering and starving South [Reconstruction]. History is just, and as Mr. Lincoln used to say, "We cannot escape history." Puritanical hypocrisy, self-adulation, and self-glorification will not save the enemies of liberty from their just punishment.

Not even Christian burial of the remains of Captain Wirz has been allowed by Secretary Stanton. They still lie side by side with those of another and acknowledged victim of military commissions, the unfortunate Mrs. Surratt, in the yard of the former jail of this city.

If anybody should desire to reply to this, I politely beg that it may be done before the first of May next, as I shall leave the country— but to return in the fall. After that day letters will reach me in care of the American Legation or Mr. Benedete Bobzani, Leipsig Street, No. 38, Berlin, Prussia.

LOUIS SCHADE

Attorney at Law.

About the Authors

JAMES RONALD (Ron) and WALTER DONALD (Donnie) KENNEDY were born and reared in Mississippi. Each received his Bachelor's degree from the University of Louisiana- Monroe. Ron holds a Master's degree in Health Administration (MHA) from Tulane University and a Master's of Jurisprudence in Health Law (MJ) from Loyola University, Chicago. Donnie is a graduate of Charlotte Memorial Medical Center School of Anesthesia, Charlotte, North Carolina.

Their book, *The South Was Right!* may be said to have initiated the modern Southern movement and has sold over 135,000 copies. Shotwell Publishing produced the third edition in 2020, updated for the 21st century. Many in the media have noted the Kennedy Twins advocacy of limited government—that is, real States' Rights—which have led to many interviews and TV appearances. The Kennedy Twins have been interviewed by numerous local and national talk radio shows including Col. Oliver North's radio show, Alan Colmes' radio show, Bill Maher's show Politically Incorrect, BBC, French National TV, Louisiana Public Broadcasting TV and Mississippi Public Broadcasting radio and TV.

Both have served as Commander of the Louisiana Division Sons of Confederate Veterans. They have received special recognition awards from the National Commander of the Sons of Confederate Veterans, the Jefferson Davis Historical Gold Medal from the United Daughters of the Confederacy, and numerous other awards from various Southern Heritage organizations. The Kennedy Twins are frequent speakers at civic associations, church groups, patriotic groups, and Southern Heritage conferences.

ADDITIONAL TITLES FROM THE KENNEDYS AND MANY OTHER **UNAPOLOGETICALLY SOUTHERN** AUTHORS

AVAILABLE AT

S HOTWELL P UBLISHING . COM

Free Book Offer

Don't get left out, y'all.
Sign-up and be the first to know about new releases, sales, and other goodies
—plus we'll send you TWO FREE EBOOKS!

Lies My Teacher Told Me:
The True History of the War for
Southern Independence
by Dr. Clyde N. Wilson

Confederaphobia:
An American Epidemic
by Paul C. Graham

FreeLiesBook.com

Southern Books. No Apologies.
We love the South — its history,
traditions, and culture — and are proud
of our inheritance as Southerners. Our
books are a reflection of this love.

www.ingramcontent.com/pod-product-compliance
Lightning Source LLC
Chambersburg PA
CBHW060830190426
43197CB00039B/2537